Myths in Austrian History: Construction and Deconstruction

Günter Bischof and Marc Landry, eds.

Christian Karner, guest editor

CONTEMPORARY AUSTRIAN STUDIES | VOLUME 29

UNO PRESS innsbruck university press

Printed in the United States of America

Cover illustration by Johannes Mahlknecht
Book design by Allison Reu and Alex Dimeff

Published in the United States by
University of New Orleans Press
ISBN: 978-1-60801-188-9

UNO PRESS

Published and distributed in Europe
by Innsbruck University Press
ISBN: 978-3-99106-020-8

iup

Publication of this volume has been made possible through a generous grant by the Federal Ministry of Education, Science and Research through the Austrian Academic Exchange Service (ÖAAD). The Austrian Marshall Plan Anniversary Foundation in Vienna has been very generous in supporting Center Austria: The Austrian Marshall Plan Center for European Studies at the University of New Orleans and its publications series. The College of Liberal Arts at the University of New Orleans, as well as the Vice Rectorate for Research and the International Relations Office of the University of Innsbruck provided additional financial support.

Bundesministerium
Bildung, Wissenschaft
und Forschung

THE UNIVERSITY *of*
NEW ORLEANS
CENTER AUSTRIA

Federal Ministry
Republic of Austria
Education, Science
and Research

universität
innsbruck

Marshallplan-Jubiläumsstiftung
Austrian Marshall Plan Foundation

Contemporary Austrian Studies

Sponsored by the University of New Orleans and University of Innsbruck

Table of Contents

POST- WORLD WAR II

NON-TOPICAL ESSAY

FORUM: SOUTH TYROL IN THE TWENTIETH CENTURY

REVIEW ESSAY

BOOK REVIEWS

Myths in Austrian History: Construction and Deconstruction

Preface

Günter Bischof/Marc Landry/Christian Karner

Austria's post-World War II "victim myth" both shaped the country's postwar history and, since its deconstruction in the aftermath of the Waldheim affair, is now a central trope in scholarly literature. This volume aims at extending the discussion of *different myths* throughout Austria's twentieth-century history and some of their continuing impact on the present. We consider "myths" to be socially, culturally, and politically consequential—though always also contestable—narratives of particular pasts and their purported meanings. Such narratives are, at best, selective in what is being remembered. At worst, they contain outright distortions that are arguably particularly topical at our present historical juncture with its concerns about the "post-factual." Distinctly interdisciplinary and focused on different realms of "myth-making," this volume casts its analytical net unusually wide. The various myths critically examined here thus include: artistic representations of "Austrian"/"German" landscapes, both before and after the "Anschluss"; Austrian narratives surrounding World War II, the Holocaust, and the much-discussed *Stunde Null*; postwar reconstructions; neutrality; the trope of postwar Austria as an *Insel der Seligen*; the relationship between myth and environment in Austria; Viennese narratives about the city's Jewish history; and *Mitteleuropa-Nostalgie* and its (transnational) manifestations in policy-making. Importantly, this volume offers different critical responses to such myths, including assessments about their political impact or usefulness, as well as thought-provoking discussions of the role and responsibilities of scholarship vis-à-vis such highly selective or positively distorting narratives.

Our volume starts with a conceptually focused outline of existing scholarship on the complex, much-debated interrelationships and differences between "myth-making" and "history-writing." Drawing on a range of disciplinary perspectives (i.e., from sociology, anthropology, religious studies, and memory studies), Christian Karner's discussion unfolds around three sets of issues: recent deconstructive efforts at rethinking binary oppositions of "myth" to "history"; questions pertaining to the political and cultural roles played by different narratives of the past; and a return to crucial questions about the responsibilities of critical historiography at a time of postmodern hyper-relativism and in the context of "mythscapes" (Duncan Bell) in which ideological self-interest all too often trumps respect for the historical record. Further, Karner's introduction ties these wider epistemological and political issues to illustrative Austrian examples. The purpose of the introduction is to both prepare important conceptual ground for the ensuing discussions and to pre-alert readers to the wide range of politically, discursively, socially, and culturally representational domains in which myth-making has unfolded throughout—as well as beyond—modern Austrian history.

Unlike Christian Karner's theoretical introduction to "myths in history and the social sciences," Peter Berger's contribution on "Myths in Recent Austrian History" takes a broad view of myth production and runs through a gamut of such concrete, twentieth-century, well-worn historical myths. Starting with Sir Karl Popper's admonition that historians had to challenge historical myths critically with rational arguments, Berger proceeds to do just that with popular historical myths generated in Austria after World War I: the myth of Austria's economic nonviability after the war, as well as Austria falling prey to foreign capitalists; the "Habsburg myth," emanated from literary production; and the myth of Clemenceau, pronouncing in Paris in 1919 "*Le reste, c'est l'Autriche*," actually having been produced by "pro-Anschluss" German nationalists. After World War II, the myth of Austria having been "the first victim" of Nazi Germany and the myth of the *Lagerstrasse* both were important instruments in building an Austrian identity. Myths were also reinforced through the censorship of critical historical works by state actors. Berger also weaves some very personal observations of his years in a Vienna *Gymnasium* and the legends taught by his German-nationalist history teacher into his learned analysis.

In his contribution focused on Vienna's Heldenplatz, Peter Stachel traces key moments in the history of one of the city's—and indeed Austria's—central *lieux de mémoire*. Stachel shows that on the Heldenplatz, as a historically and symbolically charged locality in the heart of Vienna, political communities have taken shape throughout the modern history of Austria. As significantly, the political acts that have taken place and continue to take place there span state institutions, prominent political actors, and practices of opposition and resistance. As such, Stachel shows how the Heldenplatz has been featured as Austria's quintessential political square, with noticeable functional similarities with equivalent spaces in other European cities. Beyond such parallels, Stachel's chapter documents the historical, architectural, and representational dimensions of Austria's arguably best-known and most-symbolic locality.

In his essay, Tim Corbett traces the origins and developments of "Jewish" historiography in Vienna, from its emergence in the 1840s until the 1930s. The focus here is on "histories conceived to speak exclusively about Jews and Jewish culture" regardless of their authors' spiritual beliefs.

For Corbett, it is not so much the historical veracity of this early historiography that deserves our attention. After all, much of it was infused with mythical flourishes, such as the idea that the origins of the Jewish community in Austria reach back to 1700 BCE (the oldest archeological evidence of Jewish life in Austrian territory actually dates back to the third century CE). Rather, it is the interpretive frameworks and the ideological motivations underlying the "master narratives" of this long-ignored literature that possess relevance for today. Though the line between myth and history is quite blurred in these works, they open up space for a more integrative approach to Vienna's social and cultural history.

Few Austrian individuals of the twentieth century have been so surrounded by myth as the Christian Social federal chancellor and dictator Engelbert Dollfuss. With the recent removal of the Dollfuss portrait that hung throughout much of the postwar period in the Austrian parliament, Lucile Dreidemy suggests it is time to take stock of the mythology surrounding the man. Dreidemy traces both the self-creation of a Dollfuss myth in the years 1933–34 and its development and impact on Austrian political life since then. Going hand in hand with the *Koalitionsgeschichtsschreibung* that characterized Austrian historiography after 1945, Dreidemy argues that Dollfuss apologists promoted an image of a "light and shadow figure" that has persisted despite historical findings. The result, she argues, has been a revisionist tendency that activates old mythical themes and relativizes the historic role of the Austrofascist regime in paving the way for a National Socialist takeover.

Laura Morowitz's thought-provoking article complements much that has been written about Austrian postwar myth-making. Where the latter has foregrounded Austria's much-discussed, highly problematic "victim status" and the myth of autonomous reconstruction from scratch (i.e., under the symbolic-discursive "umbrella" of the *Stunde Null*), Morowitz critically examines two earlier central myths of the Nazi era: first, quasi-millennialist propaganda portrayals of the "Anschluss" and, second, myth-like constructions of the *Ostmark* and its mountains as a "bulwark" allegedly protecting the *Volksgemeinschaft* in or from the east.

Peter Pirker presents a novel interpretation of the stubborn Austrian myth of having been Hitler's "first victim" ("*Opfermythos*"). Given the dual meaning of "*Opfer*" in German, signifying both "victim" and "sacrifice," he argues that historians have failed to recognize the importance of *sacrifice* as the crucial aspect of their "victimological memory" in their postwar politics of history. Needing to incorporate World War II veterans as victims, grand coalition politicians stressed their "sacrifice" in their "sacrificial memory regime." "*Opfer*," in this sense, meant "Austria's responsibility to make its own *sacrifices* in the struggle for liberation."

Maria Pohn-Lauggas returns us to some of the historical moments that in recent Austrian history have arguably been the most shrouded in mythical narratives (i.e., the later stages of World War II as experienced in Austria and the immediate postwar context). Focused on the much-discussed *Trümmerfrauen*, women portrayed as clearing bomb debris and hence widely seen as symbols of (self-)sacrifice in the service of national reconstruction, Pohn-Lauggas develops a critical reading of later discursive framings of the *Trümmerfrauen*, particularly as formulated in the context of the 2005 parliamentary debate that led to a federal law compensating former *Trümmerfrauen* for their "contribution to reconstruction." Pohn-Lauggas thereby also offers an insightful (re)examination of the intersection of gendered and victim discourses in parts of Austria's recent national mythscape.

Peter Berger and Günter Bischof compare the two postwar eras and the popular notion of Austria's "economic nonviability" after the breakup of the Habsburg Empire. The myth stemmed from the fact that the Habsburg Empire had been economically self-sufficient, and the small Austrian state ought to be so as well. But no less a giant of economic thinking than Joseph Schumpeter argued after the war that Austria had the resources to become economically viable in the long run, and yet many Austrians wanted to see an "Anschluss" with Germany and therefore pushed the argument of nonviability. The victorious powers in Paris prohibited "Anschluss" and gave financial aid to Austria in 1923 toward its recovery. World War II cured Austrians of any desire for "Anschluss." Nazi German investments during the war and massive American foreign aid (including the Marshall Plan) after the war guaranteed Austria's economic recovery. In the late 1950s, Austria spoke of their homegrown "economic miracle." After World War II, Austrians were much more confident in the future of their state than after World War I. The new postwar myth propagated by conservative politicians claimed that during the "heroic age" of postwar economic reconstruction, the country had become viable due to the hard work of its people.

In a wide-ranging article, Konrad Paul Liessmann explores the myth of Austria as an *Insel der Seligen* (Fortunate Isle). These famous words ("*isola felice*"), uttered by Pope Paul VI on the occasion of Austrian President Franz Jonas's visit to Rome in 1971, have come in the intervening years to characterize the entire country—though they are increasingly invoked to emphasize that Austria is *not* (or no longer) such a place. The author departs from a twofold assumption about myths. First, following Hans Blumenberg, that myths are necessary for communities to communicate about their foundation. Second, that "political myths"—narratives that may have a "historical core"—work best when they can be attached to their particular culture's reservoir of great myths. In recognition of the latter, Liessmann considers the links between ancient, old European, and Christian mythology and the idea of the "isle of the blessed." He finds that part of the reason for the staying power of this myth is its connections to utopian thought stretching back as far as Homer's Odysseus. Furthermore, the notion of an Austrian retreat into an insular existence offered a solution to the trauma of National Socialism. Liessmann ends by considering the ways in which neutrality and the social partnership fueled the belief in Austria's blessedness.

Georg Rigele turns to the Austrian environment as a source of multiple myths in contemporary Austria. If, as he suggests, there is a human need to impart political significance and attach national identities to natural landscapes, then the conditions for doing so in Austria are excellent. Austria is, after all—as its national anthem proclaims—a land of sublime landscapes. Drawing on thirty years of research into the relationship between technology and the environment, Rigele explores the influential and at times surprising myths that have arisen in connection with Austrian landscapes. After a consideration of the foundational shaping of the Austrian landscape during the First Republic, Rigele surveys the postwar Austrian landscape as portrayed in popular films, the place of skiing in Austrian national identity (as well as its environmental effects), and finally the emergence of environmentalist opposition to roads and hydropower dams. The article concludes with a reflection on how an island created by engineering artifice—Vienna's *Donauinsel*—has become a leisure paradise and one of the city's greatest development successes.

Christian Hütterer's contribution to our volume acts as a timely reminder that "mythscapes" can and do operate across a variety of geographical scales and institutional settings in which national actors play a prominent, albeit not the only, significant roles. Tracing the histories of two particular policies (i.e., the Central European Initiative and the Regional Partnership, respectively), Hütterer reconstructs earlier attempts at (re)imagining *Mitteleuropa* soon after the revolutions of 1989–91. This is followed by a discussion of the later post-EU enlargement context in which the EU Strategy for the Danube River Basin, as one of the European Union's "macro-regions," again illustrates the complex interplay of national actors and institutions, European policy makers, and various (though not always easily) coexisting historical "imaginaries."

Michael Burri examines a peculiarity—one is tempted to say irony—of the myth-making process of constructing an Austrian national identity after 1945. In the life and works of Heinrich Drimmel, one of the most instrumental elite figures in developing this new identity, Burri finds a tension between acting on behalf of the state to inculcate Austrians with national values while simultaneously criticizing these efforts. Drimmel, a conservative Catholic, was the minister of education from 1954 to 1964 under five different governments. As part of his vast portfolio, he oversaw primary and secondary education, sports, arts, and culture. His tenure was responsible for building the foundational contours of these sectors in the Second Republic. Analyzing the minister's speeches and writings, Burri identifies a "Drimmel effect"—a performance whereby he served the state and expanded its institutions and activities while expressing an anti-state posture. The Drimmel effect suggests a certain elite ambivalence about the necessity and impacts of national myths.

As the essays in this FORUM suggest, the historiography on the South Tyrol issue has commonly been written from both the patriotic/nationalist Austrian/Tyrolean and Tridentine/Italian sides. These two historiographies hardly took note of one another. In the essays published in this FORUM, the authors are going beyond such traditional patriotic/nationalist perspectives. Based on archival sources and the asking of new questions, they are incorporating the historiographies of the other side.

Finally, a brief note on a myth missing in this volume. Originally, we had intended for one contribution to deal with "Red Vienna"—a big issue with many myths spinning around it. In 2019, the Museum of the City of Vienna put on a big exhibit on "*Rotes Wien.*" It was a comprehensive exhibit on the famous public housing program of the Socialists who governed the community of Vienna after World War I and many other aspects of "Red Vienna," such as public education, cultural and leisure programs organized regularly by the city, as well as the many intellectual networks that continued to make Vienna a hub of innovation in Central Europe. The city of Vienna is very conscious of its important history and likes to construct myths around this vital past. Unfortunately, we heard too late from our Red Vienna contributor that she would be unable to produce. It was too late to ask another colleague to cover this important topic. So, this chapter is missing.

A number of people have been instrumental in making the completion of this volume possible. Christian Karner (then on leave from the University of Nottingham, now teaching at the University of Lincoln) visited Center Austria: The Austrian Marshall Plan Center for European Studies for a few weeks in the fall of 2018. He suggested the topic of doing a CAS volume on "myths in Austrian history." Günter Bischof and Marc Landry were excited about the idea, and we sat down to map out this volume and find contributors.

Christian wrote his theoretical introduction on "national mythologies" during the summer of 2019. We subsequently sent it to all contributors as a methodological introduction to "mythscapes." The volume takes an interdisciplinary approach with contributors from various fields. We are sincerely thankful to all the contributing authors for submitting their essays in a timely fashion and for responding favorably to all editing suggestions from our production team. Christian Stenico, the 2019/20 Austrian Federal Ministry of Education, Science, and Research fellow at UNO and PhD student in American Studies at the University of Innsbruck, has done a fine job in tracking every manuscript through both the copyediting and proofreading processes and toward final publication. Christian introduced a superior management system for handling manuscripts between three editors and the copy editor on Dropbox. He also has been relentless in correcting and aligning footnotes with our style sheet and humoring authors toward completion of their manuscripts. Christian also suggested to ask his friend Johannes Mahlknecht in Innsbruck to design a cover. We were very pleased with Johannes's efforts.

We would also like to thank our anonymous outside peer reviewer for their thorough and timely assessments. All three editors also reviewed every manuscript before they went to an outside peer reviewer.

Center Austria is blessed to work with two dedicated university presses on both sides of the Atlantic. Lauren E. Garcia at UNO Press put her enthusiasm into the final round of copyediting the individual manuscripts, and Alex Dimeff skillfully typeset the final text of the volume. G.K. Darby and Abram Himelstein, the leadership team at UNO Press, have been hugely supportive to spirit this volume through to final publication. At Center Austria: The Austrian Marshall Plan Center for European Studies, Gertraud Griessner, with the help of Jacqueline Wieser, conducted the center's daily business with superb efficiency to allow the coeditors to work on managing the completion of this volume. Without the dedicated teams at Center Austria and UNO Press, there would be no CAS series. At innsbruck university press, Birgit Holzner was helpful with the final round of proofreading and then producing the volume for the European market. Cooperating with her has become a big bonus in the production of these volumes. We would also like to thank all institutions on behalf of our contributors for being helpful with photo material for this volume and thereby making the volume more attractive.

As always, we are happy in acknowledging our sponsors and supporters for making the publication of the *Contemporary Austrian Studies* series possible at all—not a small matter in the age of diminishing budgets for higher education in general and the social sciences and humanities in particular.

At the Universities of Innsbruck and New Orleans, our thanks go to Vice *Rektor* for Research Ulrike Tanzer for a grant toward the printing of this volume and Matthias Schennach, Barbara Tasser, Gerhard Rampl, and Janine Köppen in the New Orleans office. At UNO, Kim Long, the dean of the College of Liberal Arts, Education, and Human Development, and Robert Dupont, the chair of the History Department, have given us green lights and much support whenever needed. We are also grateful to President John Nicklow and *Rektor* Tilmann Märk for their support of the entire UNO-University of Innsbruck partnership agenda, including its publication series. In the Federal Ministry of Education, Science and Research and its student exchange office, Österreichischer *Auslandsdienst* (ÖAD), we are grateful to Barbara Weitgruber, Christoph Ramoser, Felix Wilcek, Josef Leidenfrost, and Florian Gerhardus. Markus Schweiger, the executive secretary, and Ambassador Wolfgang Petritsch, the chairman of the board, as well as the board members of the Austrian Marshall Plan Foundation, have been our strongest supporters for more than a decade now. It is a great pleasure and privilege to work with them all and acknowledge their unwavering support of Center Austria: The Austrian Marshall Plan Center of European Studies at UNO and its activities and publications.

New Orleans/Lincoln, March 2020

Theory

National Mythologies: Theoretical Reflections, Empirical Applications

Christian Karner

In a joint interview more than three years before the opening of the Haus der Geschichte Österreich, Oliver Rathkolb and Matti Bunzl specified some of the core challenges facing museum representations of modern Austrian history: its tracing to 1848; a transcending of yesteryear's "narrow historical debates" focused on the Austrian State Treaty and neutrality; and a capturing of wider audiences by positioning Austria as "cosmopolitan and pluralistic."[1] When, in the fall of 2018, rumors of a possible renaming—from Haus der Geschichte to Haus der Republik—circulated, responses to this were justifiably strong. Critical commentators raised suspicions about this new institution's political autonomy if such a potential renaming, seen to reek of "old-fashioned national history-writing," was to go ahead.[2] Others pointed out that a Haus der Republik would be a misnomer, running the risk of "bracketing out" the crucial and darkest years in recent Austrian history, from 1934 to 1945, when Austria was precisely *not* a republic. Further, the museum's (in some political quarters) purported task, to "strengthen Austrian identity," was criticized as a "fundamental misunderstanding" of what a museum of contemporary history should enable—namely a critical engagement with collective pasts and not a reinforcing of hegemonic political narratives.[3]

Such debates serve as poignant scene-setters to this volume of *Contemporary Austrian Studies* and its thematic focus on a (re)examination of complex questions of recent history, national myth-making, and their interrelationships. The purpose of this introduction is to offer some necessary definitional and conceptual groundwork. This will involve an engagement with a range of influential scholarship on myth(ology), sampled from a diversity of disciplinary perspectives. Constraints of space do not permit detailed summaries of some of the—for many historians and empirically minded sociologists—bolder, overly abstract theorizations encountered in parts of the literature that has shaped anthropological, religious, or cultural studies perspectives on myth.[4] However, this introduction demonstrates that an extrapolation of core concepts and questions from this interdisciplinary body of scholarship bears analytical dividends for an undertaking such as ours. Providing a framework for the ensuing contributions, my discussion unfolds around three sets of issues. First, I offer a brief reexamination of the vexed question about the interrelations between myth-making and history-writing. This is followed by an outline of alternative analytical questions to be put to public, myth-like representations of the past (i.e., questions about their functions, uses, and [perceived] plausibility). Finally, I trace a recent conceptual shift from mythologies to "national mythscapes,"[5] arguing that the latter provides a more accurate lens through which to view relevant materials, in Austria as elsewhere. Throughout this discussion, I interweave conceptual propositions with relevant empirical illustrations, thereby setting the tone for our Austrian case studies in the chapters to follow.

Myth-History: Getting beyond the Binary?

In everyday commonsense, myth and history are constructed as diametrical opposites—with the former assumed to offer fictitious, or at least strongly distorted, accounts of the past, and the latter taken to be premised on objectively verifiable depictions.[6] The *Oxford English Dictionary* thus subsumes under myth traditional, purportedly explanatory stories often involving supernatural entities, "a widespread but untrue or erroneous story or belief," a "misrepresentation of the truth," as well as "a popular conception of a person or thing which exaggerates or idealizes the truth."[7] However, the beginnings of a deconstructive effort are discernible in *The Penguin Dictionary of Philosophy*, where common connotations attached to history, as myth's widely assumed (superior) opposite, are opened to scrutiny. History's ambiguity, we are reminded, entails its inclusion of both "account[s] of certain events, [and] the events themselves."[8] Turning toward more sustained academic discussions, two insights readily present themselves. First, recent decades have seen noticeable shifts toward a partial blurring of the myth-history binary. Second, one need not subscribe to any singular theoretical position provided by anthropology, religious, or cultural studies to recognize how else myth—other than as history's purported (and purportedly fictitious) "other"—may be understood. Such alternative conceptualizations, some of them emerging from the interdisciplinary field of memory studies, draw attention to the social practices and political work various narratives of the past and representations of collective memories enable and perform.

Scholars in religious studies have long insisted that both "myth and history reflect a…search for meaning" and that, whilst as approaches to the past they often differ profoundly on epistemological grounds, "history itself involves the human imagination reflecting on events and on patterns of cause and effect."[9] Some anthropologists concur, also pointing out that "myth may contain historical material"[10] or, most famously, arguing against "the simple opposition between mythology and history" since "in our own societies history has replaced mythology" as a mediating resource structuring people's collective relationship to the(ir) past.[11] More recently, in sociological quarters, Charles Lemert[12] has observed that myths, though not to be read literally, should not be misunderstood as being premised on "sheer imagination with no basis in discernible reality" either, for they can be *partially* factual and "express [some] truth." Such selective blurring of alleged opposites is given further impetus by contributions to memory studies that conceive of a dynamic relationship between myth and history. Detecting a "two-way traffic" between them, Xinzhong Yao observes both the "mythologization of history" (i.e., actual events appearing as "mythical history" or as "history forged by the logic of myths") and the "historicization of myths," whereby "imaginative myths force their way into historical records."[13] Our contributions to this volume provide ample opportunity to observe such processes and various combinations, arguably indicative of a continuum that stretches across multiple intermediaries, from pure myth-making toward epistemologically sound historiography, at work throughout Austria's recent history.

Part of a constructivist critique of positivist historiography, Claudio Fogu and Wulf Kansteiner's notion of a *poetics of history* illustrates how precisely the "mythologization" of history can unfold. This involves enduring "tropes derived from an…institutionalized historical culture," often nationally defined, that frame public memories, furnish a "poetic arsenal" relating history to the present, and reveal the "boundary between history and memory [to be] porous."[14] Austria's mythical or "poetic" arsenal is, indeed, extensive. It includes some of the best-known interpretative lenses applied to defining moments in modern Austrian history. Though grounded in *some* real experiences, such tropes make totalizing claims and *mythologize* by turning what are, at most, partial truths and (highly) selective experiences into master narratives that mask the interpretative work and distortions they entail.

For instance, we detect this in the most widely debated of Austrian myths: the country's post-1945 construction of the *Opfermythos*, premised on a self-interested and highly selective reappropriation of the Moscow Declaration of 1943,[15] as the Second Republic's identity-bestowing narrative and core component of a then-new discourse of Austrian particularism as opposed to previously dominant, pan-Germanic self-understandings.[16]

Amongst the historical sources documenting this most clearly was the 1946 *Rot-Weiss-Rot-Buch*, the preface of which made a number of newly paradigmatic assertions. Its self-defined purpose was to justify Austria's claim to the "status and treatment of a liberated state as outlined in the Moscow declaration." Additionally, reference was made to the "political and economic circumstances this state and its people" had found themselves in "due to the peace treaties" after World War I. Also, the book explicitly countered the former Nazi depiction of the Anschluss as a "peaceful unification wanted by both sides" with a portrayal of "Austria's first passive and later active resistance" against her *braune Unterdrücker*.[17] Whilst this is well-trodden historical terrain, two of these argumentative-discursive features warrant renewed attention to the backdrop of our present conceptual concerns. First, the historical narrative offered in the *Rot-Weiss-Rot-Buch* reappropriated a topos of victimhood that, as shown in a previous volume of *Contemporary Austrian Studies*, had already become culturally entrenched as a "leitmotif of the post-Habsburg Austrian self-identity"[18] in the aftermath of World War I. Put differently, a "poetical-mythical" framing of collective memories centered on the ingroup's asserted victim status already had a pre-history by 1946 and did not start with the Second Republic's highly selective and self-interested appropriation of the Moscow Declaration. Second, extreme selectivity, for all its profound problems and distortions, still needs to be differentiated from complete fictitiousness. What made Austria's postwar *Opfermythos* so effective, at least in part, was the fact that it *did* have real experiences and shared memories to allude to (e.g., of bombing raids,[19] of some 247,000 Austrian Wehrmacht soldiers who had died in the course of the Nazis' "total war,"[20] of malnutrition, rape, and exile thereafter). What made this mythical was not an act of utterly unfounded fabrication but its extreme partiality, one-sidedness, and blatant omissions. The latter surfaced most grotesquely in the ideological and institutional postwar exclusion of the real victims of the country's recent and darkest historical chapter, namely Austrian Jewish Holocaust survivors,[21] from the young Second Republic's "political architecture," newly constituted ingroup, and normative frameworks. As recently and most comprehensively shown by Barbara Serloth, these continuing exclusions manifested in reluctant, denied, or delayed restitution, the fact that those forced into exile after March 1938 were never invited back, and in discursive trivializations of the crimes of Nazism.[22]

Resistance had, of course, been a part of a minority of Austrians' wartime experience. The historical record on this is important to remember, including the fate of some 100,000 Austrians who were arrested "on political grounds" and 2,700 killed for "resistance related activities" during more than seven years of Nazi terror.[23] Much of the organized resistance, meanwhile, and the only truly effective military opposition in Hitler's "heartlands," centered on Slovene militia units that were, for a time, supported by the British Special Operations Executive.[24] When turned into the post-1945 mythical victim-master narrative, however, these very particular "sub-categories" were made to metonymically[25] stand for, or be distortedly projected onto, the much larger category of Austrians—the majority of whose wartime positions via-à-vis National Socialism are more accurately captured as having ranged from silent survival-cum-complicity via opportunism (i.e., as manifest among the direct or indirect beneficiaries of Jewish dispossession through Aryanization policies), to political commitment (i.e., NSDAP Party membership), and all the way to prominent Austrian Nazi-enthusiasts. The purposes of metonymical arguing, as cognitive linguist George Lakoff has shown, is to make "inferences or judgments"[26] to which we need to add, in light of Austrian post-1945 history, the staging of political claims and the (re)construction of collective self-understandings. Put differently, the mythical qualities of Austria's *Opfermythos* revolved around a particular combination of assumptions and highly selective interpretations: first, a form of amnesiac "erasure"—in Laura Morowitz's suggestive choice of words[27]—regarding the Holocaust, its (Austrian) Jewish victims, and its (Austrian) perpetrators; and second, combined with this, a metonymic projection, defined by its obvious selectivity, of experiences of Austrian hardship, loss, and suffering onto the entire national "ingroup," to the exclusion of the (many) other subject positions that could not be made to fit the victim narrative. The myth's highly selective memory-work—on the basis of real, though then-(metonymically) misprojected experiences and coupled to large-scale omissions and amnesias—facilitated the geopolitical strategies, as well as the ideological nation-building, that defined Austria's immediate postwar years.[28]

The myth of victimhood[29] is, as the present volume demonstrates, far from the only such selective, ideologically[30] crafted, and institutionally consequential narrative in recent Austrian history. Neutrality, in its origins, assumed merits, and identity-bestowing functions is similarly relevant here. This transpired two decades ago from some of Ruth Wodak, Rudolf de Cillia, Martin Reisigl, and Karin Liebhart's observations of the *discursive construction* of Austrian identity. More particularly, their research corroborated "neutrality's mythical character" as a "taboo-laden" conceptual pillar for the Second Republic and many of her citizens. Concurrently, however, and against the backdrop of the shifting political landscapes of the 1990s, the "meaning of neutrality" had entered into a "process of transformation," threatening to turn neutrality into a "meaningless symbol, the content of which can be defined at will."[31] This also expands our conceptual grip on how national myths operate or, more accurately, on their building blocks: as narratives focused on select historical phenomena and particular interpretations thereof, myths are also highly symbolic; and their core symbols—their condensed or "dominant symbols"[32] in anthropological terminology (i.e., political neutrality in this particular case)—are equally capable of carrying polysemic (i.e., multiple) contents as they are of turning into empty signifiers over time. More recently, in an attempt to capture the full social significance of the constitutive symbols of dominant narratives of national identification, *Profil* columnist Georg Hoffmann-Ostenhof went so far as to suggest that neutrality, along with widespread opposition to both genetically modified food and nuclear energy, furnished Austria's "national religion."[33]

Well-known aspects of Austrian collective memories and of prominent, national self-understandings clearly *work with* real historical materials, albeit highly selectively, whilst *reworking* them for particular ends. Philosopher Konrad Paul Liessmann shows this arguably most persuasively when—in relation to Austrian *political mythology* (i.e., the *Opfermythos*, the Heldenplatz as *lieu de mémoire*, and the "*Insel der Seligen*" topos)—he argues as follows: myth is "collective, narratively structured speech," which may indeed have a historical "kernel" but whose purpose lies in an appropriation of this past for present interests. This implies selectivity and reveals the "mythological moment," which "promises meaning" (*Sinnversprechen*) through its emphasis on a particular retelling of a particular history.[34] All this limits the analytical utility of thinking of "history-writing" and "myth-making" as entirely mutually exclusive processes. Instead, their entanglements raise further questions.

Functions, Uses, Plausibilities

Attempts to think beyond the simplistic, commonsensical binary that sees "myth" and "history" as diametrical opposites are not, by necessity, complicit with what one may describe as a strongly postmodernist position in historiography. The latter is epitomized in Keith Jenkins's propositions that "the truth(s) of the past elude us; history is intersubjective and ideologically positioned;...objectivity and being unbiased are chimeras;...history is...a worldly, wordy language game."[35] Against such radical relativism, later parts of this discussion will argue that the prominence and political consequences of the "mythologization of history" call for renewed and principled efforts to disentangle ideologically motivated accounts of the past from those that are supported by a critical weighing up of all available evidence. The question thus arises as to what a transcending of the myth-history binary may accomplish that is *not* tantamount to an epistemological *anything goes*.

To answer this, the terms and guiding questions of the analysis need some recalibration. This, in turn, must start by restating the crux of the argument emerging from the previous section. The latter can be paraphrased by defining as "mythical" or "myth-like" any accounts of—or claims about—select pasts, which are not, or at least not primarily, driven by concerns with substantiation through, and balancing of, evidence and which are disinterested in any ongoing, critical debate of the version of the past being offered. It is on this premise that the next questions present themselves—namely how such mythical accounts may be contextualized, interpreted, and, possibly, countered. Seminal conceptualizations of myth that were originally formulated by Bronisław Malinowski, founding father of modern social anthropology, and by Mircea Eliade, influential (and politically controversial) historian of religion, respectively, provide vital analytical momentum at this point.

According to Malinowski, myths "exercise an active influence" on the conduct of a social group. More particularly, Malinowski detects the "sociological importance" of myths in their provision of "a foundation" or "backbone of an institution."[36] Whilst this functionalist understanding attributes to myth the ability to provide a "charter for social action…[and] structure," Eliade widens the terms of the debate yet further: to him, myths even act as a "source of ontology" by providing a generally accepted "framework for organizing reality."[37] Put differently, the Malinowskian line foregrounds the political-institutional consequences of widely revered narratives, whereas for Eliade the importance of myths lies in their ability to provide compelling interpretative-cognitive frames of understanding. Philosopher Hans Blumenberg pushed the latter strand yet further by distinguishing scientific or historiographic explanations from the affective, emotionally charged work performed by myth. According to Blumenberg, then, "the function… of myth is not, as for the Enlightenment, to explain the world but to…fulfill the need 'to be at home in the world.'"[38]

Blumenberg's distinction may, at first sight, appear to provide a plausible account of the centrality of myth to popular conceptions of *Heimat*, in Austria as elsewhere. Beyond or "behind" those, this distinction arguably also resonates in the romantics' Counter-Enlightenment rediscovery of, and deep investment in, mythology,[39] whose purported purpose was precisely the provision of a center, or anchor, in a new, modern world of rational organization and emerging industrialization. However, an overly neat distinction between enlightened, universal science (and historiography), on one hand, and emotionally effective, since-localized mythology, on the other, risks resuscitating the very binary that our discussion has already called into question. Further, it overlooks important examples of history—not myth—being presented as fulfilling the very institutional and interpretative functions theorized by Malinowski and Eliade, respectively. The aforementioned Haus der Geschichte Österreich, or more accurately its *Begleitheft*, illustrates this powerfully. There, visitors-cum-readers are told[40] that "*die Republik Österreich [hat] jetzt ein Haus für ihre Geschichte—einen Ort, an dem wir darüber reden, wer oder was Österreich ist und wie wir in diesem Land zusammenleben wollen.*" Here, history is presented as holding the keys to both what Austria is and to how "we" want to organize "our" shared lives "here." The first dimension extends Eliade's conception of myth to history, which thereby acts as a "source of ontology," purporting to define Austria. The second dimension, meanwhile, reveals—in neo-Malinowskian fashion—that history, too, might act as a "charter for social action" as a blueprint for institutions and a group's political workings. Similarly noteworthy here is the use of what Michael Billig[41] has described as some of the "deictic markers" of *banal nationalism* (i.e., "we," "here," "in this country") through which nation-states, in part, are reproduced in the course of our everyday lives and beyond our conscious awareness but with our symbolic, discursive, and institutional participation. Such banal nationalism, as is corroborated by this particular example at hand, is certainly *not* the exclusive "possession" of the political right, but it cuts across the ideological spectrum. What is more, we here see that even national histories that are critically retold and debated can reveal entanglements with the workings of banal nationalism whilst performing some of the institutional and interpretative functions commonly identified with myth.

Analytically, we have now begun to sidestep—if only for the time being—the commonsensical preoccupation with historical (in)accuracy usually brought to bear on myths. Instead, and following the conceptual lines just sketched, a different set of issues opens up. These include the question as to which institutions have been underpinned by which mythical narratives in Austria. And, turning from Malinowski to Eliade, which myths have enabled which particular ontological constructions (i.e., views or framings of historical or present realities)? It is best left to our individual contributors to develop specific answers with regard to specific Austrian narratives and self-understandings in our later chapters. For the purposes of the present introduction, however, such questions about the ideational underpinnings of political institutions and widespread views of reality can be meaningfully extended through yet another social scientific concept predominantly associated with anthropology and religious studies—that of the "taboo." Conceptually connected to Durkheimian understandings of the sacred, as the "set apart and forbidden" that helps tie social groups together,[42] taboos have also been recognized as performing significant functions in variously "stabilizing" or "mobilizing" modern, democratic, and increasingly postindustrial societies. With regard to Austria, Anton Pelinka observed twenty-five years ago that whilst it would be "naïve to imagine a political culture without taboos," which he defined as its unquestioned axioms, it was also a fundamental "democratic virtue" and necessity to look beyond the distortions and simplifications taboos entail and to critically interrogate their "functionality." At the time, Pelinka mentioned the blatant omissions in Austria's *Opfermythos*, as well as in both the SPÖ's and the ÖVP's respective narratives of their *Lager*'s roles during the 1930s, as examples of (sub)culturally prominent and politically consequential taboo subjects.[43] As outlined in the previous section, Austria's postwar *Opfermythos* revealed a highly selective, distorting, self-interested, and ideologically guided reframing of historical experiences. At the same time, its public standing as a taken-for-granted, uninterrogated narrative—that in large parts of Austrian society persisted until the aftermath of the "Waldheim affair" in the second half of the 1980s—displayed distinctive features of a political taboo.[44] Yet taboos can be broken, and myths, as social anthropologists have long observed, can "die."[45] Applied to Austria and its dominant postwar self-narration, this is, of course, precisely what has happened since the tumultuous events of 1986 when a long overdue process of critical reexamination of the country's victim-myth at long last began to take hold. This process, in turn, has implicated competing positions, shifting cultural memories, and landmark events such as the commemorations of 1988 and 2005, respectively.[46]

Plenty of myths persist, as our contributors in the ensuing chapters illustrate. Some of those, in turn, are in the process of being turned into more prominent objects of discussion. One may think of recent media debates surrounding current commemorative events of *100 Jahre Rotes Wien*.[47] This started with Christa Zöchling's thought-provoking reflections in *Profil* on how Social Democracy's "utopia of the good human" and "communitarian euphoria" had subsequently been corrupted and turned against Enlightenment humanism.[48] It did not take long for this to be (mis)construed as a "grotesque" distortion of Red Vienna as a "predecessor," rather than "enemy and victim," of Austrofascism and National Socialism.[49] Who one chooses to side with in debates of this kind matters less for our present purposes than the fact that this corroborates the very conceptual lines that have framed this section: what endows certain historical memories and narrations with "mythic qualities"[50] is their ability to bind social groups—including political parties, at least for a certain period of time—and to furnish comprehensive, (sub)culturally shared frames for interpreting lived realities.[51] What is more, examples such as these also partly re-inflect Roland Barthes's argument, to whose seminal contributions to analyzing mythology I shall return shortly, that "[s]tatistically myth is on the right."[52] Whilst the next section provides further corroboration, if this was needed, of the prominence of political mythology on the political right, the Austrian example also demonstrates that myth—if understood as a "charter" for social/political action and as underpinning a shared self-understanding and view of reality—also features on the political left. Debates about "the extent to which Austrian Social Democrats mythologized [their] resistance against Austrofascism"[53] thereby acquire a new meaning, one that pertains to the party's self-definition rather than to lacunae in such narratives.

The analytical step performed in this section has been tantamount to a temporary sidestepping of the epistemological questions pertaining to myths through a foregrounding of the political and interpretative work they perform. Michael Burri, in a recent review of Katherine Arens's *Belle Necropolis*, develops a similar line of argument in tracing various "plausible restagings" by subsequent generations of Austrians of the "highly malleable [historical] material" provided by the late imperial period. With attention shifting from "veracity" to "plausibility," Burri demonstrates that "understanding myth-making" can give rise to a different kind of "historical sensibility": one cognizant of the fact that in terms of "late imperial Austrian myth-making," the historical raw materials in question are "not fixed but… continually reshaped to address new Austrian realities."[54]

Taken together, the arguments developed thus far make a strong case for conceptualizing (national) mythologies carefully and for taking them seriously as narratives selectively focused on particular pasts that perform significant cultural and political work in the present. This, however, leaves the difficult question as to how historiography might respond productively to such reevaluation of mythology as yet unanswered.

From Mythologies to Mythscapes

As already alluded to in the introduction, recent years have witnessed an additional theoretical shift that promises to enhance our discussion further. At the heart of this shift was Duncan Bell's notion, proposed as a conceptual alternative to both "memory" and "mythology," of the *national mythscape*. Bell defines this as "the temporally and spatially extended discursive realm wherein the struggle for control of people's memories and the formation of nationalist myths is debated, contested and subverted incessantly."[55] Most crucially, Bell conceives of myths in the plural and recognizes them as constituting a strongly contested political field in which "dominant" narratives and "subaltern" voices jockey for attention, agreement, and recognition. What is more, underpinning Bell's mythscape is a processual understanding of *ongoing* memory-work and myth-making. All narratives of the past, then, though they may seek a reified permanence and durability, require ongoing political efforts and a discursive presence (i.e., in a variety of institutional settings and across multiple social domains).[56]

One first and obvious implication of this line of argument is the postulate that no matter how strongly hegemonic a particular version of a contextually significant past may be (i.e., a dominant "nationalist myth"), there will be counter-memories, if only those formulated in whichever social and representational realms they can access, by the structurally marginalized and oppressed. That said, dominant majorities need to be acknowledged as being internally divided themselves, not least in terms of competing political blocks and their corresponding, subculturally variable framings of the past. To bring this back to the Austrian context, this strongly resonates with the earlier comments on the enduring, *Lager*-specific taboos and narratives concerning the 1930s. It also echoes in Heidemarie Uhl's seminal analysis of the uneasy coexistence of the "victim myth" with the commemoration of "dutiful, fallen soldiers" and the subsequent shift toward the "co-responsibility thesis" in the course of Austria's postwar history.[57] Finally, a focus on the internal struggles that furnish *any* mythscape invite more sustained attention to the marginal pockets of contestation, which occasionally did manifest in the pre-Waldheim era, of the strongly hegemonic *Opfermythos*.[58]

More generally, an analytical shift toward mythscapes—and the concurrent attention to competing historical narratives, representations, and claims this entails—can also help redefine the public role of historians and social scientists, in particular in the wider cultural context of epistemological relativism (or even nihilism) mentioned earlier. Put differently, since mythscapes are contested terrains of competing memories and myths, there is a strong case to be made that public discussion is in need of renewed stringency and critical testing vis-à-vis any of the narratives on offer. One may here remember Timothy Garton Ash's[59] "allergy to some of the ludicrous frivolities of postmodern historiography," coupled with his insistence that scholarly care (i.e., careful contextualization, a balancing of "intellectual distance" and "imaginative sympathy" with all historical actors in question) can enable "a truth…not a single absolute Truth with a capital T, but still a real…one" to emerge from the most one-sided of memories and the most self-interested documents. A relevant, recent example of how critical, historiographical engagement with prominent myths can reveal the inaccuracies and limited historical understanding contained therein is Maximilian Graf and Sarah Knoll's revelation of how, contrary to the dominant Austrian narrative on the *Ungarn Flüchtlinge* of 1956, "already in 1957 the societal attitude toward the Hungarians who stayed in Austria and did not migrate further turned negative."[60] A reading of this through the lens provided by the concept of the (national) mythscape facilitates one additional analytical step: continuing in the "presentist" vein that has defined memory studies ever since Maurice Halbwachs,[61] Duncan Bell concurs that the clashing myths that are constitutive of a mythscape are also drawn upon in the pursuit of competing politics in the here and now. Graf and Knoll's critical rethinking of the Austrian hospitality topos that has long underpinned public memories of 1956 also enables us to ask this: How has this particular myth been used since, in the context of later migratory flows, by competing political actors and in the pursuit of competing policy aims (e.g., for refugee integration or for a closing of borders respectively)? More work remains to be done on important questions such as these, not least in light of the "refugee crisis" in 2015/16 and its widely debated impact on Austria.

There are wider, even more significant issues that a recognition of the ideological battles fought over the past, which is implicit in the concept of the mythscape, raises. A postmodern relativism arguably underpins some of our era's most widely debated phenomena, including "fake news" and growing numbers of people's withdrawal to their ideological "bubbles," or "echo chambers," in which circular, unsubstantiated claims prevent critical engagement with a diversity of perspectives, one's own and others'. There are reasons to fear that ideologically motivated historical "beliefs" and "opinions," as forms of myths, are very much part and parcel of some such "echo chambers." On the radical end of the spectrum, epistemological relativism seemingly also underpins, in part, the extreme right's Holocaust revisionism. Typically and shockingly, "opinions" are thereby directly or indirectly presented as comparable or even legitimate alternatives to documented historical facts. Infamously, one may here remember the 2010

FPÖ presidential candidate Barbara Rosenkranz's indirect questioning of Austria's *Verbotsgesetz*; early in her campaign Rosenkranz thus suggested that a belief in the "freedom of opinion" meant that one had to also accept "opinions one may consider wrong, absurd or offensive."[62] If unchecked by scholarly standards for presenting evidence and for the continual, critical checking and debate of all claims, this is what national mythscapes can also entail: a self-serving hyper-relativism in which any claim, no matter how absurd, can be given discursive space. Put differently, the concept of a (national) mythscape alerts us to, and captures, the complexity of the politics of memory. At the same time, mythscapes underscore the importance of historical scholarship—in our information age seemingly more than ever before—in disentangling documented historical realities from unsupported, or positively grotesque, "opinions." This resonates with, and builds upon, several of William McNeill's propositions concerning "mythistory": first, historians achieve "truths…when they bend their minds…critically and carefully…to the task of making their accounts credible as well as intelligible to an audience"; second, this does not at all negate, but it underlines, the differences and varying degrees of accuracy separating different "mythistories" from one another; third, following from this, "our historiographical myth making and myth breaking…cumulates across time" to work toward "truer and more adequate" accounts of the past capable of "sustaining ingroups in ways that are less destructive to themselves and to their neighbors."[63]

Analysis of some of the building blocks constitutive of Austria's mythscape today can go yet further. One may, at this point, consider one of the FPÖ's most recent electoral campaigns (see figure 1) as myth-like (i.e., the party's subsequently much-discussed posters for the EU elections in May 2019, which showed an image of HC Strache, in a statesman-like posture, accompanied by calls to the electorate to "protect what we love: Austria" and to "stand up for our homeland"). This can be read through Roland Barthes's seminal analytical framework for making sense of myth as a particular "type of speech and system of communication." According to Barthes, myth is a "second-order semiological system" that reworks a fully-functioning first-order sign that consists—as any sign—of a signifier and signified. It is by using a first-order sign as a signifier for a secondary system of mythical signification (i.e., on a less directly accessible ideological level) that myth is able to perform its vital political functions: namely to "naturalize" and "depoliticize"—by "aim[ing] to cause an immediate impression"—and hence to suggest to the intended audience that a particular collection of words or an image in question are self-evident, obvious, or natural rather than arbitrary, carefully constructed, and strongly contestable.[64]

Figure 1: FPÖ, 2019 EU election campaign poster, image taken by the author.

Barthes's most famous example was the image of a young black soldier saluting the Tricolour, published on the front cover of a French magazine in the 1950s. As a first-order sign, as Barthes demonstrated, the image in question was precisely that. On its secondary ideological or mythical layer, however, the image conveyed more subtle and more elaborate ideas: that "France is a great Empire, that all her sons, without any colour discrimination, faithfully serve under her flag, and that there is no better answer to the detractors of alleged colonialism than the zeal shown by this [soldier] in serving his so-called oppressors."[65] It ought to be stressed that only careful historical contextualization is capable of seeing through the image in question to detect its subtler, mythical workings.

When applied to the FPÖ's electoral poster, Barthes's approach directs us as follows. The poster's first-order signs are easy enough to spot: a confident politician, immediately recognizable as HC Strache to all politically interested Austrians, is giving it to his fellow citizens "straight," so to speak, by interpellating them as co-members of the same ingroup (i.e., *wir*)[66] and declaring what needs to be done and for whom or what (*für unsere Heimat*).

This combination of text and image then operates, more subtly, on Barthes's second (and mythical) semiological layer. Arguably, it is there that the real message is transmitted, albeit indirectly. Deciphering this, as in Barthes's own examples, requires contextual knowledge and reflexivity. The *naturalization* accomplished by the FPÖ relates to the national community (i.e., *wir* are clearly defined in national, Austrian terms as if no other ingroups were conceivable) and to patriotic love (i.e., the latter is taken for granted as a seemingly inevitable emotional disposition). Second, a *topos of danger/threat*[67] is similarly taken as given here; Austria needs protection, so the insinuation goes, and people will inevitably know from whom or what. Third, and at least as importantly, the poster's slogans work their ideological message through implied opposites or negations. The sub-text of these slogans is that whilst "we," meaning the FPÖ and its intended audience, "love Austria" and are prepared to "stand up" for the country, others allegedly do not and are not. This does not need explicit stating or repeating. After all, this is the very "logic" written into the populist construction of "ordinary people" and the politicians in question in juxtaposition to "outside forces" and "other parties" that are purportedly out-of-touch with "us" and "our concerns."[68] A similar subtext of implied opposites has been at work in the FPÖ's self-designation as a *soziale Heimatpartei* for years. There, the (mythical) implication, which resonates subtly and does not need explicit formulation, is that the FPÖ outperforms the SPÖ on questions of social fairness and is *heimattreuer* than the ÖVP. Neither claim needs to be made explicitly, nor needs to be substantiated. It is mythical speech in its full, *naturalizing* swing.

The photograph above was taken in late April 2019. At the time, it struck me as obvious and important to include this as an example of "mythical speech," in Barthes's sense, and to include and comment on it in my introduction to this volume of *Contemporary Austrian Studies*. This was several weeks before the events that are now known as "Ibiza-gate." Rarely do political claims come crashing down as spectacularly as they did in HC Strache's case following the (undercover) revelations of the deeply troubling suggestions and promises the then-FPÖ-*Bundesparteiobmann* had made in the summer of 2017. All of a sudden, from what—or from whom—Austria might need protecting appeared in an altogether different light, one that contradicted the very claims Strache and the FPÖ had been making for years (i.e., about their own purported lack of corruption and dedication to working in Austrians' interests). The purported national protectors had, overnight, turned into actual, and in this case well-documented, threats to Austria. The detailed events of May 2019 are so well-known as to not need further retelling here.[69] However, what makes Ibiza-gate even more relevant to this discussion was the fact that through it, by blatantly contradicting the very "logic" that was extrapolated from the FPÖ poster through my Barthes-ian reading above, the FPÖ's myths about its workings and intentions were so suddenly, so completely, and so publicly disproven. These were conditions in which one might well have expected these particular myths to "die,"[70] for too blatant were the contradictions between party claims and actual events. Yet the results of the ensuing EU and national elections have, at least in part, suggested otherwise. In spite of everything, with the FPÖ receiving 17.2 percent of Austrian votes cast at the EU elections in May 2019 and 16.17 percent at the parliamentary elections in September 2019, we have reason to believe that the party's myths still have a definitive afterlife. The FPÖ's relative decline and loss of credibility after Ibiza have been palpable and, with a loss of nearly 10 percent since the *Nationalratswahl* 2017, very formidable. And the chronology of events since the spring of 2019 suggests that questions about alleged financial impropriety (i.e., the much-discussed *Spesenaffäre*) damaged the FPÖ—by undermining its self-designed image—even more than Ibiza-gate. Recent survey results thus suggest that some 80 percent of Austrian voters would now oppose any political return by Heinz-Christian Strache. Conversely, the percentage of those favoring such a potential return declined from 17 percent in June 2019 to 11 percent four months later. However, FPÖ voters continue to profess very different sentiments, with 34 percent of them hoping that Strache might still stage a political comeback.[71] Along parts of the ideological spectrum, the events and revelations of recent months notwithstanding, the FPÖ's long-cultivated myths clearly still retain some of their traction.

Concluding Reflections

In his observations of Austria's politics of memory in general, and of the *Gedenkjahr* 2005 in particular, Matthew Berg reminds us that "for historians, social scientists and cultural critics, a willingness to face difficult truths at the expense of comfortable silences or insulating myths" is imperative; and beyond the domain of critical scholarship, there is, of course, a similar need on wider societal and political levels "to question…fundamental self-conceptions…[and to] challenge the taboos that protect memory and myths from pitiless self-criticism."[72] Berg's comments echo some of the political and epistemological questions raised in this introductory contribution to the present issue of *Contemporary Austrian Studies*. To prepare the conceptual ground for the wide-ranging contributions to follow, this discussion has unfolded around three successive analytical steps. The first of these briefly outlined how an overly simplistic dichotomy juxtaposing "history" to "myth" has come to be called into question across a range of disciplines. Emerging insights into the symbolic-discursive framing, and hence a highly selective retelling of collective memories, were then brought to bear on some of the Second Republic's foundational narratives and self-conceptions, including the much-discussed *Opfermythos*. In a second step, the discussion sketched the analytical benefits of detecting myth-like qualities in various narratives, representations, and views of the past, which are best dissected for their political-institutional uses and their perceived plausibility given present circumstances and needs. Third, by turning toward Duncan Bell's concept of the *mythscape*—as the, by definition, internally contested terrain on which competing dominant and subaltern representations of the past are variously articulated, contested, and reappropriated—the analysis moved questions of the politics of historical knowledge, and of its epistemological conditions of possibility, center stage. Combined with a rejection of the hyper-relativism enabled by strong versions of postmodern history-writing, recognition of the constitutive, ideological components of Austria's mythscape[73] also underscores, yet again, the importance of critical scholarship in challenging those "comfortable silences or insulating myths" Berg mentions. The analysis then concluded with an application of Roland Barthes's semiological approach to a particular example of political myth (i.e., the FPÖ's self-portrayal as a, or rather the purportedly only, force of national "protection"). In examples such as these, myths act as subtle-but-pervasive political claims presented as though they were statements of indisputable fact. In other words, myth here indeed *naturalizes* highly political and contestable claims as though they were obvious and commonsensical.

As emerges from parts of this introduction, there is no shortage of recent discussions, both journalistic and academic, that have exposed previously largely taken-for-granted narratives, tropes, and topoi pertaining to Austria's twentieth-century history to more critical scrutiny. For instance, Austria's Haus der Geschichte, with which the present discussion opened, skillfully and self-consciously reflects upon the complexities and politics of collective remembering. It is against the multiple backdrops sketched in this introduction (i.e., thematic, conceptual, political, and epistemological) that the ensuing contributions should be read. As we are about to be reminded, Austria's recent history has indeed been shaped, and retold, through multiple "silences or insulating myths." Some of those have stretched across ideological divides, whilst others have been specific to one or the other amongst the three political *Lager* that have shaped Austrian politics since the late nineteenth century. The points of reference for some of the myths examined here and next are as varied as art, the environment, or memories of postwar "reconstruction." Whilst some such myths have indeed attempted to speak to, and thereby interpellate, all Austrians, others center on very specific localities and their histories.

As has been argued, one of the hallmarks of "the mythical" is that it offers circular claims about, and hence closed, carefully selected versions of the past that are not, or only reluctantly, subjected to debate or reexamination through relevant evidence. In this respect, today's aforementioned "echo-chambers" arguably also offer ideological and structural conditions in which myth, as defined here, thrives. Put differently, there is every reason to believe that rather than being the hallmark of a bygone era, myths, both old and new, are part and parcel of our much-discussed information age.

Endnotes

1 Matthias Dusini and Barbara Tóth, "Interview: Ein Platz für das Haus unserer Geschichte," *Falter*, Feb. 4, 2015, 14-15.

2 Barbara Tóth, "Bitte alles – nur kein Museum des nationalen Schulterschlusses," *Falter*, Oct. 31, 2018, 7.

3 Martin Tschiggerl and Thomas Walach, "Hände weg vom Haus der Geschichte," *Falter*, Dec. 5, 2018, 6.

4 For relevant overviews, see, for example, Seth Kunin, *The Logic of Incest* (Sheffield: Sheffield Academic Press, 1995), Robert Segal, *Theorizing about Myth* (Amherst: University of Massachusetts Press, 1999).

5 Duncan Bell, "Mythscapes: Memory, Mythology, and National Identity," *British Journal of Sociology* 54, no. 1 (2003): 63-81.

6 See, for example, William McNeill, "Mythistory, or Truth, Myth, History, and Historians," *American Historical Review* 91, no. 1 (1986): 1-10. McNeill outlines similar commonsensical understandings of "myth" and "history" to then offer the notion of *mythistory* as a conceptual bridge between them.

7 *OED Online*, s.v. "myth," accessed December 16, 2019, https://www.oed.com/viewdictionaryentry/Entry/124670.

8 *The Penguin Dictionary of Philosophy* (London: Penguin, 1999), s.v. "History."

9 Douglas Davies, "Introduction: Raising the Issues," in *Myth and History*, ed. Jean Holm and John Bowker (London: Pinter, 1994), 1; 6.

10 Kunin, *The Logic of Incest*, 30.

11 Claude Lévi-Strauss, *Myth and Meaning* (New York: Schocken Books, 1995), 40; 43.

12 Charles Lemert, *Globalization: An Introduction to the End of the Known World* (London: Routledge, 2015), 159ff.

13 Xinzhong Yao, "Chinese Religions," in *Myth and History*, ed. Jean Holm and John Bowker (London: Pinter, 1994), 172-174.

14 Claudio Fogu and Wulf Kansteiner, "The Politics of Memory and the Poetics of History," in *The Politics of Memory in Postwar Europe*, ed. Richard Lebow, Wulf Kansteiner and Claudio Fogu (Durham: Duke University Press, 2006), 301ff.

15 See, for instance, Günter Bischof, "Die Instrumentalisierung der Moskauer Erklärung nach dem Zweiten Weltkrieg," *Zeitgeschichte* 20 (1993): 345-366; Heidemarie Uhl, "Das 'erste' Opfer: Der österreichische Opfermythos und seine Transformationen in der Zweiten Republik," *Österreichische Zeitschrift für Politikwissenschaft* 30, no. 1 (2001): 19-34; Stefan Karner and Alexander Tschubarjan, eds., *Die Moskauer Erklärung 1943: "Österreich wieder herstellen"* (Vienna: Böhlau, 2015).

16 For example, see Peter Thaler, *The Ambivalence of Identity* (West Lafayette: Purdue University Press, 2001); Christian Karner, "The 'Habsburg-Dilemma' Today: Competing Discourses of National Identity in Contemporary Austria," *National Identities* 7, no. 4 (2005): 411-434.

17 *Rot-Weiss-Rot Buch, Erster Teil: Gerechtigkeit für Österreich. Darstellungen, Dokumente und Nachweise zur Vorgeschichte und Geschichte der Okkupation Österreichs* (Vienna: Druck und Verlag der Österreichischen Staatsdruckerei, 1946), 3. A copy of the *Rot-Weiss-Rot Buch* is on display in the aforementioned *Haus der Geschichte Österreich*.

18 Ke-chin Hsia, "'War Victims': Concepts of Victimhood and the Austrian Identity after the Habsburgs," *Contemporary Austrian Studies* 27 (2018), 245.

19 For a discussion of Austrian discursive framings of memories of the Allied *Bombenkrieg*, see Nicole-Melanie Goll, "'Terror Pilots' and 'Bombing Holocaust': Discourses on

Victimization and Remembrance in Austria in the Context of the Allied Aerial Bombardment," *Contemporary Austrian Studies* 27 (2018): 277-292.

20 Steven Beller, *A Concise History of Austria* (Cambridge: Cambridge University Press, 2006), 243.

21 More than 65,000 Austrian Jews were murdered in the Holocaust, 130,800 driven into exile. Further, some 35,000 non-Jewish Austrians (e.g. Sinti, Romani, political/ religious opponents, gays and lesbians, people with disabilities) were also murdered by the Nazis: see Oliver Rathkolb, "The Anschluss in the Rear-View Mirror, 1938-2008: Historical Memories between Debate and Transformation," *Contemporary Austrian Studies* 17 (2009): 13-14. Beller adds some 20,000 Austrian victims of the Nazi "euthanasia program" to these shocking statistics, Beller, *Concise History*, 242.

22 Barbara Serloth, *Von Opfern, Tätern und jenen dazwischen* (Vienna: Mandelbaum, 2016), 22; 75.

23 Beller, *Concise History*, 242.

24 Peter Pirker, "British Subversive Politics towards Austria and Partisan Resistance in the Austrian Slovene Borderland, 1938-45," *Journal of Contemporary History* 52, no. 2 (2017): 319-351.

25 See Georg Lakoff, *Women, Fire and Dangerous Things* (Chicago: The University of Chicago Press, 1987), 71. Metonymy (or *pars pro toto*), according to Lakoff, describes the cognitive process of "one easy to perceive aspect of something" being used to "stand for the [much more heterogenous] thing as a whole," Lakoff, *Women*, 77.

26 Lakoff, ibid.

27 Laura Morowitz, "'Heil the Hero Klimt!': Nazi Aesthetics in Vienna and the 1943 Gustav Klimt Retrospective," *Oxford Art Journal* 39, no 1 (2016): 107-129.

28 Also see Christian Karner, *Nationalism Revisited: Austrian Social Closure from Romanticism to the Digital Age* (New York: Berghahn, 2020), chapter 4.

29 It is important to remember that victim myths are not an Austrian peculiarity alone. Other national settings have most certainly known their own versions – albeit with other emphases and chronologies – of such a framing of recent historical experiences. See, for example, Bill Niven, ed., *Germans as Victims* (Basingstoke: Palgrave Macmillan, 2006).

30 I here conceptualize "ideology," a notoriously vague term, as including ideas and social practices that contribute to either the reproduction or the subversion of existing power relations. See Martha Augoustinos, "Social Representations and Ideology," in *The Psychology of the Social*, ed. Uwe Flick (Cambridge: Cambridge University Press), 156-169.

31 Ruth Wodak et al., *The Discursive Construction of National Identity* (Edinburgh: Edinburgh University Press, 1999), 65.

32 Victor Turner, *The Forest of Symbols* (Ithaca: Cornell University Press, 1967), 28.

33 Georg Hofmann-Ostenhof, "Unsere Nationalreligion," *Profil*, March 7, 2009, 73.

34 Konrad Paul Liessman, *Die Insel der Seligen* (Innsbruck: Studienverlag, 2005), 31-38.

35 Keith Jenkins, *Re-Thinking History* (London: Routledge, 1991), 67.

36 Bronislaw Malinowski, *Argonauts of the Western Pacific* (London: Routledge, 2002 [1922]), 299; 303.

37 See Kunin, *The Logic of Incest*, 36-37.

38 Cited in Segal, *Theorizing about Myth*, 145.

39 Rüdiger Safranski, *Romantik: Eine deutsche Affäre* (Frankfurt a.M.: Fischer, 2013).

40 Haus der Geschichte Österreich, *Begleitheft* (Vienna: Österreichische Nationalbibliothek, 2018), 4.

41 Michael Billig, *Banal Nationalism* (London: Sage, 1995), 94. National *deixis*, following Billig, includes those "familiar habits of language" (e.g. the use of pronouns or topographical references) that routinely and rhetorically "point at" or "flag" the nation-state and thereby aid its everyday naturalization and reproduction.

42 Fiona Bowie, *The Anthropology of Religion* (Oxford: Blackwell, 2006), 123-127.

43 Anton Pelinka, "Tabus in der Politik," in *Tabu und Geschichte: Zur Kultur des kollektiven Erinnerns*, ed. Peter Bettelheim and Robert Streibel (Vienna: Picus, 1994), 21-28; see also the classic Anton Pelinka and Erika Weinzierl, eds., *Das große Tabu: Österreichs Umgang mit der Vergangenheit* (Vienna: Edition S, 1987).

44 Cornelius Lenguth, *Waldheim und die Folgen: Der parteipolitische Umgang mit dem Nationalsozialismus in Österreich* (Frankfurt a.M.: Campus, 2013); see also Günter Bischof's review of this book in *Contemporary Austrian Studies* 24 (2015), 255-267.

45 Claude Lévi-Strauss, *Structural Anthropology II* (New York: Basic Books, 1976), 256-268.

46 See, for example, Matthew Berg, "Commemoration versus *Vergangenheitsbewältigung*: Contextualizing Austria's *Gedenkjahr* 2005," *German History* 26, no 1 (2008): 47-71; see also the essays by Katharina Wegan and Günter Bischof in the CAS-FORUM "Memory Boom: The 'Year of Reflection' 2005," in *Contemporary Austrian Studies* 15 (2007), 172-224.

47 See https://www.wien.info/de/sightseeing/rotes-wien/veranstaltungen-100-jahre-rotes-wien, last accessed 12 June 2019.

48 Christa Zöchling, "So flieg, du flammende, du rote…." *Profil*, April 19, 2019, 12-23.

49 Klaus Nüchtern, "Vom Roten Wien lernen? Basteln an einer besseren Welt." *Falter*, May 2, 2019, 6.

50 Berg, "Commemoration versus *Vergangenheitsbewältigung*," 53.

51 Also relevant here is what has been termed a recent "cognitive turn" in the study of ethnicity and nationalism. See Rogers Brubaker et al., "Ethnicity as Cognition," *Theory and Society* 33, no. 1 (2004): 31-64.

52 Roland Barthes, *Mythologies* (London: Vintage, 2000 [1957]), 148.

53 Berg, "Commemoration," 52.

54 Michael Burri, "Review: Katherine Arens, Belle Necropolis: Ghosts of Imperial Vienna," *Journal of Austrian Studies* 49, no. 3-4 (2016): 155-157.

55 Bell, "Mythscapes," 66; also see Christian Karner and Bram Mertens, "Introduction: Memories and Analogies of World War II," in *The Use and Abuse of Memory: Interpreting World War II in Contemporary European Politics*, ed. Christian Karner and Bram Mertens (New Brunswick: Transaction, 2013), 1-21.

56 Further, it is worth noting that although Bell focuses on *national* mythscapes, the concept can be put to use across other geographical and institutional scales, too. It is thus perfectly possible, and arguably desirable, to also turn analytical attention to the workings of local, regional or supranational mythscapes, in which other, though similarly contested struggles over the representation of contextually relevant pasts unfold.

57 Heidemarie Uhl, "From Victim Myth to Co-Responsibility Thesis: Nazi Rule, World War II, and the Holocaust in Austrian Memory," in *The Politics of Memory in Postwar Europe*, ed. Richard Ned Lebow, Wulf Kansteiner and Claudio Fogu (Durham: Duke University Press, 2006), 40-72.

58 Evelyn Adunka, "Antisemitismus in der Zweiten Republik: Ein Überblick anhand einiger ausgewählter Beispiele," in *Antisemitismus in Österreich nach 1945*, ed. Heinz P. Wassermann (Innsbruck: Studienverlag, 2002), 30-34; Christian Karner, "National *Doxa*, Crises and Ideological Contestation in Contemporary Austria," *Nationalism and Ethnic Politics* 11 (2005): 221-263.

59 Garton Ash, Timothy, "Trials, Purges and History Lessons," in *Memory & Power in Post-War Europe*, ed. Jan-Werner Müller (Cambridge: Cambridge University Press, 2002), 281-282.

60 Maximilian Graf and Sarah Knoll, "In Transit or Asylum Seekers? Austria and the Cold War Refugees from the Communist Bloc," *Contemporary Austrian Studies* 26 (2017), 91-112 (here 94-97).

61 Maurice Halbwachs, *On Collective Memory* (Chicago: The University of Chicago Press, 1992 [1939]).

62 Quoted in Ruth Wodak, *Politik mit der Angst* (Vienna: Edition Konturen, 2016), 124.

63 McNeill, "Mythistory," 9.

64 Barthes, *Mythologies*, 109; 114; 129-131; 142.

65 Ibid., 116.

66 This is of another example of the "deictic" workings of (banal) nationalism, through personal pronouns. See Billig, *Banal Nationalism*, 106.

67 Michał Krzyżanowski, "The Discursive Construction of Europe and Values in the Coverage of the Polish 1981 'State of War' in the European Press," in *The European Public Sphere and the Media,* ed. Anna Triandafyllidou, Ruth Wodak and Michał Krzyżanowski (London: Palgrave, 2009), 181.

68 See, for example, Wodak, *Politik mit der Angst*, 47-48. Herbert Auinger, *Die FPÖ: Blaupause der Neuen Rechten in Europe* (Vienna: Promedia, 2017), 163-171.

69 See Frederik Obermaier and Bastian Obermayer, *Die Ibiza-Affäre* (Cologne: Kiepenheuer & Witsch, 2019).

70 Kunin, *The Logic of Incest*, 44.

71 Conrad Seidl, "Jeder dritte FPÖ-Wähler wünscht sich Strache zurück," *Der Standard* (Oct. 28, 2019), accessed Nov. 6, 2019, https://www.derstandard.at/story/2000110148667/jeder-dritte-fpoe-waehler-wuenscht-sich-strache-zurueck.

72 Berg, "Commemoration versus *Vergangenheitsbewältigung*," 65; 70.

73 Christian Karner, "Multiple Dimensions and Discursive Contests in Austria's Mythcape," in *The Use and Abuse of Memory*, ed. Christian Karner and Bram Mertens (New Brunswick: Transaction, 2013), 193-210.

Myths in Recent Austrian History: About their Origins, Resilience, and Destruction

Peter Berger

Addressing Historical Myths: Rewards and Pitfalls

In a lecture devoted to the possibility of arriving at a sociological *theory of tradition*, the Austrian-born philosopher Sir Karl Popper discusses the point in history when early attempts at scientific reasoning superseded religious explanations of natural phenomena ("primitive myth-making"). This seems to have happened somewhere in Greece in the sixth or fifth centuries before Christ. Sir Popper acknowledges the fact that the new proto-scientific stories about, say, the emergence of thunderstorms at sea may have contained no less mythical elements than previous explanations referring to "the anger of Gods." But, says Popper, there was a decisive difference in that early Greek "scientists" no longer expected their audiences to blindly accept what they were told but to ask questions, to discuss matters: "The Greek philosophers invented a new tradition—the tradition of adopting a critical attitude towards the myths, the tradition of discussing them; the tradition of not only telling a myth, but also of being challenged by the man to whom it is told. Telling their myth they were ready in turn to listen to what their listener thought about it…admitting thereby the possibility that he might perhaps have a better explanation than they."[1]

Once the rationalist tradition had gained the upper hand over the uncritical acceptance of myths, the question arose of how to deal with some of the rationalists' more exaggerated claims. In what is probably Popper's most widely known work, *The Open Society and Its Enemies* (1945), he attacks, among other things, Karl Marx's philosophy of history because of its determinism. Determinism, says Popper, is untenable on many grounds even if it undeniably forms a part of the rationalist culture. Similarly, he refutes observationalism, the notion that we can understand the world by simply looking around instead of allowing ourselves to be guided by preconceived theories, which can be tested and, in case of evidence against them, disposed of. And, finally, Popper heaps scorn on the many pseudo-rational conspiracy theorists of society who, abandoning God as the prime mover of things, replace him with sinister individuals or pressure groups "who are to be blamed for having planned the great depression and all the evils from which we suffer."[2]

Obviously, conspiracy theories were at the root of many unwarranted statements about Austrian affairs, particularly in the aftermath of World War I. But before entering here into a discussion of specific examples, another point requires clarification: Is there a fundamental difference between a scientist of nature challenging irrational explanations of natural phenomena and a historian who confronts historical myths? For Karl Popper as for most devoted practitioners of the historical profession, I would believe, the answer is a clear no. Even if one remains skeptical of Sir Geoffrey Elton's claim that historians, thanks to their step-by-step accumulation of knowledge, steadily advance toward "the fortress of truth,"[3] they should certainly be capable of distinguishing historical legends from documented facts, of identifying the reason(s) why particular myths are being fabricated and handed on, and of placing their own informed narrative against what they perceive as—unintentionally or purposefully—flawed history. More often than not, their legitimate desire to question established tradition would be met with neglect, ignorance, or even stubborn resistance from the part of the orthodox faithful. But there are also examples of thinkers-against-the-grain succeeding to overturn strongly rooted but evidently problematic historical claims. One such example: the Dutch historian-journalist Chris van der Heijden, author of *Grijs verleden* (Gray past, 2001), a book about how the Dutch dealt with their complex wartime experience of 1940-45.

Van der Heijden's starting point in *Grijs verleden* is the observation that, beginning in the early 1960s, Dutch popular interest in World War II soared. Instrumental in this development was a TV documentary about the German occupation of the Netherlands that was successfully broadcast in four episodes each year until 1965. It was produced, as well as presented, by a historian and former newspaper columnist who was then in his forties, Louis "Loe" de Jong. Having survived the war in Great Britain, where he served as the director of *Radio Oranje* (the mouthpiece of Holland's government-in-exile), de Jong returned to his fatherland in 1945 and was named head of a newly founded Institute for War Documentation (RIOD), which, under a different label, still exists today. In his capacity as chief of RIOD, he set off in 1969 to write a monumental fourteen-volume collection, *The Kingdom of the Netherlands during World War II*. This work set the tone of the national war and occupation debates for decades to come, but according to Chris van der Heijden, it also sank a fatally distorted picture of wartime conditions into the minds of the Dutch public. Glorifying the heroism of Dutch resistance fighters and lashing out at the wickedness of collaborators (whose impact he, at the same time, systematically belittled), De Jong created a false impression of everyone in Holland being consciously either "black" or "white," says van der Heijden. In real life, Dutchmen during the war were, in their vast majority, neither heroes nor villains. They were just normal, weak individuals, gray mice whom the whims of fortune had left in this or that position and who tried to survive there as best as they could—avoiding any dramatic choices that might have exposed them to unknown perils.

Certainly, van der Heijden should be lauded for dismantling a legend, which blatantly contradicted important findings of mass psychology about the mental structure of average human beings. But in my view, he deserves equal praise for his insight that Loe de Jong's tale of the (many) good and the (few) bad, when it was offered to Dutch listeners, may have well been the only way of creating a stable, spiritual basis for modern democracy in the Netherlands and beyond.[4] Had the winner nations of the war on Nazism from the outset painted their victory in nothing but shades of gray, it would have been utterly difficult to master the problems of their postwar societies. As a thoughtful historian, Chris van der Heijden understood both the importance of legend deconstruction and the fact that myths may fulfill, at certain times, highly desired cohesive social functions.

But then it is also true that myths, and more precisely *national myths*, often serve the opposite purpose: that of separating individuals, or ethnic or social groups, which the myth makers consider genuine, autochthonous, and legitimate, from others believed to be intruders, imposters, and unworthy of joining the national union. It is this capacity of myths to divide that US historian Timothy Snyder had in mind when he addressed a crowd gathered in Vienna on May 9, 2019, to commemorate the defeat of the Third Reich and to honor the victims of the Holocaust. Snyder spoke of "a way to remember which leads you back to yourself, to a story of how you were always right, to a story of how you, or people like you, were always innocent." And he insisted that, in contrast to such myth-building, there "is another way of remembering, which is *history*. History allows you to take what you remember and add it to what others remember, constantly and critically compare memory with other sources and perspectives, so that you can see for what you are responsible."[5] Snyder's pleading to grant different memories equal treatment and to put what is remembered to the test of sources seems to echo Sir Karl Popper's praise of the open, critical mind. And since Snyder came to fame as a historian of Eastern Europe, his words may also be read as an encouragement to rulers in post-Communist states to allow for an intellectual climate in which myths can be challenged and critical history can prosper.

Minor Myths Versus Big Narratives

If we accept the notion that past events are subject to interpretation and that such interpretation is bound to vary depending on the outspoken or hidden agenda of the interpreter, we cannot avoid a discussion of politics of history. The term seems to have been coined in Germany around 1985 in connection with a controversy among historians over the singularity of the Holocaust (*Deutscher Historikerstreit*). In Poland, Russia, and the English-speaking world, synonyms of *Geschichtspolitik* were soon used to designate efforts at highlighting or de-emphasizing certain aspects of the past. Some historians have since forcefully pleaded against any attempt to manipulate collective memory in the interest of political pressure groups. For the German Reinhart Koselleck, politics of history is a despicable notion and tantamount to ideology. But others rushed to defend it, and as a field of scholarly activity, it has recently drawn increased interest among political scientists, sociologists, and historians, of course.[6]

As we advance from politics of history to myth-making, the concept of historical truth enters the stage. In their quest to control and direct flows of collective memory, agencies such as the state, political parties, business lobbies, or mass media sometimes resort to the fabrication or spreading of myths (i.e., they transport historical messages that are outright false or easily lend themselves to misinterpretation). In some cases, the effect on public opinion is in itself a minor one but may help to generate a distorted overall picture of the past. I propose to label historical myths with a low impact on the general public as "minor myths." To the chagrin of historians eager to debunk them, they often prove extremely resilient. Let us look at an Austrian example: the alleged quip of French Prime Minister Georges Clemenceau ridiculing the truncated post-Habsburg Alpine Republic. "The rest is Austria," Clemenceau is reported to have said.

My fellow historian at Vienna's University of Economics and Business, Manfred Zollinger, devoted a good deal of time and effort browsing through "The Tiger's" published speeches, statements at the Paris Peace Conference, and newspaper interviews, but he was incapable of finding a trace of the derisive remark in question. Instead, Zollinger found a pamphlet written in 1930 containing the infamous "the rest is..." quote. Its author was a native of Upper Austria, Hermann Neubacher, manager in the service of Vienna's Red municipal administration and convinced advocate of a union of Austria and Germany; he later entered the Nazi party to become the first mayor of Vienna after the Anschluss. In the eyes of people like Neubacher, the peacemakers of 1919 committed a crime by denying

Austrians self-determination (i.e., accession to Germany) following the demise of the Habsburg Empire, and they did not shy away from shockingly radical language to press their point. But Neubacher himself never claimed a French origin of the phrase "The rest is Austria," let alone did he ascribe it to Clemenceau. Rather, it was another figure of the Pan-German camp, historian Viktor Bibl, who did both in 1937. Since then, "*Le reste, c'est l'Autriche*," complete with Clemenceau's authorship, have become common stock of German and Austrian history textbooks. To change that may require more than just one courageous, corrective voice.[7]

A recent work of "corrective history" dealing with interwar Austrian affairs is Nathan Marcus's *Austrian Reconstruction and the Collapse of Global Finance, 1921-1931*. The book's ambition is to destroy the myth of post-1918 Austria as an easy prey of merciless foreign capitalists sitting in the League of Nations Financial Committee and the Bank of England. Its central argument that "Austria's interwar politicians retained much agency over, and thus responsibility for, the political and economic trajectory of their country"[8] is shared by an increasing number of historians. But they fight an uphill battle against both the scholarly and popular mainstream holding to the victimization narrative. The latter's longevity—and obvious similarity with the notion of Austrians being the first victims of National Socialist Germany instead of agents in their own right—warrants its treatment as a comprehensive, identity-building, big narrative designed to unite Austrians in a partnership of suffering, an "imagined community" of sorts.

Like most legends, the tale of a "financial dictatorship" weighing heavily on the young Austrian state as it emerged from the Habsburg Empire's ruins is based on some hard facts. Following the dismemberment of Austria-Hungary as an economic union, trade between its former component parts came to a near-complete standstill. The territory now forming the Austrian Republic had to cope with shortages of basic foodstuffs, as well as a massive inflow of soldiers returning from the front and civil servants formerly employed in other regions of the Dual Monarchy. Industrial production almost ceased due to lack of coal and raw materials. There were no financial means to ease the plight of the needy and keep a rudimentary state infrastructure functioning. The picture was brightened to a limited extent by the lifting of an Allied blockade in March 1919 and by the assistance that Allied governments and charitable organizations offered, in money or in kind, to save people from starvation. Subsequent Austrian chancellors vied, without much success, for substantial foreign credits to balance a state budget under permanent threat of derailing and to combat inflation caused either by currency depreciation, banknote printing presses running hot, or both. Not before September 1922, the long-awaited international reconstruction loan was agreed upon. At the same time, the government in Vienna accepted a scheme of foreign supervision of its public spending practices. Thus, Austrian inflation got "killed," and Austrian state finances stabilized some months before the first installment of the loan arrived.

In a recent contribution to *The Journal of Modern History*, I summarized the mechanism of Austrian financial reconstruction as follows:

> To attract foreign capital, holders of reconstruction bonds were offered collateral guarantees issued by, inter alia, the governments of Great Britain, France, the Netherlands, and the United States of America. But what made Austrian reconstruction unique was the fact that neither the guarantor governments nor the loan-issuing banks were entrusted with monitoring the employment of moneys lent to Austria or the adherence of that country to budgetary discipline. Instead, the powers of financial control came to rest with the League of Nations, that supranational body which had been created in 1920 to promote peace and cooperation among the nations of the world and of which Austria had become a member in the same year. The 'League label' effectively distinguished Austrian financial reconstruction from earlier efforts to 'educate' unreliable debtor nations by curbing their fiscal autonomy (like late nineteenth century Turkey). As if to prove that old style financial colonialism was definitely dead the Austrian model of financial stabilization under League auspices was, more or less successfully, replicated in Hungary, Bulgaria, Greece, and the free city of Danzig during the 1920s.[9]

Why, then, did the Austrian reconstruction model come under fire of contemporary observers and, later, of historiography? And what exactly were the grievances uttered by critics of the League scheme since its inception in 1923? To begin with, Austria's creditors were accused of exerting undue pressure upon Vienna to carry out harsh measures of economic and financial austerity. The Bank of England became a favorite bashing target of Austrians who disliked Governor Norman's recurrent appeals to raise interest rates in the pursuit of price and currency stability. And, last but not least, the League "Commissioner General" dispatched to Vienna to make sure the government adhered to the agreed terms of balancing the budget, and employing loan money was reproached of arrogance and a near-total lack of empathy with a nation in dire straits.

All these allegations have one thing in common: they are not founded on facts. While it was true that a balanced state budget formed the core of what Geneva and the community of lenders required from Austria, its government soon discovered that tax revenues far exceeded the forecasts made by League experts prior to currency stabilization. Thus, one could afford spending relatively freely while at the same time the relation between state income and expenditure improved. In other words, the fiscal belt in Austria never got tightened so as to involve substantial sacrifice. Also, it was true that Montagu Norman felt that the way Austrians managed their central bank rate held the potential of driving inflation, and he publicly denounced it. But Norman's Austrian counterpart, Richard Reisch, ignored foreign admonitions and continued to supply the economy with cheap money. And, lastly, Alfred Rudolf Zimmerman, the League's commissioner on the spot, while certainly displaying signs of an authoritarian character, was far from being a "financial dictator." Nathan Marcus calls him "largely helpless vis-à-vis the Austrian government's infringement of its international commitments"[10] and, like other historians before him,[11] notes that Zimmerman often mediated between divergent views of Vienna and Geneva instead of asking that Austrians should give in.

Toward the end of his book, Marcus offers a convincing explanation as to why distorted views of contemporary reality spill over into the later work of historians: to be challenged every now and then by more rigorous research but mostly without success. At the core of a legend's longevity, says Marcus, is the widespread urge to continue believing in fake narratives because of their inherent usefulness, political or psychological. In the case of Austria, the interwar "victimization narrative"—and its correlate, the legend of Austria locked up in the chains of irresponsible austerity policies—served multiple purposes way into the 1970s and 1980s. By pointing at the shameful way Austria got treated by the victorious Entente, the League of Nations, and international capital in the 1920s, mainstream historians after World War II offered Austrian governments, and the general public, invaluable assistance in putting the blame for the Anschluss upon foreign shoulders without explicitly having to say so. Also, the Austrian economic miracle of the late 1940s and 1950s, fueled by the positive impact of Marshall aid, could be highlighted by contrasting it with the suffocating petty greed and ignorance of Austria's interwar creditors. Finally, advocates of Keynesian deficit spending under the Socialist Kreisky administration after 1973 could and did pack their argumentative arsenal with exaggerated horror stories of "deflationism" in the 1920s and 1930s, caring little about how well founded they were.

Strategies of Self-deception: The Habsburg Myth and the Legend of a Doomed Republic

It is hardly possible to overrate the observation that historical legends are not merely slips of a scholarly pen. They help those who create them and keep them alive to ignore unwelcome realities. The best case in point is the *Habsburg myth*, which loomed large in Austrian literature and, to a much lesser extent, historiography of the nineteenth century and reached the peak of its power in the two decades following Austria-Hungary's demise. It was made popular under this name by the Italian scholar, translator, and writer Claudio Magris, a native of the Adriatic port city of Trieste, where Austrian rule (until 1918) has left its intellectual traces to this day. Magris's influential dissertation first got published in 1963 under the title *Il mito absburgico nella letteratura Austriaca moderna*. It has since seen several reprints.

The essence of the Habsburg myth, explains Magris, is to read European history against the grain and to see virtues where others see shortcomings. The Habsburg Empire had very little in common with the classical nation states emerging after the French Revolution and its British industrial namesake. It was a conglomerate of lands united by nothing except that they were ruled by the same dynasty. The empire lacked a coherent national narrative—something considered, since the nineteenth century, as a prerequisite of institutional modernization. It failed to promote one of the thirteen or so languages spoken within its borders to the rank of sole administrative language—except in the army, where German commandos had to be understood by everyone. The speed of economic development of its provinces differed widely. As a result of that, overall growth remained laggard at a time when countries like Britain, Belgium, France, or Germany developed their infrastructure and industries at a fast pace. In recent years, a number of economic historians came to the conclusion that Austrian economic backwardness might have been overestimated and that, without the catastrophe of the Great War of 1914-18, the monarchy's growth trajectory would have come to resemble that of more advanced Western countries.[12] But to imagine a similar, gradual modernization at the constitutional, political, or administrative level would have been tantamount to imagining a monarchy without Habsburg, without its cacophony of ethnical strife and multiple nationalisms, without the sloppiness and the measured pace of its bureaucracy. And since it was almost impossible to imagine all that, and also because the outcome of the war brought Habsburg's 600-year-long history to an abrupt end, some Austrian literati preferred to tell a different story of their (ex-)homeland, one that tied together its obvious anachronisms and oddities in a state idea and a lifestyle supposedly nobler, wiser, and more human than what prevailed in the rest of the world. Remember the famous description of Kakania in Robert Musil's novel *The Man Without Qualities*:

> On paper it was called the Austro-Hungarian Monarchy, but in conversation it was called Austria, a name solemnly abjured officially while stubbornly retained emotionally, just to show that feelings are quite as important as constitutional law and that regulations are one thing but real life is something else entirely. Liberal in its constitution, it was administered clerically. The government was clerical, but everyday life was liberal. All citizens were equal before the law, but not everyone was a citizen. There was a Parliament, which asserted its freedom so forcefully that it was usually kept shut; there was also an Emergency Powers Act that enabled the government to get along without Parliament, but then, when everyone had happily settled for absolutism, the Crown decreed that it was time to go back to parliamentary rule. ...
>
> There was some show of luxury but by no means in such over-refined ways as the French. People went in for sports, but not as fanatically as the English. Ruinous sums of money were spent on the army, but only just enough to secure its position as the second-weakest among the great powers. The capital, too, was somewhat smaller than all the other biggest cities of the world, but considerably bigger than a mere big city. And the country's administration was conducted in an enlightened, unobtrusive manner, with all sharp edges cautiously smoothed over, by the best bureaucracy in Europe, which could be faulted only in that it regarded genius, and any brilliant individual initiative not backed by noble birth or official status, as insolent and presumptuous.[13]

Musil worked on *The Man Without Qualities* from 1921 until his death in exile in 1942. Another great novelist with roots in the Habsburg Empire, Bosnian-born Ivo Andrić (who was twelve years Musil's junior), was appointed secretary to the consulate of Yugoslavia at the Austrian town of Graz in

1923, two years after Musil began to plot down his novel and four years after the Treaty of Saint-Germain. Graz later acquired fame as a hotbed of Pan-Germanism and National Socialism, and Andrić , who enrolled at the local university as a doctoral student, may well have noticed the enthusiasm for all things German of the *Burschenschaften*, students' corporations of the Far Right. But in his official records, another theme is paramount: that of a country (Austria) inhabited by flabbergasted monarchists.[14] He meets former officers of the Imperial Army who sport their medals of distinction and cannot understand how and why Austria-Hungary disappeared. The new Austrian state seems to be disliked by everyone. In conversations with the diplomat Andrić, some call it a *Judenrepublik* and others a *Pfaffenrepublik*. Of course, this republic continues to run a civil service and to award its functionaries offices and titles. But these titles suffer from steady depreciation, like the exchange rate of the Austrian crown, Andrić notes.[15]

In Austria, unlike in Germany, advocates of a restoration of the monarchy failed to build up political clout at the time of the First Republic. They gained some influence during the Dollfuss-Schuschnigg dictatorship when the regime tried to counterbalance increasing pressure from Nazi Germany with a renewed emphasis on Austria's glorious, imperial past. After 1933, Habsburg symbols reappeared in public life. The armed forces reintroduced the old uniforms of the Habsburg military, and the melody of Joseph Haydn's "*Kaiserhymne*" was again sung as Austria's national anthem. Aristocratic families stripped of their landed properties in the course of the "Austrian revolution" of 1918/19 were now partially compensated. But apart from such marginal gestures, there was little for Habsburg legitimists to rejoice about except maybe the works of novelists like Franz Werfel, Stefan Zweig, and Joseph Roth and of dramatists like Franz Theodor Csokor. Here, the old monarchy continued to shine—the brighter, the uglier times came to be. Tellingly, many of these authors fell victim to Nazi persecution, their works being subjected to the infamous book burnings of 1933 or purged from libraries all over the Reich. Some survived in exile (like Csokor), but others died without ever returning to Austria (like Werfel, Zweig, and Roth).

While the Habsburg myth failed to spark effective political action in interwar Austria, another contemporary legend, promoted by academic scholarship, business circles, and influential journalists, slowly but steadily unfolded its disastrous effect. The myth that Austria, as it had emerged from the war and the ensuing peace treaties, was incapable of economic survival owed its initial success to the anger and frustration of those who had trusted Woodrow Wilson's pledge to base the postwar world order on the principle of national self-determination. For Austria, this would have meant immediate union with the defeated German Reich. But, as the historian Norbert Schausberger correctly observed, the Entente powers had not fought a bloody four-year war to see German power increase by the accession of a neighboring state. Thus, they prohibited the Anschluss in both the Versailles (Art. 80) and the Saint-Germain (Art. 88) peace treaties. In reaction, Austrians showed understandable disappointment but also increased susceptibility to voices contesting the chance of a bright economic future for Austria. From 1920 onward, assertions of Austria's *Lebensunfähigkeit* (non-viability) became a regular feed for readers of Austrian newspapers and academic journals. The excitement ebbed away thanks to the transitory success of financial stabilization in 1923, but at this point it had already left an indelible mark on domestic public opinion. In the 1930s, Nazi propaganda capitalized on the deep-rooted sentiment that little Austria was a failure from the start.

As long as the Austrian state enjoyed a democratic government (1918-33), Anschluss friends could be found in all political parties. Pan-German sentiment was no doubt strongest among the *Grossdeutschen*, but leaders of the Social Democratic Party showed almost equal zeal for the German cause, notably Otto Bauer, the party's mastermind and deputy chairman. As state secretary of foreign affairs, Bauer in early 1919 hoped to negotiate a workable Anschluss deal with his German counterpart, Brockdorff-Rantzau. Upon the news that the peace treaties would ban Austro-German unification, he later resigned from his government post. But in his capacity as the Social Democrats' front man in all but name, he kept the party firmly on a pro-Anschluss track until, in January 1933, Hitler took power in Germany. Soon thereafter, references to the Anschluss were dropped from the Social Democratic Party program. Of all the political mass movements in interwar Austria, political Catholicism was certainly least attracted to the Pan-German idea. Intellectuals with Christian Socialist leanings countered the notion of Austria's economic non-viability by proposing a somewhat utopian-sounding "federation of the Danube states." As of 1933, Dollfuss and Schuschnigg, both faithful Catholics brought up to believe in German virtues and German greatness, fought for an Austrian state German in substance but independent in form, destined to represent the best of German culture threatened by Nazi barbarianism. Dollfuss was murdered in 1934 during an attempted Nazi *putsch*, and Schuschnigg failed miserably when confronting the *Führer* at Berchtesgaden. But the successful reinvention of an Austrian identity in its own right after 1945 doubtlessly owed something to intellectuals holding public functions in their authoritarian *Ständestaat*, such as Ernst Karl Winter, who was briefly a deputy mayor of Vienna (1934-36). Winter, who as a student opposed the German nationalism of the *Burschenschaften*, later eloquently pleaded for an "Austrian [as against a Pan-German, P.B.] consciousness of history" and for building bridges to the Socialist workers' movement instead of fighting it. Such views did not help strengthen Winter's position within the regime and certainly not vis-à-vis the fascist *Heimwehren* upon whose support it depended. Winter lost his job in Vienna, and his efforts to end the harassment of labor were increasingly frustrated. Shortly before the Anschluss, he fled via Switzerland, France, and Britain to New York.

Friedrich Heer, a Viennese historian and journalist whose progressive Catholicism resembled Winter's, has shed some light on the support for Anschluss ideas by Catholic Pan-Germans (*Katholisch-Nationale*) who taught at Austria's universities during the interwar period. Of all curricular subjects, history and German studies were the most impressive bastions of German nationalism, wrote Heer.[16] Understandably, few permanent faculty members embraced Nazism prior to Hitler's annexation of Austria. Since full-time professors used to be civil servants in interwar Austria, outward loyalty to the state had to go hand in hand with their Pan-Germanic *Weltanschauung*. The latter came to the fore most visibly when Jewish or "nationally lukewarm" scholars threatened to move up the academic career ladder. Such ambitions were usually nipped in the bud. Among the best-known *Deutschnationalen* employed at Austrian universities were historians Hans Uebersberger, Heinrich von Srbik, and Alfons Dopsch, along with the Germanic philologist Josef Nadler. The economic historian Dopsch in 1919 proposed to cut all commercial ties between Austria and the "Slavic" successor states of the Dual Monarchy as a preliminary to the desired union with Germany.[17] Srbik, who briefly served as Austria's Minister of Education in the democratic government of Johann Schober (1929/30), later welcomed the Anschluss as the fulfillment of a "thousand year-old dream of the German people." He happened to be the academic teacher of many prominent figures of post-1945 Austria, including Austria's federal chancellor of 1966-70, Josef Klaus, and the novelist Heimito von Doderer. About Doderer, Claudio Magris says in *Il mito absburgico*: "The main-spring of his personality as an artist remains closely connected with the Habsburg heritage. It shimmers through every facet of his work."[18] If we are to believe Magris—and there are good reasons to believe him—the poetic evocation of the atmosphere and rhythm of old Austria, instead of ending with Musil's *The Man Without Qualities*, reached new peaks in Doderer's novels. But how could the talented student of a dyed-in-the-wool Pan-German become the last guardian of the Habsburg myth in Austrian literature? The answer to this question may well be contained in a line from the jacket flap of former *New York Times* correspondent Paul Hofmann's fascinating portrait of Vienna (*The Viennese: Splendor, Twilight, and Exile*, 1988): "This enchanted land of contradictions."

The Anschluss is Dead, Long Live Austria: A New Legend is Born

On October 30, 1943, the foreign secretaries of the United Kingdom, the USA, and the Soviet Union, meeting in Moscow, solemnly signed a "Declaration on Austria." It stated that the annexation of that country by Germany was considered null and void. It affirmed the wish of the Allied powers to see the return on the map of a free and independent Austrian state, liberated from German dominance. And, most important in retrospective, it called Austria "the first free country to fall victim to Hitlerite aggression." Whatever the reasons were to issue the Moscow Declaration (some say that it aimed at encouraging anti-Nazi resistance within Austria but had no ambitions to forestall future Allied decisions concerning its status[19]), its wording certainly drove a big nail into the coffin of the myth that the Anschluss had been a legitimate and historically justified move. Following the collapse of German rule in Austria and the establishment of a provisional Austrian government under the benevolent eyes of the Red Army stationed in Vienna, State Chancellor Renner's new cabinet was more than delighted to echo the Moscow Declaration in its first official proclamation published on April 27, 1945. The document spoke of an "imposed" union of Austria and Germany now obsolete. In the following months, official Austria continued to show its determination of breaking with the country's wartime past. A decree issued in September 1945 by the head of the education department, the Communist Ernst Fischer, required public schools to rename the German vernacular "*Unterrichtssprache*" (language of instruction).[20] Until 1955, the term embellished Austrian grade sheets and drew sarcastic and sometimes angry comments from the public. Fifty years later, the German daily *Frankfurter Allgemeine Zeitung*, looking back on Austria's postwar political contortions, blamed Fischer's successor in office, Felix Hurdes (a conservative), for the language decree of 1949. The paper recalled a pun common at the time, that Austria had become "Hurdestan," and Austrians were to speak "Hurdestanese."[21] Leaving aside the question of Fischer's and Hurdes' motives (genuine belief in Austria's cultural singularity or the wish to impress the Allied Council), their actions was clearly part of a broader strategy: that of sinking the twin legends of

Austria's wartime victim status and of its un-Germanic character into the minds of foreigners and native citizens alike.

Large seagoing vessels require some time to change their direction of travel. Similarly, a new national narrative dictated from above cannot but slowly trickle down to the conscience of the individual. In postwar Austria, regular opinion polls were held to determine the intensity of national feeling current among the population. A 1956 poll for the first time asked whether Austrians should be considered a nation in its own right. Forty-nine percent answered in the affirmative, while forty-seven percent said "no," meaning that they considered themselves part of the German *Volk*. The outcome was no surprise given the short time that had elapsed since the fall of the Third Reich and the fact that Austrians had been exposed to Pan-Germanic and Nazi ideology for many decades—and to a large extent had embraced it. In 1964, deniers of Austrian nationhood were down to fifteen percent, the "yes, a nation"-group down to forty-seven percent. Fifteen percent said to have no opinion (this option had not existed in 1956), and twenty-three percent thought that Austrians "slowly began to feel like a nation."[22] From the 1970s onward, a steadily growing number of participants in opinion polls asserted their Austrian-ness: seventy-seven percent at the turn of the twenty-first century and eighty-two percent in 2008.[23] In 1988, on August 18 (which happened to be the birthday of Emperor Francis Joseph), the chairman of Austria's right-wing Freedom Party, Jörg Haider, told television reporters that the Austrian nation was tantamount to "an ideological freak" (*eine ideologische Missgeburt*) "since belonging to a state was one thing, but belonging to a *Volk* another." His fellow countrymen clearly disapproved. Only five percent of the viewers asked about their opinion said that Haider was right.[24]

It is a paradoxical aspect of the process of Austrian postwar nation-building that one of the pillars upon which its success should have rested betrayed signs of weakness. History teachers at Austrian schools (first and foremost the *Gymnasien*) in the 1950s and 1960s had in their formative years often been under the spell of *grossdeutsche* or National Socialist professors. For some of them, the day-to-day experience of living together with Germans from the Reich, either in annexed Austria or in *Wehrmacht* units at the front, may have been disillusioning.[25] But others remained faithful to their Pan-Germanic *Weltanschauung*. As Austrian civil servants, they were obliged to follow the directives of the Ministry of Education and of regional or local school councils (*Landes- und Stadtschulräte*) and to help promote "patriotic" instruction, whether they liked it or not. But as individuals in the classroom, they metaphorically crossed their fingers behind their backs to apologize to their conscience for what they had said. Some history teachers were old Nazis readmitted to school service following a final amnesty in 1948. Many had a Nazi family background. And more often than teachers of, say, mathematics or foreign languages or chemistry, historians sided politically with Austria's "third camp," the Freedom Party (formerly *Verband der Unabhängigen*/VdU), where the theory that *Staat* and *Volk* were things to keep apart and that Austrians had a state but were no *Volk* was held in high esteem.

One of these *Völkischen* taught at my *Gymnasien* when I was fourteen or fifteen years old. He was a man of about fifty at the time, bore the name of a noble family of Pomeranian descent, but nothing in the way he spoke betrayed his German roots. Probably his ancestors had at some point in the past been chosen for serving the Habsburg Crown. During his training as a historian, he had focused on the Dual Compromise of 1867, a crucial event both for Austria and Hungary, henceforth treated as "halves" of the monarchy, each with its own government and parliament but under the rule of the same Habsburg prince, who in Austria was "the Emperor" and in Hungary "the King." When addressing the class, the Hussite Wars of the early fifteenth century were among one of his favorite subjects. None of his students would remain indifferent to the lively account he gave of this conflict, which involved the Holy Roman Emperor, the Papacy, and the followers of the religious reformer Jan Hus, who was burnt on the stack for heresy in 1415. The names of the factions that formed the Hussite movement and soon started to fight each other with a fanaticism matching their hate of the Roman Catholic church—Utraquists, Taborites, and some lesser known spinoffs—for us became almost household words. Many years later, I met another historian fascinated with the Bohemian Middle Ages, the Czech František Šmahel, a reform Communist and victim of the purges following the Prague Spring of 1968. When I saw Šmahel in the 1980s, Czechoslovak authorities had just sent him to the small town of Tabor, where he was allowed to work in a tiny, local Hus-Museum and to write what would later make his fame: a four-volume history of the Hussite Revolution with many hidden (and not-so-hidden) references to Stalinism and the events of 1968. Our history teacher—let us call him X—was of a much smaller caliber than Šmahel and politically his opposite.

X's teaching of our class coincided with a period of intense coverage of the Vietnam War by Austrian media. Between 1964 and 1968, US bombs rained on North Vietnam, and television transmitted the horrors of the war theater into Austrian living rooms. This is where we have to return to the history teacher so fond of the Hussites and their violent times. To the amused bewilderment of his young listeners, X maintained that the US military avoided any action on the ground in Vietnam. Newsreels showing battle scenes were fabrications of the Hollywood movie industry, X said. In real life, American strategy rested exclusively on hitting the enemy from above, and US bombs were released from such an altitude as to minimize losses of their own aircraft. The subtext of this message could easily be deciphered: US warfare is not about heroism but about avoiding risk. And X left us in no doubt where he thought the home of true heroes was: in the German *Wehrmacht* of World War II. Anti-Americanism and the myth of the *Wehrmacht*'s untainted glory easily blended to a poisonous cocktail in the Austrian 1960s. The "third camp" in particular was susceptible to it.

Probably X was no member of the "Freedomites." After all, he enjoyed full employment as a civil servant, and in postwar Austria with its "proportional spoils system" (*Proporz*), such a privilege was usually contingent upon one's closeness to one of the two parties in government. But whatever X's strategy had been to conquer the post he held, he was a Pan-German at heart. One day we had a private conversation in front of the school. X lowered his voice and in a conspiratorial tone asked me whether I knew the first line of the Dutch national anthem. I knew it since I had spent the first years of my life in Holland and spoke Dutch. "William of Nassau I am, of German blood," I said.

"You see, the Dutch are allowed to be Germans. We Austrians are not," was X's reply.

Some years later, in the early 1970s, he was forced to retire prematurely following a disgusting anti-Semitic remark he made during one of his history classes.

Street Violence, the Arts, and a President. Myths under Fire, 1960s to Present

"In every moment of history we must decide anew, which past events should come to the light and in what context we want them to be perceived. The past is a battlefield, and the battle is about cultural hegemony. We produce images of history and let them compete for dominance in the representation of states or other political units." This statement[26] was made by the Austrian left-leaning historian Helmut Konrad in his contribution to a *Festschrift* in honor of Wolfgang Neugebauer, longtime head of the *Dokumentationsarchiv des österreichischen Widerstandes*. Former members of the Austrian resistance founded the archive in 1963. Neugebauer had recently turned sixty, and Konrad felt he should remind readers of his *Festschrift* that the forthcoming year, 2005, would see a series of official events commemorating the sixtieth anniversary of the end of World War I and the fiftieth anniversary of Austria's State Treaty. For Konrad, the government's choice of certain scholars to receive related research commissions and public subsidies clearly reflected a conservative bias. He predicted that, in dealing with the first postwar decade, these scholars would rather focus on the role played by statesmen of the People's Party (Raab, Figl) than by those of the Left (Renner, Körner, Schärf). There was no imminent danger of progressive historians losing their grip on the founding myth (*Gründungsmythos*) of the republic, Konrad assured his readers, but the struggle for sovereignty over interpretation was obviously gaining momentum.

The idea that message control belonged to the tasks of historiography was certainly not new. But in the first two decades of the Second Republic, both Socialists and Catholics agreed upon what the message would have to be: our country cannot prosper unless its dominant political forces cooperate in peace. Had not the interwar years amply demonstrated the pernicious effects of permanent mobilization of one side against the other? In a provocative and witty study of postwar Austria published in 2005, Oliver Rathkolb speaks of an awe of open conflict typical for both the People's Party and the Socialists in the 1950s and 1960s (election campaigns excepted, of course) and of the resulting "deathlike silence" that characterized Austrian domestic politics, as well as cultural life.[27] Works of historians from this period have since been classified as "coalition historiography" (*Koalitionsgeschichtsschreibung*), and the term is usually not meant as a compliment. Coalition historiography smoothed over all potentially disruptive issues in modern Austrian history, such as the Socialist workers' uprising against a repressive state in February 1934, which schoolbooks presented as a tragic episode without discussing the question of guilt. One is reminded here of Musil's quip that in old Austria things were not made but happened: "*Es ist passiert, sagte man dort.*"[28] But maybe the greatest accomplishment of coalition historians was the invention of a new legend known as *Mythos der Lagerstrasse.* It told the story of "a group of wise men," former Austrian politicians of the Left and the Right, who as prisoners in Nazi concentration camps had learnt an important lesson: rebuilding their country after the war required that they should join forces.[29] The narrative had serious flaws. Only a few leading figures in postwar Austrian politics had been detained in Nazi camps, and those who indeed had suffered often sided with their ex-torturers rather than with former fellow prisoners when their postwar political careers were at stake. But the myth proved useful in many respects. It perfectly matched with the myth of Austria as Hitler's first victim, the *Opfer* story of the 1943 Moscow Declaration. And it lent some plausibility to the Second Republic's reluctance to recognize Jewish suffering at the hand of the Nazis and to restitute Jewish property since "indigenous" victims (like Catholics of the first Dachau transport in 1938) had to come first.

In the mid-1960s, Austria entered a new stage of its postwar history. For the next twenty years, there would be no more grand coalitions of the People's and the Socialist (later Social Democratic) Parties but single-party governments, first of the conservatives and then of the Left. From 1983 to 1986, the Socialists and the Freedom Party governed together. Austria's impressive economic record (the country did well even in comparison with growth champions of the OECD) boosted national pride and put the question of how "Germanic" Austrian identity was almost entirely off the agenda. Similarly, the once-dominant narrative of Austria as a victim of Nazism and German expansionist designs seemed to slowly fade away (until it popped up again during Kurt Waldheim's successful presidential campaign of 1986).

Thirteen years of Socialist hegemony in Austrian domestic politics, commonly referred to as the Kreisky era, provided the fertile ground for a new generation of critical historians eager to challenge viewpoints, which hitherto had enjoyed near-axiomatic status. One such would-be axiom posited that in recent Austrian history, politically motivated violence had been an exclusive domain of the Right while the victims were always Socialists. In an autobiographical essay written in 2017, Gerhard Botz relates why, as a young doctoral student, he chose to put this dogma to the test, how teachers and colleagues reacted to his decision, and what his findings were.[30] Botz started to work on his dissertation in 1963 and submitted it in the fall of 1966 (when Austria had a conservative government headed by Josef Klaus, the former student of Heinrich von Srbik). A book based on the thesis came out in 1976 and found enthusiastic reviewers. At this time, Kreisky's chancellorship was already in its sixth year.

To cut a long story short: Botz's PhD supervisor, Ludwig Jedlicka—a political chameleon who had been a member of Schuschnigg's "Fatherland Front," as well as an Austrian Nazi of the first hour, but entertained good relations with Jewish and Socialist or even Communist fellow historians—supported Botz's topical choice but otherwise was not very helpful. Valuable assistance was provided, however, by the Viennese Chamber of Workers (*Arbeiterkammer*) and its staff of, in Botz's words, "non-dogmatic Marxists and Keynesians."[31] Fellow students encouraged Botz[32] and discussed his methods and findings with him. After years of meticulous quantitative research, he came to the conclusion that National Socialists and Austrofascists (a term Botz is not very happy with) had committed most acts of interwar political violence in Austria but that Socialists and Communists were also perpetrators, if to a lesser degree. Many left-leaning friends and acquaintances found Botz's conclusions shocking. A publishing house co-owned by the Socialist Party and the Austrian Trade Unions Congress refused to print his dissertation in full and would only accept the parts dealing with police violence against workers on July 15, 1927.

Another historian of fame whose career began during the Kreisky era is Oliver Rathkolb. A wider public came to know him as the ghostwriter-editor of the retired statesman's three volumes of memoirs. Early in the 1980s, Rathkolb successfully accomplished his PhD thesis, but unlike Botz's, it never went to print in Austria. As he told the daily newspaper *Der Standard* many years later, his publisher feared that disclosure of the Nazi connections of conductors Karl Böhm and Herbert von Karajan, opera singer Elisabeth Schwarzkopf, and others by an ambitious young student of the musical world might be too much for the public to swallow.[33] Ten years later, no such scruples plagued the Österreichischer Bundesverlag, a publishing house that brought out Rathkolb's bestselling *Führertreu und gottbegnadet*, a profound inquiry into the conduct of artist elites in Hitler's state. In this book, Rathkolb debunked popular myths of how artists managed to keep a safe distance from Nazi dignitaries or even perform acts of resistance. In fact, there was hardly any distance and even less opposition or moral fortitude among stars of the opera, film, or stage. When Richard Strauss resigned from the presidency of the Reich Music Chamber (*Reichsmusikkammer*), says Rathkolb, he did so not out of solidarity with his Jewish librettist, Stefan Zweig, but because he loathed working with lesser lyricists. Other prominent artists simply enjoyed being courted by a state that drove Jewish talent into exile and hence depended on support of the remaining darlings of the public. Exceptions confirmed the rule. Goebbels feared actress Käthe Dorsch because of her repeated appeals in favor of endangered Jewish colleagues. And the movie-screen embodiment of the typical grumbling Viennese, Hans Moser, managed to protect the life of his Jewish wife throughout the years of Nazi rule in Austria.[34]

Let us briefly flash back to Sir Karl Popper's demands on enlightened scholarship: to adopt a critical attitude toward myths and to challenge them with rational arguments. In Austrian historiography, thanks to the work of people like Botz, Rathkolb, and others, such a tradition was firmly established by the early 1980s. That is not to say that historical legends came anywhere close to total extinction. Tony Judt in his magisterial history of Europe since 1945, *Postwar*, cites the disconcerting results of a Gallup poll among Austrians held in 1991: twenty percent thought Jews should be excluded from "positions of authority," thirty-one percent would rather not have Jewish neighbors, and fifty(!) percent agreed to the proposition "that Jews are responsible for their past persecution." One year earlier, in 1990, Gallup had asked if Austrians considered themselves "victims of Hitler rather than his accomplices," and nearly two in five had agreed. Forty-three percent of the people polled thought that "Nazism had good as well as bad sides."[35] Into this fatal mix of ignorance and resentment, the Waldheim and "unclaimed Jewish accounts" affairs exploded in 1986 and 1998, respectively, giving a strong but short-lived boost to Austrian feelings of undeserved victimization and self-pity.

Much has been written about the 1986 presidential candidacy on a People's Party ticket of the former chief executive of the United Nations, Kurt Waldheim. It was Waldheim's second attempt to be elected into Austria's highest ceremonial office after suffering defeat against the Socialist and former mayor of Vienna, Franz Jonas, in 1971. His troubles began when the Austrian weekly newsmagazine *Profil* and the New York-based World Jewish Congress started to inquire into his wartime past. Soon it became clear that the candidate's authorized biography lacked references to his *Wehrmacht* service in Greece and Yugoslavia at a time (1942-44) when large-scale deportations of Jews and reprisals against Tito's partisans were common business there. As an aide-de-camp to the German high staffs and interpreter for several Axis generals, he must have realized what was going on. But when asked about it by reporters covering his 1986 campaign, he first denied any involvement on the Balkans and later said to have been but an uninformed subaltern officer who did his duty. Waldheim won the presidential runoff against the Socialist Kurt Steyrer in June 1986 by a comfortable margin of nine percentage points. Many people normally indifferent to domestic politics felt that the attacks on him were overblown and cast their ballots in his favor. Even in Austria's numerically insignificant Jewish community, some expressed doubts about the accusations leveled against him. Did not the fact that he had been an undisputed, though ineffective, UN secretary-general prove his innocence? And was it acceptable that the World Jewish Congress's spokesman, Israel Singer, told *Profil* on the eve of the election that *every* Austrian should reckon with the consequences if Waldheim were successful?

Indeed, serious consequences of Waldheim's triumph soon became apparent—consequences not for each individual Austrian but for the prestige of the presidential office and for the victorious candidate as a person.

Despite the verdict of a commission of internationally recognized experts on military history appointed by the Austrian government to either clear Waldheim from war crime accusations or confirm them (no signs of a direct involvement in any of the Balkan massacres were found), his reputation was irreversibly tarnished. In an unprecedented move, the US Justice Department put his name, the first of an acting head of state, on the list of aliens barred from entering American territory. Due to the absence of invitations, he made no state visits to other foreign countries except for the Vatican, Hungary, and Jordan. When Austria officially commemorated the fiftieth anniversary of the Anschluss, the federal president gave no speech. Following threats of a walkout by Socialist and other members of Parliament, Waldheim's role was reduced to that of a silent attendant.[36]

The Waldheim affair proved as divisive for Austrian society as US President George W. Bush's war on Saddam Hussein in 2003 or Donald Trump's tweets from the White House were for America. While scores of Austrian diplomats, upon orders from the Ballhausplatz, jetted from one place to another to lobby for Waldheim's rehabilitation,[37] and political heavyweights at home like former Foreign Secretary Karl Gruber or the People's Party's secretary general, Michael Graff, defended him with bravado and occasionally irritant puns,[38] many young Austrians started to wonder what their parents or grandparents had done during the war and asked them questions. And while American tourists in the streets of Vienna risked being insulted by locals when the US travel ban on Waldheim became public (I myself witnessed such incidents), Chancellor Franz Vranitzky, in a speech to the Parliament, apologized in the name of his government for the crimes committed by Austrians during the Nazi era and thus officially shelved the myth of Austrian victimization.[39] Vranitzky's words and another moving speech he gave during a state visit to Israel kindled hopes that, in the long run, the cathartic effect of the Waldheim episode would outweigh its negative aspects.

Epilogue

In his beautiful *A Little History of the World*, as written for children, the young Ernst H. Gombrich compared memory with a burning scrap of paper thrown into a bottomless well.[40] While the paper torch falls, it lights the sides of the well, and we catch a glimpse of the bricks, one layer after the other. The deeper our paper falls, the fainter our impressions until the light finally goes out, and we stop seeing anything. We can borrow Gombrich's analogy to describe the work of historians. They also throw burning torches into wells. What they see in the light produced by the flames, of course, depends on which side of the well their eyes fixate. In other words, there is no objective historiography as the direction of the historian's gaze depends on a preliminary choice. And since he cannot build on his own memories alone, the choices of all the other historians whose stories he relies on determine the scope of his work. This does not imply, of course, that angles of vision are a substitute for hard facts. If mountains appear to take on a different shape if looked at from different angles, they are still mountains (Edward H. Carr). But to look at the facts alone is not what a historian does if he wants to be more than a chronicler. True historians interconnect facts by way of interpretation. The act of interpreting, in turn, must not be blurred by a preconceived idea of the world, as it should be, or by a supposed larger meaning of history. Historians, whose interpretations are tied to whatever metanarrative, help to perpetuate myths. Solid interpretation results from an informed dialogue between evidential traces and a theoretical framework thought to be fit to increase our understanding of the past. No interpretation can do without theory. But honest historians should be open to criticism of their theoretical premises and ready to alter them if they prove untenable.[41]

Sometimes myth fabrication serves a purpose. I have tried here to do justice to historical half-truths without which the recent history of Europe might have followed another, less desirable course. Other legends, grand or minor, proved entirely out of step with factual evidence but were kept alive because of their potential for political mobilization. Take as an example the false claim that Austria's public debt was entirely the result of Socialist misgovernment in the recession of the 1970s. These charges were since repudiated by many experts but continued to pop up in the press. As late as 2007, a finance minister of the People's Party spoke of a "Kreisky handicap" weighing on the budget, which he otherwise would have straightened out.[42]

It would be utterly naïve to think of historiography without any trace of myths. People always attempt to make sense of what is happening around them. And while doing so, they are often less interested in discovering the truth than finding an explanation that will make their own personal views and choices seem legitimate.[43] The postmodernist historian Brenda Marshall goes even further, claiming that history is not about knowing the past but about chance and power.[44] But then, is it not that "*to learn what is true, in order to do what is right* is the summing up of the whole duty of a man"?[45]

Endnotes

1 Karl R. Popper, *Conjectures and Refutations: The Growth of Scientific Knowledge* (London: Routledge and Kegan Paul, 1972), 126 ff.

2 Ibid., 123.

3 Richard J. Evans, *In Defense of History* (New York and London: W. W. Norton & Company, 1999), 41.

4 Chris van der Heijden, *Grijs verleden: Nederland en de Tweede Wereldoorlog* (Amsterdam and Antwerpen: Uitgeverij Contact, 2001), 16.

5 Timothy Snyder, "Judenplatz 1010: A speech to Europe," *eurozine.com* (May 13, 2019), accessed November 11, 2019, http://eurozine.com/Judenplatz-1010/. Italics added by me, P. B.

6 *Docupedia.de*, s.v. "Geschichtspolitik," last modified August 04, 2014, http://docupedia.de/zg/Geschichtspolitik.

7 Andrea Stangl, "Myths and Narratives: 'The Rest is Austria!'... Or Something Like That," *habsburger.net*, accessed November 11, 2019, https://ww1.habsburger.net/en/chapters/myths-and-narratives-rest-austria-or-something.

8 Nathan Marcus, *Austrian Reconstruction and the Collapse of Global Finance 1921-1931* (Cambridge, Mass.: Harvard UP, 2018), 338.

9 Peter Berger, *Journal of Modern History* 91, no. 3 (2019), 725-28.

10 Marcus, *Austrian Reconstruction*, 338.

11 The first in-depth study of Zimmerman's duties and conduct in Vienna was Jacques Bosmans, *De Nederlander Mr. A. R. Zimmerman als Commissaris-Generaal van de Volkenbond in Oostenrijk, 1922-1926* (Nijmegen, 1973). Before coming to Vienna, Zimmerman acted as mayor of the city of Rotterdam and earned himself a reputation as a critic of Socialism. Following his return from Vienna, he expressed sympathy for Mussolini and the fascists.

12 See for example David Good, *The Economic Rise of the Habsburg Empire 1750-1914* (London: University of California Press, 1984).

13 Robert Musil, "The Man Without Qualities," in *Modernism: Representations of National Culture: Discourses of Collective Identity in Central and Southeast Europe 1770–1945: Texts and Commentaries*, ed. Ahmet Ersoy, et. al. (Budapest: Central European University Press, 2010), http://books.openedition.org/ceup/1081.

14 Michael Martens, *Im Brand der Welten: Ivo Andrić, Ein europäisches Leben* (Vienna: Zsolnay, 2019), 145.

15 Ivo Andrić, *Durch Österreich (1923)*, quoted in Martens, *Im Brand*, 145-46.

16 Friedrich Heer, *Der Kampf um die österreichische Identität* (Vienna: Böhlau, 1981), 373.

17 Ibid., 378.

18 Magris, *Der habsburgische Mythos*, 354.

19 Peter Berger, *Kurze Geschichte Österreichs im 20. Jahrhundert* (Vienna: Facultas.wuv, 2008), 225.

20 "Ernst Fischer," *Austria Wiki* (August 30, 2019), accessed November 25, 2019, https://austria-forum.org/af/AustriaWiki/Ernst_Fischer_%28Schriftsteller%29.

21 *FAZ* of 11 February 2004, cited in *ostaririchi.com*, accessed November 25, 2019, https://www.ostarrichi.com/wort/Hurdestanisch.

22 Christian Pichler, *Österreich in Europa: Eine Studie zur Transformation der nationalen Identität*, 66.

23 Oliver Pink, "Eine schwere Geburt," *Die Presse* (October 25, 2013), accessed November 27, 2019, https://www.diepresse.com/eine-schwere-geburt.

24 Nicole Schmidt, "profil vor 25 Jahren: Jörg Haider und Österreich als deutscher Staat," *profil.at* (August 27, 2013), accessed November 27, 2019, https://www.profil.at/home/25-jahren-joerg-haider-oesterreich-deutscher-staat-365015.

25 Cf. Wolfgang Benz, "Aus deutscher Perspektive: Österreich im 20. Jahrhundert," in *Aussenansichten: Europäische (Be)Wertungen zur Geschichte Österreichs im 20. Jahrhundert*, ed. Oliver Rathkolb (Innsbruck: StudienVerlag, 2003), 307 f.

26 Helmut Konrad, "Der Februar 1934 im historischen Gedächtnis," in *Themen der Zeitgeschichte und der Gegenwart: Arbeiterbewegung – NS-Herrschaft – Rechtsextremismus: Ein Resümee aus Anlass des 60. Geburtstags von Wolfgang Neugebauer*, ed. DÖW (Vienna, 2004), 13. My English translation of the quote is not word-for-word, P.B.

27 Oliver Rathkolb, *Die paradoxe Republik: Österreich 1945 bis 2000* (Vienna: Paul Zsolnay, 2005), 329 f.

28 Robert Musil, *Der Mann ohne Eigenschaften*, Erstes Buch, Kapitel 8, *Projekt Gutenberg*, accessed December 3, 2019, https://www.projekt-gutenberg.org/musil/mannohne/chap008.html.

29 "Säulenheiligenscheine," *profil.at* (January 22, 2005), accessed December 3, 2019, https://www.profil.at/home/saeulenheiligenscheine-103295.

30 Gerhard Botz, *Zeitgeschichte im Spannungsfeld zwischen Politik, Biografie und Methodik: autobiografische Anmerkungen*. Historical Research Supplement 28 (2nd ed.), 23-102. https://doi.org/10.12759/hsr.suppl.28.2017.23-102

31 Ibid., 46 f. Botz mentions the journalist Josef Toch, Theodor Prager, a Communist, the Social Democrat Ferdinand Lacina, later to become Austria's finance minister, and Eduard März, an economist, bank historian, and authority on Rudolf Hilferding, inventor of the theory of finance capitalism.

32 Among them was Peter Huemer, whose own dissertation about Chancellor Engelbert Dollfuß' legal adviser Robert Hecht, murdered by the Nazis in 1938, is another brilliant example of corrective historiography. Peter Huemer, *Sektionschef Robert Hecht und die Zerstörung der Demokratie in Österreich: Eine historisch-politische Studie* (Vienna: Verlag für Geschichte und Politik, 1975).

33 Oliver Rathkolb, "Historiker Oliver Rathkolb: 'Wir Müssen Uns Vom Geniekult Verabschieden.'" interview by Fritz Neumann, *derstandard.at*, January 26, 2018. https://www.derstandard.at/story/2000073018453/historiker-oliver-rathkolb-wir-muessen-uns-vom-geniekult-verabschieden.

34 Burkhard Jellonnek, review of *Führertreu und gottbegnadet: Künstlereliten im Dritten Reich*, by Oliver Rathkolb. *Archiv für Sozialgeschichte* 34 (1994): 706 f.

35 Tony Judt, *Postwar: A History of Europe Since 1945* (New York: Penguin, 2005), 812 f.

36 Hofmann, *The Viennese*, 328.

37 Ibid., 327.

38 According to Graff, Waldheim had to be considered innocent "until we have proof that he strangled six Jews with his own hands." As a consequence of this slip of the tongue he lost his party job. Wolfgang Zaunbauer, "Michael Graff: Mocks General mit Ecken und Kanten ist tot," wienerzeitung.at (August 7, 2008), accessed December 6, 2019, https://www.wienerzeitung.at/archiv/portraets/77919-Michael-Graff.html.

39 "Der 'Opfermythos' in Österreich: Entstehung und Entwicklung," *demokratiezentrum.org*, accessed December 5, 2019, http://www.demokratiezentrum.org/wissen/timelines/der-opfermythos-in-oesterreich-entstehung-und-entwicklung.html

40 Ernst Gombrich, *A Little History of the World* (New Haven, London: Yale University Press, 2005), 2.

41 Richard J. Evans, *In Defense of History* (New York, London: W. W. Norton, 1999), 198.

42 Wolfgang Petritsch, *Bruno Kreisky: Die Biografie* (St. Pölten: Residenz, 2010), 11.

43 Marcus, *Austrian Reconstruction*, 340.

44 Brenda Marshall, *Teaching the Postmodern* (London: Routledge, 1992).

45 Thomas Henry Huxley, "On Descartes' 'Discourse Touching the Method of Using One's Reason Rightly and of Seeking Scientific Truth'", 1870.

First Republic

Austria's Main Square and Political Stage: The Heldenplatz in Vienna[1]

Peter Stachel

On October 18, 1865, the second equestrian monument built by the sculptor Anton Dominik Fernkorn (1813–1878) was revealed on the *Äußeren Burgplatz* (Outer Castle Square) next to the *Hofburg* (Imperial Castle) in Vienna. After the Habsburgian Archduke Charles (1771–1847), who had defeated Napoleon in the Battle of Aspern in 1809, had a monument erected in his honor on the same square five years earlier, now Austria's secular patron saint Prince Eugene of Savoy (1663–1736) was being honored. The date of the opening was in some ways unusual, for it was the 202nd birthday of the prince. This showed that the erection of the monument did not happen exactly the way it had been planned. And strictly speaking, this second monument had not been built by Fernkorn, who, due to mental illness, was unable to work anymore and was thus only the titular director of the *Kaiserliche Kunsterzgießerei* (Imperial Foundry for Works of Art) in Vienna's Gusswerkstrasse. But besides these obstacles, the supporting program was impressive and public enthusiasm overwhelming. Some newspapers wrote that because of the second monument, the Outer Castle Square should get a new name: *Heldenplatz*, or Hero's Square. And the satiric journal *Zwischen-Akt* (*Intermission*) wrote in its volume from October 19, 1865, with abundant self-confidence, that even this square would not be large enough to commemorate all Austrian heroes of the past.[2] It is interesting that, as far as we know today, neither in 1865 nor until much later did the square officially get renamed as Heldenplatz. Until the mid-1970s, the official street directory of the city of Vienna used both names interchangeably—Äußerer Burgplatz and Heldenplatz. This might be the explanation for the fact that, although it is a large square in the very city center of Vienna, no postal address "Heldenplatz number so and so" exists. But where the Heldenplatz lies and what kind of meaning it has for Austria in past and present times is something every Austrian knows without an official street directory.

The Main Square of Austria

The Viennese Heldenplatz is nothing less than the main square of Austria. Situated in the very city center of the capital city, it is surrounded by some of the most important political and cultural institutions of the Republic of Austria. The president of the republic has their seat directly in the Hofburg,[3] in the former sleeping room of Maria Theresia. The bureau of the chancellor, as the head of the government, and the *Ministerratssaal* (meeting hall of the ministers) lies on the Ballhausplatz in direct vicinity of the Heldenplatz. Also, the Ministry of Foreign Affairs, Austrian Parliament, and Vienna City Hall are in sight, as are the legendary Burgtheater, the *Kunsthistorisches Museum* and *Naturhistorisches Museum* (Museum for Art and Museum for Nature), the users' area of the Austrian National Library, and the newly created House of Austrian History, which are all situated directly on the Heldenplatz. Both for its size but mainly because of its very central position, the Heldenplatz is the location where, in the course of the history of the Republic of Austria, political communities have taken shape in public space. This applies to all kinds of official acts of state. On the square, presidents have been sworn in, as well as soldiers, on October 26, Austria's National Day, official acts of commemoration are held in the so-called *Heldengedenkstätte* (Heroes' Memorial) inside the monumental castle gate that leads from the Ringstrasse to the Heldenplatz. The "heroes" who are commemorated here are different and various: soldiers of the Habsburg Army from World War I, soldiers of Austrian origin who fought and died in the German *Wehrmacht* in World War II, and victims of National Socialism. Obsequies for representatives of the state happened here, or their funeral processions passed the square. Two services from popes took place here; the so-called *Papstkreuz* (Pope's Cross) from the *Europavesper* in 1983 still stands next to the Burgtor.

But the Heldenplatz is also the most important place for oppositional acts, such as demonstrations and commemorations—from the obsequy for the first political dead of the Second Republic, the funeral of the Communist Ernst Kirchweger, who had been killed while taking part in a demonstration by a right-wing counterdemonstrator in 1965, to the *Lichtermeer* (Sea of Lights) against FPÖ leader Jörg Haider (1950–2008) in 1993 in which about 300,000 people took part. The latter event was the biggest group of people that had ever assembled on the square, as one of the organizers, the artist André Heller, proclaimed. After the formation of the first coalition government involving the conservative People's Party and the far-right Freedom Party in 2000, the so-called *Donnerstagsdemonstrationen* were organized on the Heldenplatz every Thursday. For every act of resistance and for every demonstration that has a meaning for the Austrian state, the Heldenplatz is *the* obvious stage, and it is highly important that demonstrations focus on this square. As a stage, the square charges events with specific symbolic meanings. The importance of the specific act of protest is measured by the number of people filling the square and "conquering" it temporarily. In other words, the Viennese Heldenplatz is an archetypical example of what I call a *political square.*

Political Squares

Such political squares do exist in most states. In many cases, it is, in fact, one single square, but sometimes several squares share this function in a different way. In Paris, for example, official acts of state take place on Place de l'Étoile (renamed the Place Charles de Gaulle in 1970) at the Arc de Triomphe. Oppositional demonstrations also regularly lead from the Place de la Bastille—with its connection to the revolutionary past of France—to the Place de la République. In Berlin, it is the Pariser Platz with the Brandenburg Gate. In London, its Trafalgar Square with Nelson's Column that fulfill the function of political stages. The example of Paris is especially interesting as in this city, the transmission of historical and political symbols into the social space of the city is exceptionally observable insofar that a relatively clear ideological border runs through the area of the city. The monuments of the revolution and the republic include the Pantheon, the *Colonne de Juillet* (July column) on the Place de la Bastille, the *Monument to the Republic* on the Place de la République, the *Triumph of the Republic* statue on the Place de la Nation, and *le Mur des Fédérés* (the Wall of the Communards) on the Père Lachaise Cemetery, located in the east. There are the patriotic and military ones, such as the Arc de Triomphe and the Tomb of the Unknown Soldier on the Place de l'Étoile, the monument for Georges Clemenceau on the Avenue des Champs-Élysées, Les Invalides with the grave of Napoleon, and the Column of the Grand Armée with the Napoleon statue, made of the material of captured cannons, on the Place Vendôme, situated in the west of the city. This spatial-political division of the city dates back to the times of the city planning of Georges-Eugène Haussmann (1809–1891) in the nineteenth century, and it can also be observed in the voting behavior of the citizens.[4]

In London, it is Trafalgar Square, located at the very center of the imperial metropolis which serves as the urban area, that is the traditional place for big meetings and demonstrations. It is one of the largest inner-city squares, located at the meeting point of four deployment streets: the Strand, Regent Street, the Mall (the connection to Buckingham Palace and the Horse Guards Parade, the traditional place for military parades), and Whitehall (with the Cenotaph at which on each November 11, the tribute to the fallen of the World Wars takes place). Among the many events that happened on that square, only a few can be mentioned here: "Bloody Sunday" (November 17, 1887), the celebrations of Armistice Day (1918), and the Poll Tax Riots (March 31, 1990). The square is named after the Battle of Trafalgar, where the British fleet under the command of Admiral Lord Horatio Nelson (1758–1805) destroyed the French fleet in 1805. Accordingly, Nelson's Column, the fifty-six-meter-high pillar with the statue of Lord Nelson on top, is placed in the center of the square. The monument, following the model of a statue in the Temple of Mars Ultor (Mars, the Avenger) in imperial ancient Rome, was erected in 1843. The bronze reliefs on the pedestal, showing scenes from Nelson's military triumphs and his dead in the Battle of Trafalgar, are made of the material of captured French cannons. The column is surrounded by bronze lions and by the statues of other "heroes" of British military history on top of the pillar and at The National Gallery. The whole area, built between 1830 and 1850 on the place of former Royal Mews and including the medieval Eleonor Cross (Charing Cross), had been planned by the architect John Nash (1752–1835) as an expression of imperial power, an "emblem of empire."[5] Canada House and South Africa House were included in that planning, and the representations of other (former) colonies were placed near the square. The building of such a monumental square so near to the most important political institutions (i.e., the parliament, Downing Street, and Buckingham Palace) was part of a fundamental rearrangement of the whole city of London to underline its function as the capital of a global empire: "The public art and architecture of London together reflected and reinforced an impression, an atmosphere, celebrating British heroism on the battlefield, British sovereignty over foreign lands, British wealth and power, in short, British imperialism."[6] The focused assembly of important political or religious institutions in one urban area is, of course, not a new invention. One might think of the Roman Forum in ancient Rome, which functioned as the center of the whole empire.[7] But in the cases of nationally encoded public squares, their meaning and function are different. In many cases, these squares were consciously constructed as national sanctuaries. Additionally, the forms and structures might not be different from classical architecture of mastery, such as triumphal arches or monumental gates. The best example of a switch from the classical meaning of mastery to a national sanctuary is the area of Unter den Linden–Pariser Platz–Brandenburg Gate in Berlin. This urban space had been, in the beginning of its planning, a typical form of representation of mastery from pre-nationalist times. The

Brandenburg Gate,[8] built according to the model of the Propylaea of the Athenian Acropolis, was erected as a symbol of Prussian "Hohenzollern" power and as a monument of victory for the war in the Netherlands in 1787. Its handing-over to the public traffic had been a pure act of administration, without a feast or ritual and without the king taking part. The displacing of Johann Gottfried Schadow's (1764–1850) quadriga, which is situated on top of the gate, to Paris by Napoleonic troops in 1806 became interpreted as an act of national embarrassment, and the restoration of the quadriga after the Battle of Leipzig in 1813 became celebrated as a national German triumph. To the figure of the horse-driving Victoria, an iron cross was added, and the date "1813" was engraved into the gate. The whole gate thus turned into a national monument.[9] Nowadays, the urban space Unter den Linden–Pariser Platz–Brandenburg Gate serves as the public square of Germany in good, as well as in bad, times: It was here that Hitler's coming to power was celebrated on January 30, 1933, and here where the division of Germany symbolized by the building of the wall in 1961 was shown visually. It was here where the wall tumbled and fell in 1989. From a symbol of separation and isolation, the Brandenburg Gate turned into a symbol of overcoming the division and accomplishing reunification.

The oldest examples of squares, which were in their planning loaded with national meanings and connotations, are the Place de l'Étoile with the Arc de Triomphe and Avenue des Champs-Élysées in Paris and Trafalgar Square in London.[10] The triumphal arch in Paris, erected according to ancient models, was ordered by Napoleon in 1806, but the forty-nine-meter building was finished much later in 1836. It got its prominent spot at the intersection of twelve streets in the second half of the nineteenth century during the reordering of the city of Paris under Napoleon III, which is connected with the name of Baron Georges-Eugène Haussmann. The Avenue des Champs-Élysées, which is the deployment area to the national sanctuary of the Place de l'Étoile and the Arc de Triomphe, in former times had been a parkway with elm trees and a recreation area closed to the city with cafés and dancing halls. The Arc de Triomphe itself is mainly a monument of the French Army, especially commemorating the times of the Napoleonic Wars and the two World Wars. As a memorial for the fallen of World War I, the first Tomb of the Unknown Soldier with the "eternal flame of remembrance" ("*Flamme du Souvenir*") (1920) was added to the memorial.[11] A form of remembrance for the victims of industrialized types of warfare, similar themes were picked up in most of the states involved in the twentieth century's cataclysms and added to existing national sanctuaries, such as the Heldenplatz in Vienna, the *Hősök tere* (Heroes'

Square) in Budapest, the *Václavské náměstí* (Wenceslas Square) in Prague, the *Monumento Nazionale a Vittorio Emanuele II* (the Victor Emmanuel II National Monument) in Rome, the *Neue Wache* (New Guardhouse) in Berlin (which houses the remains of an unknown soldier and an unknown KZ prisoner), the Alexander Gardens in Moscow, the Piłsudski Square in Warsaw, the Syntagma Square in Athens, and Arlington National Cemetery in Washington, D.C., USA.

Fig.1: The "outer castle door" (Äusseres Burgtor) with the controversial war monument (Photo: Peter Stachel).

Napoleonic Traces

As mentioned, political squares do not differ from older dynastic-monarchist squares in their architecture but in their function as political stages, which are a result of the politization of a broader public through (and since) the Napoleonic Wars. Consequently, the oldest symbolic elements on these squares refer to these wars. This can be said for the Brandenburg Gate. In the cases of the Arc de Triomphe and Nelson's Column, the reference to the Napoleonic Wars is evident. However, in the case of the Viennese

Heldenplatz, not only the monument of Archduke Charles but the oldest symbolic elements also deal with the commemoration of the war against France. This begins with the origins of the square itself, which came into existence because of the fact that the Napoleonic troops destroyed a part of the Viennese fortification in 1809 before leaving the city. In that area, the Heldenplatz, the *Volksgarten* (People's Garden), and the *Burggarten* (private garden of the emperor) were built—seemingly according to ideas of the architect Ludwig Gabriel von Remy (1776–1851). The new *Burgtor* (Castle Gate) and the Theseus Temple were erected as monuments intended to remind passersby of the victory over Napoleon.

The Burgtor was built in 1824 under the architect Pietro Nobile (1774–1854) and based on construction plans of Luigi Cagnola (1762–1833), who had also designed the Arco della Pace for the Foro Buonaparte in Milano. It seems that his plans for Vienna were influenced by the model of the Brandenburg Gate, which itself followed the archetype of the Propylaea from the Athenian Acropolis. The Burgtor was built in the "roman style," as newspapers explained at the time,[12] meaning that it was erected not by professional stonemasons but by soldiers. This clearly marked the gate as a monument of the army, and as a matter of fact, it was the property of the Austrian Army not only during the Habsburg Monarchy but also during the First and Second Republic of Austria. Importantly, the gate was opened to the public on the (eleventh) anniversary of the Battle of Leipzig in which Napoleon had been defeated in October 1813. The gate has five gateways, based on Doric pillars, intended to symbolize both social equality and hierarchy. The middle gateway was not open for public use but only for the use of the emperor (it became opened to the public after the 1960s), but the other four gateways are absolutely identical to the middle gateway.

The Burgtor changed its look several times. The inscriptions "*Franciscus I. Imperator Austriae MDCCCXXIV*" and "*Justitia Regnorum Fundamentum*" ("Law is the Fundament of Ruling," the motto of the regime of Emperor Franz) date back to the time of the construction of the gate. The inscription "*Laurum militibus lauro dignis*" ("Glory to the Soldiers, that have earned merits") was added during World War I, as were the laurel collars that are nowadays seen as the typical ornaments of the gate. On the street side of the gate, four golden laurel sprigs are fixed with golden belts on which the names of the donors can be read: Franz Joseph I of Austria, Wilhelm II of Germany, Ferdinand I of Bulgaria, and Sultan Mehmed V of the Ottoman Empire—the four monarchs whose countries where allied in World War I.

In 1934, the inner part of the gate converted into the so-called *Österreichisches Heldendenkmal* (Austrian Heroes' Monument), which commemorated the fallen soldiers of World War I and two Habsburgs: Archduke Franz Ferdinand, who was presented as the first victim of the war, and the last emperor, Charles I, who died in exile. After World War II, as in many local war memorials, simply the dates "1939–1945" were added. Later, a memorial for the victims of Nazism was added. The central piece of the war memorial from 1934 is the Tomb of the Unknown Soldier, following the model of Paris. The architect of the tomb in the Burgtor was the sculptor Wilhelm Frass (1886–1968), who later became a prominent official of Nazi cultural politics. After the Anschluss of Austria to Nazi Germany in 1938, Frass boasted that he had smuggled a pro-Nazi message into the monument. In 2012, the tomb was opened, and such a message was really found. Although this message is removed now, the finding caused discussions about the function of the whole monument that are still ongoing.

The Theseus Temple in the Volksgarten, a copy of the Theseion of the Acropolis, is also a monument that commemorates the victory over Napoleon; but to understand its function, it is necessary to know the circumstances of its construction. The temple had been built as a location for a marble monument made by the Roman sculptor Antonio Canova (1757–1822)—that of Theseus killing a centaur. This monument had been ordered by Napoleon for the Corso of Milano, the planned Foro Buonaparte, which was meant to signify and celebrate the new function of the city as capital of Italy, where Napoleon's stepson, Eugène, should have ruled as vice king. Another monument that had been designated to be part of the Foro Buonaparte was a three-and-a-half-meter-high marble statue of *Napoléon en Mars désarmé et pacificateur* (Napoleon as Mars, who laid down his weapons and brought peace). The statue, which references antique Roman traditions of the deification of the emperor, was also produced by Canova. Shortly after Napoleon's definitive defeat at Waterloo in 1815, this sculpture was bought by the English Parliament and donated as a gift to the Duke of Wellington (1769–1852), who had been commander of the British troops at Waterloo. The duke had it placed in his Palais Apsley House in London, nowadays a museum, where it still stands today.

It seems that this example motivated the Austrian Emperor Franz I (1768–1835) to buy the Theseus Group for Vienna to convey that he, too, had defeated Napoleon. On the occasion of a visit from Emperor Franz to Rome in 1819, he met with Canova and bought the monument. It was logical that the monument was added to the transfiguration of the area near the Hofburg, and so the plan of the Theseus Temple came into existence. As Canova's monument was moved to the newly built Kunsthistorisches

Museum in 1890, the Theseus Temple lost its original meaning. Nowadays, even most Viennese do not know that this temple had been built as a memorial for the victory over Napoleon.

In December 1857, Emperor Franz Joseph I (1830–1916) issued the order to remove the now-obsolete fortifications of the city of Vienna. From this moment on up to the last years of the existence of the Habsburg Monarchy, the city center of Vienna was one big construction site. The key element of the planning was the *Ringstrasse* (ring road) that surrounds the old city center and radiates streets to the outer parts of the city. The formulation of Franz Joseph's order illustrates his intentions. He envisaged the enlargement of the inner city—and the "inner city" implied the Hofburg, noble families' palais, churches, and monasteries. The Votivkirche was the first official building erected on the Ringstrasse, a church that was meant as a votive offering for a failed assassination attempt against Franz Joseph. It was planned that this church should also serve as a garrison church for those parts of the army stationed near the inner city of the capital. In other words, the Votivkirche was meant as a visual symbol for the alliance of the old ruling powers: nobility, church, and army. But due to political changes, the Ringstrasse happened to become the visible symbol for the new, economically dominant middle class (the term *Ringstrassengesellschaft*, or Ring Street society, refers to this development).[13] As a counterpoint to this development, the idea of a gigantic *Kaiserforum* (Emperor's Forum) arose, which would not only include the Heldenplatz but the whole space to the mews of the court (nowadays the Museum Quarter). According to plans by the prominent architect Gottfried Semper (1803–1879), two new wings of the Hofburg were planned, which would enlarge the building to the Ringstrasse. Two triumphal arches over the street would link the Hofburg to the two museum buildings that were under construction at the time.[14] This project, atypical for the Habsburgs in its gigantism, never came into existence. The only part of it that was finished (in the year 1913) was one of the planned two new wings of the Hofburg: the so-called *Neue Burg* (New Hofburg), which nowadays houses the users' part of the National Library, and the House of Austrian History. The planned opposite wing of the Hofburg was never built, and this fact gives the Heldenplatz its characteristic open form. While it is architecturally closed on one side, the other side flows into the Volksgarten, and the view to the Burgtheater and Vienna City Hall is open. This motivated the Austrian writer Jörg Mauthe (1924–1986) to call the Heldenplatz the most beautiful square in the world—because it has no borders.[15]

Fig 2: Full view of the Heldenplatz with the "Neue Burg" and the promontory, where Hitler gave his "Anschluss" speech on March 13, 1938 (Photo: Peter Stachel).

The Anschluss Rally

One characteristic of many political squares is their connection to ruptures or violent events in the history of the country. On some of these squares, people have been killed in political conflicts. These traumatic events give these squares their specific social meanings and turn them into something like "holy grounds." But in all religions, sacred space is also a *locus terribilis*: it is awesome and sometimes frightening, and it points to dramatic and traumatic experiences in the history of a group. One might think of Tlatelolco with its Plaza de las Tres Culturas in Mexico City, whose name stands for the massacre against 300 students committed by police and army forces in 1968. Or one might think about the *Tiān'ānmén Guǎngchǎng* (Square of Heavenly Peace) in Beijing, which refers to the massacre of 1989 (there, the squarc is either closed to the public or strictly controlled by the authorities on each June 4, the anniversary of the tragic event). The Brandenburg Gate reminds us of the Nazis coming to power in 1933. Many other examples could be mentioned.

The Viennese Heldenplatz definitely is such a square, which similarly refers to a traumatic event that can exactly be named and dated. At the so-called *Anschlusskundgebungen* (Annexation rally) on March 15, 1938, Adolf Hitler (1889–1945) proclaimed from the balcony of the New Hofburg to a jubilating mass of people on the Heldenplatz Austria's annexation by Nazi Germany. Nobody was killed right then and there, but "The Heldenplatz," as this event is sometimes called, marks the beginning of years of political persecution, war, and genocide. More than this, in the pictures and film scenes from March 15, 1938, the compliance, active participation, and the ethical capitulation of a part of Austrian society before Nazism is documented. This was far from the first political rally on the Heldenplatz, which had been used for political purposes many times before, but it became the quintessential political event and remains the main defining element in the square's history to this day. The day after the rally, the *Völkischer Beobachter*, the official newspaper of the Nazi Party, was published in Austria for the first time, and its editorial article was a text about the Heldenplatz, its historical meaning in the past, its architectural and artistic meanings, and the new significance the square had gained in the eyes of the Nazis through the Anschluss rally. The square where the Anschluss officially had been proclaimed would become the central ceremonial square of the NS regime in the *Ostmark* (former Austria). Several plans were made, most of them including an architectural demarcation of the square toward the Volksgarten. The whole square would become cobbled, the Burgtor would be moved to the center of the square, and the Theseus Temple would be placed on an artificially built hill, as per the "role model" of the Walhalla near the city of Regensburg in Bavaria. According to the memories of Hitler's childhood friend August Kubizek (1888–1956), young Adolf had criticized the buildings of the Hofburg because they had been built up by bricks and not by stones, which would be more solid. Thus, the buildings were to be replaced by new stone buildings in a similar style.[16] Fortunately, none of those ideas and plans ever came into existence as the beginning of World War II stopped all these projects.[17] At the end of the war, the square had changed its look as the two equestrian monuments were shielded from bomb damage by brick walls, and a huge fire protection pond filled with water was placed in its center. After the war, during a period of extreme food shortages, parts of the Heldenplatz and especially the surrounding gardens were used for gardening potatoes and vegetables. This use of the square became restaged in a reenactment in 2005.

All events that have happened on the Heldenplatz since March 15, 1938, temporary political acts or demonstrations and permanent constructions of monuments alike, have to refer in one way or another to this cardinal point of modern Austrian history. It also has to be remembered that to this day, the pictures produced by Nazi propaganda frame the optical memory of the event. The cameramen and photographers of NS propaganda, of course, were interested in presenting the square as filled to the brim and the people as invariably enthusiastic. This explanatory comment should not be misinterpreted as an act of relativization but as a reminder that highly emotional pictures are not a product of happenstance, but, rather, they are produced and selected with care for specific reasons and with intended impacts.

It is noteworthy that the optical memory of the balcony scene from March 15, 1938, would in due course be partly overwritten by another important balcony scene in Austrian history. On May 15, 1955, the Austrian State Treaty (or Austrian Independence Treaty) between the four occupation armies (United States, Great Britain, Soviet Union, and France) and the Republic of Austria was signed at Belvedere Castle in Vienna. After the ceremony, the five ministers of foreign affairs (John Foster Dulles, Harold Macmillan, Vyacheslav Molotov, and Antoine Pinay for the occupation countries and Leopold Figl for Austria) greeted the people waiting in front of the castle from its balcony. Figl showed the signed treaty to the public. The picture of that moment is iconic for Austrians, who all know that Figl shouted "*Österreich ist frei*" ("Austria is free") from the balcony—something that he, in fact, never did (the image was produced by an editor of the *Austria Wochenschau*, a newsreel that was shown in all cinemas before film screenings).[18] It is interesting to compare the two iconic scenes as they are presented in pictures and on film. At the Anschluss rally, the crowded Heldenplatz is seen from above, from the position of power—Hitler's position. Here, he is acclaimed by the masses. In the case of the signing of the Austrian State Treaty, the view is exactly opposite—from below to the balcony with the ministers. And in the images of the Heldenplatz rally, military elements can be seen elsewhere, while these are totally missing in the second case. The ministers are wearing civilian garb, they are laughing, and they are waving to the public with their handkerchiefs.[19]

For the tenth anniversary of the event, it had been planned that the scene should be reenacted by the present ministers but with the very popular Leopold Figl, a member of the conservative People's Party (ÖVP) who had been imprisoned in concentration camps during most of the Nazi years, as a central figure. Unfortunately, Figl died six days before the planned event. For the funeral service, his coffin was not placed in front of Belvedere Castle nor at the Ministry of Foreign Affairs but at the Heldenplatz exactly under the balcony, where Hitler had held his speech. This position was chosen with care, as the preface of a book with Figl's political speeches published shortly after his death explained: the memory of the "bad Austrian" Hitler should become replaced with that of the "good Austrian" Figl.[20]

The Heldenplatz as a Topos in Austrian Literature

The term "Heldenplatz" in Austria does not necessarily or only signify the concrete square in Vienna. It can also be used as code for an ethically contaminated and burdened chapter of Austria's past. It is in exactly this sense that the term has been used in Austrian literature several times.[21] The first example was a novel by Ernst Lothar (1890–1974), written in exile in the United States and published in 1945 in a German and an English edition. It is interesting that only the original German version is entitled *Heldenplatz*, while the English translation got the title *The Prisoner*.[22] It is evident that everybody reading the German version would know the meaning of the term "Heldenplatz," while the same could not be guaranteed for readers of the English translation. The narrator of the novel is a Viennese author in exile who teaches at an American college—as Lothar himself did. He gets to know a young man from Vienna, who is imprisoned in a prisoner of war camp in the United States and fears that he will be killed by a Vehmic court of fanatical Nazis among the prisoners, armed with the knowledge that he is an opponent of Nazism. The main part of the novel is the story of that young man, named Toni, who had been a Nazi himself but became disillusioned by several events—among them, a talk with an old Jewish man, whom he met one night on the Heldenplatz.

Another example for a literary use of the term is the poem "*wien: heldenplatz*" from June 4, 1962, by Austrian poet Ernst Jandl (1925–2000). It is one of the best-known examples of modern Austrian poetry, and it is printed in most school textbooks in Austria.

"*wien: heldenplatz*" by Ernst Jandl

der glanze heldenplatz zirka / versaggerte in maschenhaftem männchenmeer / drunter auch frauen die ans maskelknie / zu heften heftig sich versuchten, hoffensdick / und brüllzten wesentlich.
verwogener stirnscheitelunterschwang / nach nöten nördlich, kechelte / mit zu-nummernder aufs bluten feilzer stimme / hinsensend sämmertliche eigenwäscher.

pirsch! / döppelte der gottelbock von Sa-Atz zu Sa-Atz / mit hünig sprenkem stimmstummel. / balzerig würmelte es im männechensee / und den weibern ward so pfingstig ums heil / zumahn: wenn ein knie-ender sie hirschelte.[23]

the gloryomplete heldenplatz, approximately / refounderd in ablundand manikinmain / 'mong them women that on the masculknee / tried to pin themselves fiercly and hopethick / and inheatroared substantially.
adoughious foreheadpartingunderswing / needly northly, panted / with a slam-numbering bloody foldsold voice / scything some selfwashers.
stalk! / doubolloped the goddygoat from ss-entence to ss-entence / with a giantic spreak stump of a voice / it wormed matingly inside the manikinsea / and the females felt so penetrecostal 'round the heil / especianny: when a knee-ender stagged them.

(The translation is provided by the author of the article in the interest of comprehensibility. It has not been authorized by the author of the poem.)

Jandl, who as a thirteen-year-old boy had been witness to the Anschluss rally, presents the event as a grotesque drama, loaded with violence and with sexuality. It is interesting to realize that although the literary presentation is highly alienated, in a Brechtian sense, the key word "*heldenplatz*" in the title of the poem leaves no doubt as to which event is being described.

The third example is Thomas Bernhard's (1931–1989) drama *Heldenplatz* from 1988,[24] which was intended as the official commentary of the Burgtheater on the fiftieth anniversary of the Anschluss. The play presents a Jewish family by the name of Schuster, who came back to Austria after 1945 to discover that the political situation fifty years after the Anschluss was getting more and more similar to the situation in 1938. The symbol for that resemblance is the "*Sieg Heil!*" chants from the Heldenplatz (from March 15, 1938) that one of the characters believes to be hearing again all the time. At the end of the play, the chants can be heard by the visitors of the theater as well. This was arguably the best-known dramatic use of the concrete place, where the drama was staged for the first time. The Burgtheater is so close to the Heldenplatz that on March 15, 1938, the chants from the square must have been heard inside the theater as well.

Contested Space

As the most important stage of public politics in Austria, the Heldenplatz is at the same time a sometimes virtually, sometimes tangibly contested space. On April 13, 2002, when about 200 participants of a right-wing demonstration protested on the Heldenplatz against an exhibition about the war crimes of the German *Wehrmacht*, participants of an unofficial counterdemonstration—among them politicians of the Socialist Party and the Green Party—tried to break through the police block to attack the demonstrators. The day after, Austrian newspapers reported street fighting and heavy riots on the Heldenplatz and unanimously criticized that the authorities had allowed the right-wing demonstration on that square—elsewhere, maybe, but not on the Heldenplatz with its political and historical burden.

Also, for other more or less right-wing acts and demonstrations, it is often demanded that the Heldenplatz should not be allowed to be their stage. For example, the annual "Honoring of the Fallen (of World War II)" in front of the Burgtor on May 8 (the anniversary of the capitulation of the German *Wehrmacht* in 1945)—as organized by the Viennese *Korporationsring*, an association of German nationalist academic fraternities—has not been allowed to take place there since 2013. Now on that date, the spot is occupied by a vigil of the Austrian Army and a concert from the Vienna Symphonic Orchestra, as organized by the Mauthausen Committee Austria as a *Fest der Freude* (Festival of Joy).

In other words, conflicts about the legitimacy of a temporary "occupation" or use of the Heldenplatz by some political groups turns out to be a conflict about the authority of interpretation regarding collective memory in Austria. The Heldenplatz is a central stage of these conflicts, and so it is the political square and the main square of the Republic of Austria. Who is allowed to use the Heldenplatz as a stage and who shall or shall not, according to some commenters, use it for that purpose are important political and symbolic questions. Historical knowledge is helpful for this, but it is mainly not history itself but the moral evaluation of history from the vantage point of present times that is at stake here. But this simultaneously means that such disputes are not settled by historical facts nor by moral understandings, but they also implicate political power and the implementation of one's own position as the legitimate one. Those who are able to fill the Heldenplatz up with people in public acts for their ideals and try to keep other positions from the square also attempt to demonstrate their dominance. The fact that such conflicts in Austria often focus on the Heldenplatz shows and reinforces its function as a symbolic focal point for Austrian identity.

Endnotes

1 See Peter Stachel, *Mythos Heldenplatz: Hauptplatz und Schauplatz der Republik* (Vienna: Molden, 2018).

2 "Vor dem Theater. (Kleine Wochen Plaudereien)," in *Zwischen-Akt*, October 19, 1865, 3.

3 For the history of the castle see: *Die Wiener Hofburg*, 5 vols., ed. Artur Rosenauer (Vienna: Verlag der Österreichischen Akademie der Wissenschaften, 2012-2018).

4 See Maurice Agulhon, "Paris: La traverse d'est en oust", in *Lieux des mémoire*. III. *Les France*, 3. *De l'archive à l'embléme*, ed. Pierre Nora (Paris: Gallimard, 1992), 869–909.

5 Rodney Mace, *Trafalgar Square: Emblem of Empire* (London: Lawrence and Wishart, 1976).

6 Jonathan Schneer, *London 1900: The Imperial Metropolis* (New Haven–London: Yale University Press, 2001), 19. See as well: David Cannadine, *Ornamentalism: How the British Saw Their Empire* (London: Penguin UK, 2001).

7 See Theodor Kissel, *Das Forum Romanum: Leben im Herzen Roms* (Düsseldorf: Artemis, 2004).

8 See Hans Juergen Scholz, "Deutschlands Portal: Das Brandenburger Tor (1791)," in Hans Juergen Koch, *Wallfahrtsstätten der Nation: Von Brandenburg bis Bayern* (Frankfurt/Main: Fischer, 1986), 15-24; Gustav Seibt, "Das Brandenburger Tor," in *Deutsche Erinnerungsorte 2*, ed. Étienne Francois and Hagen Schulze (Munich: Beck, 2001) 67–85.

9 See Godehard Janzing, "Die Quadriga auf dem Brandenburger Tor: Bildwerk und Verteidigungsidentität," in *Denkmale und kulturelles Gedächtnis nach dem Ende der ost-west Konfrontation*, ed. Gabi Dolff-Bonekaemper and Edward van Voolen, (Berlin: Jovis, 1999), 73–84.

10 See Marc Gaillard, *The Arc de Triomphe* (Paris: Martelle, 1998); Roland Pozzo di Borgo, *Les Champs-Élysées: Trois siècles d' histoire* (Paris: Editions de La Martinière, 1999).

11 See Jan-François Jagielski, *Le soldat inconnu: Invention et postérite d'un symbol* (Paris: Imago, 2005).

12 See, e.g., *Österreichisch Kaiserliche privilegierte Wiener Zeitung*, Oct. 16, 1824, 1.

13 See Carl E. Schorske, "The Ringstrasse, Its Critics, and the Birth of Urban Modernism", in Carl E. Schorske, *Fin-de-siècle Vienna: Politics and Culture* (New York City: Alfred A. Knopf, 1979), 24–115. In general, see *Die Wiener Ringstrasse*, 11 vols, (Vienna: Böhlau, 1969–1981).

14 See Margaret Gottfried, *Das Wiener Kaiserforum: Utopien zwischen Hofburg und Museumsquartier* (Vienna: Böhlau, 2001).

15 Jörg Mauthe and Paul Flora, *Wien für Anfänger: Vorläufige Bruchstücke zum Entwurf einer Skizze über Land und Leute* (Innsbruck: Haymon, 2016).

16 See August Kubizek, *Adolf Hitler: Mein Jugendfreund* (Graz: Leopold Stocker Verlag, 1953).

17 See Ingrid Holzschuh, *Wiener Stadtplanung im Nationalsozialismus von 1938 bis 1942: Das Neugestaltungsprojekt von Architekt Hanns Dustmann* (Vienna: Böhlau, 2011); *Wien – Die Perle des Reiches. Planen ür Hitler* (Vienna: Architekturzentrum Wien, 2015).

18 See Peter Stachel, "Oesterreich ist… Die Inszenierung kollektiver Erinnerung am Beispiel des Österreichischen Staatsvertrags," in *Inszenierung und Gedächtnis: Soziokulturelle und ästhetische Praxis*, ed. Hermann Blume, Elisabeth Grossegger, Andrea Sommer-Mathis, and Michael Roessner (Bielefeld: transcript, 2014), 83–103.

19 See Hans Petschar and Georg Schmid, *Erinnerung & Vision: Die Legitimation Österreichs in Bildern. Eine semiohistorische Analyse der Austria Wochenschau 1949–1960* (Graz: ADEVA, 1990), 47.

20 See Ludwig Reichhold, "Politiker mit christlicher Verantwortung," in Leopold Figl, *Reden für Österreich: Mit einem Vorwort von Ludwig Reichhold* (Vienna: Europa Verlag, 1965), 11.

21 See Johann Sonnleitner, "Heldenplatz und die Folgen: 1938 – 1988," in *Der literarische Umgang der Oesterreicher mit Jahres- und Gedenktagen*, ed. Wendelin Schmidt-Dengler (Vienna: Österreichischer Bundesverlag, 1994), 242–251.

22 Ernst Lothar, *The Prisoner*, trans. James A. Galston (Garden City: Doubleday, 1945).

23 Ernst Jandl, "wien: heldenplatz," in Ernst Jandl, *Laut und Luise* (Olten: Walter Verlag, 1966), 46.

24 Thomas Bernhard, *Heldenplatz* (Frankfurt/Main: Suhrkamp, 1988).

Das jüdische Fabelreich in der Ostmark: "Jewish" Historiography and the Question of Origins in Vienna before the Holocaust

Tim Corbett

One of the first modern historiographic works on the Jews of Vienna was published in 1847 by the writer and political figure Ludwig August Frankl.[1] The timing is conspicuous, his work appearing in the years when the first halting steps were being taken toward the legal emancipation of Jews across the Habsburg Empire and just a few years before the provisional statutes of the *Israelitische Kultusgemeinde* (IKG), the Jewish community organization in Vienna, were enacted in 1852—the first time in almost two centuries that Vienna's Jews were once again allowed to formally organize their community. Frankl was well situated to undertake his work when he did, for he was the nascent Jewish community organization's *Aktuar* at the time, a position combining secretary and archivist roles, and in this capacity had substantially expanded and organized the collections of the community's budding archive during the 1840s—reputedly the oldest Jewish communal archive in the world.[2] Although the origins of the IKG itself constitute the subject of both myth and confusion in the copious historiography on Vienna's Jews, despite the organization's central role in the city's Jewish history, the quest for origins generally has underpinned the historiographic engagement with the Jews of Vienna since first it emerged.[3] Thus, Frankl paradigmatically opened his *Geschichte der Juden in Wien* with a reference to various "myths" and "traditions" recorded by the "eldest chroniclers of Austria," according to which Jews had been living "in a *Judenreich* [Jewish realm] in the land below the Enns"—the heartland of historic "Austria," roughly corresponding to the federal state of Lower Austria today—since about 1700 BCE, a realm that by about 200 BCE had purportedly been ruled by altogether "72 princes of Jewish descent."[4]

This is a rather fanciful notion, not least of all given that the earliest archaeological evidence of Jewish life in the territory of modern Austria dates no earlier than the third century CE: an amulet discovered in 2008 in a Roman burial ground in Halbturn in Burgenland with the Hebrew words "*sh'ma Israel*" ("Hear, O Israel," the opening words of the monotheistic credo from Deuteronomy 6:4) engraved in Greek characters.[5] To be sure, this groundbreaking discovery, which did, in fact, provide evidence of Jewish life in Austria centuries earlier than previously documented, proved a number of points, the most consequential being that Jews (and I use the term throughout this article strictly in reference to adherents of the Jewish faith) had already been living in the territory of modern Austria at a time when not even the concept of "Austria," never mind an "Austrian majority society," had yet come into existence, not even in embryonic form. After all, even the generously far-sighted, post-Nazi Austrian myth of origin only dates itself back to 966 CE on the basis of the obscure "Ostarrichi document."[6]

More than half a century after Frankl's early work, the Jewish historian Ignaz Schwarz showed that the "myths" and "traditions" Frankl had cited could actually be traced back to the sixteenth-century Viennese polymath Wolfgang Lazius, a non-Jew (quite significantly for our purposes here) who had completely misread the Hebrew inscriptions of a number of actually medieval Jewish gravestones discovered in his time. Then, in his 1546 work *Vienna Austriae*—incidentally the first ever published history of the city of Vienna—he used this wildly erroneous data to locate the origins of Jews in Austria long before classical antiquity.[7] Thereby, Schwarz refuted what he called the "*Hypothese von dem jüdischen Fabelreiche in der Ostmark*" ("the hypothesis of a mythical Jewish realm in the Eastern March")—himself intriguingly employing a glaring anachronism of medieval origin (the term *Ostmark*) in his refutation.[8]

Perhaps, as Schwarz opined, Frankl's "mythical narrative" constituted an attempt to prove "that the respective Jewish population of this swath of land, as the descendants of a tribe that had immigrated in prehistoric times, was innocent of Jesus' death by crucifixion" and was thus intended to refute the centuries-old charge of deicide levied against "the Jews" as a collective, thereby securing their equality, finally, with their non-Jewish compatriots in the age of emancipation.[9] Whatever the "facts" may be regarding the origins of Jewish life in Austria, Frankl's "mythical narrative," which he had resurrected from the first ever history of Vienna, penned by a non-Jewish scholar as far back as the sixteenth century, undoubtedly served a deeper function for the more immediate, present-day concerns of the mid-nineteenth century: to consolidate the notion, as the Zionist historian Ludwig Bato also remarked decades later, "that Jews have since time immemorial belonged in the mind of the people to the aboriginal population of this swath of land."[10] If the Zionist movement—like antisemitism—had already cast doubt on this aboriginal belonging in the early twentieth century, then the Nazi Holocaust sought to negate it entirely. In the aftermath of genocide, the early origin myths of Vienna's Jews gave way to a new historiographic metanarrative and, in time, were all but forgotten. This article revisits early "Jewish" historiography in Vienna to see how it informs present-day discourses on Jews and "Jewish" history in the Austrian context.

"*Quellenauffrischung*": The Genealogy of "Jewish" Historiography in Vienna and Its Uses for the Present

The past, as the American literary historian Van Wyck Brooks postulated in the early twentieth century, should be "usable" to the present, and, should "the past that survives in the common mind of the present" be "without living value," it follows that a "usable past" can and should be created.[11] It is no coincidence that the post-Napoleonic era in Europe—characterized as it was by colossal upheavals in the political and social fabric of the continent, rapid acceleration in communications and everyday life, mass migration and urbanization, industrialization and severance from the land, and the pervasive sense of rootlessness that took hold as a result—should have witnessed the rise of a fervent new engagement with the past that would soon culminate in the establishment of a new academic discipline: histor(iograph)y.[12] In keeping with the romanticist sensibilities of the time, this new discipline was intended to scientifically substantiate the quest for the "essence" of ostensibly "national" cultures in the emergent "nation" states of Europe and to validate their (often invented) "traditions."[13]

This historical turn also manifested itself among Europe's various Jewries, as Yosef Hayim Yerushalmi explored in his foundational work on Jewish history and memory, with a modern, secular "Jewish" historiography soon becoming, as Yerushalmi formulated it somewhat romantically himself, the "faith of fallen Jews."[14] Certainly, the general decline in formal religiosity and in the authority of religious institutions in Europe—coupled with the gradual legal, political, and social emancipation of Europe's Jews—increasingly rendered the older, inherited biblical narratives of Jewish "peoplehood" and this people's purported exile from the Land of Israel insufficient to serve the needs of Europe's diverse Jewries in the optimistic, "progress"-oriented, and most crucially nationalized atmosphere of the nineteenth century. This is the context in which a modern historiography—and with it, a set of historical origin myths—concerning Jews in Vienna first emerged, driven, as this article will show, by a network of academic and popular scholars crucially of both Jewish and non-Jewish backgrounds and with diverse motivations to craft a historical "master narrative" of Jews in Vienna.

One of the major long-term consequences of National Socialism and the Holocaust was the deep rift it created in the perception of Jews and their place in Central European culture, society, and history. This rift would profoundly shape—but arguably also distort—historiography for decades to come. On a microcosmic scale in the Viennese context, the older body of Jewish historiography was largely forgotten, despite the fact that its sources and findings had laid the groundwork for the development of the field in subsequent generations. On the macroscopic level, meanwhile, "Jewish" history—a misleadingly essentializing concept that should really be specified as the history of Jews[15]—was segregated from the "general" postwar historiography of the German-speaking world and largely reduced to the history of antisemitism, persecution, expulsions, and, of course, genocide. This "lachrymose conception of Jewish history," as Salo Baron famously diagnosed it as early as the 1960s, allowed, in turn, for the tacit resuscitation in serious scholarship of the traditional biblical "mythistories" of Jewish peoplehood, diaspora, and exile.[16] In this narrative, Jews hardly played a role in "general" Central European history except as a passive, mostly abstracted, and crucially discrete and essentially segregated "people," ghettoized in social, cultural, and sometimes also physical isolation from the "majority" or "mainstream" (implying non-Jewish) societies in which they lived—a view that still dominates in fields such as Holocaust and antisemitism studies today.

This "lachrymose" narrative found its counterpart in the inner-Jewish narrative predominating in Jewish studies that, while predicated on the same essential sense of Jewish "difference,"[17] focused on the ostensibly failed and in any case misguided attempts by the Jewish population of Central Europe before the 1930s to "assimilate" to a "German" *Leitkultur*—including, notably, in Austria.[18] Indeed, Austrian culture is not essentially distinguishable from German culture in the dominant Jewish studies perspective. Certainly, the distinction is not an important one to the "assimilation" argument, which relies on reductive essentialisms to validate its monocultural explanatory models. As Dirk Rupnow remarked in a collection of critical essays on the Holocaust and memory, this broad post-Holocaust development has meant that the complex "points of interaction between the Jewish and non-Jewish realms of experience" of previous generations were for the longest time lost from sight.[19] This finding applies aptly to the pre-Holocaust historiography of Jews in Vienna that is the focus of this article—the reinvestigation of which may then well provide a fresh impetus to rethink this perennial area of scholarly and popular interest.

To briefly consider a closely related study by way of comparison, the historian Markus Wenninger examined an expansive body of pre-Holocaust "Jewish" historiography in the Austrian provinces, where Jews had for the longest time prior to the emancipatory era of the nineteenth century been forbidden from settling. He found that this work was mostly the product of rabbis and Jewish amateur historians who aimed thereby to cultivate a sense of continuity that, given the historical circumstances of pogroms, repeated persecutions, and later mass migration, had never, in fact, existed.[20] This provincial paradigm, which would seem to confirm the conventional narrative of Jewish immigration and "assimilation" in Austria, moreover suggesting that before the Holocaust, the writing of "Jewish" history was exclusively the preserve of Jewish historians, does not apply so easily to Vienna, where a Jewish community has existed despite pogroms and expulsions and with very few interruptions since at least the High Middle Ages—and where historiographic romanticizations of the Jewish past demonstrably coincided and crucially also intersected with historiographic romanticizations of Vienna's past generally. In fact, they often emerged in tandem with one another, just as the fabulous myth of a prehistoric *Judenreich* in Austria was first espoused in the earliest ever published history of Vienna by a sixteenth-century non-Jewish humanist scholar.

In reality as in myth, the tangible, provable origins of Vienna's Jewish history coincide with the emergence both of "Austria" as a discrete political entity and of Vienna as a political center of note. Austria, which at the time meant the territory essentially comprising the modern states of Upper and Lower Austria, was elevated from a mere march of the Holy Roman Empire to a duchy, with Vienna as its new residential capital, only in the twelfth century, mere decades before the earliest Jewish resident in Vienna's recorded history—Shlom, master of the mint to Duke Leopold V—resided there with a number of coreligionists.[21] Since then, Vienna has repeatedly ranked among the most significant Jewish population centers in Central Europe—first in the late Middle Ages, then in the mid-seventeenth century, and then again from the late nineteenth century onwards, when the city was home to one of the largest and culturally most influential Jewish populations worldwide until their sweeping destruction in the Holocaust. In summary, Vienna's "general" history and the history of its successive Jewish populations are intimately and inextricably bound up with each other—this concatenation moreover accounting for a significant part of the relevance of modern Austrian history to European and even global history: from the proliferation of "Austrian" cultural and intellectual capital across the world due to the mass exodus of Jewish Austrians through to the abysmal roots of National Socialism and the Holocaust in Austria.[22] Seen in this manner, it becomes deeply problematic to speak of a discrete "Jewish" history when the history of Jews in Vienna/Austria cannot be disentangled from the broader Viennese/Austrian historical context.

This article follows the theoretical framework outlined by Christian Karner in the introduction to this volume in viewing myth and history, narrative and fact, not as diametrically opposed, but as intricately interwoven products of the quest for historical meaning—or in other words, the search for a "usable past." From this perspective, the historical veracity of the early historiography of Jews in Vienna is of less interest than the interpretative frameworks and, importantly, the ideological motivations underlying the "master narratives" developed by successive generations of historians working in this field before the Holocaust. This article traces the origins and developments of "Jewish" historiography—here meaning histories conceived to speak exclusively about Jews and Jewish culture, though not necessarily authored by Jews—in Vienna from the 1840s into the 1930s. While this corpus of works laid the foundations for the field that later generations of historians would continue to build on, these seminal works have been largely lost from sight or dismissed outright in post-Holocaust historiography, partly because their findings became outdated (as evident in the outlandish origin myths outlined above) but also surely because their "master narratives" conflicted with the ideological needs and hypotheses of more recent scholarship, or even because they were simply forgotten.

From the earliest works of history on Jews in Vienna, this article traces in broad strokes the genealogy of pre-Holocaust historiography in diachronic succession while locating the respective scholarly impulses in their contemporary contexts. It thus follows a methodology discussed by William Johnston in his groundbreaking work on the origin of the *homo austriacus*, namely *Quellenauffrischung*, the "revitalization of sources." As Johnston explained: "This method follows the course upstream, so to speak, to the source of tradition," aiming to arrive at an "amalgamation of old and new sources," the purpose of which is "to reinvigorate ossified traditions" in historiography.[23] Beginning with the emergence of a "Jewish" historiography in the context of the mythologization of *Alt-Wien* (Old Vienna), this article traces the ideological impulses, authorship, and later institutional embedding of this historiography through the era of the antisemitic Mayor Karl Lueger, into the interwar period, and ending in the short-lived era of "Austrofascist" rule in order to see what such a *Quellenauffrischung* might reveal. Perhaps the older historiography can, in fact, inform the newer and lead to deeper insights into this already well-trodden area of modern Austrian history. While the subject matter is thus moving "upstream" to the source of an older historiographic tradition, the ultimate focus of this article is very much on the established narratives and perspectives on Vienna's "Jewish" history today. In the conclusion, I will return to the question of "general" versus "Jewish" historiographies and argue that a *Quellenauffrischung* of Jewish Viennese historiography does indeed open up space for a more integrative approach to Vienna's social and cultural history and that the "mythistory" of Jewish particularism—of a "diasporic," alien people living in shunned social and cultural isolation in foreign lands, as expressed most tenaciously in the assimilationist model of Jewish history—perhaps no longer suits our present uses of the past.

Intercultural Engagements with Jewish History in *Alt-Wien*

As a groundbreaking exhibition at the Wien Museum explored in 2004, a general "documentary historical interest" in Vienna's history could already be discerned around the year 1800, which then blossomed during the *Vormärz* and after into a downright "wistfully nostalgic attitude" toward the city's romanticized past. These are the origins of the myth of *Alt-Wien*, pertinently characterized by the Wien Museum as "the city that never was."[24] As Klaus Hödl recently showed, Vienna's Jews readily participated in this project of historical romanticization, utilizing *Alt-Wien* (for example through idealized portrayals of the old "ghetto," itself a mythologizing term, in the Leopoldstadt, Vienna's second district with Jewish roots reaching back to the early modern period) as a means to counter the widespread view, with antisemitic undertones, that Jews were a recently "immigrated" and therefore not an "autochthonous" population group.[25] This view, which still persists in historiography today, obscures the crucial point that Vienna in the nineteenth century was an immigration hub for peoples from all over the Habsburg lands and not just for Jews, of whom a large number did indeed immigrate from the crownlands during the latter half of the century.[26] The topography of *Alt-Wien*—which would rapidly disappear under the construction boom of the *Gründerzeit* at exactly the same time that it was being zealously documented—thus served Jews and non-Jews alike to stake their claims to a mythologized past and, thereby, to ground their sense of belonging in the *k. k. Reichshaupt- und Residenzstadt*, which was fast becoming one of the world's largest and most influential metropolises in its day.

This is the sociohistorical context in which a modern historiography of Jews in Vienna and/or Austria first emerged, and the underlying dynamics of mass migration, urbanization, and perceived rootlessness go a long way toward explaining the quest for mythical origins that we saw in Frankl's early contribution to this nascent field. However, recalling Markus Wenninger's paradigmatic claim with regard to provincial Austrian historiography that it was primarily Jews themselves who, before the Holocaust, were involved in the production of Jewish history, it is remarkable that the first standalone history of Jews in Vienna was, in fact, not written by Frankl or any other Jew, but by a non-Jew: Gerhard Robert Walter von Coeckelberghe-Dützele. A Flemish-Austrian writer, he published *Die Juden und die Judenstadt in Wien* under the pseudonym "Realis" in 1846, one year before Frankl's *Geschichte der Juden*. In the preface to this remarkable work—published even before the game-changing 1848 revolutions—Realis explained why this "strange people" (here referring collectively to "the Jews,"), of whom "half a million" lived scattered across the Austrian Empire, deserved such a "reminiscence" as he offered here. After all, according to him, Europe "largely owes its moral and religious formation to the Jews"—in other words, the foundations of the Christian religion. Though Realis opened the first chapter with the traditional biblical narrative of "dispersion" from ancient Israel and stated that the "shocking severity" with which the here ethnically construed "people of Israel" had repeatedly been persecuted through the ages was "often not without [their] own fault"—a moral judgment that echoes with post-Holocaust Austrian victim/perpetrator reversals—he traced Jewish history in "Austria" (using the term anachronistically) back to the age of Charlemagne, his work thus underlining (rather philosemitically) the rootedness of both Jewish (religious) culture and, crucially, of Jews themselves in Europe over more than a millennium.[27]

Such an apologist justification for the benevolent treatment of Jews and Jewish history on account of the historical relationship between Jewish and Christian scripture, ethics, and religious culture can naturally be traced back to Enlightenment thinking as exemplified in Gotthold Ephraim Lessing's "Ring Parable" in *Nathan der Weise* (1779). Indeed, it is no coincidence that Vienna's Judenplatz is today dominated, alongside Rachel Whiteread's Holocaust memorial, by a statue of Lessing, which was placed there in the early 1930s, melted down by the Nazis in the late 1930s, and then replaced in its original location in the 1980s.[28] Jewish intellectuals of the nineteenth century were understandably eager to express their admiration for—and implicitly also their keen familiarity with—the classical canon of European culture, and not just with "German" high culture. As a case in point, Frankl's 1847 history of Jews in Vienna—which was published the year after Realis's pioneering work on the subject and actually focused on the city's oldest preserved Jewish cemetery in the Seegasse in the ninth district as a topographic metonym for the longevity and thus "historicity" of Jewish life in the city—opened with a German translation of the final couplet of Lord Byron's "Oh, Weep for Those" (1815): "The wild-dove hath her nest, the fox his cave, / Mankind their country,—Israel but the grave!"[29]

Such acts of quotation evince the intercultural engagements between Jewish and non-Jewish European intellectuals, both on the level of contents and authorship already at this early stage in emancipatory history, as embodied here in Byron's engagement with a (rather romanticized) Jewish history and Frankl's engagement, in turn, with Byron.

Such intercultural engagements recurred throughout the burgeoning Jewish historiography in Vienna in the latter half of the nineteenth century. On the occasion of the opening of the Jewish section of the city's Central Cemetery in 1879—a highly symbolic moment utilized by various religious leaders to emphasize the newly consolidated status of Vienna's Jewish community and its integration into the city's confraternity of cultures, as embodied materially in the integration of the Jewish section within the general Central Cemetery[30]—Gerson Wolf, the first serious scholar of Vienna's Jewish history, published the first standalone history of the city's older Jewish cemeteries in the Seegasse and in Währing, Vienna's eighteenth district. Wolf opened his groundbreaking work with a quote from Johann Wolfgang von Goethe's *Iphigenie auf Tauris* (1779): "How blest is he who his progenitors / With pride remembers, to the list'ner tells / The story of their greatness, of their deeds. / And, silently rejoicing, sees himself / Link'd to this goodly chain!"[31]

This reference to Goethe was indubitably a demonstration of Wolf's intercultural erudition, but notably also functioned as a means to infer, in turn, the "essence" of the Jewish cult of ancestors that is so integrally linked to Jewish religious sepulchral culture (as in the concept of "burial with the fathers"; see, for example, Genesis 47:30, Judges 2:10, and 2 Chronicles 16:13, as well as more broadly Nehemiah 2:3, from which the modern Hebrew term for "cemetery", *beit qvarot*, is derived). Wolf thereby established a poignant link between modern "secular" humanist literature (Goethe) and ancient Jewish religious scripture (the Hebrew Bible). If this reference to Goethe seems rather clichéd,[32] then the preamble to an earlier publication by Wolf from 1861 on the foundation of the IKG in Vienna, by contrast, included an English-language passage from an anonymous "great writer," namely William Shakespeare ("Let us be sacrificers but no [sic] butchers"—from *Julius Caesar*, 1599), and was signed "on Moses Mendelsohn's [sic] birthday, 1860."[33] With this publication, Wolf wished to register the historic times he was living through, juxtaposing the era of emancipation with Vienna's less magnanimous Jewish past while simultaneously shrugging off, as the Shakespeare quote was intended to encapsulate, the dusty vestiges of that very past and looking forward to a bright future of continuous progress, as befitting the optimism of his time. He thereby incidentally also adopted an explicitly progressive position in the struggle between orthodoxy and reform that was raging in his time, which would later be framed as a struggle between "tradition" and "assimilation." In fact, many Jewish historians writing in the late Habsburg era adopted explicit positions regarding the assimilation paradigm. For example, they would emphasize pointedly that Vienna's successive Jewries since the late Middle Ages had spoken German as their mother tongue, not Yiddish (since then already the language of East European Jews), never mind Hebrew (predominantly a liturgical language), thus highlighting the rootedness of Jews in Vienna and/or Austria in contrast to the popular narratives of diaspora and perceptions of Jewish difference.[34]

As Wolf remarked in yet another of his histories published a few years later, this one on the seventeenth-century *Judenstadt* (the "ghetto") in what is today the second district, the "pleasing upturn of the political circumstances of the Jews" in his age would "not remain without an impact on Jewish historiography."[35] This observation appears, in hindsight, to foreshadow the profound yet often overlooked engagement with Vienna's Jewish history and heritage by non-Jewish historians beginning in the late nineteenth and snowballing into the twentieth century. As early as 1859, Carl Hofbauer, a *Heimatforscher* (an idiosyncratic type of usually amateur local antiquarian), included an open and sympathetic account of the capricious history of Jews in Vienna in his topography of the Rossau, the area in today's ninth district where the Jewish cemetery in the Seegasse is located.[36] Then, in 1891, the painter and amateur historian Conrad Grefe self-published a work on the Jewish cemetery in the Seegasse in which this burial ground once more served as a physical metonym for Vienna's Jewish history, which Grefe significantly traced all the way back to the Roman era. Grefe thus underlined—like his Jewish peers and in contradistinction to the widespread antisemitic views of his day—the historical longevity of Jewish life in Vienna by contrast to the notion of Vienna's Jews as an "immigrated" population group. Grefe's aesthetic appreciation of the old cemetery, formulated in words that would resound in many works to follow, moreover implicitly grounded Vienna's Jewish heritage in the cultural and topographic canon of *Alt-Wien* as part and parcel of Vienna's cultural heritage generally:

> In the midst of this modern life lies this 'good acre' [a tacit reference to a Yiddish euphemism for cemeteries]; silent and peaceful, filled with ineffable poetic allure, thickly shadowed by closely

> intertwined, high, mighty trees, creepers climbing aloft on all sides, the ground covered in lush herbs, grasses, and leaves, with many of the partly or entirely sunken gravestones disappearing almost completely below this green blanket, this is indisputably one of the most curious and interesting landmarks of *Alt-Wien*.[37]

This remarkable text, in which a non-Jew elevated an old Jewish cemetery to an aesthetic emblem of mythical *Alt-Wien*, was accompanied by a series of sepia-toned photographs—to my knowledge the earliest photographic documentations of this old, tombstone-studded burial ground that would later be all but destroyed during the Holocaust.

Grefe's work was followed by numerous similarly inclusive topographic works on the fabric of *Alt-Wien* by non-Jewish authors, remarkable already for the fact that they appeared at a time when the subject matter—the city's old streets, squares, buildings, as well as cemeteries—had largely disappeared in the construction boom of the *Gründerzeit* (as in the bon mot: *Wien demoliert sich zur Weltstadt*, Vienna is demolishing itself into a metropolis). They were moreover remarkable for their open and benevolent inclusion of sites of Jewish heritage in their efforts to canonize *Alt-Wien*. The year 1904 alone witnessed several such engagements with Vienna's Jewish heritage,[38] most notably entailing the inclusion of the old Jewish cemetery in the Seegasse in August Stauda's expansive photographic documentation of *Alt-Wien*, an oeuvre encompassing over 3,000 shots which constitutes probably the most detailed engagement with the cultural and historical stock of the Viennese cityscape in its day and which forms an aesthetic, visual cornerstone of the myth of *Alt-Wien*.[39]

This flurry of topographic and historiographic engagements with Jewish history by non-Jewish historians and antiquarians, whereby Jewish heritage was documented and incorporated as part and parcel of Viennese heritage, coincided directly with Karl Lueger's mayoralty, when Vienna was both pervaded by and governed in an atmosphere of open antisemitism.[40] The very proliferation of proactive, benevolent engagements by non-Jews with Jewish heritage in the city at this time underlines the necessity of a more nuanced and inclusive examination of Jewish/non-Jewish relations during this crucial era beyond the crass Jewish/non-Jewish divide that continues to be perpetuated in historiography, as Klaus Hödl has repeatedly emphasized.[41]

Jewish Historiography Institutionalized in the Lueger Era

The Lueger era actually witnessed a major milestone in the development of Jewish historiography in Vienna: the establishment of the "Historical Commission" of the IKG. In the mid-1900s, the IKG board contacted Arthur Goldmann, an archivist in the *Haus-, Hof- und Staatsarchiv* (State Archives), to discuss research into Vienna's Jewish history on the basis of the expansive materials held there. Goldmann opined that comprehensive expertise, including knowledge of Hebrew, was a necessary prerequisite for sustained research with the archival materials, which finally prompted the establishment of the commission in 1906.[42] Over the years, the IKG's Historical Commission counted among its members some of the leading Jewish scholars in Vienna (some of whom were moreover community rabbis), such as Alfred Francis Přibram, Max Grunwald, Moritz Güdemann, Josef Samuel Bloch, Wilhelm Jerusalem, and Bernhard Wachstein.[43] Yet, as its origins in collaboration with the State Archives show, the commission was from the outset not merely an inner-Jewish affair, emerging, rather, in close cooperation with the most important institutions and individuals of the Viennese historiographic scene of the day, as also becomes evident in the string of publications that ensued.

Over the three decades of its existence, the Historical Commission published altogether eleven volumes on Vienna's Jewish history, many of which constitute foundational works in their respective subject areas, in a series entitled *Quellen und Forschungen zur Geschichte der Juden in Deutsch-Österreich* (Sources and Research on the History of the Jews in German-Austria; note the name applied here to the German-speaking Habsburg territories already before World War I). The series was initially published by the prestigious Braumüller publishing house, which was endowed with imperial privilege as the *k. k. Hof- und Universitäts-Buchhändler*, and included Ignaz Schwarz's above-cited work on the early modern "ghetto" (Volume 2, 1909), Bernhard Wachstein's monumental two-volume history of the cemetery in the Seegasse (which appeared as Parts I and II of Volume 4 in 1912 and 1917, respectively),[44] and Alfred Francis Přibram's equally monumental two-volume compilation of documents concerning Vienna's Jews spanning from the sixteenth into the nineteenth centuries (published simultaneously as Parts I and II of Volume 8 in 1918).[45] In fact, Bernhard Wachstein, the IKG's librarian and an important proponent of Vienna's Jewish sepulchral history, had tellingly published his first work in 1907 with a non-Jewish publisher on the basis of the proceedings of a seminar he had chaired at the Austrian Academy of Sciences in December

1906, demonstrating an interest already at this time in the niche field of Jewish sepulchral history amongst a largely non-Jewish academic public.[46] Compare the paradigmatic claim by the sepulchral historian Reiner Sörries in a landmark volume on Jewish cemeteries from 2011 that "historians and other humanities scholars" had shown "hardly any interest" in the topic "until the mid-twentieth century"—that there had, in fact, been "no (scholarly) sympathy for the cultural and artistic heritage of Jews until the 1920s."[47]

The earlier works in the series of the Historical Commission, to be sure, were all authored by Jewish historians and members of the IKG. Yet the interwar period would witness a spate of publications in the series by non-Jewish historians, by which time it was being published with the *Deutscher Verlag für Jugend und Volk*, a publishing house funded by the Social Democratic government of Vienna with the intent of promoting public education. The series thus evinces the widespread engagement with and reception of Jewish historiography among Jews and non-Jews in Vienna alike, reaching right into the late interwar period. The reception of the Historical Commission's publications in the general Viennese press in the early twentieth century points to an even broader, non-academic engagement with and interest for this field among the largely non-Jewish population of the city. Examples of this include the positive review of Ignaz Schwarz's *Das Wiener Ghetto* in the *Arbeiter-Zeitung*, the major organ of Social Democracy in Austria,[48] or of Bernhard Wachstein's magnum opus on the cemetery in the Seegasse in the *Wiener Zeitung*, Vienna's oldest daily and simultaneously the official gazette of the Austrian government, which notably praised Wachstein's work as a valuable contribution to "Viennese local history" or, in other words, to Vienna's "general" history.[49]

The late Habsburg era thus witnessed the emergence of a lively historiographic engagement with Vienna's Jewish past, booming significantly during the era of Karl Lueger's open if lackadaisical antisemitic rule, when it transcended the realm of the strictly academic into the popular sphere and was driven by an intense interaction between Jews and non-Jews, academics and amateur historians alike. In a separate publication from 1913 (not a part of the series), Ignaz Schwarz offered the first critical overview of Jewish historiography published in Vienna to date, deploring the mistakes he claimed had snuck into the field in the earliest histories of the mid-nineteenth century, which were then diligently copied by later historians (a charge that could be made of historiography in any context), criticizing especially the "mythical" accounts of the origins of Austria's Jewish population as discussed earlier. In this respect, he singled out Ludwig August

Frankl's seminal efforts as "sadly rather unsuccessful," praising Gerson Wolf, by contrast, as the first serious historian of Jews in Vienna and characterizing the establishment of the Historical Commission appropriately as having paved the way for "pertinent research" within "a strictly critical historiographic framework."[50] If, therefore, the earlier narratives of a Jewish *Fabelreich in der Ostmark* had been dismissed by this point for what they were—mere myths—then the respective historians, Jewish and non-Jewish, seem to have largely agreed on at least this important point: Vienna's Jewish heritage extended back as far as the Middle Ages, if not further, and was inextricably bound up in the cultural, not to mention topographic, fabric of *Alt-Wien* and of Austria more broadly.

This is exemplified in a notable reference to the old Jewish cemetery—which, it must be repeated, was engaged throughout this period as a metonym for the longevity and rootedness of Jewish life in the city—in the influential *Kunsthistorischer Atlas der K. K. Reichshaupt- und Residenzstadt Wien*, published in 1916 by the geographer Hugo Hassinger, who characterized the cemetery in terms that had by then become ubiquitous as "one of the most peculiar historical memorial sites of the city and one of its most picturesque corners."[51] This reference is remarkable not least of all due to Hassinger's ideological orientation: During the interwar period, he turned increasingly toward National Socialism and eventually, together with a team of spatial researchers at Vienna University, went on to lay the scholarly foundations for the expansionist and ultimately genocidal *Lebensraum* policies of the "Third Reich."[52] This case anticipates the surprisingly complex relationship between Jewish and non-Jewish scholarship and the reception of Jewish cultural heritage that manifested itself in the beleaguered sociopolitical context of the interwar period.

Right-Wing Historians and Jewish Historiography in Interwar Vienna

Despite the traumatic collapse of the Habsburg Empire, the struggle for survival of the young Austrian republic, and all the attendant conflicts that ensued, Jewish historiography continued to unfold through the interwar period and was even coproduced to a greater degree by non-Jewish professional scholars than had been the case hitherto—many of whom, strikingly, came from unlikely corners of the political spectrum. In 1926, for example, the historians Hans Rotter and Adolf Schmieger published a new history of the early modern "ghetto" in the Leopoldstadt with the prestigious Burgverlag publishing house, which remains a textbook on the subject to this day. Not only were neither of these historians Jewish, Hans Rotter moreover represented the Christian Social Party in the Viennese municipal council—the party founded by Karl Lueger, which would within a few years establish the "Austrofascist" dictatorship and which continues to be cast in even the most recent historiography as essentially, even exclusively, antisemitic.[53] On the basis of the textual heritage as well as surviving gravestones of the time, Rotter and Schmieger concluded that Vienna's Jews in the early modern period had roots all over the German-speaking world and spoke German as their mother tongue, thus emphasizing that even in the pre-emancipatory era, this was not a culturally or even linguistically "ghettoized" population group, a finding based on hard evidence that belies the "assimilationist" narratives of Jewish historiography that came to dominate after the Holocaust.[54]Following in this vein, the tenth volume published by the IKG's Historical Commission—a compilation of documents relating to Vienna's medieval Jewish history, which appeared in 1931—was edited by the non-Jewish historians Rudolf Geyer and Leopold Sailer. Both were historians in the City Archive, of which Sailer would be appointed head by the Nazi *Reichsstatthalter* in 1939, a position that, following Sailer's death in 1944, his colleague Geyer would assume and hold on to through to the postwar period, indicating striking lines of intersection and continuity between Jewish and non-Jewish scholarship before, during, and after Nazi rule in Austria.[55] The volume included an introduction by the non-Jewish historian Otto Hellmuth Stowasser, a member of the board of the *Verein für Geschichte der Stadt Wien* (Association for the History of the City of Vienna) since 1918, who stressed the connection between "Jewish" and "general" history in the city, as well as between the activities of the association and the IKG's Historical Commission. This volume, he stated finally, had emerged from "many conversations with Jewish historians," thereby emphasizing, in turn, that the volume was essentially the product of non-Jewish historians.[56]

Continuing this survey briefly into the period of "Austrofascist" rule, I came across a self-published guide to "Jewish historical sites in Vienna and the Austrian federal states" by Josef Pick, a Jewish municipal religious studies teacher who would later perish in the Holocaust. It opens with a foreword by the rabbi and historian Max Grunwald that refers intriguingly to a sadly unnamed "field trip guide for middle schools" published by the Lower Austrian state educational authority, which "also called attention to memorials to Jewish history." In other words, the "Austrofascist" educational authorities were showing Lower Austrian schoolchildren Jewish historical sites in Austria as part of a curriculum to educate them about "general" Austrian cultural heritage.[57] Such research and publications on Vienna's Jewish history by conservative, non-Jewish historians suggests a certain degree of philosemitism among Austria's non-Nazi right wing during the interwar period, or at least a high degree of fluidity when it came to positions regarding right-wing ideology, antisemitism, and the place of "Jewish" history in "general" historiography. The manifold instances of positive interaction between Jews, Jewish culture, and the "Austrofascist" movement in the 1930s certainly remain a direly underexplored area in modern Austrian history.[58]

Conclusion

In 1933, the cultural historian Hans Tietze, who a few years later would be driven into exile, published his milestone work *Die Juden Wiens*, which would set an important precedent for the post-Holocaust development of historiography on the Jews of Vienna.[59] In contrast to the dominant focus on inner-Jewish community life and politics by the historians who preceded him, a major innovation of Tietze's enduring work was that it highlighted like never before the reciprocal—what Steven Aschheim would later call "co-constitutive"[60]—relationship between Vienna's Jews and Viennese/Austrian culture over the centuries, but especially during the incisive era that is today celebrated as the fin-de-siècle. As he remarked in the preface, Tietze was moved to write this study following his general cultural history, *Wien: Kultur, Kunst, Geschichte*, published in 1931, through which he had first come to realize the import of the central—yet to date unexamined—role of Jews in Vienna's "general" cultural history.[61]

The trajectory of Tietze's thinking was for a long time overshadowed by the Holocaust, yet it presaged the discussions kicked off by Carl Schorske's groundbreaking work in the 1970s on Vienna's modernist culture that would lead, amidst a general boom of new historiography on Vienna's Jews, to a conflicted and as yet unresolved discussion on how this fruitful, yet calamitous and therefore vexing history of meetings between the "Jewish" and the "non-Jewish" was to be properly understood—including discussions of how "Jewish" is Austria's modern culture.[62] As Klaus Hödl pointed out, it was non-Austrian, mostly American historians who from the 1980s onwards provided this new impetus in Jewish Viennese historiography, citing Marsha Rozenblit, Robert Wistrich, and Steven Beller as prime examples. Yet these historians, he continued, were also responsible for reorienting the interpretative framework of Vienna's Jewish history toward the hypothesis of Jewish assimilation.[63] As a result, Jews continue to be cast as a discrete "people" foreign to a purported "German-Austrian" culture who only immigrated at a late stage to Vienna and whose attempts to "assimilate"—though these may have fostered the flowering of modernist culture in Vienna around 1900—ultimately failed to secure their place in Austrian society, as the Holocaust proved devastatingly.

As Hödl went on to point out, this historiographic model has been challenged in recent years by a growing body of work from the German-speaking world that aims to overcome the tenacious Jewish/non-Jewish divide in historiography and to achieve a more inclusive understanding of modern (Austrian) culture.[64] Indeed, it is becoming ever more commonplace in "general" Austrian historiography—and in societal discourses more broadly—to highlight the pivotal role played by Jews in the generation of Austrian culture.[65] Yet "Jewish" history still has some way to go before it becomes truly integrated into "general" or "national" Austrian historiography, owing not least of all to the tenacity of the central tenets of the "assimilation" paradigm concerning notions of inherent Jewish "difference." Perhaps, as Hödl diagnosed succinctly, this tenacity reflects a "fear of losing the Jewish and non-Jewish binary." There remains a "persistent dichotomous thinking among scholars who, contrary to all their research findings, continue to divide Jews and non-Jews into two mutually exclusive categories. This is due in part to concerns that abandoning it would conflate Jews and non-Jews, erase all traces of Jewish distinctiveness and consequently mark the end of Jewish studies as well as the professional self-understanding of scholars in this field."[66] Yet the tenacity of assimilationist thinking has also engendered a fundamental inability to perceive and account for the many dynamic points of intersection between Jews and non-Jews in modern Austrian history—as demonstrated in this article, if only briefly, with regard to the role of non-Jews in the genesis of "Jewish" historiography in Vienna, most strikingly in the case of right-wing historians in the interwar period.

Writing in the 1980s, Yosef Hayim Yerushalmi pointed out that the Zionist narrative of Jewish history—according to which Jewish "assimilation" into the "non-Jewish" European cultures had failed, with Israel now holding the promise of Jewish "national" redemption—has proven itself insufficient as a usable "mythistory" for the postwar Jewish world, which continues to be characterized by dispersion, diversity, and integration into local contexts all over the globe. Jews the world over, he concluded, "seem to await a new, metahistorical myth."[67] In this article, I traced the origins of Vienna's Jewish historiography back to its origins to demonstrate that the intersections between Jews and non-Jews as both agents and subjects of historiography in modern Austria run much deeper than postwar historiographic paradigms of difference, separation, and universal Jewish particularism would have us believe. This older body of historiography from before the Holocaust, including its origins in a complex network of Jewish and non-Jewish scholarship, could well serve as a metahistorical blueprint for how to write more inclusive histories in the future without losing sight of the specificities of the Jewish context within Viennese culture and society. In an age of resurgent nationalism, particularism, separatism, as well as religious and political extremism and the perils these worrying developments entail for diversifying societies such as Austria and Europe more broadly, a greater focus on the dynamic process of intersectional, intercultural becoming, as I feel this case study of early "Jewish" historiography in Vienna evinces, could offer us a new "usable past" to suit the needs of our pluralistic present.

Endnotes

1 Ludwig August Frankl, *Zur Geschichte der Juden in Wien: 1. Der alte Judenfreithof* (Vienna: Bei Mörschner's Witwe und W. Bianchi, 1847). All translations into English in this article, unless otherwise stated, are my own.

2 See Susanne Uslu-Pauer, "Das Archiv der Israelitischen Kultusgemeinde Wien: Jüdisches kulturelles Erbe zwischen Vergangenheit und Zukunft," in *Jüdische Archivalien: Die Wiege des österreichischen und europäischen Judentums*, ed. Israelitische Kultusgemeinde Wien (Vienna: Israelitische Kultusgemeinde Wien, 2016), 14–15.

3 Historiography old and new, including many of the works cited throughout this article, evinces surprisingly little consensus, and thus an astounding lack of sustained reflection, on the IKG's origins, with "foundation years" ranging from as early as 1792 to as late as 1896. This broad range in and of itself demonstrates that the IKG was in fact the product of a long-term and peculiarly Austrian political and legal development, the history of which must be reserved for a future publication.

4 Frankl, *Zur Geschichte der Juden in Wien*, 4.

5 "Ältestes Zeugnis jüdischen Lebens in Österreich im Fokus der Experten," *Die Gemeinde*, May 2009, 39.

6 See *Das Buch Österreich: Texte, die man kennen muss*, ed. Hans Rauscher (Vienna: Braumüller, 2005), 92.

7 The oldest Jewish cemetery in Vienna, probably dating back no earlier than the thirteenth century, was destroyed in the *Gesera*, the great pogrom of 1421, its gravestones then being purloined as building materials. They would resurface repeatedly over the centuries during excavations and construction projects around the city. See Bernhard Wachstein, *Hebräische Grabsteine aus dem XIII.-XV. Jahrhundert in Wien und Umgebung* (Vienna: Hölder, 1916).

8 Ignaz Schwarz, *Geschichte der Juden in Wien bis zum Jahre 1625* (Vienna: Gilhofer & Ranschburg, 1913), 29. See also: Ignaz Schwarz, *Das Wiener Ghetto: Seine Häuser und seine Bewohner*, (Vienna: Braumüller, 1909), 54.

9 Schwarz, *Geschichte der Juden in Wien*, 3–4.

10 Ludwig Bato, *Die Juden im alten Wien* (originally published 1928, this edition Vienna: Metroverlag, 2011), 6.

11 Van Wyck Brooks, "On Creating a Usable Past," *The Dial* (Apr. 11, 1918): 337. Brooks, whether wittingly or not, was echoing Friedrich Nietzsche's earlier, more sustained reflections on the uses of history. See Friedrich Nietzsche, *The Use and Abuse of History* (originally published 1874, this edition trans. Adrian Collins, Indianapolis: Bobbs-Merrill, 1957).

12 See Peter Fritzsche, "Specters of History: On Nostalgia, Exile and Modernity," *The American Historical Review* 106, no. 5 (Dec. 2001): esp. 1590–1591.

13 To cite the well-worn but still pertinent bon mot from *The Invention of Tradition*, ed. Eric Hobsbawm and Terence Ranger (Cambridge: Cambridge University Press, 1983).

14 Yosef Hayim Yerushalmi, *Zakhor: Jewish History and Jewish Memory* (Seattle: University of Washington Press, 1982), 86.

15 On the underlying epistemological issues of "general" as opposed to "Jewish" history, see the commentary by Klaus Hödl, "'Jewish History' as Part of 'General History': A Comment," *Medaon: Magazin für jüdisches Leben in Forschung und Bildung* 12, no. 22 (2018).

16 Salo Baron, "Newer Emphases in Jewish History," *Jewish Social Studies* 25, no. 4 (Oct. 1963): 240.

17 Here borrowing the analytical concept developed by Lisa Silverman, *Becoming Austrians: Jews and Culture between the World Wars* (Oxford: Oxford University Press, 2012).

18 A narrative expounded most influentially with regard to Jews in Vienna by Marsha Rozenblit, *The Jews of Vienna 1867–1914: Assimilation and Identity* (Albany: State University of New York Press, 1983), esp. 1–2, still cited as a textbook in the field today.

19 See Dirk Rupnow, *Aporien des Gedenkens: Reflexionen über "Holocaust" und Erinnerung* (Freiburg: Rombach, 2006), 14, see also generally 12–13.

20 Markus Wenninger, "Jüdische Studien in der österreichischen 'Provinz'," in *Jüdische Studien: Reflexionen zu Theorie und Praxis eines wissenschaftlichen Feldes*, ed. Klaus Hödl (Innsbruck: Studienverlag, 2003), esp. 26.

21 See Max Grunwald, *Vienna*, trans. Solomon Grayzel (Philadelphia: Jewish Publication Society, 1936), 2.

22 As I outlined in more detail in "Once 'the Only True Austrians': Jews and Austrian Culture in the Early Twentieth Century," in Diane Butler et al., *The Binghamton Nuvolone: Restoring an Object in Six Parts* (Binghamton: Binghamton University Art Museum, 2019).

23 William Johnston, *Der österreichische Mensch: Kulturgeschichte der Eigenart Österreichs* (Vienna: Böhlau, 2010), 282.

24 *Alt-Wien: Die Stadt, die niemals war*, ed. Wolfgang Kos and Christian Rapp (Vienna: Czernin, 2004), this quote in "Katalogteil," 333.

25 Klaus Hödl, *Zwischen Wienerlied und Der Kleine Kohn: Juden in der Wiener populären Kultur um 1900* (Göttingen: Vandenhoeck & Ruprecht, 2017), 145–149.

26 As explored in a by now classic study by Michael John and Albert Lichtblau, *Schmelztiegel Wien – Einst und Jetzt: Zur Geschichte und Gegenwart von Zuwanderung und Minderheiten* (Vienna: Böhlau, 1990).

27 Gerhard Robert Walter von Coeckelberghe-Dützele, *Die Juden und die Judenstadt in Wien: Fragmente von Realis* (Vienna: Lechner's Universitäts-Buchhandlung, 1846), 3–5, 9–10.

28 See Reinhard Pohanka, "Judenplatz (Jew's Square [sic]) after 1421," in *Judenplatz: Place of Remembrance*, ed. Gerhard Milchram (Vienna: Pichler, 2000), 116–117.

29 Frankl, *Zur Geschichte der Juden in Wien*, 2.

30 See Tim Corbett, "Culture, Community and Belonging in the Jewish Sections of Vienna's Central Cemetery," *Austrian Studies* 24 (2016).

31 Gerson Wolf, *Die jüdischen Friedhöfe und die "Chewra Kadischa" (heilige Brüderschaft) in Wien* (Vienna: Hölder, 1879), iii. This English translation quoted from "Iphigenia in Tauris," trans. Anna Swanwick, in *Dramatic Works of Goethe* (London: Bohn, 1860), 165.

32 See characteristically *Goethe in German-Jewish Culture*, ed. Klaus Berghahn and Jost Hermand (Rochester: Camden House, 2001).

33 Gerson Wolf, *Geschichte der Israelitischen Cultusgemeinde in Wien (1820–1860)* (Vienna: Braumüller, 1861), unpaginated.

34 See as a case in point Max Grunwald, *Geschichte der Juden in Wien 1625–1740* (Vienna: Gilhofer & Ranschburg, 1913), 6–7; and Grunwald, *Vienna*, 69–72.

35 Gerson Wolf, *Die Juden in der Leopoldstadt ("unterer Werd") im 17. Jahrhundert in Wien* (Vienna: Herzfeld & Bauer, 1864), 1.

36 Carl Hofbauer, *Die Rossau und das Fischerdörfchen am oberen Werd* (originally published 1859, this edition Vienna: Dirnböck, 1866), 107–109.

37 Conrad Grefe, *Der alte Friedhof im IX Bezirke aus dem 16 Jahrhundert* (Vienna: Selbstverlag, 1891), 9, see also 3.

38 For example Karl Eduard Schimmer, *Alt und Neu Wien: Geschichte der österreichischen Kaiserstadt* (Vienna: Hartleben, 1904), which includes detailed discussions of Jewish history and sites of memory, for example in vol. 1, 379–383; and Leopold Donatin, *Der Alsergrund*

einst und jetzt: Für die Jugend und das Volk geschildert (Vienna: Selbstverlag, 1904), which includes Jewish history as part and parcel of the *Vaterstadt* Vienna, see esp. 114, 147.

39 The photographs are stored under the title "Wien 9, Seegasse 9" in the August Stauda Sammlung, Österreichische Nationalbibliothek, ST 1688-91Je F, ST 1689, ST 1690 F, etc. On Stauda's oeuvre generally, see Susanne Winkler, "Die 3000 Wien-Ansichten des August Stauda: Ein Wiener 'Alt-Stadt'-Dokumentarist um 1900," in *Alt-Wien*, ed. Kos and Rapp.

40 Lueger has rightly been identified as an influence on Adolf Hitler. See Brigitte Hamann, *Hitler's Vienna: A Portrait of the Tyrant as a Young Man* (London: Tauris Parke, 2011).

41 For example in Klaus Hödl, "'Jewish History' Beyond Binary Conceptions: Jewish Performing Musicians in Vienna around 1900," *Journal of Modern Jewish Studies* 16, no. 3 (2017).

42 See Merethe Aagaard Jensen, "Traditionen der Forschung: Die Historische Kommission der Israelitischen Kultusgemeinde Wien 1901–1938," in *Ordnung muss sein: Das Archiv der Israelitischen Kultusgemeinde Wien*, ed. Felicitas Heimann-Jelinek, Lothar Hölbling, and Ingo Zechner (Vienna: Jüdisches Museum Wien, 2007), 35–36.

43 See Israelitische Kultusgemeinde Wien 1907, 55442, YIVO Institute for Jewish Research; *Israelitische Kultusgemeinde 1913* (Vienna: Liebermann, 1913), 10; and *Bericht der israelitischen Kultusgemeinde Wien über die Tätigkeit in der Periode 1925–1928*, ed. Israelitische Kultusgemeinde Wien (Vienna: Verlag der Israelitischen Kultusgemeinde Wien, 1928), 9.

44 Bernhard Wachstein, *Die Inschriften des alten Judenfriedhofs in Wien, 1. Teil 1540 (?)–1670* (Vienna: Braumüller, 1912); and Bernhard Wachstein, *Die Inschriften des alten Judenfriedhofs in Wien, 2. Teil 1696–1783* (Vienna: Braumüller, 1917).

45 Alfred Francis Přibram, *Urkunden und Akten zur Geschichte der Juden in Wien, 1526–1847* (Vienna: Braumüller, 1918).

46 Bernhard Wachstein, *Wiener hebräische Epitaphien* (Vienna: Hölder, 1907).

47 Reiner Sörries, "Friedhof und Denkmal in Deutschland: Historischer Beitrag und Erbe der jüdischen Kultur," in *Jüdische Friedhöfe und Bestattungskultur in Europa*, ed. ICOMOS Deutschland und Landesdenkmalamt Berlin (Berlin: Bäßler, 2011), 20.

48 "Das Wiener Ghetto," *Arbeiter-Zeitung*, Jul. 11, 1909, 8.

49 "Die Inschriften des alten Judenfriedhofes in Wien," *Wiener Zeitung*, Sept. 29, 1912, 2–4.

50 Schwarz, *Geschichte der Juden in Wien*, 1–3, 29.

51 Hugo Hassinger, *Kunsthistorischer Atlas der K. K. Reichshaupt- und Residenzstadt Wien* (Vienna: Anton Schroll, 1916), 170.

52 Gottfried Pirhofer, "Die raumpolitischen Leitbilder," in *Wien in der nationalsozialistischen Ordnung des Raums: Lücken in der Wien-Erzählung*, ed. Siegfried Mattl, Gottfried Pirhofer, and Franz Gangelmayer (Vienna: New Academic Press, 2018), 45, 52.

53 See characteristically the recent, almost 1200-page volume *Antisemitismus in Österreich 1933–1938*, ed. Gertrude Enderle-Burcel and Ilse Reiter-Zatloukal (Vienna: Böhlau, 2018).

54 Hans Rotter and Adolf Schmieger, *Das Ghetto in der Wiener Leopoldstadt* (Vienna: Burgverlag, 1926), esp. 52.

55 As Dirk Rupnow showed, the relationship between Nazi *Judenforschung* and the emergence of Jewish studies in Central Europe is much more entwined than is usually acknowledged by the latter field. See Dirk Rupnow, *Judenforschung im Dritten Reich: Wissenschaft zwischen Politik, Propaganda und Ideologie* (Vienna: Nomos, 2011), as well as the discussion "'Keine Disziplin' an dieser Universität: Wissenschaft des Judentums, Jüdische Studien und Judaistik. Ein Gespräch mit Klaus Davidowicz, Susanne Plietzsch, Dirk Rupnow und Julius H. Schoeps," in *Die Universität: Eine Kampfzone*, ed. Werner Hanak-Lettner (Vienna: Jüdisches Museum Wien, 2016), 197–208.

56 Rudolf Geyer and Leopold Sailer, *Urkunden aus Wiener Grundbüchern zur Geschichte der Wiener Juden im Mittelalter* (Vienna: Jugend & Volk, 1931), vii–xv.

57 Max Grunwald, "Geleitwort," in Josef Pick, *Jüdisch-geschichtliche Stätten in Wien und den österreichischen Bundesländern* (Vienna: Selbstverlag, 1935), 5.

58 For a preliminary study of this issue, see Tim Corbett, "Once 'the Only True Austrians': Mobilising Jewish Memory of the First World War for Belonging in the New Austrian Nation, 1929–1938," in *Jewish Experience of the First World War*, ed. Edward Madigan and Gideon Reuveni (London: Palgrave Macmillan, 2019).

59 Hans Tietze, *Die Juden Wiens* (Vienna/Leipzig, E.P. Tal, 1933). The enduring impact of this work is evinced by its republication in 2007 by the Mandelbaum publishing house.

60 Steven Aschheim, *In Times of Crisis: Essays on European Culture, Germans, and Jews* (Madison: University of Wisconsin Press, 2001), 87.

61 Hans Tietze, *Wien: Kultur, Kunst, Geschichte* (Vienna: Epstein, 1931).

62 See Carl Schorske, *Fin-de-Siècle Vienna: Politics and Culture* (New York: Vintage Books, 1981). On the so-called "Beller-Gombrich debate" about Jews and Austrian culture, compare Steven Beller, *Vienna and the Jews, 1867–1938: A Cultural History* (Cambridge: Cambridge University Press, 1990); and Ernst Gombrich, *The Visual Arts in Vienna Circa 1900: Reflections on the Jewish Catastrophe* (London: Austrian Cultural Institute, 1997). On this issue generally, see the early, yet still highly pertinent critique by Michael Steinberg, "Jewish Identity and Intellectuality in Fin-de-Siècle Austria: Suggestions for a Historical Discourse," *New German Critique* 43 (Winter 1988).

63 Hödl, *Zwischen Wienerlied und Der Kleine Kohn*, 35–37.

64 See paradigmatically Hödl's own work such as *Wiener Juden – Jüdische Wiener: Identität, Gedächtnis und Performanz im 19. Jahrhundert* (Innsbruck: Studienverlag, 2006).

65 I think here most recently of the trailblazing work by William Johnston on the development of the *homo austriacus*, a striking facet of which concerns how many of the subjects discussed throughout were of Jewish origin. Johnston, *Der österreichische Mensch*, see esp. 301.

66 Hödl, "'Jewish History' as Part of 'General History'," 3.

67 Yerushalmi, *Zakhor*, 98.

Dollfuss´s Place in the Austrian National Mythscape

Lucile Dreidemy

"The most controversial personality in Austrian history in the 20th century"—this is how the historian and journalist Peter Huemer described the Christian Social federal chancellor and dictator Engelbert Dollfuss in 2008.[1] The dispute over the interpretation of Dollfuss's politics and personality has shaped the historical-political discourse of the Second Austrian Republic like hardly any other. The conservative ÖVP celebrated him as a heroic chancellor and resistance fighter against National Socialism, while the Social Democrats, Communists, and later the Greens denounced the dictatorial and Fascist character of the regime Dollfuss had initiated, and they sought to rehabilitate the victims of his repressive policies. An oil painting of Dollfuss, which had been placed in the club rooms of the ÖVP after 1945, became the focal point of the controversy for years.

The last decade, however, brought some groundbreaking measures in the field of history policies. In January 2012, the so-called "Abolition and Rehabilitation Act" for the rehabilitation of the democratic victims of Austrofascism, which was called an "unjust regime" in the wording of the law, was passed with the votes of all five parliamentary parties. The next historical-political "bang" followed in 2017 when the ÖVP took the rebuilding of the parliament as an opportunity to remove the controversial portrait of the Austrofascist dictator Engelbert Dollfuss.[2]

With the removal of the controversial portrait, the central basis for the ritualistic controversy that had kept the Dollfuss myth alive throughout the Second Republic disappears. Whether this measure could result in a definitive historicization of the figure of Dollfuss and an end to the myth can be doubted given the characteristic mutability and adaptability of mythical discourses. "Historical raw materials are not fixed but...continuously reshaped to address new Austrian realities," Christian Karner recalls in the introduction to this volume.[3] Against this background, the removal of the controversial portrait appears to be a welcome occasion to take stock of the context-specific transformations of the Dollfuss myth since its creation in the years 1933–34 and of its historical-political consequences.

Dollfuss, Creator of His Own Personal Myth

An often-underestimated dimension of the Dollfuss myth is that it did not originate with the posthumous cult of the dead leader but was actively shaped by Dollfuss and his followers as early as the dictatorial turn of 1933. Dollfuss's understanding of his political function went beyond that of an autocrat. This is evident in the fact that, from the time of the dissolution of parliament, he worked very consciously on his self-staging and thus also de facto on the establishment of a personal myth. This can be seen first and foremost in his systematic tendency to transfigure his own path in life and to reinterpret its unpleasant or inglorious facets—or to conceal them. The most significant phase in Dollfuss's life was undoubtedly World War I, during which the engagement as overzealous soldier was a way to compensate for both his illegitimate origins and his height (he was only 4'11"). This may explain why he exaggerated the duration of his service on the front, always mentioning thirty-seven months, whereas it was actually only just under twenty-nine months.[4] The imprint of the war was also reflected in the increasingly belligerent rhetoric that Dollfuss used after the dissolution of parliament and with which he portrayed himself, for example, as a warrior whom "a physical danger does not shake much."[5] In accordance with this militant rhetoric, Dollfuss began to appear more and more often in public in the uniform of the *Kaiserschützenoberleutnant*. An example of this is the staging of his programmatic speech at Vienna's Trabrennplatz on September 11, 1933.

By resorting to the war uniform, Dollfuss undoubtedly imitated the appearance of the neighboring dictators.[6] In comparison to Adolf Hitler or Benito Mussolini, however, Dollfuss seemed from the outset to be more concerned with defusing, or rather "humanizing," the image of the fearsome dictator by means of a humbler image. Accordingly, an essential characteristic of the Dollfuss cult was that, in contrast to Hitler or Mussolini, its mobilization strategy was based less on fear than on identification and sympathy. One thinks, for example, of the numerous representations of Dollfuss in the role of husband and family man, which were printed in the illustrated press, in propaganda brochures and on postcards even before his death. The decisive role that image propaganda played in the staging of the "humane leader" is also exemplified by the visual coverage of the first assassination attempt against Dollfuss on October 3, 1933:

Fig. 1: *Wiener Bilder*, 8.10.1933, 1.

This photo was taken in the study of Dollfuss's apartment on the evening of October 3 and published on the cover of the weekly newspaper *Wiener Bilder* four days later, not even a month after the martial images of the uniformed dictator at the lectern of the Vienna Trabrennplatz. Here, Dollfuss was captured in a state of shock and in pajamas. Sitting next to the *director* of programs at the Austrian *broadcasting* company (RAVAG) and the eventual main propagandist of the Dollfuss cult, Rudolf Henz, who had to bend down to speak into the microphone, Dollfuss seemed even smaller than he appears normally. This visual staging clearly intensified the image of the simple, blameless man and sympathetic "victim chancellor." The propagandistic value of this appearance was already recognized by the contemporary American journalist John Gunther, who recognized in the attack of October 3, 1933, and its mediatization, retrospectively, the beginning of a tactically well-thought-out martyr myth:

> [Dollfuss's] luck, until the end, was always of phenomenal quality, but at two-fifteen p. m. on October 3, 1933, the luckiest thing of all happened: he was shot. At two-fourteen he was only a chancellor; at two-sixteen, he became a martyr, and a living martyr at that. Only good luck stood between his heart and the two bullets fired at less than a yard's range. It was his great sense of occasion that made him

> deliver a radio speech from his bedside which turned him into the world's favorite convalescent. The would-be assassin was discovered to be a slightly Van-der-loony Nazi. How Hitler must have wanted to choke him for having made a hero of his own worst enemy![7]

In fact, the radio address mentioned above was entirely under the sign of martyr rhetoric: "I am truly convinced that by a providence of God I have now escaped a grave danger,"[8] Dollfuss affirmed. Even if there is no doubt that he was deeply convinced of this divine mission, it is also clear that this sense of duty and mission became an extremely favorable instrument of justification for Dollfuss's dictatorial policy because it presented Dollfuss as an instrument of Providence and from then on minimized his own responsibility.

The Beginnings of Dollfuss's Mythical Afterlife: The National Death Cult until 1938

After his death, Dollfuss's sense of mission led to an almost apotheosis of the dead "*Führer.*" According to the motto "You are not dead to us" ("*Du bist für uns nicht tot*"), an imposing state cult was dedicated to the regime's founding father. On the political stage, the metaphor of immortality was materialized by omnipresent busts, reliefs, and portraits of the dead leader. This visual and sculptural staging of political immortality corresponds in many respects to the theory of the "Two Bodies of the King" by the German historian Ernst H. Kantorowicz, according to which, as early as the Middle Ages, artificial, lifelike representations of the deceased ruler were placed in political and public spaces as symbolic placeholders in order to give overt character to the immortality of his spirit and his work.[9] Through this mise-en-scène, the new leader Kurt Schuschnigg, in particular, was able to compensate for his own lack of charisma. By staging himself as the only legitimate successor to the eternal leader, he was also able to counteract the political ambitions of the *Heimwehr*. In addition, the myth of the dead leader was used as a "social model"[10] to demand from each individual not only a profession of loyalty to Dollfuss but also a willingness to make sacrifices and to follow his political legacy (i.e., the regime).[11]

The apotheotic component of the cult of the dead leader was also demonstrated by the fact that Dollfuss's death was often compared with the death of Christ. "Holy" Dollfuss thus took on the form of a savior, a renewer of Austria after the collapse of the Habsburg Monarchy and the presumed chaos of the postwar period. The association of Dollfuss and Christ correlates with the political instrumentalization of the Christ-King ideology from which the regime under both Dollfuss and Schuschnigg legitimized the rejection of pluralistic democratic society in religious terms. In an attempt to elevate Dollfuss to the status of a political saint, the propagandists also resorted to the figure of Saint Engelbert. These sacral references became a central component of the regime's monument policy. Countless Dollfuss martyrs and crosses (but also statues of Saint Engelbert) were erected throughout Austria, memorial churches and chapels were built, and existing churches were rededicated. The appropriation of the existing cults of saints compensated for the failure of the canonization procedure that had been initiated in order to raise Dollfuss to the holy rank of his namesake on the basis of alleged miracles attributed to him, most notably the "miracle of Austria." Dollfuss did not become a saint in the strict Catholic sense, but the official and public worship nevertheless elevated him to the status of political pillar saint (*Säulenheiliger*).

The commemorative policies around the dead leader became a political refuge for the regime. *Vaterländische Front* and government tried in vain to hide the increasingly acute domestic and foreign policy crisis by increasing the number of symbolic acts of worship for the patriotic martyr Dollfuss. But apart from the Catholic-conservative rural areas where the official cult apparently found resonance—in many farmhouses, a picture of Dollfuss was placed in the family shrine (*Herrgottswinkel*)[12]—the disproportionate commemorative policies could not curb the growing popular resentment against the Austrofascist regime. On the contrary, it ultimately played into the hands of the much more profane and concrete Nazi mobilization propaganda.

Dollfuss Myth and Worship during World War II

Immediately after the Anschluss, most of the Dollfuss memorials were destroyed, and the official worship discourse was overwritten with a counter-cult for the thirteen executed Nazi *Juliputschisten*. The destruction of the symbols of the official cult was often used for political demonstrations of power and public humiliation against local actors of the defeated regime. The climax of this symbolic assumption of power was the great carnival procession in Vienna on February 19, 1939, that took the form of a final symbolic reckoning with the overthrown Austrofascist regime.[13]

In spite of extensive destruction and repression measures, the Dollfuss cult continued to be cultivated underground by its followers and soon took on the form of a real act of political resistance. Through the influence of conservative exile circles, it was also exported abroad and adapted to the requirements of a new discursive context. This is when the myth of the "first resistance fighter" and "first victim of National Socialism" began to take shape, fully in line with the stance of conservative exile groups that sought international recognition of Austria as the first victim of National Socialism. A decisive role in this context was played by the legitimists under the leadership of pretender-to-the-throne Otto Habsburg, who had arrived in the US in 1940. At his suggestion, July 25, 1942, was declared "Austrian Day" in several states and was celebrated as a day of remembrance of Dollfuss's death and Hitler's first defeat.[14]

After the 1943 Moscow Declaration, and especially in view of the required contribution of the Austrians to their liberation, the mythical transfiguration of the dictator as a venerable resistance fighter gained even more argumentative weight. This is reflected in a Dollfuss obituary by the founder of the legitimist "Austrian League" in London, Otto Hecht, who shortly before the end of the war drew a wishful picture of the future Austria in which much space was to be given to the veneration of the supposedly fearless patriot, martyr, and inventor of Austria:

> An Austria that has found itself will recognize the infinite values that lie in tradition and in the veneration of native heroes. This Austria will honor Engelbert Dollfuss as a freedom fighter. The world will learn to understand that Dollfuss was a martyr of Austria's eternal mission, which is to lead Europe in the fight against invading barbarian hordes.[15]

However, the immediate political development in postwar Austria was in stark contrast to Hecht's ideas. With the return of parliamentary democracy and the beginning of a groundbreaking grand coalition between the former political enemies, there was no longer any room for an official worship of Dollfuss as a national martyr. The official "truce" nevertheless required a compatible memory between the former enemies. Two complementary paradigms played a decisive role in this new discourse: on the one hand, the so-called "thesis of shared guilt," and on the other hand, the collective victim thesis.

The Dollfuss Myth in the Political Discourse of the Second Austrian Republic

Based on a one-sided interpretation of the Moscow Declaration, the myth of Austria as the first victim of National Socialism and the thesis of collective resistance in Austria became a central tenet in the self-representation of the grand coalition.[16] These paradigms were meant to contribute simultaneously to domestic political reconstruction and to international rehabilitation. At the same time, the former civil war opponents agreed on the thesis of the shared guilt of the Christian Socials and Social Democrats for the destruction of the First Austrian Republic, according to the motto that the democrats had not been patriotic enough and the patriots not democratic enough.[17] This paradigm was accompanied by the myth of the *Lagerstrasse*, according to which the shared traumatic experience in the Nazi concentration camps had led to a reconciliation of the former political enemies. These paradigms were particularly beneficial to the ÖVP because they made it possible to leave unmentioned the question of responsibility in the political repressions before 1938. In 1947, one final and fierce public debate took place during the high treason trial against Austria's last foreign minister before the Anschluss, Guido Schmidt.[18] The entire ÖVP elite was put on the witness stand. Although Schmidt was politically condemned, he was ultimately acquitted for lack of concrete evidence. All other functionaries of the Austrofascist regime also remained unindicted.[19] Many of them were even reinstated to positions of state responsibility, such as the 1953–61 Federal chancellor and ÖVP-politician Julius Raab, often celebrated as "State Treaty chancellor," who had been the leader of the Fascist home guard of Lower Austria from 1928–31 and who had accumulated several leadership roles in Austrofascism, including as a member of the leadership council of the *Vaterländische Front*.

The Dollfuss supporters in the ÖVP were also able to rely on the paradigm of shared guilt in order to rehabilitate Dollfuss's policy and to legitimize the continuation of the Dollfuss worship. One of the first steps in this direction was made when a portrait of Dollfuss was placed in the office of the ÖVP parliamentary group after 1945.[20] Several former representatives of the Austrofascist regime and active ÖVP politicians commemorated the anniversary of Dollfuss's death on July 25, either at his grave or during the ceremonies in the Votivkirche or Michaelerkirche and later in the Dollfuss Church on the Hohe Wand, near Wiener Neustadt (Lower Austria). The Catholic *Cartellverband* and the *Bauernbund*, which had been among the central bearers of the official cult of the 1930s, also took an active part in the annual commemorations throughout the Second Republic. The ÖVP-*Kameradschaft der politisch Verfolgten und Bekenner für Österreich* (ÖVP comradeship of the victims of political persecution and supporters of Austria), founded in 1948, became a genuine "Dollfuss lobby group" within the ÖVP and a decisive driving force of the Dollfuss cult.

As a reaction to the continuing Dollfuss worship in the ÖVP, a counter-narrative arose in the SPÖ, which soon went beyond the factual-critical deconstruction of the conservative myth but acquired its own mythical component. According to the "mythologics" theoretically grasped by Roland Barthes (cf. Karner in the introduction to this volume), a typical "second-order semiological system" emerged in which "a signified," in this case dictatorship, authoritarianism, and fascism, was associated with the "signifier" Dollfuss in a "self-evident way"; Dollfuss became the personification of Austrofascism. The tendency to blame all evil on this single scapegoat clearly shows how much the discourse memory of the Social Democrats was shaped by the traumas of the civil war generation. This tendency correlates with the observations made by the later SPÖ Federal chancellor Bruno Kreisky, according to whom in the Social Democracy of the 1930s, "[t]he hatred of Dollfuss was stronger than the fear of everything else."[21]

The Dollfuss cult gained new momentum under the ÖVP government of Joseph Klaus (1966–70). This was partly due to the influence of the radical-conservative "Reform" wing of the party and the *Cartellverband* in the government. As early as 1967, the government implemented an annual memorial mass for Dollfuss in the chapel of the federal chancellery.[22] The further history of this mass is a striking example of the longer-term consequences of the grand coalition's policy of history. In 1970, Bruno Kreisky, himself a victim of the Austrofascist regime, became the head of an SPÖ government. His handling of the Austrofascist regime was marked by a blatant dichotomy between radical criticism and compromise-oriented piety. On the one hand, he clearly opposed the myth of shared guilt. In March 1973, for instance, at a symposium organized on the occasion of the fortieth anniversary of the dissolution of the Austrian Parliament, he stressed "that the so-called 'Dollfuß-Straße', onto which Austria had been forced, led straight into the Nazi dictatorship and thus into the abyss of war."[23] In the federal chancellery, on the other hand, he maintained the annual commemorative Dollfuss mass for the entire duration of his thirteen-year-long mandate. On the occasion of the fortieth anniversary of Dollfuss's death in 1974, he legitimized his government's reverent handling of Dollfuss's memory according to the motto "The dead man is no longer our enemy."[24]

This positioning reflects Kreisky's claim to present himself as chancellor of the political middle ground. This forbearance was without a doubt part of a political strategy aimed at sending a clear signal to the ÖVP voters, but eventually it contributed in no small measure to the fact that the Dollfuss cult developed an undreamt-of tenacity in the following decades. Chancellor Fred Sinowatz (SPÖ), who was five years old when Dollfuss died, and after him chancellor Franz Vranitzky (born in 1937) followed Kreisky's example and thus maintained a stage for dubious political commemorative events at the chancellery. The piety for the prominent Nazi victim had thus made the homage of a dictator politically acceptable. The mass was finally abolished in 2010 under chancellor Werner Faymann (SPÖ)—even then only after the daily *Der Standard* had openly questioned this commemorative tradition.[25]

While Kreisky and his Social Democratic successors in the federal chancellery chose to let piety prevail over confrontation, parliament often became the stage for open confrontation between the ÖVP and the SPÖ regarding the legacy of Austrofascism and, in particular, of Dollfuss. A frequent source of controversy was the Dollfuss portrait in the parliamentary club of the ÖVP.[26] Just as the myth was cultivated in the official cult through ritualized celebrations, it was from now on for a good part these almost-ritualized Dollfuss controversies between the ÖVP and the SPÖ that kept the myth alive. Through the mediatization of these controversies, the myth also radiated more and more into public discourse and ultimately survived the erosion of the partisan identities based upon antagonistic historical narratives. A noticeable sign of the effectiveness of the Dollfuss myth beyond party lines is, for example, the widespread tendency in public discourse to personify the Austrofascist regime through Dollfuss while at the same time excluding the historical role of his successor, Schuschnigg, for instance. This cross-party tendency to reduce the historical discourse on Austrofascism to Dollfuss may be one reason why the ÖVP made the maintenance of the Dollfuss image in its parliamentary club a kind of unimpeachable matter of honor, although this stubborn defiance was increasingly contradicting its own concessions about the unjust character and dictatorial dimension of Dollfuss's policies.

Scientification of the Dollfuss Apologetics

In view of the continuous progress in research on Austrofascism from the 1960s and 1970s onward, Dollfuss's followers came under increasing pressure to justify themselves. They therefore adapted their argument to the new discursive mainstream. Those images of history that no longer corresponded to the new political and cultural conditions were retouched. The "true German man" of the Austrofascist propaganda moved into the shadow of the anti-Nazi resistance fighter and the spiritual father of the Austrian nation, the "*Führer*" with a human face was transformed into the peasant democrat, and the hallowed victim ultimately became the "secularized" first victim of National Socialism. The political scientist Gottfried-Karl Kindermann played a pioneering role in this discursive evolution. From the early 1980s onward, he sought to rehabilitate the Austrofascist regime by presenting it as the first state that had resisted against National Socialism, thus celebrating Dollfuss as its figurehead.[27] The modern argument of Dollfuss's followers is also characterized by a segmented pattern of interpretation that is typical of mythical discourse. Accordingly, only those events and sources are consulted of which support the authors' partisan pleas. This "carefully selected version of the past" is then treated as "objective," factual basis and in a further step transformed into a demand for "justice" for Dollfuss.[28] Through this typical mixture of scientific categories and value judgments, every form of critical approach is finally branded—in a consistently paradoxical manner—as political propaganda and thus dismissed as unscientific. The benevolent Dollfuss biography by historian Gudula Walterskirchen from 2004 and her latest book, *The Blind Spots of History: Austria 1927–1938*, inscribe themselves into exactly this line of reasoning.[29] Instead of, as she announces, opening up new perspectives, Walterskirchen seems to be primarily concerned with rehabilitating the politics of the bourgeois camp of the 1920s and 1930s. This is done, for example, by overemphasizing the Social Democrats' mistakes (keyword: Karl Renner's "Yes" to the Anschluss) or, as shown in the last book, by relying on meager and questionable sources to reinterpret the February struggles as an attempted coup orchestrated by the National Socialists. Proven experts, such as Emmerich Tálos, are again labelled "unscientific."[30]

The political significance of these modern forms of apologetics is exemplified by the contradictory statements of the ÖVP politician Andreas Khol since the early 2000s. On the one hand, Khol was one of the first prominent ÖVP politicians to show groundbreaking impulses toward a critical assessment of the Austrofascist regime. In 2003, for example, as president of the Austrian Parliament, he explicitly distanced himself from the thesis of the "self-liquidation" of the parliament in March 1933. Instead, he spoke of a coup d'état and of an "authoritarian regime based on a juridical white lie."[31] Ten years later, he even added: "Of course, Dollfuss was a dictator who was responsible for a coup and—today one would say—for state terrorism."[32] Despite these critical insights, Khol never completely distanced himself from the victim and resistance narrative coined by Kindermann.[33] In 2014, during a panel discussion at the Wien Museum about the monograph *The Dollfuss-Mythos. Eine Biographie des Posthumen*, written by the author of this contribution, Khol spoke of a revisionist study and in the same breath took up again the thesis of Dollfuss as the "first victim" of National Socialism, which had long since been overcome in the scientific mainstream discourse. This episode once again showed how much the emotional logic of the myth resists rational arguments. Even if more and more scientific findings about the Austrofascist regime are accepted by the ÖVP, Dollfuss remains, to quote Khol, a "pillar saint"[34] of the party.

Traces of the Myth in the Austrian Memory and Museum Landscape

There are still about twenty Dollfuss monuments throughout Austria, most of them in Lower Austria and Tyrol. Instead of removing them, there has been a tendency in recent years to supplement them with explanatory plaques. This solution appears problematic in that these discreet additions alone cannot bring about a reversal of the functionality of these monuments—from signs of homage to memorials. Instead, they de facto legitimize the presence of symbols of worship for a dictator, even in the democratic context of the present.

A similar compromise was initially chosen in 2014 for the Dollfuss portrait in the parliamentary club of the ÖVP. In the course of yet another debate about the painting, which took place during the commemorations for the eightieth anniversary of the uprising in February 1934, ÖVP representatives started to argue that the portrait should be retained out of a duty of remembrance and because it documented the party's critical reassessment of its past. "I cannot simply detach myself from a part of my history by side-lining certain persons," declared the chairman of the parliamentary group, Reinhold Lopatka.[35] In the light of this argument, the party decided to place a plaque beneath the portrait explaining that it was not honoring the leader but that "the good as well as the bad features" of his leadership needed to be told.[36] The transition to dictatorship was once again presented as a response to the rise of Nazism, while other aspects of Dollfuss's personality and political program, such as his anti-parliamentarianism, his negotiations with the Nazis, and his admiration for Mussolini, were not even hinted at. The text ended by recalling his death during an attempted Nazi coup, thereby reviving the old myth of the martyred chancellor. The decision to keep the portrait and add an explanatory note reaffirmed the legitimacy of the portrait's presence in the office of the conservative parliamentary group and de facto in the parliament itself—the very parliament that Dollfuss wanted to permanently abolish in 1933.[37]

Just as in the case of the commemorative mass in the federal chancellery, it was an external event, namely the necessary move as a result of the renovation work in the parliament, which ultimately prompted the party to take down not only that very picture but all historic portraits that had been hanging there. Since then the painting has been part of the permanent exhibition *The Contested Republic. Austria 1918–1938* in the H*aus der Geschichte Niederösterreich* in Sankt Pölten, which was opened in September 2017.

The portrait is indeed an ideal museum exhibit as its long and controversial history gives it an incomparably expressive documentary and testimonial character. The process of the painting's creation takes us back to the phase of the creation of the *Führerkult* under Dollfuss. Its visual message (i.e., the dictator's relaxed pose as a modern bureaucrat) illuminates the characteristic features of the Austrofascist dictator's self-presentation and at the same time invites us to reflect on the longer-term effects of this self-staging on the later reception and interpretation of the regime. The portrait, which was reproduced under strict control after Dollfuss's death, is also exemplary of the diverse material forms of expression of the official, posthumous Dollfuss cult—from the classical portraits and reliefs to the most diverse devotional objects and memorabilia (i.e., postcards, coins, cups, calendars, etc.). But it is also a political history of the Second Republic that the portrait conveys to us. Its placement in the parliamentary club of the new ÖVP after 1945 raises the question of the political genealogy of the new People's Party. The debates repeated from the 1970s onward also shed light on the development of the historical-political discourse on Dollfuss and Austrofascism in the Second Republic at various levels: at the official level (keyword: coalitionary historiography), in the context of party confrontations, but also in the context of internal party controversies in the ÖVP and the SPÖ. The added explanatory plaque in 2014 also stands as an example for the current compromise solutions in dealing with the remaining Dollfuss monuments; it therefore offers an ideal occasion to discuss the consequences of consensual history policies.

However, none of these aspects are to be found in the chosen mise-en-scène. The curators were apparently anxious not to create any historical-political stir. The portrait is displayed together with several small plaques representing a variety of opinions expressed by politicians and academics.

Two contrasting statements, by the historians Florian Wenninger and Kurt Bauer, respectively, are worth quoting: "When dictators are glorified as defenders of the fatherland, tyranny is trivialized and treated as an acceptable sin"; and "Dollfuss...was not a mean guy, perhaps a bad politician, probably just a mediocre one. The wrong man at the wrong place at the wrong time." In addition, a patchwork of selected book and journal covers offers a selective insight into the relevant scholarly production. By refraining from any critical embedding, let alone commentary, it is left to the visitors to form their own opinion on the basis of these statements or to come to the suggested conclusion that Dollfuss could be seen "one way or another"—or, in other words, that the interpretation of his historical responsibility is a matter of opinion, so to speak. In the Haus der Geschichte, which opened in November 2018 in Vienna, a similar reserve dominates the discourse on Austrofascism. By means of a turning clock, the most discussed designations for the regime are presented, but the keyword-like explanations of the different terms are limited to grossly simplistic, if not outright false, assertions. Austrofascism theory, for example, does not ignore the differences to German and Italian Fascism. These shortcomings imply that the installation is not suitable as a basis for knowledge, let alone discussion. At this point of the exhibit, the Haus der Geschichte fails to meet the claim outlined in the introduction of this volume, which is to promote critical engagement instead of reinforcing hegemonic political narratives.

Fig. 2: Facebook post by SPÖ Deputy Robert Laimer, January 26, 2019.[38]

Conclusion and Outlook: The Persistent Dollfuss Myth, or the Devastating Consequences of Modern Historical Relativism

At the beginning of 2019, the Facebook post from SPÖ Deputy Robert Laimer caused a brief media stir. The post was a collage based on two Dollfuss stamps, one of which had Kurz's head pasted over Dollfuss's head. "Putschist chancellor, Austro-fascism, Mussolini's Friend" was under the original version; "Silent chancellor, Beer Capitalism, Kickl's Friend" was under the altered picture. After the expected outcry from the ÖVP, the post was deleted.[39] This incident suggests that the ritualistic Dollfuss dispute is far from over, even after the controversial portrait has been taken down. Such media-political flashes in the pan, however, are nothing but anecdotal.

The much more explosive relevance of the Dollfuss myth is demonstrated by the seemingly unbridgeable gap between the rational grasp of Dollfuss's anti-democratic politics and the constant, irrational exaggeration of his victim status. Over the last decades, the modern Dollfuss apologetics have promoted the image of a historical "light and shadow figure" as an apparent concession to the progress of historical research. Due to its consensual dimension, the theme has now also established itself in media and museum discourse. The compromised solutions regarding the remaining Dollfuss monuments, and the over-cautious treatment of Dollfuss in the newly opened Haus der Geschichte, bear witness to the far-reaching impact of this consensual approach. From the perspective of promoting knowledge, however, this narrative is sterile. From a historical-political perspective, it is even dangerous. The last authoritarianism survey from 2007 warns of the devastating consequences of such a historical relativism. At that time, barely half of the thousand respondents could associate Dollfuss with the establishment of a dictatorship in Austria.[40]

In view of this alarming situation, one can only stress with Karner that "there is a strong case to be made that public discussion is in need of renewed stringency and critical testing vis-à-vis any of the narratives on offer."[41] Indeed, even recent academic publications on Dollfuss and Austrofascism exemplify this lack of stringency and critical examination. This is best illustrated by the monographs of Lothar Höbelt and Anton Pelinka at the occasion of the commemorative year 2018 in which insights from decades of historiographical progress are ignored and instead old myths revived. For example, both already suggest in the titles of their books that the First Austrian Republic lasted until 1938, thus de facto denying (1) that the destruction of the democratic, pluralistic constitutional state was already underway from 1933 under Dollfuss and (2) that the gradual integration of the "very nationals" ("*Betont Nationalen*") under Schuschnigg from 1936 onward unmistakably paved the way for the Nazis to take power.[42] The result is a revisionist tendency that reactivates old mythical themes (especially the thesis of shared guilt or the idea that Dollfuss and Schuschnigg "had nothing against democracy per se")[43] and relativizes the historic role of the Austrofascist regime in paving the way for a National Socialist takeover. These narratives can be considered as the long-term consequences of the "*Koalitionsgeschichtsschreibung*" that was coined in the early postwar period. Regarding this recent evolution and in light of the growing influence of the "post-truth" paradigm in political discourse, it is high time for a radical critique of this corporatist mode of writing history and for a general reassertion of the accountability and responsibility of historians by acknowledging and engaging with scientific findings instead of just alluding to different opinions.

Endnotes

1 Peter Huemer, cited from Oliver Rathkolb, *Fiktion "Opfer" Österreich und die langen Schatten des Nationalsozialismus und der Dollfuß-Diktatur* (Innsbruck: Studien Verlag, 2017), 97.

2 On the author's terminological positioning, see Lucile Dreidemy, "Austrofaschismus," in *100 x Österreich: Neue Essays aus Literatur und Wissenschaft*, ed. Monika Sommer, Heidemarie Uhl and Klaus Zeyringer (Vienna: Haus der Geschichte Österreich, 2018), 29–33.

3 Christian Karner, "National Mythologies: Theoretical Reflections, Empirical Applications," in this volume, p. 21-42.

4 See his statement at the celebration of Vienna's liberation from the Turks, Schönbrunn castle, May 14, 1933, published in *So sprach der Kanzler: Dollfuß'Vermächtnis*, ed. Anton Tautscher (Vienna: Baumgartner, 1935), 141.

5 Dollfuss's address to Austrian soldier associations gathered in Mauer near Vienna, June 17,1934, in ibid., 146.

6 On the visual aspects of the Dollfuss myth, see Lucile Dreidemy, "A Dictator with a Human Face? The Portraits of the Austrian Chancellor Engelbert Dollfuss" in *The Political Portrait: Leadership, Image and Power*, ed. Luciano Cheles and Alessandro Giacone (New York: Routledge, 2020), 98—115.

7 John Gunther, *Inside Europe* (New York: Harper, 1940), 382.

8 "Nun spricht Bundeskanzler Dr. Dollfuß," anon., *Linzer Volksblatt*, Oct. 5, 1933, 2.

9 Ulrich Pfisterer, "Zwei Körper des Königs" in *Handbuch der politischen Ikonographie: Abdankung bis Huldigung*, ed. Uwe Fleckner et al. (Munich: Beck, 2011), 559–566 (here 560). On that phenomenon, see also *Heilige in Europa: Kult und Politik*, ed. Herbert Nikitsch (Vienna: Österreichisches Museum für Volkskunde, 2010).

10 Karin Liebhart, "Zur Funktion von Mythen für politische Inszenierungen" (PhD diss., University of Vienna, 1998), 232.

11 Herfried Münkler, "Das Reich als politische Vision" in *Macht des Mythos – Ohnmacht der Vernunft?*, ed. Peter Kemper (Frankfurt am Main: Fischer, 1989), 336–358 (here 343).

12 Gerhard Jagschitz, *Der Putsch: Die Nationalsozialisten 1934 in Österreich* (Graz: Styria, 1976), 193.

13 "Wiens erster großer Faschingszug," *Völkischer Beobachter, Wiener Ausgabe*, Febr. 20, 1939, 1. On the political significance of carnival, see Ruth Mateus-Berr, *Fasching und Faschismus: Ein Beispiel: Faschingsumzug 1939* in Wien (Vienna: Praesens-Verlag, 2007), here especially 287–288.

14 It is not clear how many states took part in the commemorations. According to Habsburg, there were 8. See transcript of the interview of James G. McDonald with Otto of Austria on Austrian Day, July 25, 1942, over NBC Blue Network and Station WMAL in Washington, D. C., 1–4: 3; DÖW 4773, Documentation Centre of Austrian Resistance (DÖW), Vienna. On July 26, 1942, *The New York Times* spoke about 13 states. Quoted in *Österreicher im Exil 1934–45: Eine Dokumentation*, vol. 1, ed. Peter Eppel (Vienna: Deuticke, 1995), 216. OSS-sources mention 18 states, see Eppel, 216.

15 Otto Hecht, "Engelbert Dollfuss," *Donau-Echo*, July-August 1944, 1, DÖW-Bibliothek 3057 E/2.

16 See *Rot-Weiß-Rot-Buch: Gerechtigkeit für Österreich. Darstellungen, Dokumente und Nachweise zur Vorgeschichte und Geschichte der Okkupation Österreichs (nach amtlichen Quellen)*, (Vienna: Verlag der Österreichischen Staatsdruckerei, 1946), 26. On the political significance of the victim theory in the Austrian Second Republic, see Anton Pelinka, "Die geänderte Funktionalität von Vergangenheit und Vergangenheitspolitik. Das Ende der

Konkordanzdemokratie und die Verschiebung der Feindbilder," *Österreichische Zeitschrift für Politikwissenschaft* 30, no. 1 (2001), 35–47 (here 38); Heidemarie Uhl, "Das 'erste Opfer': Der österreichische Opfermythos und seine Transformationen in der Zweiten Republik," *Österreichische Zeitschrift für Politikwissenschaft* 30, no. 1 (2001), 19–34 (here 21).

17 This phrase was coined by Communist politician Ernst Fischer who was editor-in-chief of the coalition newspaper *Neues Österreich: Organ der demokratischen Einigung*. See Ernst Fischer, "Der 25. Juli 1934," *Neues Österreich*, July 25, 1945, 1. This paradigm soon became a much-quoted phrase, especially in the conservative camp, and its 'communist' authorship was quickly forgotten. On the later reuse of this quotation, see for example Gorbach's speech on the occasion of the official commemorations of the civil war in February 1964, quoted in Paul Pennerstorfer, "Das Gedenken an die Februarkämpfe 1934: Geschichtsbilder und Geschichtspolitiken von ÖVP und SPÖ 1946–1964" (Diplomarbeit, University of Vienna, 2012), 123.

18 Between the July Agreement of 1936 and 1938, Schmidt had worked on a settlement with Hitler's Germany, which ultimately paved the way for the Anschluss. For a detailed analysis of the process, see Madgalena Neumüller, "Diskursanalyse des Hochverratsprozesses gegen Dr. Guido Schmidt" (Diplomarbeit, University of Vienna, 2012).

19 Oliver Rathkolb, *Fiktion 'Opfer' Österreich und die langen Schatten des Nationalsozialismus und der Dollfuß-Diktatur* (Innsbruck: Studien Verlag, 2017), 92–93.

20 When exactly the picture was hung up could not be determined as of yet. Andreas Khol mentioned 1945 in an interview with the chief editor of the daily *Die Presse*, Michael Fleischhacker, "Wer ist schon makellos?" *Die Presse*, March 5, 2005, 2.

21 Bruno Kreisky, *Zwischen den Zeiten: Erinnerungen aus fünf Jahrzehnten* (Berlin: Siedler 1986), 207.

22 "Gedenken an das erste Opfer," anon., *Der Freiheitskämpfer: Organ der Kämpfer für Österreichs Freiheit*, September/October 1967, 4.

23 Bruno Kreisky, "Zur Ausschaltung des Nationalrates vor 40 Jahren," in *Vierzig Jahre danach: Der 4. März 1933 im Urteil von Zeitgenossen und Historikern*, ed. Anton Benya (Vienna: Dr.-Karl-Renner-Institut 1973), 21–23 (here 21).

24 Bruno Kreisky, "Der Tote ist uns kein Feind mehr," *Arbeiter Zeitung*, July 25, 1974, 3.

25 Michael Völker, "Dollfuß-Gedenken im Kanzleramt," *Der Standard*, July 6, 2010, 6.

26 See Lucile Dreidemy, *Der Dollfuß-Mythos: eine Biographie des Posthumen* (Vienna: Böhlau, 2014), 239–241.

27 On Kindermann´s publications, see ibid., 257–261; on his argumentative strategy, see Anton Pelinka, "Opfer, Täter, Widerstand? Zur Komplexität des Österreich-Bildes," in *Soziokultureller Wandel im Verfassungsstaat: Phänomene politischer Transformation. Festschrift für Wolfgang Mantl zum 65. Geburtstag*, vol. 2, ed. Wolfgang Mantl and Hedwig Kopetz (Vienna: Böhlau 2004) 949–960 (here 952).

28 See Emmerich Tálos, "Deutungen des Österreichischen Herrschaftssystems 1934–1938: Am Beispiel des 'Ständestaats-Paradigmas,'" in *Geschichte macht Herrschaft: Zur Politik mit dem Vergangenen*, ed. Florian Wenninger (Vienna: Braumüller, 2007), 199–213 (here 202); Siegfried Mattl, "Vergangenheitspolitik und Geschichtsrevisionismus – Februaraufstand 1934, Dollfuß-Mord und Austrofaschismus", in ibid., 215–226.

29 On Walterskirchen's publications, see Dreidemy, *Der Dollfuß-Mythos*, 268-270.

30 Gudula Walterskirchen, *Die blinden Flecken der Geschichte: Österreich 1927-1938* (Vienna: Kremayr & Scheriau, 2017), 176.

31 Khol in an interview with *Kronen Zeitung* journalist Dieter Kindermann, quoted in Oliver Rathkolb, "1933: Ein (noch) geteilter Erinnerungsort, der im Dunkeln der Geschichte verschwindet," ORF-Science (Feb. 29, 2008), accessed Jan. 27, 2020, http://science.orf.at/science/news/150949.

32 Quoted in Gerald John, "Unser Held, der Terrorist," *Der Standard*, Feb. 8, 2014, 38.

33 In April 2003, Khol organized a public presentation of Kindermann's new book in the Austrian Parliament. See "Österreich gegen Hitler: Nationalratspräsident Khol stellt neues Buch im Hohen Haus vor," *Parlamentskorrespondenz* no. 175, April 2, 2003, accessed Jan. 27, 2020, http://www.parlament.gv.at/PAKT/PR/JAHR_2003/PK0175/index.shtml

34 Andreas Khol, quoted in John, "Unser Held."

35 Herbert Lackner, "Man kann Geschichte nicht verleugnen," interview with Reinhold Lopatka, *Profil.at*, February 3, 2014, accessed December 29, 2019, https://www.profil.at/oesterreich/reinhold-lopatka-dollfuss-bild-oevp-klub-372252.

36 See "Dollfuß-Porträt im ÖVP-Klub soll Infotaferl bekommen," anon., *DerStandard.at*, February 5, 2014, accessed December 29, 2019, http://derstandard.at/2000003446272/OeVP-informiert-ueber-Dollfuss-Portraet. On this occasion, the SPÖ leadership reiterated its wish to see the portrait removed from the ÖVP-Parlamentsklub. See the position adopted by the party leader and then chancellor, Werner Faymann, "Dollfuß-Bild gehört nicht ins Parlament," *Kurier*, February 9, 2014, 4.

37 In a speech he made on September 11, 1933, he declared: "This parliament is such a poor way of governing our people; it must not, under any circumstances, be allowed to return." Quoted from *Dollfuß an Österreich: Eines Mannes Wort und Ziel*, ed. Edmund Weber (Vienna: Reinhold, 1935), 26.

38 Screenshot Facebook, quoted from *Kurier.at*, accessed on Jan. 29, 2020, https://kurier.at/politik/inland/vergleich-von-kurz-mit-dollfuss-erzuernt-oevp/400391522.

39 "Dollfuß-Vergleich mit Kurz erzürnt ÖVP," Austria Press Agency, Jan. 29, 2019.

40 Rathkolb, "1933 – ein noch geteilter Erinnerungsort." On this survey, see also *Authoritarianism, History and Democratic Dispositions in Austria, Poland, Hungary and the Czech Republic*, ed. Oliver Rathkolb and Günther Ogris (Innsbruck: Studien Verlag, 2010), especially 43–50.

41 Karner in this volume, p. 21-42.

42 Lothar Höbelt, *Die Erste Republik 1918-1938: Das Provisorium* (Vienna: Böhlau, 2018); Anton Pelinka, *Die gescheiterte Republik: Kultur und Politik in Österreich 1918-1938* (Vienna: Böhlau, 2018).

43 Pelinka, *Die gescheiterte Republik*, 126. The same tendency can be found in Kurt Bauer's monograph *Der Februaraufstand 1934: Fakten und Mythen* (Vienna: Böhlau, 2019). See Florian Wenninger's book review in: *H-Soz-Kult*, accessed 13.3.2019, https://www.hsozkult.de/publicationreview/id/reb-27953.

World War II

Hitler as Liberator, *Ostmark* as Bulwark, and other Myths of the Anschluss

Laura Morowitz

In 1938, to speak of the *Ostmark* was to speak in the language of myth. With the Anschluss, a host of laws were enacted to shift the administrative and legal status of the First Republic of Austria into the Reich territory of the *Ostmark*.[1]

But the new entity of *Ostmark* existed above all in the Nazi imagination as a mythical site. It existed as myth not only in the sense of historical fallacy, and what Duncan Bell defines as the "perpetually mutating repository for the representation of the past for the purposes of the present,"[2] but the creation of *Ostmark* also functioned as myth in fulfilling what was seen as a pre-destined and God-given mission.

While there has been much written about myths that served to *erase* the Anschluss—namely the myths of the *Stunde Null* and the *Opfernation*[3]—in this paper I examine two myths arising *out of* the Anschluss, created in the years of its unfolding. One myth involves the genesis of the Anschluss, the annexation of the formerly independent nation of Austria into the Third Reich beginning on March 12, 1938. The other explores the myth of the mountainous geography of Austria (*Ostmark*) as the "bulwark against the East." The myths are bound together, for the enactment of the Anschluss was embedded in the landscape itself; the Austrian mountains were portrayed as stone barriers shielding the *Volksgemeinschaft* and demarcating the last frontier of the "not East." Both myths trade human time for a different one—in one case the divine, cyclical time of fate and predestination, the other the millennial stretch of geological time. The first concerns a mythic event, the other a mythic place.[4] Both ensured that the political act of the Anschluss, driven by entirely human and politically calculated decisions, would be inscribed in a transcendent realm beyond human error.

The following paper looks at how these myths were fortified and transmitted into the collective or cultural memory. I will focus largely on the content rather than the function of the myths, which on the most elemental level, like other Nazi myths, served to strongly delineate the history and future of the *Volksgemeinschaft* from all others groups—in other words, to enable social binding.[5] National myth, according to Bell, "simplifies, dramatizes and selectively narrates the story of a nation's past."[6] Its effectiveness relies upon repetition and replication through discourse, both verbal and visual. I therefore examine a wide range of sources in the Nazi propaganda apparatus, including scholarly texts and popular books, paying special attention to their use of language. A large-scale exhibition containing over 800 works of art, held at the Künstlerhaus in 1939, served to promulgate these ideas. Thus, I also explore the way in which imagery, from photographs to large landscape paintings, were used to persuade and stir people—in other words, to help them not only understand these myths but to believe in them.

Anschluss

While it would be framed as an event outside of time, in fact the events of the Anschluss were carefully planned and can be clocked to the hour.[7] At 2:45 p.m. on March 11, 1938, Hermann Göring repeated on the telephone an ultimatum from Hitler to Austrian Chancellor Kurt Schuschnigg. The ultimatum had originally been made months before at a meeting between the chancellor and Hitler at Berchtesgaden. Included among the demands was the replacement of Schuschnigg and his cabinet by Nazi-approved figures and the cancellation of a nationwide plebiscite scheduled for March 13. Failure to meet the demand, Göring warned, would result in German invasion. Austrian President Wilhelm Miklas refused to yield, and by 7:30 that evening Schuschnigg gave his farewell radio address to the Austrian populace, declaring that in order to avoid bloodshed, the Austrian military would put up no resistance to the invading troops.[8] To legitimize the invasion, Göring had fabricated a telegram from Schuschnigg requesting help from Germany in restoring order after mob violence. In truth, Hitler had given orders hours earlier for the German 8th Army to begin amassing at the border. As darkness fell, Nazi gangs unleashed their terror. After a night of violence and beatings, the screaming gave way to church bells greeting the German Army. By the end of the week, thousands of people, mostly Social Democrats, Communists, and Jews, had been arrested and dragged to prison.

Through newsreel and ecstatic newspaper coverage, each event in the Anschluss became part of a mythic narrative in the making, enshrined in the cultural memory in real time. At four in the afternoon, Hitler crossed into Austria at the place of his birth, Braunau am Inn, going on in the next days to his adopted hometown of Linz. His victorious entry culminated in his speech at the carefully chosen public site of the Heldenplatz on March 15, where he greeted 200,000 cheering followers in the language of epic and of myth: "I now proclaim for this land its new mission. It fulfills the aim called for by the German settlers of every district [*Gau*] of the *Altreich*. The age-old *Ostmark* of the German people should henceforth be the newest bulwark of the German nation and the German Reich."[9]

In the weeks that followed the dismantling of Austria, the process of *Gleichschaltung* (assimilation and coordination) were carried out in earnest.[10] The operations were led by Josef Bürckel, Reich Commissioner for the Reunification of Austria with the German Reich. Old administrative divisions were dissolved, and by October former Austria divided into seven *Reichsgaue*, each headed by a *Reichsleiter/Reichsstatthalter* (Governor): Upper Danube, Lower Danube, Vienna, Styria, Carinthia, Salzburg, and Tirol-Vorarlberg.[11]

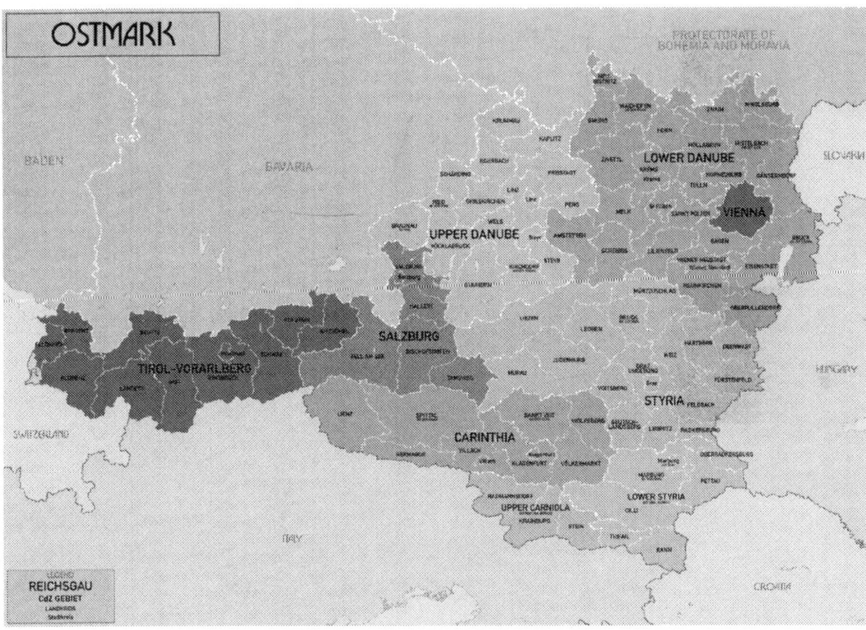

Fig. 1. Administrative map of Ostmark in 1941 showing Reichsgaue

(By 1942, even the name of *Ostmark* carried a whiff of separatism. From then on, the term would be banished, and the regions referred to only by *Gau*.) Among the earliest laws enacted were those which persecuted Jews, expropriating their property and stripping them of citizenship.[12] Five months after the declaration of Anschluss, the Mauthausen Concentration Camp was opened outside Linz.

Fig. 2 Ad for A. Hermansky, *Die Pause* 4/5, p. 11

Creation of the *Ostmark*

The creation of a political and administrative entity of *Ostmark* was paralleled in the cultural sphere: it was given a history, literature, folklore, and a set of aesthetic characteristics. While Vienna had been the heart of Austria, the city was now downplayed by the *Altreich*, which worried about Viennese separatism, especially under *Reichsstatthalter* Baldur von Schirach.[13] In the construction of *Ostmark*, the Nazis engaged in what Jeffrey Olick and Daniel Levy refer to as "instrumental constraints," reshaping and reconstructing the past to serve their needs, and the creation of a mythscape.[14]

Beginning in the days following the Anschluss, a propaganda campaign was set into motion. The personal memories of Austria's inhabitants would be replaced by a constructed cultural, or public, memory. Individual cities now had specific roles to play for the Reich: Salzburg became the "*Festspielstadt*" (Festival City), Linz, the "*Führerstadt*," etc.[15] Attention was shifted from the cosmopolitan culture of Vienna to the "Alpine" culture of the *Ostmark* through *Landesbauernschaften* (Regional Farmers Associations), which promoted the wearing of *Dirndln* and *Trachten*, and the renewal of regional folk songs through *Dorfabende* and *Singabende*.[16]

This shift was echoed in popular films like *Konzert in Tirol* (1938) and *Hotel Sacher* (1939).[17] By 1940, those who entered the Wiener Rathaus could see two frescos, carried out by future Künstlerhaus President (and Nazi Party member) Rudolf Hermann Eisenmenger, depicting *Die Rückkehr der Ostmark* (*The Homecoming to Ostmark*) and *Die Gaben der Ostmark* (*Gifts of the Ostmark*).[18]

In the academic realm, scholars and historians such as Heinz Kindermann, Franz Koch, and Josef Nadler reached back into the past to reattach *Ostmark* culture to that of the *Altreich*, creating what one scholar has called "Community, Germandom, Volkishness, Race, Blood, Soil, Destiny, Courage, Loyalty and Allegiance to the *Führer*."[19] Josef Nadler's *Literaturgeschichte des Deutschen Volkes: Dichtung und Schrifttum der deutschen Stämme und Landschaften* (*Literary History of the German People: Poetry and Writing of the Germanic Tribes and Landscapes*) (1938-41) purported to prove that the same blood flowed in the veins of Germans and *Ostmärkers*.[20]

Mythic Time: The Portrayal of the Anschluss and Hitler as Redeemer

A tidal wave of new publications and celebrations of the *Ostmark* appeared in the two years following the annexation. In nearly all of them, no matter what topic they covered, past events had led auspiciously to the Anschluss. Some of the authors adopted a scholarly, scientific tone, setting the record straight on the "real" history of the *Ostmark*, which they implied had been repressed or twisted to benefit the enemies of *Deutschtum*. These texts abounded with data, facts, statistics on natural resources, genealogical charts, etc. The very existence of the First Republic of Austria was cast as a cruel intervention in the life of the region. But the majority of these publications spoke in the language of myth. The Anschluss was not a political act, not a military phenomenon, not a strategic or planned event by a leader or government in power. Hitler was less its architect than its heroic vehicle. The Anschluss was an act of predestination. As such, the pre-history of it was of less importance than the sacred act itself. Like all myths, the story of the Anschluss was presented as one that simply was, that always had been, rather than something constructed by an author. In his introduction to this issue, Christian Karner speaks of the "selective blurring" between myth and history. Indeed, such texts offer us myth masquerading as history, just as many Nazi texts offered ideology masquerading as science. The veneer of objective academic jargon (almost) hides the irrational and purely subjective content beneath.

Typical of these texts are Günther Schwab's *Österreich: die Deutsche Ostmark* (1938)[21] and Friedrich Lange's *Unsere alte Ostmark Österreich* (1941),[22] which follow the arc of the Anschluss myth: a recounting of the region's history, beginning with the brave Germanic tribes settling the land, the destruction of *Ostmark* under Habsburg perfidy, and the redemption and salvation under Hitler. (We will later return to how the mountainous geography of the region had assured the racial purity of the *Ostmärkers* despite the threats from the East.) After an initial period of prosperity and peace, the German *Ostmark* was betrayed:

> No other German land was as much a plaything in the hands of foreign powers as Austria. These powers set aside the organic laws of the Reich and her people, indeed in opposition to them, without scruples they served their own personal interests of power in this part of Germany. And no German tribe had to bear the crime of so much foreign blood streaming beside her.[23]

The mythic tale of the Anschluss relied on the great suffering of the Austro-German people, traumatized by St. Germain. It replaced a lived national identity and experience with a cultural, communal, and invented one. One very important part of this myth was a (constructed) shared past of oppression and trauma. The separation of Austria from Greater Germany was a wound, the soldier's lost limb projected onto the body of the nation. This was laid out even before the Anschluss by historians like Alfred Rapp, who popularized Nazi ideas, noting that in the perception of every German, the loss of the German-Austrian lands could be characterized as follows: "Germany must sacrifice the freedom of its Austrian tribe in Habsburg bondage. In the perception of all Germans, the loss of the German-Austrian lands can be characterized 'as the loss of an arm and a leg.'"[24]

Despite the common reference to Germany as the Fatherland, in discussions of the separation of Austria, the country was portrayed as a maternal body. Hitler described the loss of Austria as a "*Missgeburt*" (miscarriage), and Rapp referred to the "great renunciation of German blood and German soil on the Danube" as the "Caesarian section of 1866."[25] This established the Anschluss as both a birth and a resurrection.

With the "miraculous entrance" of Hitler onto the historical stage, the true fate of the German people was claimed to have been realized.

> But the time had arrived. The development which had followed fixed laws still mysterious to us, was now at an end. The hour was here. One man raised his hand and henceforth came the German miracle, streaming over the green fields of the borders of the Mark; it overflowed, cheered on by the hearts of millions, who rushed into the streets, screaming, laughing, sobbing, with raised hands, drunk with bliss and unaware of their good fortune. Free *Ostmark*! German *Ostmark*![26]

In *Volk auf dem Marsch: Die Junge Ostmarkreihe* (1941), Anton Hadwiger described "*Das Deutsche Wunder*" (The German Miracle), which had brought *Deutschtum* to its "sacred destiny":

> In these times, when the German *Führer* moves through his Heimatland in Austria, the German Soul is brought once again to full life. ...The German people join together the last of their scattered and far flung limbs into the pure, everlasting Unity of Desire and Feeling.[27]

The tone is nothing short of Messianic. Now the fully restored limbs move in unison as if those of one body. Like a mythic hero, Hitler is the enactment of the will of his people, both those that have lived before and those currently alive.

In Robert Körber's *Rassesieg in Wien, der Grenzfeste des Reiches* (1939), the history of the Anschluss is written in millennia, not in the banal language of calendars or diaries, and stretches both forward and backward at once.

> This is the historical and cultural work of salvation of the *Führer*, that in a single day and without bloodshed, he ended the millennial war between Germans and Judaism in the *Ostmark* in triumph and at the same time gave his people the fiercely desired Greater Germany![28]

So, too, as in myth, the texts speak not of nations or civilians but of brothers, of tribes:

"Then the *Führer* came, just at the right time, and with his newly built *Wehrmacht* cut down the borders between German and German."[29] Thus, the Anschluss had succeeded in blowing away the *falsely* constructed barriers between Austrians and Germans: "The new Unity is beautifully sealed with blood."[30] Another publication on *Ostmark's* history, *Der Freiheitskampf der Ostmark-Deutschen: Von St. Germain bis Adolf Hitler* (*The Struggle for Freedom of the Ostmark Germans: From St. Germain to Adolf Hitler*) (1942), reads like a fairytale of sons and brothers:

> The same dark forces, who sought by all means to separate the *Ostmark* Germans from their brothers, wanted to annihilate the unified German people and the resulting Greater German Reich, which the *Führer* first created, and crush the people and empire into everlasting powerlessness and need. In defense of the newly-won Greater German Reich, the sons of *Ostmark* and their brethren from all tribes and *Gaue* of the Reich took part in the fight with old-time bravery and dedication.[31]

With astonishing speed, "eternal salvation" was established between the two brothers of the *Volk*.[32]

One book so completely mythologizes the events of the Anschluss that it functions much like a hagiographic legend or illustrated manuscript devoted to the *Nibelungenlied* or *Kalevala*. *Wie die Ostmark ihre Befreiung erlebte: Adolf Hitler und sein Weg zu Grossdeutschland* (*How the Ostmark Experienced its Liberation: Adolf Hitler and his Path to Greater Germany*) (1940) was the work of Hitler's favored photographer and member of his inner circle, Heinrich Hoffmann.[33] The book opens to a full-page close-up of Hitler in uniform, facing a quote ascribed to him on the day of the Anschluss, written in large Gothic font: "If Providence once sent me from this city in order to prepare me for leading the Reich she must have endowed me with one Mission, and it can be only one Mission: to restore my beloved homeland to the German Reich."[34]

The first pages of the book make apparent how this destiny is embedded in the landscape itself. Along with photos of the peasantry are tipped-in photographs resembling those from a home camera, "*Von den Ahnen und dem Land seiner Ahnen*" (From his Forefathers and the Land of his Forefathers).

Von den Ahnen und dem Land seiner Ahnen

Fig. 3 "*Von den Ahnen und dem Land seiner Ahnen*," from Hoffmann, p. 9

The rather banal images show us different features of the Waldviertel. An almost mystical and reverent tone characterizes the text, which speaks of "eternal laws" and "a noble, incomprehensible Meaning, which gives to us a difficult destiny, a Fate, and yet viewed in the mirror of the millennium, appears only as the linking together of the members of an eternal chain."[35]

Throughout the book, photos of places and objects associated with Hitler, such as the bed he slept in as a struggling young artist in Vienna, are transformed, like the relics of a saint, from banal objects to heroic symbols. The narrative leads, inexorably, to the days of the Anschluss, written as redemption myth: "There in the dark, in the deepest layers of the nation's soul, it bid its time, until the prodigious Will, beyond comprehension at that time, delivered itself to the intention of a single, chosen Man, and became in him Will and Purpose and Deed."[36] In such accounts, even Hitler was portrayed as only the instrument of a larger destiny.

Mythic Place: *Ostmark* as Bulwark and the Alpine *Abwehr*

If the events of the Anschluss were enshrined in myth, so, too, was the land in which it unfolded. The *Ostmark* was many things: the lost ancestral homeland, a treasure chest of natural resources, a bestowal of mines, waterworks, steel mills, etc. But in Nazi mythology, its most important feature was its mountains. The Austrian mountains were the geographical border guards, protecting the *Volksgemeinschaft.* (If the actual location of the mountains did not neatly map onto this narrative, such was of little concern and provides an example of what Christian Karner references as "history forged by the logic of myths.")[37] In nearly every realm, from political speech to popular journals, *Ostmark's* landscape was referred to as the "*Bollwerk des Reiches.*" The mountains were believed to simultaneously shelter and contain the racially "pure" while shielding against the physical breach by Slavic and Eastern hordes. The role of *Ostmark* in German history, wrote S.S. education leader D. Bornstedt in 1940, was *die Abwehr* (Defense), *der Schutz* (Protector), and *der Wächter* (Watchtower) all at once. [38]

These national myths did not begin with the Anschluss but are rooted in the *Ostforschung* of writers like Hermann Aubin in the 1930s, who hailed the mountain's role in protecting the German tribes that settled them.[39] Körber noted how the recent "swarm from the East"—the (largely Jewish) immigrants from the Habsburg Empire—had challenged "the natural mission of the *Ostmark* to be the Eastern bulwark of the Reich."[40]

Publications focusing on the Anschluss nearly always contained photos of the landscapes of the *Gaue*, especially bucolic scenes of rugged mountains often combined with peaceful farmland. Festivals and regional occupations were photographed in picturesque villages nestled at the foot of snow-covered peaks. The tall mountains in the distance were reassuring symbols of containment and enclosure. The very character of the *Ostmärker* was inseparable from the economic, spiritual, and racial guardianship of the mountains. The repeated imagery, from children's illustrations to travel guides and history books, strengthened the myth, naturalizing what was, in fact, a constructed narrative, to draw on Roland Barthes definition of myth.[41]

This defensive role of the Austrian mountain as border guard was mapped onto the spiritual or mystical character of this landscape that had come to the fore in the *Heimat* photography and *Bergfilme* of the 1930s.[42] Just as the mythic image of the *Führer* as redeemer in the Anschluss drew on Christian symbolism, the myth of the *Ostmark* geography drew on a history of sacred mountains in the Judeo-Christian tradition.[43] The natural fortifications of mountains lends itself easily to nationalist myth, as noted by Olick and Bell:

> The spatial dimension tends to be rooted in particular constructions of an often-idealized bounded territory, for example a romanticized national landscape: in pastoral English villages, rugged American frontiers or bucolic German forests. ...Time and place combine and are encoded in nationalist representational strategies, shaping the feelings of community and the construction of an inside/outside distinction, framing national identity in terms of a story about history and (a specific, often imagined) location. [44]

No cultural production did more to certify this metaphor of the mountain as stronghold against racial corruption than the 1939 exhibition *Berge und Menschen der Ostmark.*

Fig. 4. Photo of Exhibition Installation, *Berge und Menschen der Ostmark*, Künstlerhaus, Vienna, March 4 to April 20, 1939.

Fig. 5 Robert Angerhofer, *Almabtrieb*, 1938, oil on canvas

Held at the Künstlerhaus in Vienna in the spring of 1939, the show included over 800 works by 238 artists. Grouped by mountain regions (*Gebirgsgruppen*), the works occupied all sixteen rooms of the building.[45] Landscapes of the *Ostmark* were rendered in oil paintings, tempera, etchings, watercolors, woodcuts, and color pencil and charcoal drawings. The majority of images showed Alpine landscapes in a tremendously wide variety of styles and moods, from distant to close-up, serving for recreation, spiritual renewal, and agricultural labor. While many were sublime and empty, other scenes included peasants, farmers, loggers, harvesters, skiers, and miners. Some had been created under the Austrofascist regime, revealing the deep roots of this myth. Robert Angerhofer's *Almabtrieb* (1938) creates a fairy-tale-like scene of a farmer and his *Dirndl*-clad wife strolling with a group of cows through a forest clearing.

Layer upon layer of snowy mountain peaks ring the scene. The crystalline outlines and deep blue of the sky recall sixteenth-century German artists like Albrecht Altdorfer. The work is a virtual encyclopedia of Germanic myths, from local peasant *Trachten* to wooded forests to *Ostmark* mountains. Angerhofer was a member of the NSDAP and was often exhibited at the Haus der Deutschen Kunst.[46]

The exhibition catalogue for the show was written by Karl Strobl, who had begun as a visual artist but became well known for his fantasy and horror stories. A devoted Nazi, Strobl turned his attention to pro-Nazi propaganda following the Anschluss and became head of the *Reichsschrifttumskammer* (Writers Division of the Reich Chamber of Culture) beginning in April 1939.[47] His essay explored the way in which the mountain landscape had shaped the German character and the *Volk*. "And all this," wrote Strobl, "may contribute to the knowledge and understanding of the importance of Austria for the *Volksgemeinschaft* [national/racial community] of eighty million Germans."[48] At the heart of the show, claimed Strobl, were two central questions: "What do men create from the mountains?" and "What do the mountains bring forth from men?" Such an exhibition had at its center an important ideological aim. Numerous images of peasantry, all of good Aryan stock, attempted to answer these questions and confirmed the success of the mountains in isolating the bloodlines of *Ostmark* Germans. Etchings like Alfred Cossmann's *Two Peasants from Pinzgau* (1900) show men whose faces are as rugged, strong, and time worn as the mountains themselves.

Fig. 6 Alfred Cossmann, *Two Peasants from Pinzgau*, 1900

In late spring, the show traveled to Berlin, occupying the Funktower in Charlottenburg, where it served as a kind of "cultural ambassador," introducing the *Ostmark* to the *Altreich*. Now entitled "*Berge, Menschen und*

Wirtschaft der Ostmark," the show displayed not only fine art but folk art and fashion, as well as exhibits on forestry, agriculture, and economic history, offering regional specialties in a specially built cafe.[49] A special issue of the popular journal *Die Pause* was published to accompany the show, highlighting everything about the *Ostmark Gaue*, from their art history to their local costumes and customs.[50]

The first full-length article in the journal set the myth into motion: "*Ostmark als Bollwerke des Reiches*" ("*Ostmark* as Bulwark of the Reich"). The author, Rudolf Kremser, began by recounting the conquest of the mountains by numerous Germanic tribes. Already serving as "the strong border fence against the storm of people from the East," the mountains also served to provide the economic opportunity for trade beyond the region. However, in Kremser's account, with the weakening of the empire (attributed to foreign powers like the Habsburgs), this border became porous:

> With the advancement of time, this important role of *Ostmark* as protector and supporter of the Reich became ever more difficult and severe. On the other hand, the inner cohesion of the Reich under the last Hohenstaufen, the Habsburgs, and Luxemburgs became weaker and weaker. The weakness of the empire, becoming worse under the Habsburgs, caused the *Länder* of *Ostmark* to be ever-less capable of carrying out their mission of delimiting the borders and allowed them [the Habsburgs] to gain the support of all of Germany.[51]

These cracks in the border became a breach, with the invasion of the Turkish hoards, as the *mohammedanische Eroberervolk* (Muslim conquerors) streamed in, and for two centuries the population of *Ostmark* was forced to "suffer unspeakably cruel enemies." Through it all, *Ostmark* kept up its task as *Grenzschutz* (border guard), a *Wehrmauer im Osten* (military wall in the East). Finally, the essay concludes with the role and function of the *Ostmark* mountains, which operate as the *Führer's* geological border guards: "*Ostmark* has the task of being the sustainer and protector of the land of the Volk... to be the bulwark of the Reich from which it emerged, the defender des *Volkes* from whose work and blood it arose."[52] Thus, the task prophesized by Hitler on the Heldenplatz for the "age-old" *Ostmark* had come to pass.

Conclusion: From Bulwark to *Alpenfestung*

If many Nazi ideologues, scholars, and historians believed the particular geographic characteristics of *Ostmark* had been a bulwark, a transformed version of this myth came to be held by the Allies as well. Already by 1944 both British and US Intelligence believed that the war would not end without a powerful underground Nazi resistance, whose headquarters would be an Alpine fortress. The myth of the *Alpenfestung* was so entrenched as to be determinative of Allied military strategy. We know from the detailed research of Timothy Naftali that the Joint Intelligence Committee believed 500,000 Germans would spearhead the underground resistance.[53] In the fall of 1944 and spring of 1945, there were numerous faulty intelligence reports and equally erroneous assumptions about various Germans who would lead the widespread resistance. On December 12, 1944, a Bavarian police chief living in Switzerland and working for both the US and Britain gave an intelligence report detailing the planned action. "He suggested that the heart of German resistance to Allied occupation would be the mountains of Vorarlberg, the Tirol, Salzburg and Bavaria."[54] Such a *redoute*, or resistance, did not come to pass, in part because the Nazis could not, or would not, admit defeat until far too late for such plans to be operationalized. But the assumption that a Nazi resistance would be centered in the same Austrian mountains that had mythically protected the *Volksgemeinschaft* throughout the centuries made a kind of perfect logic and brought the myth full circle. The snow-capped *Berge*, which were lauded in 1938 for stemming the tide against the Eastern hordes and alien peoples, would now do so again, this time warding off the Red Army and the mongrel Jew-infiltrated troops of the United States military. Ironically, this time it was the "invaders" themselves who fueled the myth and invested in it. On the other side of the mountains, the Austrian politicians, as well as plenty of ordinary Austrians, were busy formulating the new myth of the *Opfernation* that would prove to be more potent, and far more useful, than any dreamed-of mountain bulwark.

Endnotes

1 Hermann Hagspiel, *Die Ostmark: Österreich im Grossdeutschen Reich, 1938 bis 1945* (Vienna: Braumüller, 1995); Thomas Weyr, *The Setting of the Pearl: Vienna under Hitler* (Oxford University Press, 2005); Austrian scholar Gerhard Botz has written on nearly all aspects of the Anschluss, for example Gerhard Botz, *Nationalsozialismus in Wien: Machtübernahme, Herrschaftssicherung, Radikalisierung, 1938/9* (Mandelbaum Verlag: 2008). On the changes rendered to ordinary life see Hagspiel.

2 Duncan S.A. Bell, "Mythscapes: Memory, Mythology and National Identity," *British Journal of Sociology* 54, no. 1 (March 2003): 66.

3 Günter Bischof, "Founding Myths and Compartmentalized Past: New Literature on the Construction, Hibernation and Deconstruction of WWII Memory in Postwar Austria"; Heidemarie Uhl, "The Politics of Memory: Austria's Perception of the Second World War and the National Socialist Period"; Anton Pelinka, "Taboos and Self-Deception: The Second Republic's Reconstruction of History," in *Austrian Historical Memory and National Identity*, Contemporary Austrian Studies, vol. 5, ed. Günter Bischof and Anton Pelinka (New Orleans, 1997): 95-102. For myths surrounding the Anschluss specifically see Peter Utgaard, *Remembering and Forgetting Nazism: Education, National Identity and the Victim Myth in Postwar Austria* (New York: Berghahn Books, 2003), 74-89.

4 Here I draw on the definition of myth in relation to anthropological and religious studies, as well as the notion of myth as a widely held but "false" belief. Throughout this paper I argue for both aspects of myth in the phenomena I explore. For the complexity of defining myth see the opening essay of this volume. Also see the essays of Laurie Honko, G.S. Kirk and Raffaele Pettazzoni in *Sacred Narrative: Readings in the Theory of Myth*, ed. Alan Dundes (Berkeley: University of California Press, 1984).

5 See the discussion of this issue in Karner, introduction.

6 Bell, "Mythscapes," 75.

7 On the seizure of power and Hitler's demands, communicated largely by telephone through Hermann Göring, see Botz, *Nationalsozialismus in Wien*, 62-81; On the unfolding of the events of the Anschluss see Hagspiel, *Die Ostmark*, esp. chapter three, "Österreich zwischen Ende und neuem Beginn," 17-58. See also Weyr, *Setting*, chapter one.

8 Kurt von Schuschnigg, radio broadcast (March 11, 1938), "Anschluss," *Spartacus Educational*, accessed June 4, 2019, http://spartacus-educational.com/2WWanschluss.htm

9 "Ich proklamiere nunmehr für dieses Land seine neue Mission. Sie entspricht dem Gebot, das einst die deutschen Siedler aus allen Gauen des Altreichs hierher berufen hat. Die älteste Ostmark des deutschen Volkes soll von jetzt ab das jüngste Bollwerk der deutschen Nation und damit des Deutschen Reiches sein…"Adolf Hitler, speech on the Heldenplatz, March 13, 1938, quoted in Anton Hadwiger, *Volk auf dem Marsch: Die Junge Ostmarkreihe.* (Vienna: Deutscher Verlag für Jugend und Volk, 1941), 8. On the political use of the Heldenplatz see Peter Stachel, *Mythos Heldenplatz: Hauptplatz und Schauplatz der Republik* (Vienna: Molden Verlag, 2018).

10 *Gesetz über die Wiedervereinigung* Österreichs *mit dem Deutschen Reich*. 13 März 1938. *DocumentArchiv.de*, accessed June 4, 2019, http://www.documentarchiv.de/ns/1938/anschluss_oesterreich_deutsches-reich.html. There would continue to be problems with the double system of Party and Government, often leading to overlapping roles and conflicts.

11 The system became official on October 6, 1939. Hagspiel, *Die Ostmark*, 49-57.

12 Josef Fränkel, ed., *The Jews of Austria: Essays on their Life, History and Destruction* (London: Valentine Mitchell, 1967) and Gertrude Schneider, *Exile and Destruction: The Fate of Austrian Jews 1938-1945* (Westport: Praeger, 1995). Wolf Gruner, *Zwangsarbeit und Verfolgung. Österreichische Juden in NS Staat 1938-1945* (Innsbruck: Studien Verlag, 2000).

13 On von Schirach and worries about Austrian separatism see Morowitz, "'Heil the Hero Klimt': The 1943 Gustav Klimt Retrospective and Cultural Politics in Nazi Vienna," *Oxford Art Journal* 39, no. 1 (March 2016): 107-129.

14 Jeffrey Olick and Daniel Levy, "Collective Memory and Cultural Constraint: Holocaust Myth and Rationality in German Politics," *American Sociological Review* 62, no. 6 (December 1997): 922. On Bell's concept of the mythscape see introduction, 31-34.

15 Hagspiel, *Die Ostmark*, 195.

16 Hagspiel, *Die Ostmark*, 192-3.

17 Robert Dassanowsky, "Snowblinded: The Alps contra Vienna in Austrian Entertainment Film at the Anschluss," *Austrian Studies* 18 (August 2010): 106-123; Johann Hüttner, "Austria and the Austrians as Seen Through the Films of Nazi Germany After the Anschluss," *Modern Austrian Literature* 32, no. 4 (1999): 204-212.

18 Peter Stachel, "Vom NS-Leiter des Künstlerhaus zum Gestalter des Eisernen Vorhangs der Wiener Staatsoper: Rudolf Hermann Eisenmenger (1902-1994)," in *Das Wiener Künstlerhaus: Kunst und Institution*, ed. Peter Bogner, Richard Kurdiovsky, and Johannes Stoll (Vienna: 2015), 154.

19 "Gemeinschaft, Deutschtum, Volkstümlichkeit, Rasse, Blut, Boden, Schicksal, Lebenskraft, Mut, Treue und Führergefolgschaft." Hans. H. Hiebel, "Der Anschluss der Ostmark an das Reich: Zur präfaschistische Germanistik in Österreich," in *Austrian Writers and the Anschluss: Understanding the Past, Overcoming the Past,* ed. Donald G. Daviau (Riverside: Ariadne Press, 1991), 70.

20 Josef Nadler, *Literaturgeschichte des deutschen Volkes. Dichtung und Schrifttum der deutschen Stämme und Landschaften*. 4 vols. Berlin: Im Propyläen-Verlag, 1938-1941.

21 Günther Schwab, *Österreich: die Deutsche Ostmark* (Berlin: Karl Specht Verlag, 1938).

22 Friedrich Lange, *Unsere alte Ostmark Österreich* (Berlin: Nibelungen Verlag, 1941).

23 "Kein anderes deutsches Land war so wie Österreich Spielball in den Händen volksfremder Mächte, die unter Hintansetzung der Lebensgesetze des Reiches und des Volkes, ja in Gegensatz zu ihnen, diesen Teil Deutschlands skrupellos ihren persönlich Machtinteressen dienstbar machten. Und kein deutscher Stamm hat so wie dieser den Einbruch so vieler fremder Blutströmer zu ertragen." Schwab, *Österreich*, 7.

24 "Als den Verlust eines Armes und eines Beines...." Alfred Rapp, *Die Habsburger: Die Tragödie eines halben Jahrtausends deutscher Geschichte* (Stuttgart: Frankische Verlagshandlung, 1936), 263.

25 Ibid., 263.

26 "Aber die Zeit war um. Die Entwicklung, die bestimmten, uns noch unbekannten Gesetzen folgt, war abgelaufen. Die Stunde war da. Ein Mann hob die Hand und das Deutsche Wunder kam, strömte feldgrün über die Grenzen der Mark; quoll rauschend, jubelnd aus der Herzen von Millionen, die auf die Straßen eilten, schreiend, lachend, schluchzend, mit erhobenen Händen, wonnetrunken und die Ungeheuerlichkeit, dieses Glück nicht fassend. Die Ostmark frei, die Ostmark deutsch!" Schwab, *Österreich*, 14.

27 "In diesen Tagen, da in Österreich der deutsche Führer durch sein Heimatland zog, ist die deutsche Seele zu vollem Leben wieder ausgemacht.... und auch die letzten seiner verirrten und versprengten Glieder zu vollen, bleibende Einheit des Wollens und des Fühlens zusammengebracht." Hadwiger, *Volk auf dem Marsch: Die Junge Ostmarkreihe* (Deutscher Verlag für Jugend und Volk, 1941), 26.

28 "Darin besteht das geschichtliche und kulturelle Erlösungswerk des Führers, dass er den tausendjährigen Krieg zwischen Deutschtum und Judentum in der Ostmark an einem einzigen Tage und ohne Blutvergießen siegreich beendet und gleichzeitig seinem Volke das heiß ersehnte Grossdeutsche Reich geschenkt hat!" Robert Körber, *Rassesieg in Wien*

der Grenzfeste des Reiches (Vienna: Universitäts Verlag Wilhelm Braumüller, 1939), 289. Körber was a committed anti-Semite and Nazi long before the Anschluss and remained one until his death in 1980. Norbert Sahrhage, "Der Mann, der nach dem Zweiten Weltkrieg Nazi-Größen nach Bünde holte," *Neue Westfälische.* July 25, 2019, accessed August 2, 2019, https://www.nw.de/lokal/kreis_herford/buende/22516621_Der-Mann-der-nachdem-Zweiten-Weltkrieg-Nazi-Groessen-nach-Buende-holte.html

29 "Da kam der Führer, nun doch gerade zur rechten Stunde, und überschritt mit seiner neu aufgebauten Wehrmacht die Grenze zwischen Deutschen und Deutschen." Lange, *Unsere alte Ostmark,* 47.

30 "Schon ist die neue Einheit mit Blut besiegelt worden." Ibid, 7.

31 "Dieselben dunklen Mächte, die mit allen Mitteln bestrebt waren, die Ostmark-Deutschen von ihren Brüdern zu trennen, wollten das geeinte deutsche Volk und das entstandene Grossdeutsche Reich, das der Führer erst schuf, vernichten und Volk und Reich in ewige Ohnmacht und Not stürzen. Zur Verteidigung des neugewonnenen Grossdeutschen Reiches zogen die Söhne der Ostmark mit den Brüdern aus allen Stämmen und Gauen des Reiches mit altgewohnter Tapferkeit und Einsatzbereitschaft in den Kampf." Otto Reich von Rohrwig, *Der Freiheitskampf der Ostmark Deutschen von S. Germain bis Adolf Hitler* (Vienna: Leopold Stocker Verlag, 1942), 5.

32 "In unglaublicher Schnelligkeit wurden diese Verträge zunichte gemacht, die nichts anderes wollten, als einen ewigen Keil zwischen die beiden Brüder des gleichen Volkes zu stossen." Reich von Rohrwig, *Der Freiheitskampf,* 465.

33 Heinrich Hoffmann, *Wie die Ostmark ihre Befreiung erlebte: Adolf Hitler und sein Weg zu Grossdeutschland* (Vienna: Austria Tabakwerke, 1940).

34 "Wenn die Vorsehung mich einst aus dieser Stadt heraus zur Führung berief des Reiches, dann muss sie mir damit einen Auftrag erteilt haben und es kann nur ein Auftrag gewesen sein, meine teure Heimat dem Deutschen Reich wiederzugeben." Quote attributed to Adolf Hitler on March 12, 1938. Hoffmann, *Wie die Ostmark*, opening page.

35 "...eine hohe, unbegreifliche Sinngebung, die uns oft ein schweres Schicksal, ein Verhängnis und doch, im Spiegel der Jahrtausende betrachtet, nur wie das Aneinanderfügen von Gliedern einer ewigen Kette erscheint." Ibid, 7.

36 "Dort im Dunklen, im tiefsten Grunde der Volksseele, konnte es nun warten, bis seine Zeit kam, bis der ungeheure Wille jenseits unseres Begreifens sich in den Sinn eines einzelnen, erlesenen Menschen senkte, in ihm Wille und Wert und Tat wurde." Ibid, 8.

37 See Karner, introduction, 37.

38 Wilhelm Bornstedt, *Die österreichische Ostmark in der deutschen Geschichte* (Breslau: Heinrich Handels Verlag, 1940). Despite his membership in the S.S., Bornstedt continued his career in education until 1980. Hans-Christian Harten: *Weltanschauliche Schulung der SS und der Polizei im Nationalsozialismus: Zusammenstellung personenbezogener Daten* (Paderborn: Verlag Ferdinand Schöningh, 2017), 54.

39 See for example Hermann Aubin, *Geschichtlicher Aufriss des Ostraumes* (Berlin: Hugo, 1940).

40 "So vollzog sich besonders im letzten Jahrhundert im Gegensatz zur natürlichen Sendung der Ostmark, Bollwerk des Reiches im Osten zu sein..." Körber, *Rassesieg in Wien*, 36.

41 Roland Barthes, *Mythologies*, trans. Annette Lavers (New York: Farrar, Strauss and Giroux, 1972). For Barthes, myths are "depoliticized speech," that is, they present as natural and innocent that which has been human-made.

42 Elizabeth Cronin, *Heimat Photography in Austria* (Salzburg: Fotohof Editions, 2015); Roman Giesen, *Der Bergfilm der 20er und 30er Jahre* (Frankfurt am Main: Johann Wolfgang Goethe-Universität, 2008).

43 Anne Naess, *Mountains and Mythology* (Durban: Trumpeter, 1995).

44 Olick and Bell, 76.

45 For the content of the show see the published catalogue, *Berge und Menschen der Ostmark*, 4. März bis 30. April 1939 (Vienna: Genossenschaft der bildenden Künstler Wien, 1939). For a detailed analysis of the exhibit see Laura Morowitz, "Erasing the City: 'Berge und Menschen der Ostmark, March 4 to April 30, 1939'", forthcoming.

46 Angerhofer received his training at the Munich Academy of the Fine Arts and became a member of the Vienna Künstlerhaus in 1937 and a member of the NSDAP. He was well received by the Nazi establishment, appearing in the 1937 "Großen Deutschen Kunstausstellung" in Munich and winning the Oberdonau Gaukulturpreis für Malerei in 1941. His work fell into obscurity after the war. For a brief biography on Angerhofer see Norbert Loidol, "Holzknechte im Windbruch," http://wwwg.uni-klu.ac.at/kultdoku/kataloge/39/html/2953.htm, accessed May 12, 2019. Text taken from Julius Stieber, ed., *Land der Hämmer. Heimat Eisenwurzen. Region Phyrn-Eisenwurzen. Katalog der Oberösterreichischen Landesausstellung* (Salzburg: Residenz-Verlag, 1998), 533.

47 On Strobl see Ernst Klee, *Das Kulturlexikon zum Dritten Reich: Wer war was vor und nach 1945* (Frankfurt am Main: S. Fischer, 2007), 601.

48 "Und dies alles mag auch wieder Beitrag sein zur Kenntnis und Erkenntnis der Bedeutung Österreichs für die Volksgemeinschaft der achtzig Millionen deutschen Menschen im Herzen Europas." Strobl, *Berge und Menschen,* unpaginated.

49 The show was in Berlin from May 26 to June 25, 1939.

50 *Die Pause* 4/5 (1939).

51 "Mit fortschreitender Zeit wurde diese wichtige reichsschützende und reichserhaltende Rolle der Ostmark immer schwerer und ruhmvoller... Demgegenüber wurde der innere Zusammenhalt des Reiches unter den letzten Hohenstaufen, den Habsburgern und Luxemburgern immer schwächer... Aber die unter den Habsburgern immer größer werdende Reichsschwäche bewirkte es, dass die östmärklichen Länder bei der Lösung ihrer Grenzmarkenaufgabe immer weniger auf den Rückhalt am Gesamtdeutschtum rechnen durften." Kremser, "Ostmark als Bollwerk des Reiches," *Die Pause* 4/5 (1939), 20.

52 "Er hat die Aufgabe, Mehrer und Schützer deutschen Volksbodens zu sein.... Der Führer hat die Ostmark wieder zu der Bestimmung zurückgerufen, zu deren Erfüllung sie geschaffen wurde: Bollwerk des Reiches zu sein, aus dem sie hervorgegangen, Schutzwehr des Volkes zu sein, aus dessen Arbeit und Blut sie erstanden ist." Ibid., 21 .

53 Timothy Naftali, "Creating the Myth of the Alpenfestung: Allied Intelligence and the Collapse of the Nazi Police State," in Bischof and Pelinka, 203-246.

54 Ibid, 219.

The Victim Myth Revisited: The Politics of History in Austria up until the Waldheim Affair

Peter Pirker

Introduction

Over the last thirty years, no other concept has defined the politics of history concerning Austria's Nazi past to a greater extent than the concept of the Austrian "victim myth." The term emerged in the mid-1980s as part of an effort to expose the victim hypothesis formulated in the Declaration of Independence of April, 27, 1945—namely that Austria was occupied by Nazi Germany in March 1938 and became, along with its population, a helpless and defenseless victim of German repression, exploitation, and warmongering—as an "existential lie," a "fiction," and a "state mythology."[1] The exposure of the "victim myth" profoundly changed Austria's "national mythscape" (Duncan Bell). Today, one could well claim that it has become a widely shared component of the national memory regime, which has moreover taken on a legitimizing function on the level of governance. This became especially clear in the 2018 memorial year after the Austrian People's Party (ÖVP), under the leadership of Sebastian Kurz, had entered into a coalition government with the right-wing Austrian Freedom Party (FPÖ) despite the fact that the latter has made a name for itself with rather different attitudes regarding the politics of history, especially in relation to the service of Austrians in the *Wehrmacht*, as well as with repeated revisionist, antisemitic, and racist statements made by its functionaries. Now, the "new" politics of memory went hand in hand with a decisively right-wing politics directed against refugees and immigrants, with Austria and the Austrians being stylized as victims that needed protection from an unbridled—and, in the anti-Semitic discourse of the FPÖ, even targeted—invasion by foreigners. In contrast to the original intention of the critics of the victim myth, namely to liberalize a problematic and antiquated national politics of memory in pursuit of a new political culture of self-reflection, the demarcation of the victim myth now served to instrumentalize the politics of history as the flank guard of a right-wing conservative political turn.

In the introduction to this volume, Christian Karner called in reference to Duncan Bell for a "processual understanding of ongoing memory-work and myth-making." This naturally also applies to the discovery of the victim myth and its function as a "master narrative" of Austria's politics of history. In what follows, I will therefore examine some of the elements of this explanatory model as an impetus to rethink the "victim myth" as the central lens through which to approach the Austrian politics of memory up until the Waldheim years. I will begin with the central problem of the theory of the victim myth—namely the deficiencies in differentiating conceptually between various meanings of the German term *Opfer*, which can, in fact, be translated into English either as "victim" or "sacrifice." This distinction, I argue, can serve to analyze the politics of history in Austria more precisely while overcoming the aporias inherent to the concept of the "victim myth." To this end, I will develop the hypothesis that the most significant engagements with the past that occurred during the first two decades after the war on the state and civil society levels revolved around the question of "sacrifices made" (*erbrachte Opfer*) rather than "victimization" (*Opferwerdung*). On the civil society level, the competing positions in this debate reflected the views of the organizations of former resistance fighters and political opponents of National Socialism on the one side and of *Wehrmacht* veterans on the other. The central question here was who could claim to have made the greatest sacrifice for Austria during the Nazi era. This approach challenges the hypothesis that the victim myth was not just a "foundational myth supportive of the state" but moreover led to a "public consensus" and laid the groundwork for a "process of victimization" through which the "true victims of National Socialism" were marginalized.[2] Even though, as Heidemarie Uhl and Günter Bischof have emphasized, the relationship between different narratives of victimization were not necessarily consensual—and there were, in fact, various "competing Austrian victim myths"[3]—the vanishing point and broad reception of the narrative pattern of victimization were ultimately grounded in its postulation of "generalization," "universalization," "leveling," and "homogenization" of the category of victimhood in relation to various societal groups, some of whom had been deeply involved in the Nazi system.[4] Walter Manoschek and Thomas Geldmacher characterized the politics of history in the first ten years after 1945 altogether as the political implementation of "Austrian identity as a collective of victims."[5] In the final section of this paper, I will describe, by contrast, the crystallization of a state-implemented sacrificial memory regime, which ultimately allowed for Kurt Waldheim to be elected federal president in 1986. In summary, this paper presents the hypothesis that Austria's national formation through the politics of history should be understood as a process in which the recognition of *sacrifice* was the crucial issue, while the turn toward a victimological memory only occurred following Waldheim's election and his international isolation.

Conceptualizations of Victimhood in the Waldheim Context

The meaningful distinction between the two dimensions of the German concept of *Opfer*, which is linguistically clearer in English through the correspondence of this term to either "victim" or "sacrifice,"[6] was recognized in the discussions surrounding the victim myth but not systematically differentiated in the corresponding analyses.[7] Aleida Assmann's distinction between sacrificial and victimological forms of remembrance is pertinent in this context. The conceptual consequences are clear: A perspective focusing on sacrificial efforts places the subject's motivations to act at center stage in the politics of history, posing questions such as "to what end" and "in opposition to what" they acted. Meanwhile, a focus on sacrifice opened up a broad space for the search for meaning, the process of victimization being far more difficult to make sense of. As Svenja Goltermann addressed, "victimhood was hardly ever an attractive subject position" until the latter third of the twentieth century.[8] Neither in Europe nor in the US was it of particular moral benefit to describe oneself as a victim after enduring an act of violence. The victim position was "loaded with reservations" as it was perceived as a result of weakness and therefore implied a certain co-responsibility in the act of aggression, particularly in cases concerning Jews and women.[9] This also entailed the mechanism of guilt reversal, which typified both the secondary antisemitism of the post-1945 era, whereby the Jews' ostensible political and economic power was identified as the reason for their persecution,[10] along with sexist perceptions of victimhood, which identified sexual impulses as the cause of violence against women.[11]

As scholars of nationalism have shown, collective identities throughout much of the twentieth century were formed through the construction of collective sacrificial efforts and their recognition by the state—in other words, through sacrificial memory regimes. As early as the nineteenth century, during the era of civil emancipation, the notion arose that the "highest duty [of the citizen] consisted in sacrifice and death for the fatherland."[12] Ernest Renan described the honorific recognition of "sacrifices that have been made" as the most significant moment in the process of national integration. This was the symbolic remuneration from state and society for the fulfillment of duty, greater still than the material remuneration in cases of invalidity or death. National remembrance, to paraphrase Benedict

Anderson, was grounded in the selective memory not so much of having killed but of having willingly died.[13] As I will demonstrate shortly, this thinking is precisely what underlies the antagonistic self-representations of veterans of the resistance and veterans of the *Wehrmacht* between the late 1940s and the mid-1960s. What these opponents had in common, though, was that they did not seek recognition as victims but as martyrs for Austria.

The quest for meaning in the commemoration of victims of antisemitic and racist persecution is a more recent phenomenon, a consequence of the turn toward recognition of the victims that began in the 1960s when new social movements started to campaign for victims' rights and to give them a voice. A greater recognition of the victims' perspective in criminal and trial law also only emerged in the 1960s as the attribution of co-responsibility to the victims and/or disregard for the victims began to be criticized, for example, by the feminist movement.[14] In Holocaust research, too, the victims only began to emerge from the shadows as a result of the Auschwitz trials in Germany during the 1960s. It was not before the early 1970s that survivors of the Shoah in Europe began to receive medical treatment for post-traumatic stress disorder.[15] The global transmission of the American TV series *Holocaust* in the late 1970s finally broke the embargo on remembering Jewish victims of the Holocaust in mass media.[16] Investigations conducted into the psychological aftereffects of soldiers' wartime experiences, for example during the Vietnam War, meanwhile led to a reevaluation of the victimization of soldiers in wartime contexts and consequently to a de-heroization of death and suffering among soldiers.[17] Another aspect of shifting perspectives on victimization was the struggle for human rights from the 1970s onwards and the worldwide lobbying on behalf of victims of human rights infractions. This empowerment of victims finally also affected the perspective on perpetrators, focusing attention on their identities and motives.

A terminological differentiation of the concept *Opfer* can help open the way for a clearer analysis of the Austrian politics of history that occurred from the 1950s to the 1980s, the period during which an Austrian national consciousness began to be consolidated. However, the most influential monographs and edited volumes published after Waldheim's election focused on the immediate postwar years or on the Waldheim debate itself.[18] The victim hypothesis emerging from the Allied Declaration on Austria of 1943 and the Austrian Declaration of Independence of 1945 did, indeed, play a major role in both temporal contexts. It was first deployed as a means to distance Austria from Nazi Germany. Then, following decades of meaninglessness, it was resurrected in 1986 to deflect criticisms of Austria's engagement with the Nazi past. The timestamps of the criticisms then and now were the years 1945 and 1986—a time frame that became foundational for the theorization of the entire politics of history of the Second Republic. Criticisms of Austria's self-representation as a victim and the exposure of this narrative as a myth were important, yet they were only partially able to account for the transmission and continued propagation of values and attitudes in the new democratic order that had been shaped by Fascism and National Socialism. A differentiation between "victim" and "sacrifice" is therefore also a suitable frame within which to understand the constellation underlying the politics of history that led to the exposure of the "victim myth" in the mid-1980s.

In Austria, the turn toward a memory of victimhood began on the political level with some delay following the Waldheim affair. Kurt Waldheim did not present himself in his election campaign as a victim of National Socialism but as someone who, like hundreds of thousands of Austrian *Wehrmacht* soldiers, had "done his duty." He deployed a rhetoric that had already been promoted by the Austrian Union of Comrades (*Österreichischer Kameradschaftsbund*, ÖKB) in the 1950s and was adopted into the official historical narrative of the republic in the 1960s. It had moreover already been utilized as a justification first by the former *SS-Obersturmführer* and FPÖ politician, Friedrich Peter, in 1975[19] and then again by the emerging right-wing politician Jörg Haider in 1985 to defend the former SS officer Walter Reder when he returned to Austria in 1985 following a prison sentence served for war crimes in Italy.[20] In his election speeches, Waldheim added the phrase "we were decent" to this rhetoric.[21] According to Robert Knight, the first historian to astutely analyze the "Waldheim context,"[22] Waldheim's success thus contravened the "myth about the foundation of the Austrian republic," for "decency" and the "fulfillment of duty" did not number among the topoi of the anti-Nazi victim narratives of the period from 1943 to 1946, whether in the Declaration on Austria, the Declaration of Independence, or the *Rot-Weiss-Rot-Buch*, a 1946 government-issued work intended to document Austria's status as a country occupied by Nazi Germany. However, it would also be missing the mark to characterize the "fulfillment of duty" narrative as a kind of subcutaneous popular tradition and as a populist countermyth that stood for a long time in covert contradistinction to the state victim myth.[23] Waldheim was speaking in the context of a sacrificial regime of honor that had been promoted by government politicians since 1955 and had become entrenched as the *leitmotiv* of patriotic memory. The ÖVP only cast Waldheim as a victim during the presidential campaign in response to the criticisms of this narrative of sacrifice in the line of duty, which in the context of the new historical paradigm of the

Holocaust predominating outside of Austria (as well as among a minority within Austria) had come to be regarded as a structural contribution to the murder of European Jewry, as well as to the stability of the Nazi regime. The victimological turn only became evident after the election when Waldheim ceased employing the terminology of a "proper fulfillment of duty" that had won him the election. Meanwhile, the unavoidable recognition of the persecution of Austria's Jewish population was accompanied by representations of the non-Jewish population in various victim roles, particularly of the civilian population as those who had severely suffered through the bombing war.[24] Soldiers were also included among the ranks of the victims, although the positive recognition of the soldiers' fulfillment of duty remained highly resilient right into the 2000s.

In light of the new attention paid to the "true" victims, both these forms of victimization of *Wehrmacht* soldiers and civilians rightly began to be viewed by a younger generation of intellectuals as an illegitimate appropriation that, in relation to present discourses as well as to historical foundational documents, needed to be deconstructed as myths. In fact, the reactivation of the victim hypothesis also demanded an adaptation by state representatives to suit the new context of victimological remembrance. If, in 1945, the Germans alone could be identified as the perpetrators (along with a highly treasonous minority of Austrian Nazis), the new victimization of the Austrians now also raised the question of Austrian perpetrators. Under these circumstances, Waldheim became the first leading politician to admit that many Austrians had enthusiastically embraced National Socialism and become Nazi perpetrators.[25] However, this acknowledgement of co-responsibility only received a degree of credibility after the Waldheim years in the 1990s when Austria was preparing itself for accession to the European Union.

The Fading of the Victim Hypothesis in the International Context

The resurrection and rejuvenation of the victim hypothesis was not only an issue for the ÖVP in the grand coalition, which was established once more in 1986 after a more than twenty-year hiatus. This position was also adopted with particular zeal by Foreign Minister Peter Jankowitsch of the Social Democratic Party (SPÖ), who after Waldheim's election reminded critics of Austria abroad "that this country did not just become the victim of verbal aggression, but that hundreds of thousands of Austrians had to give their lives during World War II in Adolf Hitler's concentration camps and on his generals' battlefields."[26] He thus harked directly back to the rhetoric of the 1945 Declaration of Independence. However, the reanimation of Austria's victim status found little appeal amongst the Western Allies. The UK government had already implemented diplomatic sanctions against the Austrian federal government a year earlier and indefinitely postponed a planned visit of Defense Minister Friedhelm Frischenschlager as he had personally welcomed the above-mentioned convicted war criminal, Walter Reder, back to Austria with a handshake.[27] Despite vocal international criticism, Frischenschlager did not resign. Moreover, at the grand ceremonies organized in Vienna in May 1985 to mark the thirtieth anniversary of the signing of the State Treaty, the foreign ministers of the UK and the US, Geoffrey Howe and George Shultz, did not address Austria as the "first victim of National Socialism." Only French Foreign Minister Roland Dumas and his Soviet counterpart, Andrei Gromyko, described Austria as the "first victim of Hitlerite aggression" and as the "first victim of National Socialism," respectively.[28] Dumas jumped to Austria's defense because France had itself been battling challenges to its own longstanding resistance myth for a number of years already, which after 1945 had sidelined French collaboration with the German occupation in the persecution of the resistance and the deportation of Jews.[29] For the Soviet Union, meanwhile, the State Treaty and the neutrality of the Austria it enshrined had constituted a significant success for post-Stalinist foreign policy and for the political architecture of Europe. Due to the rumblings then occurring in various states of the "East Bloc," Gromyko had no interest in damaging these cornerstones of Soviet diplomacy.

The fact that the UK and the US did not support the victim hypothesis in 1985 did not actually represent a policy turnabout. The victim hypothesis had already ceased being of relevance to the leading Western states after 1955. No supporting statements by their diplomats can be found in the stream of news reports by the *Austria Press Agency* (*APA*) during this period. Statements characterizing Austria as the "first victim" were uttered exclusively by representatives of the Communist regimes in Yugoslavia, Czechoslovakia, and the Soviet Union. Of the Western democracies, only neutral Sweden and France can be found to have made statements to this effect—and then only very rarely. The US and the UK had—since the beginning of their open, systemic competition with the Soviet Union from 1947 onwards—been cultivating a different image of Austria, which was not that of a victim. The US in particular continued to characterize Austria as a model for the Central and Eastern European states of the East Bloc. The victim role was not suitable to this end. Quite on the contrary, the point was to demonstrate how a small country could overcome the victim role: through accepting the aid offered by the Marshall Plan, resisting the Soviet Union's claims to power, and adopting a democratic solution to societal conflicts, market-based modernization, and religious tolerance. Inversely, only a few *APA* reports demonstrate an emphasis on the victim status in statements by Austrian foreign affairs politicians after 1955. This finding suggests that Austria's external nation-building process, meaning the positioning of the country in the international context, was already detached from the anti-German victim doctrine. The politics of neutrality that set in after 1955 guided this external nation-building process out of the shadow of the Nazi past and into the context of the Cold War, the decolonization and non-alignment movements, as well as the North/South divide.[30]

The two most significant Allied powers therefore did not participate in the Austrian resuscitation of the victim doctrine. On the contrary, their leading media became the first in 1985 to attack the "victim myth."[31] This dissonant constellation, with the US and UK distancing themselves from the victim doctrine at precisely the time that Austria was attempting to resuscitate it, had a great impact on the views of the critics. This led to an exceptionalist interpretation of the victim hypothesis as a specific national product of the Austrian politics of memory—as something specifically Austrian.[32]

A Reevaluation of the Declaration on Austria and Its Problems

A major scholarly foundation for this development was the influential reevaluation of the Allied Declaration on Austria of November 1943, as presented by the historian Robert Keyserlingk in 1988.[33] In his greatly abbreviated reconstruction of the origins of this document, Keyserlingk arrived at the conclusion that it by no means constituted a declaration of intent on behalf of the Allies to reestablish Austria. According to Keyserlingk, this document was nothing more than a short-term propaganda instrument of psychological warfare designed to promote resistance in Nazi Austria. Keyserlingk's line of argumentation was adopted by most historians working on the "victim myth," although Gerald Stourzh proffered a convincing critique of his analysis.[34] For critics of Austria's politics of history, Keyserlingk's "demystification" of the Declaration on Austria came at just the right time. If the Allies had not actually described Austria in earnest as a victim of Nazi Germany, then the responsibility for this portrayal lay exclusively with the first generation of the political elite of the Second Republic, who therefore became the subject of criticism. The adoption of the victim hypothesis in the Declaration of Independence now appeared as an immoral instrumentalization designed to externalize all guilt and responsibility for the crimes of National Socialism onto Germany. Undoubtedly, Keyserlingk's work stimulated a meritorious body of literature on the early Austrian politics of history and its protagonists. However, these reevaluations significantly distorted the underlying historical power relations. The Allies were now cast as weak agents from whom the victim hypothesis had essentially been wangled by cunning and/or opportunistic Austrian postwar politicians.

The deconstruction of the Declaration on Austria additionally entailed the deconstruction of the Declaration of Independence, the *Rot-Weiss-Rot-Buch*, and the preamble to the State Treaty. Like dominoes, one document after the other succumbed to this process of demystification. In the Declaration of Independence, the state founders had obfuscated the reference to Austria's co-responsibility for the German war effort, excluded the Jews as the largest group of victims, and instead transformed the *Wehrmacht* soldiers into victims of the Germans. In the *Rot-Weiss-Rot-Buch*, the government then grossly exaggerated the scope of the resistance. Previously celebrated in national historiography as a masterwork of diplomacy, the complete expungement of Austria's "responsibility" from the preamble of the State Treaty was reevaluated as the final affront to the "true" victims of National Socialism.

These deconstructions reproduced a negative of the Austro-centric perspective, meaning that the problems of writing a national historiography were perpetuated. For example, the fact that the Declaration on Austria was just one of four declarations made by the Allies during the Moscow Conference in October 1943 was completely overlooked. As late as 1996, Keyserlingk opened his essay on the "Moscow Declaration" in the foundational edited volume *Österreich im 20. Jahrhundert* (*Austria in the Twentieth Century*) with the two counterfactual research questions of why the Allied foreign ministers had chosen Austria of all countries "as the first and only country for which a decisive postwar policy was formulated" and how this political declaration fitted in with the "otherwise exclusively strategic military character of this conference."[35] Aside from the central strategic military declaration on the continuation of hostilities until the "unconditional surrender" of the German armies had been achieved and the political declaration on the reestablishment of Austria, two further, decisively political declarations were made. The "Statement on Atrocities" formulated the principles of the judicial action that was to be taken against the German perpetrators for the atrocities, massacres, and mass murders committed in the context of the war and the occupation of foreign countries. Naturally, this declaration also applied to civilians and soldiers from Austria who, as the Declaration on Austria stated, had fought on the side of Germany. In the "Declaration Regarding Italy," the foreign ministers formulated seven principles of action with which Fascism was to be overcome, a guide that was absent in the Declaration on Austria. In contrast to Italy, Austria had a longer democratic history upon which it could build. In Austria's case, the key challenge was its territorial separation and national dissociation from Germany. Thus, the authors of the drafts of the Declaration on Austria from the British Foreign Office came up with the strategy of pointedly describing Austria as the "first free country *to fall a victim* [my emphasis] to Hitlerite aggression." However, victimization alone is not enough for the construction of a national identity. The authors therefore also included a formulation that aimed, first of all, to relativize the main hypothesis by ascribing to Austria "a responsibility for the participation in the war on the side of Hitlerite Germany." Thus, a second form of *Opfer* was introduced—namely Austria's responsibility to make its own *sacrifices* in the struggle for liberation. The path from being victimized to making a sacrifice, from a negative identity to a positive identity, was idealistically preordained in the Declaration on Austria. The Declaration of Independence can be read as the first official response on behalf of the provisional government. It began by quoting in full the victim hypothesis and the clause for the reestablishment of the republic. However, not surprisingly, Austrian politicians here broadened the victim hypothesis by portraying the "participation in the war" on the side of Germany as coerced and the Austrian *Wehrmacht* soldiers as some sort of war slaves of the Germans. Yet the transition to a positive identity formation turned out to be weak indeed. The document evinces no heroization of the resistance, rather excusing its meager contribution in this regard by pointing to the debilitation of the people and the despoliation of the country.

Austria's top diplomats ultimately encouraged the government to adopt this line as general foreign policy since they expected this to result in preferential treatment by the Allies.[36] In December 1945, the parliament cemented the victim hypothesis as foreign policy doctrine. The Allies accepted this legislation because—entirely in contrast to the situation in 1918—this narrative elevated Austria's dissociation from Germany to a basic consensus of the political elites. Whether the formulations of these documents correlated to historical facts is somewhat irrelevant. Rather, both documents should be viewed entirely as political declarations drafted and based on partly counterfactual knowledge: they aimed at a transformation of an unpleasant past and present into an outline for a better future. In other words, they were products of the politics of history.

In preparation for negotiations over full sovereignty, the Austrian government tried to overcome the shortcomings of a pure victimization narrative through the *Rot-Weiss-Rot-Buch* of 1946, which documented civilian and military resistance, as well as the martyrdom of opponents of National Socialism. Concerning war service, the fallen Austrian soldiers were counted among the victims of the German occupation. The government thereby tried to entirely recreate the two dimensions of *Opfer*—victimhood and sacrifice—proffered by the Declaration on Austria.[37] At this point, the Allies were still invested in interrogating the shift from victimization and collaboration to resistance, this issue therefore playing a prominent role in the negotiations concerning reparations, as well as the transferal of "German property" from Austria to the Soviet Union.[38] As has been demonstrated by Ulrich Nachbaur, the government was thoroughly aware that the *Rot-Weiss-Rot-Buch* was not particularly impressive.[39] The relatively low scale of resistance corresponded to the expectations of British diplomats in 1943. The price for freedom was thus ultimately not fixed according to a historical judgment but according to the present interests of the Allies. At first, the Soviet Union massively escalated its demands in the general context of systemic confrontation between the powers, resulting in the initial conclusion of negotiations in 1949 stipulating the loss of the petroleum industry. Ultimately, however, Austria profited from the formalization of antagonistic military alliances in Europe, the NATO and the Warsaw Pact, in 1955. As part of its attempts to improve the relations with "strategically important 'floating' European countries,"[40] the Soviet Union agreed both to strike the responsibility clause from the preamble of the 1947 draft of the State Treaty and to completely relinquish its property claims against Austria.

The Failure of the Victim Hypothesis in Austrian Society

In an article from 1988, Robert Knight distinguished between two functions performed by the Declaration on Austria—namely a tactical function designed to legitimize the separatist foundation of the state as a victim of Nazi Germany through which the Austrian population was detached from their entanglements with the "Third Reich," as well as a legitimizing function for the "creation of a national myth."[41] However, he was unsure whether the "legitimizing" function had like the "tactical" function, in fact, been realized, for one of his theories was that Waldheim's electoral victory must be regarded not as a paradox of the Austrian success story but as an integral component thereof. Knight had already argued that the "official myth about Austria as a victim, including [its] resistance" had not provided "a sufficient basis for a national consensus in postwar Austria."[42] Waldheim's electoral victory was thus precisely not a "confirmation of the victim hypothesis by the majority of the electorate."[43]

Knight was here referring to the difference between exterior and interior processes of national formation. He thereby questioned whether the victim myth developed in the international political context had been fertile in the domestic societal context. In other words, while on a diplomatic level the readiness to lie in unison was sufficient for politicians to reach a consensus amongst themselves, such negotiations do not translate onto the inner relations of a representative democracy. The state-founding parties could propagate certain historical narratives in society but not dictate them. Knight noted the sensitivity of the governing politicians to the resonance of historical pronouncements among the general population in his analysis of the minutes of cabinet meetings relating to discussions on the restitution of Jewish property and/or compensation for "Aryanized" property. The governing politicians of the ÖVP and SPÖ in 1946 already entertained significant doubts about the usefulness of the vocabulary of the victim doctrine as a legitimization for the new state.

Knight therefore interpreted the curtailment and deferment of reparations as a "balancing act between maintaining the victim hypothesis in foreign policy and finding consensus in domestic policy."[44] This suggests that the very first elected postwar government already considered the logical consequences of the victim doctrine to be difficult to implement among the broader population. With specific regard to the small group of Jewish survivors in Austria and their meager societal influence, the government moreover did not consider them worth realizing. A strategy in this context consisted of placing the victimization of the non-Jewish population on a par with the persecution of the Jews by presenting Austria's "occupation" as a process of unlawful expropriations of Austrian state property, implying that the systematic despoliation of the Jewish population was not a unique phenomenon. This genuinely did constitute an "instrumentalization" of the Declaration on Austria and of the Declaration of Independence,[45] for neither of these documents evinced such a political relativization of victimhood. In fact, these discussions made visible the continuity of antisemitic attitudes both on the government level and among the general population since the belonging of Jews to the "Austrian" collective of victims addressed in the Declaration of Independence was implicitly challenged.

Aside from the relativization of the persecution of the Jews, victimization was ultimately a short-lived phenomenon of postwar politics with a low societal impact, as Bertrand Perz also noted.[46] Initially, the attempt to document the scale of resistance was complemented by an emphasis on the sacrifices made by resistance fighters, as evinced by the temporary anti-fascist exhibition "*Niemals vergessen!*" ("Never Forget!") and by the first *Opferfürsorgegesetz* (Victim Welfare Act), which exclusively benefited resistance fighters. Not until 1949 were victims of racist persecution integrated and then only on a subordinate level.[47] However, the various portrayals of resistance soon led to conflicts between the SPÖ and ÖVP when it came to dealing with the Austrian dictatorship between 1933 and 1938. Another line of conflict was the anti-communism being enforced in the context of the Cold War, which divided the SPÖ from the Communist Party of Austria (KPÖ). An analysis of the first wave of anti-fascist memorials in Vienna reveals that anti-fascist and/or anti-Nazi commemorations of sacrifice did not achieve a national, patriotic dimension but rather remained stuck in reconstructed partisan identities.[48] In addition, there is absolutely no empirical knowledge concerning the dissemination and influence of the *Rot-Weiss-Rot-Buch* among the Austrian population.[49] Its function as a "manifesto"[50] of the victim myth is thus far from self-evident.

At the same time, the victim myth offered no suitable resources to integrate on a national level the 1.3 million Austrian veterans of the *Wehrmacht*. The first edition of the veteran newspaper *Der Kamerad* announced programmatically on the front page in April 1950 that the political establishment had to date failed to show the frontline soldiers the "illustrious gratitude of the fatherland."[51] In 1951, the ÖKB, an umbrella organization for *Wehrmacht* veterans founded with the help of the ÖVP, demanded a positive recognition of the fulfillment of duty performed in the *Wehrmacht* and the *Waffen-SS*. The dominant position evinced by former *Wehrmacht* soldiers was identification with the *Wehrmacht* and its supreme commandment of fulfillment of duty.[52] An important development was the welfare provided to some 505,000 disabled veterans and the next of kin of fallen soldiers by the *Kriegsopferversorgungsgesetz* (Law Concerning Welfare for the Victims of War) of 1949. However, the soldiers were here by no means generally transformed into victims.[53] The attribution of victimhood related only to specific injuries that diminished the veterans' capacity to work. Of all the parties, the SPÖ clung to a soldierly victim myth the longest. The Socialists thereby built on their post-1918 victim narrative,[54] cultivating an image of soldiers that conformed to the binary model of oppression postulated by Marxist theories of Fascism. A radio speech held by the SPÖ deputy and former resistance fighter, Rosa Jochmann, in March 1949, which has frequently been cited as evidence for the successful assertion of the victim myth, also needs to be placed in this Socialist—not national—context. Her mantra that "we were all victims of fascism" was intended to include *Wehrmacht* soldiers, the civilian population, those driven into exile, concentration camp inmates, and Jews.[55] However, she did point explicitly to the uniqueness and ruthlessness of the antisemitic persecution—a fact that is often omitted when it comes to supporting the hypothesis of the victim myth.[56] Her intention was, in fact, to justify to the general population the inclusion at long last of Jews in the victim welfare system. Nevertheless, Jochmann elevated the anti-fascist martyrs above all other victim groups. This Socialist hierarchy of martyrdom over victimization was dismantled by the ÖVP in the 1950s. Following the removal of SPÖ-friendly Leopold Figl in 1953, the ÖVP pursued a different path in their struggle with the *Verband der Unabhängigen* (Federation of Independents, VdU, the predecessor party of the FPÖ)[57] for hegemony in the right-wing political camp and in preparation for the establishment of a federal army. As in the 1930s, the conservatives thus moved away from the victimization of the military toward a sacrificial portrayal of wartime service. This paradigm shift was expressed pointedly in a speech by future Federal Chancellor Alfons Gorbach of the ÖVP, a former concentration camp inmate, held before parliament in December 1954. In an argument concerning the question over "who was in fact a hero and who was a traitor: the Austrian resistance fighters or such Austrians who were loyal to their oaths and fulfilled their bitter duty up until the final hour in the German *Wehrmacht*,"[58] Gorbach defended the fulfillment of duty as a meaningful patriotic and anti-Bolshevist service, praised the loyalty shown to the oaths that had been made, and advocated the necessity of unconditional obedience. Gorbach thereby transferred the sacrificial memory cultivated by the ÖKB in the civil society sphere to the representative sphere of the state. His position was consolidated on an official state level in November 1955 by Ferdinand Graf of the ÖVP, a former inmate of the Dachau Concentration Camp and the state secretary responsible for the Austrian Armed Forces, during the first official military memorial service at the Austrian Heroes' Memorial on the Heldenplatz in Vienna since 1945. The Heroes' Memorial had been created in 1934 by the Austrofascist regime to honor the fallen soldiers of World War I, a function it continued to serve under the Nazi regime, which until March 1945 used the site for the commemoration of fallen *Wehrmacht* soldiers as well. Now, after the end of the Allied occupation, Graf demanded that the site become a "national memorial" dedicated to Austrian soldiers of both World Wars. In front of veterans of World War II and the first troops of the Austrian Armed Forces under the command of Erwin Fussenegger—a former *Wehrmacht* colonel, bearer of the Knight's Cross, and member of the Nazi *Soldatenring* organization—Graf declared that it was necessary "in the now free and sovereign Austria to give a new voice to the commemoration of heroism."[59] Under the political partnership emerging between the ÖKB, the Ministry of Defense, and the armed forces, a new mythology was cultivated around fallen *Wehrmacht* soldiers as martyrs in the struggle for Austria's freedom.

This constituted a parallel development on the state level in Austria of what Norbert Frei called the "secondary affirmation" of the Nazi *Volksgemeinschaft* with regard to the rehabilitation of the *Wehrmacht* on the societal level in West Germany in the 1950s.[60] However, while the West German state then also began a new judicial reckoning with the crimes committed in the context of the war, the Austrian state more or less terminated postwar prosecutions in 1957. If we cease adopting the "victim myth" as an a priori paradigm for our analyses of the politics of history in postwar Austria, the concept of a "secondary affirmation" also becomes evident in the "denazification" process. As Siegfried Göllner has demonstrated, the amnesty granted to former Nazis from 1948 onwards was shot through with positive evaluations of their "idealism"—in other words, a recognition of their subjective sacrifices for the idea of National Socialism.[61] Ina Markova demonstrated recently that the images of soldiers returning home conveyed not just wartime suffering but also heroic endurance, anti-communist self-justifications, and admonitions against the Soviet internment of POWs. They moreover served a reconstruction of masculinity that ran contrary to the assumption of a powerless victim role in the war.[62]

The Sacrificial Memory Regime

The politics of history spearheaded by the ÖVP promoted a new hierarchy of sacrifices over victims, which, in turn, intensified the conflicts between the veterans' associations and the associations of resistance fighters. The violent riots that erupted during the so-called Borodajkewicz affair in 1965 marked the nadir of a deep polarization after Austria obtained full sovereignty. During this first grand memorial year of the Second Republic—marking twenty years since the foundation of the state and ten years since the State Treaty—the governing coalition of ÖVP and SPÖ was faced with the central challenge of overcoming the memory conflict over the question of who had made the true sacrifice. On April 27, 1965, the federal government extended the Austrian Heroes' Memorial with a memorial room for the "*Opfer im Kampf für Österreichs Freiheit*" in order to honor the sacrifices made by the resistance fighters alongside the sacrifices made by the *Wehrmacht* soldiers. A few months later, the parliament established October 26, the anniversary of the implementation of the Declaration of Neutrality in 1955, as Austria's national holiday. The Austrian Heroes' Memorial was chosen as the site for the state ritual to be enacted on this new national holiday. Although the ÖVP and SPÖ had agreed during the two previous years to settle their differences concerning the politics of the past, this day became the locus of renewed conflicts regarding the evaluation of the behavior of Austrian citizens during the era of Nazi rule. The coalition was only able to agree on laying a wreath in the memorial room for the resistance at the first state ritual but not on a ceremony to take place in the crypt dedicated to the *Wehrmacht* soldiers.[63] A coequal commemoration of freedom fighters and *Wehrmacht* soldiers evidently did not meet with the approval of the SPÖ ministers. Yet the ÖVP continued to emphatically demand a commemoration on equal terms of sacrifices made. Alfred Maleta of the ÖVP, the president of the National Council, used his ceremonial address in the parliament to rally for a general recognition of *all* the sacrifices made and called for everything that divided the nation to be forgotten in the interests of national formation. He regarded the context of sacrifice as offering a "common understanding"—"if we do not understand and affirm Austria as a mere community of material benefit, but as an *Opfergemeinschaft*."[64] With this term, Maleta was precisely not speaking of a community of *victims* but a community of people who had made various *sacrifices*. These included, he continued, the "*Opfergang* [in the sense of martyrdom] of the patriots" in the concentration camps on the basis of which "the idea of Austria" had been reborn, before adding the "courage to make sacrifices to the point of self-renunciation" in the period of Allied occupation, and finally integrating the former *Wehrmacht* soldiers and Nazis into his summation: "we do not aim to limit the sacrifices made by Austrians to the patriots, but rather to also integrate those sacrifices into our state consciousness that Austrians made during World War II, whether from force or from inner conviction, in the service of an idea they thought to be right." Distinctions between different forms of sacrifice and questions regarding their meaning he dismissed as "sophistry." The assertion of the sacrificial community in the state ritual at the Heroes' Memorial was finally enabled by the end of the Grand Coalition in April 1966 when the ÖVP for the first time achieved an absolute majority in the general election. From then on, the heads of state laid wreaths in both the memorial room for the resistance and the crypt for the *Wehrmacht* soldiers.[65] The ÖVP's majority government under Federal Chancellor Josef Klaus thus institutionalized Austria's "sacrifices" as a new "imaginative horizon" in the memory of National Socialism and of World War II.[66] On a theoretical level, the government's policy can be understood as "a hegemonic process whereby the official narrative promoted by state agencies operates so as to 'frame' war memories articulated from below, in forms which serve the interest of that nation-state."[67] The subsequent majority government led by Bruno Kreisky of the SPÖ maintained this principle. One characteristic of the sacrificial memory regime was the authoritarian circumscription and appeasement of the various contradictory forms of recognition of sacrifices to the state that existed among *Wehrmacht* veterans and resistance associations. In return for recognition, all mutual contestation was to cease. Only then did an authoritarian element of "identity consolidation 'from above'" become effective, which it can hardly be said to have done previously through assertion of the victim hypothesis.[68]

In contrast to the victim myth, the myth of sacrifice had the potential to connect to the social memory of a "dominant milieu" (Anton Pelinka) of which the mindset was characterized not by demarcation from but, rather, continuity with National Socialism. The tactical function of the victim myth (namely, dissociation from Germany) was the sign under which the sacrificial memory regime, including the recognition of supportive and conformist behavior under National Socialism, could be established. It externalized guilt to Germany, as Rainer Lepsius argued, while simultaneously also creating the conditions for what could, in reference to a contemporary finding of Theodor W. Adorno, be termed the afterlife of National Socialism in Austrian democracy.[69] The flipside of the authoritarian pacification of memory conflicts was the continued marginalization of those victims who had been "harmful to the community," who had been not "Germanizable," meaning Jews, Sinti and Roma, *Wehrmacht* deserters, so-called "asocials," homosexuals, and Carinthian Slovenes. Their marginalization was less an expression of a repression of guilt as of manifest continuities of social rejection and state discrimination. They could only be recognized as "true" victims once the sacrificial memory regime had eroded, and the struggles for recognition of the social movements in the 1970s and 1980s had extended discussions of their legal discrimination and social denigration into the politics of history too.

Endnotes

1 See Anton Pelinka: "…so leben wir mit zwei Geschichtsbildern," *ORF Nachlese Extra*, 1985, 15–17 (here 17); Heidemarie Uhl, *Zwischen Versöhnung und Verstörung: Eine Kontroverse um Österreichs historische Identität fünfzig Jahre nach dem "Anschluss,"* (Vienna: Böhlau, 1992), 15–16; Oliver Rathkolb, *Fiktion "Opfer": Österreich und die langen Schatten des Nationalsozialismus und der Dollfuß–Diktatur* (Innsbruck: Studien Verlag, 2017) 11; Günter Bischof, "'Opfer' Österreich? Zur moralischen Ökonomie des österreichischen historischen Gedächtnisses," in *Die politische Ökonomie des Holocaust: Zur wirtschaftlichen Logik von Verfolgung und "Wiedergutmachung,"* ed. Dieter Stiefel (Munich: Oldenbourg, 2001), 305–335 (here 307); Robert Knight, "Besiegt oder Befreit?" in *Die bevormundete Nation: Österreich und die Alliierten 1945–1949*, ed. Günter Bischof, Josef Leidenfrost (Innsbruck: Haymon, 1988), 75–92 (here 77). There is a vast literature on the "victim myth." Due to lack of space, I can only refer to some of the key literature here. I wish to thank Tim Corbett for the translation of this article and his critical comments.

2 See e.g. Brigitte Bailer, "Alle waren Opfer: Der selektive Umgang mit den Folgen des Nationalsozialismus," in *Inventur 45/55: Österreich im ersten Jahrzehnt der Zweiten Republik*, ed. Wolfgang Kos (Vienna: Sonderzahl, 1996), 181–200 (here: 185).

3 Bischof, "'Opfer' Österreich," 319; Heidemarie Uhl, "Of Heroes and Victims: World War II in Austrian Memory," *Austrian History Yearbook* 42 (2011): 185–200 (here 185).

4 Gerhard Botz, "Geschichte und kollektives Gedächtnis in der Zweiten Republik: 'Opferthese,' 'Lebenslüge' und 'Geschichtstabu' in der Zeitgeschichtsschreibung," in *Inventur 45/55: Österreich im ersten Jahrzehnt der Zweiten Republik* (Vienna: Sonderzahl, 1996), 51–86.

5 Walter Manoschek, Thomas Geldmacher, "Vergangenheitspolitik," in *Politik in Österreich: Das Handbuch*, ed. Herbert Dachs et al. (Vienna: Manz, 2006) 448–464 (here 453); Helga Embacher and Maria Ecker, "A Nation of Victims: How Austria Dealt With the Victims of Authoritarian Ständestaat and National Socialism," in *The Politics of War Trauma: The Aftermath of World War II in Eleven European Countries*, ed. Nannet Mooij, and Jolande Withuis (Amsterdam: aksant, 2010) 15–47 (here 15); Barbara Serloth, *Von Opfern, Tätern und jenen dazwischen: Wie Antisemitismus die Zweite Republik mitbegründete* (Vienna: Mandelbaum, 2016), 128–129; Ernst Hanisch, *Männlichkeiten: Eine andere Geschichte des 20. Jahrhunderts*, (Vienna: Böhlau, 2005), 316; Evan Burr Bukey, *Hitler's Austria: Popular Sentiment in the Nazi Era, 1938–1945* (Chapel Hill and London: The University of North Carolina Press, 2000), 228–230. I do not exclude myself from this critique: Peter Pirker, *Subversion deutscher Herrschaft: Der britische Kriegsgeheimdienst SOE und Österreich*, (Göttingen: Vienna University Press, 2012), 219–220.

6 See Aleida Assmann, *Der lange Schatten der Vergangenheit: Erinnerungskultur und Geschichtspolitik* (Munich: Beck, 2006), 73, 76; Cathleen M. Guistino, "Behind the Opfermythos: Fascism, Agency, and Accountability in Twentieth–Century Austria," in *Austrian Environmental History*, ed. Marc Landry, Patrick Kupper, and Verena Winiwarter (New Orleans: UNO Press, 2018), 293–297 (here 294–295).

7 See e.g. Uhl, "Of Heroes and Victims," 185–186; Cornelius Lehnguth, *Waldheim und die Folgen: Der parteipolitische Umgang mit dem Nationalsozialismus in Österreich* (Frankfurt/Main: Campus, 2013), 64–*68*; Kathrin Hammerstein, *Gemeinsame Vergangenheit – getrennte Erinnerung? Der Nationalsozialismus in Gedächtnisdiskursen und Identitätskonstruktionen von Bundesrepublik Deutschland, DDR und Österreich* (Göttingen: Wallstein, 2017), 60–62; Siegfried Göllner, *Die politischen Diskurse zu "Entnazifizierung," "Causa Waldheim" und "EU–Sanktionen": Opfernarrative und Geschichtsbilder in Nationalratsdebatten* (Hamburg: Kovač, 2009).

8 Svenja Goltermann, *Opfer: Die Wahrnehmung von Krieg und Gewalt in der Moderne* (Frankfurt/Main: S. Fischer, 2017), 182.

9 Goltermann, *Opfer*, 177.

10 See John Bunzl, and Bernd Marin, *Antisemitismus in Österreich: Sozialhistorische und soziologische Studien* (Innsbruck: Inn–Verlag, 1983), 206–208.

11 Karin Stögner, *Antisemitismus und Sexismus: Historisch–gesellschaftliche Konstellationen* (Baden–Baden: Nomos, 2014), 50.

12 Ernest Renan, *Was ist eine Nation?* (Vienna: Folio, 1995), 57.

13 Benedict Anderson, *Imagined Communities: Reflections of the Origin and Spread of Nationalism* (London: Verso, 2006), 7.

14 Goltermann, *Opfer*, 192.

15 Annet Mooij, and Jolande Withuis, "Conclusion," in *The Politics of War Trauma: The Aftermath of World War II in Eleven European Countries*, ed. Annet Mooij and Jolande Withuis (Amsterdam: aksant, 2010), 323–332 (here 325).

16 See e.g. Frank Bösch, *Zeitenwende 1979: Als die Welt von heute begann* (Munich: C.H. Beck, 2019), 363–395.

17 Jolande Withuis, "Introduction: The Politics of War Trauma," in *The Politics of War Trauma: The Aftermath of World War II in Eleven European Countries*, ed. Annet Mooij and Jolande Withuis (Amsterdam: aksant, 2010), 1–11, 2.

18 See Robert Knight, *"Ich bin dafür, die Sache in die Länge zu ziehen": Die Wortprotokolle der österreichischen Bundesregierung von 1945 bis 1952 über die Entschädigung der Juden,* 2nd ed. (Vienna: Böhlau, 2000); *Das große Tabu: Österreichs Umgang mit seiner Vergangenheit*, ed. Anton Pelinka, and Erika Weinzierl (Vienna: Böhlau, 1987); *Die bevormundete Nation: Österreich und die Alliierten 1945–1949*, ed. Günter Bischof, and Josef Leidenfrost (Innsbruck: Haymon, 1988); *Kontroversen um Österreichs Zeitgeschichte: Verdrängte Vergangenheit, Österreich–Identität, Waldheim und die Historiker*, ed. Gerhard Botz and Gerald Sprengnagel (Frankfurt/Main: Campus 1994).

19 Ingrid Böhler, "'Wenn die Juden ein Volk sind, so ist es ein mieses Volk': Die Kreisky–Peter–Wiesenthal–Affäre 1975," in *Politische Affären und Skandale in Österreich: Von Mayerling bis Waldheim* ed. Michael Gehler, and Hubert Sickinger (Thaur: Kulturverlag, 1995), 502–531 (here 519).

20 Austrian Press Agency, 11 February, 1985.

21 *Waldheims Walzer: Ein Film von Ruth Beckermann* (Vienna: edition Filmladen, 2018).

22 Robert Knight, "Der Waldheim–Kontext," in *Kontroversen um Österreichs Zeitgeschichte: Verdrängte Vergangenheit, Österreich–Identität, Waldheim und die Historiker*, ed. Gerhard Botz, and Gerald Sprengnagel (Frankfurt/Main: Campus 1994), 78–88 (here 81).

23 Gerhard Botz, "Die 'Waldheim-Affäre' als Widerstreit kollektiver Erinnerungen, in *1986: Das Jahr, das Österreich veränderte*, ed. Barbara Toth and Hubertus Czernin (Vienna: Czernin, 2006), 74–95 (here 86); Uhl, "Of Heroes," 186.

24 See Nicole–Melanie Goll, "'Terror Pilots' and 'Bombing Holocaust': Discourses on Victimization and Remembrance in Austria in the Context of the Allied Aerial Bombing," in *Austrian Environmental History*, ed. Marc Landry, Patrick Kupper, and Verena Winiwarter (New Orleans: UNO Press, 2018), 277–292, 286.

25 Kurt Waldheim, "Fernsehansprache anlässlich der 50. Wiederkehr der Besetzung Österreichs, 10.3.1988," in *Jahrbuch der österreichischen Außenpolitik* (Vienna: Bundesministerium für Auswärtige Angelegenheiten, 1988), 459–462.

26 "Vortrag von Außenminister Peter Jankowitsch am 11. November 1986 zum Thema 'Von der Unentrinnbarkeit der Außenpolitik: Österreich in der Welt von heute,'" in *Österreichisches Jahrbuch für Internationale Politik* (Vienna: Böhlau, 1986), 343–353 (here 352).

27 "Frischenschlager-Besuch in Großbritannien verschoben," APA, March 15, 1985.

28 "Grußadressen der Außenminister der vier Signatarstaaten bei den Feierlichkeiten zum 30. Jahrestag der Unterzeichnung des österreichischen Staatsvertrages am 15. Mai 1985 im Wiener Belvedere," in *Österreichisches Jahrbuch für Internationale Politik* (Vienna: Böhlau, 1985), 293–296.

29 Katharina Wegan, *Monument – Macht – Mythos: Frankreich und Österreich im Vergleich nach 1945* (Innsbruck: Studien Verlag, 2005), 324–325.

30 See also Thomas U. Berger, *War, Guilt, and World Politics after World War II* (Cambridge: Cambridge University Press, 2012), 101–107.

31 Michael Gehler, *Österreichs Außenpolitik der Zweiten Republik: Von der alliierten Besatzung bis zum Europa des 21. Jahrhunderts* (Innsbruck: Studien Verlag, 2005), 539.

32 Christian Gerbel et al., "Einleitung: Transformationen gesellschaftlicher Erinnerung. Zur 'Gedächtnisgeschichte' der Zweiten Republik," in *Transformationen gesellschaftlicher Erinnerung: Studien zur 'Gedächtnisgeschichte' der Zweiten Republik*, ed. Christian Gerbel et al. (Vienna: Turia + Kant, 2005), 7–20 (here 11).

33 Robert Keyserlingk, *Austria in World War II: An Anglo–American Dilemma* (Quebec: McGill-Queen's University Press, 1988).

34 See e.g. Günter Bischof, "Die Instrumentalisierung der Moskauer Erklärung nach dem 2. Weltkrieg," in *Zeitgeschichte* 20 (1993): 345–366; Thomas Albrich, "'Es gibt keine jüdische Frage': Zur Aufrechterhaltung des österreichischen Opfermythos," in *Der Umgang mit dem Holocaust. Europa – USA – Israel*, ed. Rolf Steininger (Vienna: Böhlau, 1994), 147–166; Heidemarie Uhl, "Das 'erste' Opfer: Der österreichische Opfermythos und seine Transformationen in der Zweiten Republik," in *Österreichische Zeitschrift für Politikwissenschaft* 30, no. 1 (2001): 19–34, 21; Barbara Serloth, *Von Opfern, Tätern und jenen dazwischen: Wie Antisemitismus die Zweite Republik mitbegründete* (Vienna: Mandelbaum), 81; Bukey, *Hitler's Austria*, 207; Peter Utgaard, *Remembering and Forgetting Nazism. Education, National Identity, and the Victim Myth in Postwar Austria* (New York: Berghahn, 2003), 123–124. For a critique, see Stourzh, *Um Einheit und Freiheit*, 25-28; Richard Mitten, "Jews and other Victims: The 'Jewish Question' and Discourses of Victimhood in Postwar Austria," in *Austria in the European Union*, ed. Günter Bischof, Anton Pelinka, and Michael Gehler (New Brunswick: Transaction Publ., 2001), 223–270 (here 230); Peter Pirker, "British Subversive Politics towards Austria and Partisan Resistance in the Austrian–Slovene Borderland, 1938–1945," in *Journal of Contemporary History* 52, no. 2 (2017): 319–351.

35 Robert H. Keyserlingk, "1. November 1943: Die Moskauer Deklaration – Die Alliierten, Österreich und der Zweite Weltkrieg," in *Österreich im 20. Jahrhundert: Vom Zweiten Weltkrieg bis zur Gegenwart, vol. 2*, ed. Rolf Steininger and Michael Gehler (Vienna: Böhlau, 1997), 9–38.

36 Rathkolb, "Fiktion Opfer," 48–49.

37 *Rot-Weiss-Rot-Buch: Darstellungen, Dokumente und Nachweise zur Vorgeschichte und Geschichte der Okkupation Österreichs nach amtlichen Quellen* (Vienna: Österr. Staatsdruckerei, 1946), 3.

38 Stourzh, *Um Einheit*, 73–74.

39 Ulrich Nachbaur, *Österreich als Opfer Hitlerdeutschlands: Das Rot–Weiß–Rot–Buch 1946 und die unveröffentlichten Vorarlberger Beiträge* (Regensburg: Roderer 2009), 70.

40 Ian Kershaw, *Roller-Coaster: Europe, 1950–2017* (London: Penguin, 2019), 9–10.

41 Knight, "Besiegt oder Befreit?," 77.

42 Knight, "Der Waldheim-Kontext," 81.

43 Rathkolb, *Fiktion "Opfer,"* 31.

44 Knight, *Ich bin dafür*, 46.

45 See Albrich, "Es gibt keine jüdische Frage," 160.

46 Bertrand Perz, "Österreich," in *Verbrechen erinnern: Die Auseinandersetzung mit Holocaust und Völkermord*, ed. Volkhard Knigge and Norbert Frei (Bonn: Bundeszentrale für politische Bildung, 2005) 170–182 (here 177).

47 Brigitte Bailer, *Wiedergutmachung kein Thema: Österreich und die Opfer des Nationalsozialismus* (Vienna: Löcker, 1993), 26–27.

48 See Peter Pirker, Philipp Rode, and Mathias Lichtenwagner, "From Palimpsest to Memoiré: Exploring Urban Memorial Landscapes of Political Violence," in *Political Geography* 74 (2019), https://doi.org/10.1016/j.polgeo.2019.102057; and the digital map www.porem.wien.

49 Nachbaur, *Österreich als Opfer*, 108.

50 Hammerstein, *Gemeinsame Vergangenheit*, 59.

51 "Was will 'Der Kamerad,'" in *Der Kamerad* 1 (1950): 1.

52 Felix Römer, *Kameraden: Die Wehrmacht von innen* (Munich: Piper, 2014), 117, 136; Richard Germann, "'Österreichische' Soldaten im deutschen Gleichschritt?," in *"Der Führer war wieder viel zu human, viel zu gefühlvoll": Der Zweite Weltkrieg aus der Sicht deutscher und italienischer Soldaten*, ed. Harald Welzer and Sönke Neitzel (Frankfurt/Main: Fischer, 2011), 217–233 (here 218).

53 Walter Manoschek and Günther Sandner, "Die Krieger als Opfer: Das Kriegsopferversorgungsgesetz (KOVG) in den Debatten des österreichischen Minister- und Nationalrats und in österreichischen Printmedien," in *Wie Geschichte gemacht wird: Zur Konstruktion von Erinnerungen an Wehrmacht und Zweiten Weltkrieg*, ed. Hannes Heer et al. (Vienna: Czernin, 2003), 109–144 (here 115).

54 See Ke–chin Hsia, "'War Victims': Concepts of Victimhood and the Austrian Identity after the Habsburgs," in *Austrian Environmental History*, ed. Marc Landry, Patrick Kupper and Verena Winiwarter (New Orleans: UNO Press, 2018), 245–252 (here 249).

55 Rosa Jochmann, "Für die Opfer des Faschismus," *Arbeiter–Zeitung*, March 1, 1949, 1–2.

56 See Serloth, *Von Opfern*, 129–130; Bailer, "Alle waren Opfer," 185; Sandner and Manoschek, "Krieger," 131–132; Hammerstein, *Gemeinsame Vergangenheit*, 62.

57 The VdU was founded in 1949 and consisted largely of 'former' National Socialists, see Margit Reiter, *Die Ehemaligen: Der Nationalsozialismus und die FPÖ* (Göttingen: Wallstein, 2019), 96–101.

58 "Rede des Abg. Gorbach, 54. Sitzung des Nationalrates, VII. GP.," Dec. 3, 1954, www.parlament.gv.at. For the provinces, see Heidemarie Uhl, "Erinnerung als Versöhnung: Zur Geschichtspolitik der Zweiten Republik," in *Zeitgeschichte* 23, no. 5/6 (1996): 146–160.

59 Austrian Press Agency, Nov. 6, 1955.

60 Norbert Frei, *Vergangenheitspolitik: Die Anfänge der Bundesrepublik und die NS-Vergangenheit* (Munich: Beck, 2012), 304.

61 Göllner, *Die politischen Diskurse*, 212.

62 Ina Markova, *Die NS-Zeit im Bildgedächtnis der Zweiten Republik* (Innsbruck: Studien Verlag, 2018) 46–47.

63 Amtsvermerk, Schmückung des Weiheraumes, Zl. 2279/65, Burghauptmannschaft Österreich (BHÖ).

64 Festsitzung am 26. Oktober 1965, www.parlament.gv.at.

65 Militärkommando Wien, Oct. 20, 1966, Zl. 2265/66, BHÖ.

66 Oliver Marchart, "Das historisch-politische Gedächtnis: Für eine politische Theorie kollektiver Erinnerung," in *Transformationen gesellschaftlicher Erinnerung: Studien zur 'Gedächtnisgeschichte' der Zweiten Republik*, ed. Christian Gerbel et al. (Vienna: Turia + Kant, 2005), 21–49 (here 40).

67 T. G. Ashplant, Graham Dawson, and Michael Roper, "The Politics of War Memory and Commemoration: Contexts, Structures and Dynamics," in *The Politics of War Memory and Commemoration*, ed. idem (London: Routledge, 2000), 3–85 (here 53).

68 Hammerschmitt, "Gemeinsame Vergangenheit," 65.

69 Theodor W. Adorno, "Was bedeutet: Aufarbeitung der Vergangenheit," in *Eingriffe: Neun kritische Modelle* (Frankfurt/Main: Suhrkamp, 1963), 125–146 (here 126).

Victimization and Gender: The Myth of the *Trümmerfrauen* and Its Present Use(fulness)

Maria Pohn-Lauggas

1. Introduction

It is an iconic image that has a firm place in Austrian (visual) memories: groups of women clearing away debris in the cities with their own hands after World War II and manifestly beginning the work of reconstruction. They have been remembered as *Trümmerfrauen*[1] ever since the postwar period, and in public discourses, they are referred to as victims of the war. There is something heroic in this image of victimhood that, however, cannot be concretized any more than the homogenizing construction of the *Trümmerfrauen* in the collective memory, which disregards the fact that women had multiple options to act in the Nazi period.

Two recent events show that, after so many years, social reality in Austria is still influenced by the myth of the *Trümmerfrauen*.

In 2019, the first *Stolperstein* (a commemorative brass plaque set in the pavement) in Tyrol was to be laid in the Ziller Valley in memory of Hans Vogl, a resistance fighter who was executed by the Nazis. Originally, the initiators had also wanted to lay a *Stolperstein* for Hilde, his widow, but this idea was blocked in the local council by the Austrian People's Party (*Österreichische Volkspartei*, ÖVP) and the Austrian Freedom Party (*Freiheitliche Partei Österreichs*, FPÖ). These two parties argued that they would give their approval only if a *Stolperstein* could be laid for all war widows in the village.[2]

One year previously, in October 2018, the FPÖ, under the leadership of the then Vice-Chancellor Heinz-Christian Strache, unveiled a memorial for the *Trümmerfrauen* in Vienna. It consists of the bronze figure of a naked woman sitting on a heap of rubble with the inscription "Austria's *Trümmerfrauen* 1943–1953." The years stand for the beginning of bombings in Austria and the approaching end of foreign occupation and the great hardships of the postwar period. According to Strache, the FPÖ had made a proposal for the erection of such a memorial in the Vienna City Council as long ago as 1986.[3] That was the year in which the controversy over Kurt Waldheim, an Austrian presidential candidate who was suspected of having been involved in Nazi war crimes, served to problematize the established praxis of trivializing and denying Austria's National Socialist past.

Thus, from the 1980s onward, the national myth of victimization (*Opfermythos*) was shaken to its foundations, yet these examples show a continuity, unbroken since 1945, in the construction of women as victims of the war and its effects, a construction which completely disregards the country's National Socialist past. In 2005, a federal law was passed that reinforced and legitimized this idea by providing for "a one-off compensation payment for women in recognition of their special contribution to the reconstruction of the Republic of Austria"[4] (BGBl I 2005/89). The year 2005 was Austria's "Commemorative Year," so passing the law at this time was not a coincidence but suggests that it had a particular social function in connection with the way Austria treats its Nazi past. In this paper,[5] I will discuss the parliamentary debate on this federal law to show the arguments used to legitimate it, and I will formulate these in respect of its function in Austrian memory culture. But before this, it is necessary to place the *Trümmerfrauen* myth in the overall context of Austrian memory culture after 1945.

2. On "Unpolitical" Women and the Invisibility of Women's Freedom to Act

The separation of National Socialism and World War II, which is constitutive of the hegemonic Austrian memory culture in which the war is not seen as a consequence of National Socialism, makes it possible to construct non-persecuted women exclusively as "victims of the war" and to glorify their contribution to reconstruction. The separation of war and National Socialism is also at the basis of the national *Opfermythos*, which has been problematized since the 1980s by critical scholars, Nazi survivors, and journalists.[6] The term *Opfermythos* has been used by historians and political scientists to describe the national construction of victimhood, which influences the way the majority of Austrians regard the Nazi past. Reversing perpetrator and victim[7] and externalizing crimes served here as strategies to evade responsibility. Austria saw itself as the first victim of Hitler's Germany, a political and social doctrine that survived into the 1990s and was only transformed in the course of the Waldheim affair.[8] This was followed in 1991 by a declaration from Franz Vranitzky, the Austrian chancellor, admitting Austria's complicity in Nazi crimes. This ended the taboo on speaking of "Austria as a perpetrator country" and led to broad public discussion of the issue. Today there is consensus that the theory of national victimization has been transformed into a thesis of co-responsibility[9] so that insisting on the former is no longer a simple matter.

The role of women, however, has largely been ignored, both in critiques of the *Opfermythos* and in public debates.[10] This omission of women from discussion of Nazi crimes, together with the establishment of the national theory of victimization, has been described by historians Irene Bandhauer-Schöffmann and Ela Hornung as a double myth of victimization (*doppelter Opfermythos*).[11] Women's self-descriptions are also characterized by attempts to construct themselves as "non-political" and not responsible because they were not part of Nazi military structures.[12] Thus, Bandhauer-Schöffmann and Hornung observe that "most women did not develop any awareness of the way domestic work was militarized and functionalized by National Socialist organizations for women and girls (BDM, NSF, DFW and NSV)."[13] In her biographical study of the Hitler Youth organization in Germany, Gabriele Rosenthal found that joining the *Wehrmacht* (the German Army) or being discharged from it, or periods spent as a prisoner of war, were experiences shared by all men, which could be interpreted in collective terms as a phase "that belongs to the life of a man."[14] In Austria, in addition to this, the national theory of victimization provided a pattern of interpretation in which responsibility for Nazi crimes could be evaded. But unlike men, women did not have any collective pattern of this kind.

The positioning of non-persecuted women as being uninvolved, non-political, and thus not responsible for the establishment and maintenance of Nazi society, was reinforced by the fact that those women who faced criminal charges because they had worked as guards in concentration camps, for instance, were described as "beasts,"[15] which is just another construction of the non-political woman, or in this case "bad" woman. But above all, it is also a construction that denies female perpetrators[16] their womanliness—here, in the sense of being unaggressive and caring—and separates them from the mass of women who, because of their gender, cannot be held responsible for atrocities.

Thus, with respect to the role of women in National Socialism, constructions of victimhood that correlate with the image of *Trümmerfrauen* dominate to this day and have become inscribed in the collective memory: women handing bricks to each other, bending down in the rubble with a shovel, tugging a cart along together, smiling at the camera. The collective female effort of clearing and reconstructing is present in every picture. The important thing about this image is that those events that could tell another story of women in National Socialism remain hidden. We do not see, for instance, that some of the women in the photographs had been active supporters of National Socialism and for this reason were forced by the Allies to help with the work of clearing the rubble.[17] No one ever mentions the presence of these women in the pictures.[18] The iconic photographs of *Trümmerfrauen* in the cities suggest instead that their tireless devotion to this work is certain knowledge. But there are things that are not seen—for instance, in reality, the main burden of removing the rubble was not borne by these women. In her comprehensive study of the "myth of the *Trümmerfrauen*" in Germany—with results that can also be applied to Austria—Leonie Treber (2014) shows that the "knowledge" transported by these photographs (i.e., that the main burden of clearing away the rubble was borne by women) can be refuted by other photographic material. For there are photographs in the archives that show that this work did not start in 1945 but that it was continually performed during the war by various actors.[19] Before 1945, debris was cleared by laborers from the Reich Labour Service (*Reichsarbeitsdienst*, RAD) and military commandos, for instance, as well as by prisoners from concentration camps. After the end of the war, the pictures show groups of men both with and without women. Many photographs also show the use of heavy machinery.[20] After 1945, this diversity did not become an integral part of the visual, written, and oral memory culture, either in Germany or in Austria.[21]

Thus, the question of who these women were and the question of their Nazi past are not concrete issues in the image of the *Trümmerfrauen* and its associated narrative any more than the reason why they helped with the work of reconstruction, which was simply that they had to work to survive. That they are exclusively women who were not persecuted is accepted as an intrinsic part of the concept of the *Trümmerfrauen*. This is part of the implicit stock of knowledge of Austrians.

3. The Commemorative Year 2005 and the "Discovery" of Women

In an interview with *The Jerusalem Post*, Wolfgang Schüssel (ÖVP), chancellor of the first ÖVP-FPÖ government in the Second Republic, made the following remark: "The Nazis took Austria by force. The Austrians were the first victims" (September 11, 2000). The fact that this statement was made by the highest-ranking conservative politician shows that although the national *Opfermythos* has been transformed into a thesis of co-responsibility, it can be revived at any time and will find acceptance in the middle of Austrian society. The renewal of the national theory of victimization reached its peak in the "Commemorative Year 2005." This was in memory of the signing of the State Treaty in 1955 and the end of the war in 1945. By contrast, there was no commemoration of the period of National Socialism so that the chief aim of the "Commemorative Year 2005" was clearly to rehabilitate the so-called reconstruction generation, a rehabilitation that could only be constructed by disregarding the victims of the Nazis. The effect was to reinforce the separation of National Socialism from World War II. The Nazi perpetrators in Austrian society were erased from the collective memory by suppressing their victims, "by overwriting their place with other narratives, namely the perpetrators' 'own' narratives of victimhood ('how we suffered'), so that in the end there were only victims left and no perpetrators at all."[22] Thus, the "Commemorative Year 2005" can be seen in the continuity of perpetrator reconciliation,[23] which began in 1945 with the establishment of the national theory of victimization and the marginalization of Nazi resistance. The essential point is that Austria was not celebrating the fact that it existed again after 1945 but that it had ceased to exist between 1938 and 1945, and for this reason it was itself a victim.

The rehabilitation of the so-called reconstruction generation can be read as a further essential aspect of the envisaged perpetrator reconciliation. In the book *Texts for the Jubilee Year* that was published at the beginning of 2005, we read:

> This extraordinary achievement deserves our gratitude and respect, respect for the suffering and hard work of those who did the work of reconstruction. Anyone who is earnestly grateful must accept responsibility: responsibility for a past which gives cause for pride and humility, but also for reflection—for instance on one's own share of blame for the horrors of the 20th century. The act of thanking is an encounter between the generations. It is not free of separation and grief: after fifty years we have to remember that many people who suffered during the war and helped to rebuild Austria have passed away.[24]

This formulation renders visible the coexistence of the theory of victimization and the theory of co-responsibility, as well as the fact that the theory of victimization will not be completely reactivated. In the light of events since Waldheim, it is no longer possible not to speak of "blame" in an official publication of the Austrian Republic in 2005, but it becomes shallow in the context of the "horrors of the 20th century." National Socialism as a concrete event disappears in the vague notion of the "past." Here, we find the same patterns of interpretation produced in the national discourse of victimization. They contain constructions of victimhood based on the perception of Austrians as victims of the war and of occupation by the Allies, especially the Red Army. This construction depends on the separation of National Socialism and the war, a separation that makes it possible to speak of suffering during the war while ignoring the fact that the war was a direct expression of National Socialist expansionist ambitions.

The federal law enacted in 2005 on the "provision of a one-off compensation payment for women in recognition of their special contribution to the reconstruction of the Republic of Austria" (BGBl. Nr. 89/2005) can be seen as one aspect of rehabilitation. This law was part of a "Nazi package," which also included a federal law on the recognition of services for the Austrian resistance movement and a federal law on the definitive elimination of National Socialist acts of injustice. For the first time, this law recognized people who had been categorized as "asocial" and who had been convicted as deserters by the Nazis as victims of the Nazi judicial system. In addition to this extended recognition and rehabilitation of murdered or surviving victims of Nazi crimes, and the above-mentioned "compensation payment" for women, changes were also made in the law on compensation for prisoners of war, the law on war victims, and the law on protection of the armed forces. If we consider that the federal law addresses women who were *not persecuted*, we can see that its enactment fits into the Austrian praxis that started in the 1940s. Restitution and compensation payments for Nazi victims were "tied to payments to other groups of people who had been affected in some way by war and the consequences of war in Austria since the 1940s," which amounts to a "compensation business that completely shuts out a perpetrator perspective."[25] The simultaneous enactment of these laws as part of a "Nazi package" is a further instance of the strategy of shutting out the perpetrators and their actions by deliberately blurring the boundaries between victims and perpetrators. But for the first time, non-persecuted women were now included as a separate group.

It is thus worth taking a closer look at the parliamentary debate that preceded the enactment of this law in order to reconstruct what function it fulfilled, how the discourse on the *Trümmerfrauen* was constituted, and what strategies were followed.[26]

4. The Gendered Discourse on Victimization: A New Positioning of the Theory of Victimization

The law on compensation payments for so-called *Trümmerfrauen* was discussed controversially in a public debate. One side spoke of very late recognition, while others argued that this law was a continuation of the national discourse of victimhood and complained that it was focused on only one gender.

4.1 On Continuity

The counter-discourse to the *Opfermythos* developed by critical scholars, journalists, and Nazi survivors has transformed Austrian policy with regard to commemorating historical events in such a way that it is now necessary to speak of "co-responsibility" in public contexts. This is still a contested sphere characterized by the discursive practice of shutting out the perpetrators, a practice that has been followed for decade. Thus, in connection with the enactment of the federal law in 2005, unclear and ambiguous expressions continued to be used (i.e., when people spoke of the "horrors of the 20th century" or of a "dark age,"[27] expressions that leave room for interpretations influenced by a desire for exoneration and exculpation).[28]

In the parliamentary debate, there was a suspicion in the air that was also mentioned by the opposition and in which played a role in the discussions—namely, that this federal law would represent a form of exculpation. It was important to remove this suspicion in order to legitimize enactment of the law.

With regard to arguments in favor of the payment of compensation to the *Trümmerfrauen*, a specific way of speaking about National Socialism reveals a basic strategy of the ÖVP and the FPÖ. Besides the use of formulations such as "terrible time" or "darkest chapter of our history," which are so fuzzy that they admit broad interpretation, speaking about National Socialism is always combined with speaking about the war or other historical events, such as the expulsion of Germans and Austrians from areas liberated by the Allies. Conversely, only the war alone is talked about without mentioning the racist and anti-Semitic expulsion, persecution, and murder of different groupings that took place under National Socialism. This is a long-established way of talking that lets the speaker relativize his or her Nazi activities and reproduces fragments of the national victimization discourse. As a demonstration of this kind of argument, we may quote Ursula Haubner (FPÖ), the then federal minister of social security, generations, and consumer protection, who said, with reference to the terror attack in London on July 7, 2005:

> Before I begin, let me express my personal sympathy with the victims of the cowardly terror attack in London. I think that this attack has shown once again how terrible the effects of violence against innocent people can be. Passing these laws today means taking seriously our responsibility for the victims of the darkest chapter of our history. These draft laws are a consequence of reappraising the dark side of our history and a sign of our deepest sympathy and respect for the victims of Nazi injustice and war.[29]

After this, Haubner mentions different groupings that were victimized by the Nazis, such as Jews or homosexuals, and finishes by arguing in favor of giving women a compensation payment since her own generation heard "contemporary accounts, first-hand accounts of the war," and so it is important "not to forget any group from that time when it comes to paying compensation, reevaluating the past, but especially showing admiration and respect."[30] This sequence of topics again results in ambiguities and blurred boundaries and a continuation of the national discourse of victimization, which lets those who were responsible for the suffering of others disappear behind expressions like "Nazi injustice and war" or "from that time."

4.2 A Broader Understanding of Victimhood

In the parliamentary debate, a specific element appears beside these continuities. While National Socialism is never referred to without simultaneously mentioning the war, the grouping of female resistance fighters is increasingly included in the debate (no other female Nazi victims are mentioned). Thus, for instance, Anna Franz from the ÖVP stresses how important it is to recognize "services for the Austrian resistance"[31] since "all victims deserve our respect and our sympathy."[32] Female Nazi victims are not mentioned in any other debate, not even in commemorative speeches, which refer to Nazi victims in general and where gender differentiation serves no function. Through the explicit placing of female resistance fighters, as persecuted women, beside women who were not persecuted and who played a role in Nazi society, the latter are inscribed in a victim collective. Recognizing their services for the Republic of Austria as being equivalent to those of female resistance fighters follows the familiar strategy of equating victims and perpetrators, which legitimizes the demand for payment to non-persecuted women with reference to the reconstruction of the Austrian nation. Non-persecuted women and female resistance fighters stand side by side. While women are not otherwise explicitly referred to as Nazi victims, they are now made more generally visible for the purpose of producing a gendered victim discourse. Women are constructed as a separate group of victims only in connection with resistance *and* war and in connection with the "reconstruction" of the nation or the struggle for its sake. Victims of the Shoah and of racist persecution are not part of this narrative on the reconstruction of Austria, which again points to the fact that this construction is primarily aimed at veiling Austria's complicity, which gives it its legitimation. Women are placed in the subject position of Nazi victims (resistance fighters) or victims of the war. This enables the establishment of a new concept of victim that embraces more than the concept of Nazi victim since the latter excludes *Trümmerfrauen*. This "more" includes the grouping of non-persecuted women. The broad concept of victim that is produced here again lets female perpetrators disappear from view; they are not thematized as such.

Of interest at this point is the information that was published by the Federal Social Welfare Office in countless national and regional media (i.e., daily newspapers, local newspapers, etc.) after the law was passed.[33] This explained the conditions for applying and added that "women whose behavior in word and deed was incompatible with the idea and the objectives of a free Austria" were excluded from the scheme. In the application form, this very general formulation was concretized by requesting the applicant to sign a declaration that she had never been "convicted of an offence relating to the events of the war or the Nazi regime—in particular under the law on war crimes or under the law banning Nazism—by a court of the Republic of Austria, a court of the four allied occupation powers, or a court of any other country." This declaration was included following pressure from the opposition and shows that perpetrators were defined purely in terms of criminal convictions. This definition excludes the many different ways in which women played active roles in Nazi society[34] and does not ask, for example, if they were registered members of the NSDAP, which could be proved.[35] Due to the exclusion of such possible activities, no further checking of the applicant's background was necessary.

4.3 The Construction of Mothers as Victims

There was also another kind of exclusion. Compensation was payable only to women who had given birth to a child before 1951. With this restriction, the construction of victimhood is legitimized in terms of family and social policy. Marialuise Mittermüller from the FPÖ argued as follows:

> The law we are considering today which provides for a one-off compensation payment to mothers in recognition of their contribution to the reconstruction of the Republic of Austria after 1945 is a sign of our appreciation. ... I don't quite understand the criticism. Today, the double burden of job and family is uncontested in all parties.[36]

The compatibility of job and family as demanded by supporters of women's rights is successfully integrated but is given a moral dimension. This strategy of linking an emancipatory policy with a moral dimension that says mothers cannot be denied recognition is a way of rebutting the criticism put forward by the opposition that this law is a continuation of the image of "Austria as a victim." Still more, even if the criticism relates mainly to the construction of non-persecuted women as victims by shutting out their Nazi past, the opposition cannot, at this point, fall behind its own goal, which is to give social recognition to women's reproductive work. Thus, the Austrian Social Democratic Party (*Sozialdemokratische Partei Österreichs*, SPÖ) and the Greens are not fundamentally opposed to the payment of compensation, but they are critical of the visibly problematic attitude to Austria's Nazi past and especially of the way women are reduced here to their role as mothers.

Another function is fulfilled by this restriction. It enables two constructions of mothers as victims: "silent national heroes" and "moral victims." Ms. Turkovic-Wendl from the ÖVP, for instance, says:

> In Vienna—and that's where I was in May 1945—we had hardly anything. No electric power, no water, very, very little food, sometimes none at all, and many people had no roof over their heads. And obviously grown-up people could understand the situation, could explain why there were these shortages, but how can a mother

> explain to her children why she has no food for them and nowhere to sleep? ... Today we are grateful to those women because in those days they gave us an image—and it's an image that impressed me deeply—that life goes on, that they can manage, that they can cope. I think this had a big effect on me when I was young: we can do it. Women can do it. They look to the future, they don't complain. And at this moment I feel grateful to these role models.[37]

This "silent hero" image constructs non-persecuted women as people who bear every burden and are willing to make sacrifices. This goes together with the idealization of their generation as those who "fought hard for freedom and democracy...and accepted hardships, because they always believed in this Austria,"[38] as Haubner (FPÖ) puts it. This is an explicit mixing of the deeds of female resistance fighters with those of the *Trümmerfrauen*.

This succeeds because the undifferentiated "special contribution" that is to be given recognition by the federal law is integrated in a national context and described as "believing in" and "fighting for" Austria. The focus on motherhood is related to powerful gender discourses in which women are reduced to their power of reproduction and are constructed in their role as mothers as self-sacrificing, protective, and uncomplaining women. By creating a link between motherhood and nation, mothers who care for their offspring are imagined as protecting and nurturing the nation.

Through the focus on mothers, whose multiple burdens and suffering no one would contest, a moral dimension is introduced that ensures that the true suffering of mothers is respected while making a distinction between them and those with a Nazi past. This moral dimension removes the distinction between victims of the war and victims of the Nazis, a distinction that has been demanded by scholars, critical media, and the opposition, and established a new concept of victimhood: "when the legislators express their respect and sympathy for victims, then it is justifiable to understand the concept of victim in a very broad sense" (Maria Theresia Fekter, ÖVP).[39] Herbert Haupt, member of parliament for the FPÖ, says:

> I think that, in view of our experience of dealing with victims and different groups of victims, we should be careful—sixty years after the end of the Second World War—not to make great distinctions and stress the differences when assessing the suffering, the pain and the subjective pain of individual people in those days.[40]

Thus, what critics had demanded for Nazi victims should now be applied to all victims, morally legitimized by the argument that no one has the right to judge different kinds of suffering. Minister of Justice Karin Miklautsch (ÖVP) argues that "we want to show our respect and our appreciation for all victims of this terrible war regime, although we are well aware that there are different victims, that there are victims who were directly persecuted by the Nazi regime."[41] With this focus on suffering and the formulation of a new concept of victimhood, active participation in Nazi society disappears, and a continuation of the national theory of victimization is produced through the construction of mothers as a "new" victim collective. In contrast to the national *Opfermythos* and as a way of underlining the close intertwining of the construction of victimhood with gender, I choose to speak of a gendered discourse on victimization.

This demand by members of the ÖVP-FPÖ government for a broad concept of victimhood was a response to the criticism that many Nazi victims were neglected for far too long, such as people who were categorized as "asocial" or "homosexual" or deserters, and they reversed it by arguing that a broad concept of victimhood would abolish the risk of "overlooking" certain groups of victims.

5. "Heroized Victims" and the Disappearance of the Perpetrators

The debate on the federal law can be read as a renewal and a perpetuation of existing discourses on the way Austria deals with its Nazi past, but it also reflects current shifts. In the national theory of victimization, the question of who is a victim was negotiated, and supporters of the Nazi regime and those responsible for Nazi crimes were positioned as victims through a reversal of perpetrator and victim. But in the gendered discourse, we see a shift toward another concept of victimhood. This shift is connected with the different meanings of the term *Opfer* in German: renunciation, offering, sacrifice in the religious sense, or one who is made to suffer (i.e., the victim).[42] The term *Opfer* can be used in all these senses. With reference to women, a religious connotation is introduced by adding the idea of "making an offering or sacrifice," a familiar concept from Austria's Catholic tradition (*Opfer-Erbringen*), to the idea of being a victim (*Opfer-Sein*). In times of great hardship, women's struggles were a kind of self-sacrifice for the sake of their children (and the nation). When these meanings are linked, as I have shown in the case of the parliamentary debate, and the term *Opfer* is used without a concrete context (i.e., without specifying that Nazi victims are meant), and in a next step the same term is used to refer to those who made selfless sacrifices (*Opfer-Erbringen*), then everyone is a victim—the victims of National Socialism and the Shoah, as well as non-persecuted women who greeted National Socialism enthusiastically and worked for it in different ways. In this way, an extremely broad concept of victimhood, a concept that has been weakened and blurred, was introduced into the public debate and can be applied to many different groupings. This runs counter to the demands made over many decades by critical scholars and journalists: that "Nazi victims" should be distinguished from those who were not persecuted by the Nazis. In the federal law, a new interpretation was given to the concept of victim.

This is a repositioning that is linked to the (constructed) social role of women as people who are willing to make sacrifices, a link that permits a moral legitimation of this repositioning. But the gendered discourse on victimization is also legitimized by the fact that with the resulting interpretation of mothers as "heroized victims," it produces a new victim collective but does not return to the way things were discussed before the 1980s.

Thanks to this moral dimension, the unspeakable can be avoided. Mothers cannot be *not* respected, and their contribution to the reconstruction of the Republic of Austria cannot be questioned. The view that women did this work because it was a sheer necessity if they were to survive and not—as suggested in the parliamentary debate—because they wanted to contribute to reconstructing the Austrian nation is relegated to the margins. The social disadvantages of mothers are the subject of a powerful public discourse, while knowledge gained from research on the multiple options open to non-persecuted women for participating actively in Nazi society is again pushed into the category of what cannot be spoken out loud. As a result, women as Nazis disappear completely.

The special feature of the parliamentary debate in 2005 is thus that the recognition of (other) Nazi victims was linked to recognition of the suffering (due to the war) of non-persecuted women. This linking of victimhood and gender makes it possible to use fragments of the national *Opfermythos* in current discursive disputes over commemoration. This shows that deflecting the blame is still a common practice and can be read as an indication of the extent to which deflecting the blame and denying responsibility permeate Austrian society to this day: as an immanent part of family dialogues, public commemoration, and individual memories.

The image of the *Trümmerfrauen* was always part of the *Opfermythos*, and thus of the Austrian memory, but the question of why, in 2005, sixty-five years after the end of National Socialism, this image was revived, extended and turned into a topic of public interest, which—as shown by the examples presented here—is obviously still of importance today. The critical counter-discourse had exposed the patterns of perpetrator-victim reversal, trivialization, or reconciliation as ways of deflecting blame but had always made reference to a male perpetrator collective in which women were only implicitly included, without making them visible as purposeful subjects. But treating non-persecuted women as victims creates a new victim collective to which the families of those who were not persecuted, the families of perpetrators and participants, can now feel that they belong. Almost every Austrian family that was not persecuted by the Nazis can apply the interpretation pattern of the "heroized victim" to their (great-)grandmothers. Events such as the Waldheim affair or the *War of Annihilation: Crimes of the Wehrmacht 1941 to 1944* exhibition have broken with the myth of the "clean Wehrmacht" and have made it impossible to see "men" exclusively in roles that correspond to the victim narrative as "returnees" or "ordinary soldiers." Rather, they became visible as Nazi perpetrators and as being actively involved in Nazi society—at least in the public discourse. By contrast, the *Trümmerfrauen* were always part of the Austrian memory in which National Socialism is trivialized, but in 2005, women were finally made visible as people willing to make self-sacrifices and thus perpetuated as victims.

Endnotes

1 This term exists only in memory cultures in Germany and Austria, and has a specific meaning and function in these two post-fascist societies. It is left untranslated here for this reason.

2 See *Der Standard*, September 21/22, 2019, and the detailed online report by Steffen Arora, "Zell am Ziller erhält Tirols ersten Stolperstein und verhindert zweiten," *derstandard.at* (September 21, 2019), accessed Dec. 23, 2019, https://www.derstandard.at/story/2000108883619/zell-am-ziller-erhaelt-tirols-ersten-stolperstein-und-verhindert-zweiten.

3 See "Strache enthüllt Denkmal für Trümmerfrauen in Wien," *diepresse.at* (Oct. 01, 2018), accessed Dec. 23, 2019, https://www.diepresse.com/5505798/strache-enthullt-denkmal-fur-trummerfrauen-in-wien.

4 Bundesgesetz, mit dem eine einmalige Zuwendung für Frauen als Anerkennung für ihre besonderen Leistungen beim Wiederaufbau der Republik Österreich geschaffen wird.

5 This paper is a brief summary of the results of an analysis of the gendered victim discourse from the point of view of the sociology of knowledge, which I carried out as my doctoral dissertation project (Maria Pohn-Weidinger [Lauggas], *Heroisierte Opfer: Bearbeitungs- und Handlungsstrukturen von "Trümmerfrauen" in Wien*, 2nd ed. (Wiesbaden: Springer VS, 2014)). In this study, I combined discourse analysis methods from the sociology of knowledge (Reiner Keller, "The Sociology of Knowledge Approach to Discourse (SKAD)," *Human Studies* 34, no. 1 (2011): 43–65) with social-constructivist biographical research (Gabriele Rosenthal, "Biography Research," in *Qualitative Research Practice*, ed. Clive Seale, Giampietro Gobo, Jaber F. Gubrium and David Silverman (London: Sage, 2006), 48-64) to study the self-constructions of *Trümmerfrauen* in Vienna.

6 On this very broad debate, see for example: Gerhard Botz, "Krisen der österreichischen Zeitgeschichte," in *Kontroversen um Österreichs Zeitgeschichte: Verdrängte Vergangenheit, Österreich-Identität, Waldheim und die Historiker*, ed. Gerhard Botz and Gerald Sprengnagel (Frankfurt a.M.: Campus, 1994), 16-77; Gerhard Botz, "Geschichte und kollektives Gedächtnis in der Zweiten Republik: Opferthese, Lebenslüge und Geschichtstabu in der Zeitgeschichtsschreibung," in *Inventur 44/55: Österreich im ersten Jahrzehnt der Zweiten Republik*, ed. Wolfgang Kos and Georg Rigele (Vienna: Sonderzahl, 1996), 51-85; Anton Pelinka and Erika Weinzierl, eds., *Das große Tabu: Österreichs Umgang mit seiner Vergangenheit* (Vienna: Verl. der Österr. Staatsdr., 1987); Meinrad Ziegler and Waltraud Kannonier-Finster, *Österreichisches Gedächtnis: Über Erinnern und Vergessen der NS-Vergangenheit* (Innsbruck: StudienVerlag, 2016); Peter Pirker in this volume.

7 See for instance Ruth Wodak, *Wir sind alle unschuldige Täter: Diskurshistorische Studien zum Nachkriegsantisemitismus* (Frankfurt a. M.: Suhrkamp, 1990).

8 When questions about then-presidential candidate, and in due course elected president, Kurt Waldheim's proximity to, knowledge of, or even potential involvement in Nazi war crimes were being raised, he reacted by saying: "In the war I did nothing different from hundreds of thousands of other Austrians, namely I fulfilled my duty as a soldier" (quoted after Heidemarie Uhl, "Denkmäler als Medien gesellschaftlicher Erinnerung: Die Denkmallandschaft der Zweiten Republik und die Transformationen des österreichischen Gedächtnisses," in *Nationen und ihre Selbstbilder: Postdiktatorische Gesellschaften in Europa*, ed. Carola Sachse, Edgar Wolfrum, and Regina Fritz (Göttingen: Wallstein Verlag, 2008), 62-89 (here 82). For the Waldheim-affair see also Richard Mitten, *The Politics of the Antisemitic Prejudice: The Waldheim Phenomenon in Austria*, (Boulder, Colorado: Westview Press, 1992). The concept of "fulfilling one's duty" subsequently became the central reference category in a debate carried on by critical historians and political scientists, and raised the question "whether it is possible to speak of duty in the service of a criminal regime" (Ruth Wodak,

Florian Menz, Richard Mitten, and Frank Stern, eds., *Die Sprachen der Vergangenheit: Öffentliches Gedenken in den österreichischen und deutschen Medien* (Frankfurt a. M.: Suhrkamp, 1994), 200). This discussion reached its peak in 1995 with the exhibition entitled "War of Annihilation: Crimes of the Wehrmacht 1941 to 1944," organized by the Hamburg Institute of Social Research, which threw serious doubt on the image of the 'clean' Wehrmacht (see for instance Hannes Heer, *Vom Verschwinden der Täter: Der Vernichtungskrieg fand statt, aber keiner war dabei* (Berlin: Aufbau Verlag, 2004)).

9 See Heidemarie Uhl, "From Victim Myth to Co-Responsibility Thesis: Nazi Rule, World War II, and the Holocaust in Austrian Memory," in *The Politics of Memory in Postwar Europe*, ed. Richard Ned Lebow, Wulf Kansteiner, and Claudio Fogu (Durham: Duke University Press, 2006), 40-72.

10 Here, the academic discourse followed traditional research, in which women are neglected. And even in early women's and gender studies, *Trümmerfrauen* were sometimes presented in positive terms as female role models, and as an alternative to the "male reconstruction myth enshrined in traditional historiography" (Irene Bandhauer-Schöffmann and Ela Hornung, "Das Geschlecht des Wiederaufbaus," *erinnerungsort.at* (2005), accessed Jan 16, 2020, http: www.erinnerungsort.at/dokumente/hornung.pdf, 3). Moreover, *Trümmerfrauen* were victims of the patriarchal policies of National Socialism. The academic discourse did not change until the 1980s, when new light was thrown on the multiple options open to women, and scholars began to criticize the idea that they were exclusively victims (for a review of the discourse, see Christina Herkommer, "Der Diskurs zur Rolle von Frauen im Nationalsozialismus im Spiegel feministischer Theoriebildung," in *Täterinnen und/oder Opfer: Frauen in Gewaltstrukturen*, ed. Christine Künzel and Gaby Temme (Hamburg: Lit-Verl., 2007), 25-45).

11 Bandhauer-Schöffmann and Ela Hornung, "Vom 'Dritten Reich' zur Zweiten Republik: Frauen in Wien der Nachkriegszeit," in *Frauen in Österreich: Beiträge zu ihrer Situation im 19. und 20. Jahrhundert*, ed. David Good (Vienna: Böhlau, 1994), 225-246 (here 225-226).

12 Erika Thurner, "Frauen-Nachkriegsleben in Österreich – im Zentrum und in der Provinz," in *Wiederaufbau weiblich: Dokumentation der Tagung 'Frauen in der österreichischen und deutschen Nachkriegszeit,'* ed. Irene Bandhauer-Schöffmann and Ela Hornung (Vienna/ Salzburg: Greyer-Ed., 1992), 3-14; Bandhauer-Schöffmann and Hornung, "Vom 'Dritten Reich' zur Zweiten Republik," 226); Pohn-Weidinger [Lauggas], *Heroisierte Opfer*.

13 Bandhauer-Schöffmann and Hornung, "Vom 'Dritten Reich' zur Zweiten Republik," 226.

14 Gabriele Rosenthal, *"... wenn alles in Scherben fällt ...": von Leben und Sinnwelt der Kriegsgeneration: Typen biographischer Wandlungen,* Biographie und Gesellschaft, vol. 6 (Opladen: Leske und Budrich, 1987), 380.

15 Ulrike Weckel and Edgar Wolfrum, eds., *"Bestien" und "Empfehlsempfänger": Frauen und Männer in NS-Prozessen nach 1945,* (Göttingen: Vandenhoeck & Ruprecht, 2003).

16 In this paper, I do not refer to the broad debate on "complicity" – especially in women's and gender studies (see Herkommer 2007, Gravenhorst/Tatschmurat 1990) – which means running the risk of making inadmissible generalizations. Since my arguments here relate to the level of public hegemonic discourses, I use this term to show that it marks the place of the unspeakable in discursive struggles over interpreting the Nazi past in Austria (see also Pohn-Weidinger [Lauggas], *Heroisierte Opfer)*. On the level of concrete biographies, this term needs to be differentiated according to different forms of participation, specific family history and biographical contexts, or institutional options, to mention only a few important aspects.

17 There are no academic studies showing what criteria were used in Austria for forcing women to perform this kind of labour, or how the responsible authorities reached their decisions. In a study relating to Dresden, for example, Leonie Treber says that former

members of the NSDAP or any of its associated organizations were (forcibly) made to help with the work of clearing rubble on the basis of orders by the state administration of Saxony. These women and men had to register with the labour office. (Leonie Treber, *Mythos Trümmerfrauen: Von der Trümmerbeseitigung in der Kriegs- und Nachkriegszeit und der Entstehung eines deutschen Erinnerungsortes* (Essen: Klartext, 2014), 202.)

18 Few pictures show women who were stigmatized with a crossed out swastika during their work (Peter Eppel, *Frauenleben 1945: Kriegsende in Wien*, (Vienna: Eigenverl. d. Museen der Stadt Wien, 1995)).

19 By mentioning the year 1943, the FPÖ memorial acknowledges that the work of clearing debris began before 1945, but without mentioning that this work was done by different groupings.

20 See Treber, *Mythos Trümmerfrauen*, 417ff.

21 In Austria these photographs were used only from the 1960s onwards, for example in magazines or school textbooks (see https://warofpictures.univie.ac.at/truemmerfrauen, accessed Dec 23, 2019).

22 Oliver Marchart, "Die ungezählten Jahre: Opfermythos und Täterversöhnung im österreichischen 'Jubiläumsjahr' 2005," in *Rebranding images: Ein streitbares Lesebuch zu Geschichtspolitik und Erinnerungskultur in Österreich*, ed. Martin Wassermair and Katharina Wegan (Innsbruck: Studien-Verl., 2006), 51-60 (here 57).

23 Ibid.

24 Bundeskanzleramt Österreich, *Österreich 2005: Das Lesebuch zum Jubiläumsjahr, mit Programmübersicht*, ed. Teresa Indjein (St. Pölten: Residenz-Verl, 2004), no page numbers.

25 Eva Blimlinger, "Wer ist Täter, wenn alle Opfer sind? Die Viktimisierung der österreichischen Gesellschaft nach 1945," *erinnern.at* (2009), accessed December 23, 2019, http://www.erinnern.at/bundeslaender/oesterreich/e_bibliothek/seminarbibliotheken-zentrale-seminare/7-zentrales-seminar-internationale-konferenz/Eva%20Blimlinger%2C%20Wer%20ist%20Tater%2C%20wenn%20alle%20Opfer%20sind.pdf/view, 1.

26 The analysis presented in this paper is based on the text of the federal law and the minutes of the 116th session of the National Council of the Republic of Austria, which contain a record of the parliamentary discussion on this law.

27 See Teresa Distelberger, Rudolf de Cillia and Ruth Wodak, "Österreichische Identitäten in politischen Gedenkreden des Jubiläumsjahres 2005", in *Gedenken vom 'Gedankenjahr': Zur diskursiven Konstruktion österreichischer Identitäten im Jubiläumsjahr 2005*, ed. Rudolf de Cillia and Ruth Wodak (Innsbruck: Studien-Verl., 2009), 29-71 (here 40-45).

28 See Ruth Wodak et al., eds., *Zur diskursiven Konstruktion nationaler Identität* (Frankfurt a. M.: Suhrkamp, 1998).

29 Verbatim record of the 116th session of the National Council of the Republic of Austria (July 7, 2005), 166.

30 Ibid.

31 Here, too, reference is made to the national thesis of victimization, because in the first two post-war decades efforts were focused on making the "Austrian resistance" visible (but not the communist or Jewish resistance), in order to present Austria to the outside world as a country that had stood up against Nazi tyranny, which came from outside.

32 Verbatim record of the 116th session of the National Council of the Republic of Austria (July 7, 2005), 175f.

33 See "Information über die Zuwendung für Frauen als Anerkennung für ihre besonderen Leistungen beim Wiederaufbau der Republik Österreich," in Maria Pohn-Weidinger [Lauggas], *Heroisierte Opfer*, 382 (Appendix 1).

34 In particular scholars in women's and gender studies have initiated research on the different roles and fields of action of non-persecuted women. In the case of Austria, studies have been made for instance of a former Nazi woman (Ingrid Bauer, "'Ich hab' geglaubt, die Welt fällt zusammen ...' Notizen zu einem nicht einkalkulierten Dialog mit einer Nationalsozialistin," *Zeitgeschichte* 9/10 (1988): 388-402), of the League of German Girls (*Bund Deutscher Mädel*) (Johanna Gehmacher, "Biografie, Geschlecht und Organisation: Der Bund Deutscher Mädel in Österreich," in *Die BDM-Generation: Weibliche Jugend in Deutschland und Österreich im Nationalsozialismus*, ed. Dagmar Reese (Berlin: Verl. f. Berlin-Brandenburg, 2007), 159-214), and of denunciations (Christina Altenstraßer, *Handlungsspielraum Denunziation: Alltag, Geschlecht und Denunziation im ländlichen Oberdonau 1938 bis 1945* (Munich: in press, 2005); Ela Hornung, "Denunziation, 'Wehrkraftzersetzung' und Geschlecht," in *Frauen- und Geschlechtergeschichte des Nationalsozialismus*, ed. Johanna Gehmacher and Gabriella Hauch (Innsbruck u.a.: Studien-Verl., 2007), 169-185).

35 In 1947, a total of 471,689 people were registered as Nazis as defined in section 4 of the law banning Nazism, of whom 124,648 were women (see Dieter Stiefel, *Entnazifizierung in Österreich* (Vienna: Europa-Verlag, 1981), 218).

36 Verbatim record of the 116th session of the National Council of the Republic of Austria (July 7, 2005), 165.

37 Ibid., 177.

38 Ibid., 168.

39 Ibid., 148.

40 Ibid., 151.

41 Ibid., 154.

42 *Wörterbuch der deutschen Gegenwartssprache*, s.v. "Opfer," accessed Jan 16, 2020, https://www.dwds.de/wb/wdg/Opfer. The term "victim" initially denoted sacrifice in the performance of religious rituals, later the meaning had turned to a "person who is hurt, tortured, or killed by another" (see *Online Etymology Dictionary*, s.v. "victim," accessed Jan 16, 2020, https:www.etymonline.com/word/victim)

Post-World War II

"Nicht lebensfähig?": Austria's Economic Viability after the Two World Wars

Peter Berger/Günter Bischof

Introduction

After World War I, the myth was born and became widespread in intellectual circles and beyond that Austria was "nonviable" ("*nicht lebensfähig*"). After the turmoil of World War I, when economic life was disrupted due to war production and the lack of manpower in agriculture—along with the collapse and breakup of the Habsburg Monarchy in 1918—the bulk of German speakers were stranded in the small state of Austria, one of the new successor states of the Dual Monarchy. Austrians, particularly the Viennese, were poor and destitute. In the fall of 1918, thousands of them got infected with Spanish influenza, without any chance of receiving medical assistance.[1] (Egon Schiele and his wife, Edith, were among the numerous victims of the disease.) As the cultural critic George Prochnik put it: "Few people believed that enough of Austria remained after World War I to survive on its own." He adds: "The truncation of empire inspired many Viennese to retreat further into phantasy. 'I shall live on with the torso, and imagine it is the whole,' Freud wrote in a letter, capturing the mood in the former imperial capital."[2]

Cut off from its traditional agricultural hinterlands in what became the new states of Hungary, Poland, Rumania, and Yugoslavia, the once-affluent Austrian capital could not even feed its children. In 1919, Herbert Hoover's American Relief Administration ran twenty-three "people's kitchens" in every corner of Vienna, offering 150,000 warm meals per day to boys and girls under the age of fifteen.[3] Hunger was not the only problem in the winter of 1918/19. Coal from the Ostrava mines and other production sites now situated in Czechoslovakia failed to reach Austrian households and the energy-ridden industry as a result of protectionist measures of the Prague government—and also because Austria lacked the means to pay for it. High tariffs levied by the succession states vis-à-vis Austrian exports disrupted the usual trading patterns. Inflation skyrocketed in the early 1920s. Fortunes were lost and made in the inflation economy. Austrian industrial production and the financial sector needed years to achieve precarious recovery. Only with foreign financial aid did the country survive. Currency stabilization and balanced budgets came thanks to a massive intervention of the League of Nations. It was welcomed by the conservative coalition government of Chancellor Ignaz Seipel but met with strong resentment on the part of the political Left and generally of all those who believed that Austria could only prosper if allied (or even united in an "Anschluss") with Germany.

After World War II, the Austrian economy went through a difficult recovery period of postwar adjustment lasting into the early 1950s. Severe bottlenecks in transport and in the labor force, along with drastic shortages in raw materials (i.e., coal, electricity, etc.) and food, needed to be overcome before launching economic reconstruction. The rubble needed to be cleaned away in the cities. Only foreign food aid (from the US Army, the United Nations Relief and Rehabilitation Administration, and American Interim, Congressional, and Marshall Plan aid) managed to allow for the survival of the population. Yet Nazi German investments in Austrian industry during the war actually left the country in better shape (i.e., Hitler's "Marshall Plan" for Austria). Unlike during the post-World War I period, the country's elites were confident in 1945 and thereafter that Austria would recover and was economically "*lebensfähig*." Yet new myths came into being, such as that of the hard work of the Austrian population single-handedly rebuilding the country without any foreign aid during the "heroic age" of postwar reconstruction.

Post-World War I: The First Republic

Looking back on the disaster of the lost Great War, Count Ottokar Czernin, Austria-Hungary's foreign minister until April 1918, recalled his impressions about the country he had served without success. "We were bound to die," he wrote in the 1920s, "and the only choice we had was one of the manner of our death." And not without self-criticism he added: "We chose the most terrible one."[4]

In hindsight, the obsession of high-ranking representatives of the Habsburg regime with Austria's impending doom (proof of which can be detected long before 1914) strangely mirrored the convictions of anti-Habsburg radicals among the non-German subjects of the Dual Monarchy. In an epic tale about a fictitious Croatian noble family at the turn of the nineteenth century (written by the Yugoslav novelist Miroslav Krleža), the son of a Hungarian civil servant of Croatian descent embraces both South Slav Irredentism and Socialism. He tries to convince his father, whose loyalty to the Crown is beyond doubt, that Austria is a zombie state: "Don't you see it already lies on its deathbed? No matter how you toss or turn it, it is like squaring the circle!"[5]

When the leading Entente statesmen gathered in Paris and handed over, on June 2, 1919, the peace terms to an Austrian delegation, "representing a morsel of what had once been a great Empire,"[6] the delegates, as well as public opinion at home, were shocked and dismayed. Both the territorial and economic clauses of the treaty, which Austria was expected to sign, stripped that country of every chance to survive in dignity, at least in the opinion of most (if not all) of its citizens. They rendered it "*lebensunfähig*," incapable of living. Now the bygone days of the Habsburg Monarchy suddenly appeared as an era of milk and honey, when domestic agricultural and industrial resources were plenty, when reasonable living standards for the majority could be achieved without bothering about a foreign trade surplus, when the currency was stable and banks were safe. As late as 1941, Stefan Zweig, in his memories published under the title *The World of Yesterday*, echoed the pains of a loss of security felt by a generation of Austrians who had witnessed both prewar Habsburg rule and the struggle for survival of the fledging First Republic. In retrospect, their (and Zweig's) Habsburg nostalgia clearly missed the point, just as the legend of a historically inevitable decline of Austria-Hungary was nothing but that: a legend. It must not be forgotten that between the fall of Napoleon and the Balkan Wars of 1912/13, most political observers thought of the Habsburg Empire as a guarantor of stability in Central and Eastern Europe.[7]

While Habsburg nostalgia failed to spark effective political action in interwar Austria, the new legend of Austrian nonviability, promoted by academic scholarship, business circles, and influential journalists, slowly but steadily unfolded its disastrous effect. The myth that Austria, as it had emerged from the war and the ensuing peace treaties, was incapable of economic survival owed its initial success to the anger and frustration of those who had trusted Woodrow Wilson's pledge to base the postwar world order on the principle of national self-determination. For Austria, this would have meant immediate union with the defeated German Reich. But, as the historian Norbert Schausberger correctly observed, the Entente powers had not fought a bloody four-year war to see German power increase by the accession of a neighboring state. Thus, they prohibited the Anschluss in both the Versailles (Art. 80) and the Saint-Germain (Art. 88) peace treaties. In reaction, Austrians showed understandable disappointment but also increased susceptibility to voices contesting the chance of a bright economic future for Austria. From 1920 onward, assertions of Austria's *Lebensunfähigkeit* (nonviability) became a regular feed for readers of Austrian newspapers and academic journals. The excitement ebbed away thanks to the transitory success of financial stabilization in 1923, but at this point it had already left an indelible mark on domestic public opinion. In the 1930s, Nazi propaganda capitalized on the deep-rooted sentiment that little Austria was a failure from the start.

Adherents to the dogma of Austrian economic nonviability could advance some seemingly strong arguments in their favor. More than anything else, inflation and the interruption of regular business between Habsburg's former dominions actively played into their hands, as Schausberger and others have pointed out.[8] The breakup of a largely self-sufficient economic unit, Austria-Hungary, forced its seven successor states to henceforth compete both for essential imports and for markets capable of absorbing their surplus production. In Austria's case, grain, meat, coal, and a range of semi-finished products were in desperately short supply. Industry struggled with fuel shortages but also with a penchant for protectionism in many states of Eastern and Southeastern Europe. Of course, a return to normal in commercial relations was more than a remote possibility and did in fact support economic recovery throughout the Danube Basin after 1924. But soon after the war, Czechs, Hungarians, and Yugoslavs were hesitant to strike deals with Vienna. Hence, the popular, but unfounded, reasoning that nothing but unification with Germany and its consequentially renewed Great Power status could save Austrians from disaster.

As this CAS volume amply demonstrates, historical myths always pop up when they serve somebody's interests. So, what about the notion that Austria, under the conditions defined by the Treaty of Saint-Germain, would necessarily end up in failure? Who saw a benefit in propagating Austrian nonviability, and was there any "scientific" justification to do so? In the earliest days of Republican Austria, domestic public opinion did not bother much about the future viability of the rump state inhabited by ethnic Germans of Vienna and the Alpine provinces. Cassandra like the Socialist elder statesman Viktor Adler, who in the Provisional National Assembly spoke of an impossible mission to develop the economy of a truncated fatherland, were largely ignored.[9] The main concern of the man in the street was mere physical survival when everybody was threatened by hunger, cold, and the lack of employment opportunities. The father of the composer Ernst Krenek, who had been a quartermaster general of the Habsburg Army before and during the war, ultimately managed to find a job as a clerk in a Viennese shoe shop. He belonged to the lucky few. His later-famous son, born in 1900, left us a volume of memoirs, published posthumously in 1998, in which reference is made to the nonviability issue as it presented itself in the early 1920s—when Austrian embarrassment about the Paris Peace Treaties reached a peak. All and sundry, writes Krenek, now believed in the axiom of "*Lebensunfähigkeit*," from the state secretary down to the last chimney sweep. But did anybody take the pains to dispassionately analyze the question? No, says Krenek, or else the theory of nonviability must have become untenable. Post-1919 Austria was certainly capable of performing an "economic miracle" and, to a certain extent, did so in the second half of the 1920s when bigger and wealthier countries envied it for its achievements. The talk of its nonviability originated in the false conception that states had to be economically self-sufficient. But autarchy in times of peace made no sense, Krenek asserted, since the world market offered more products than any domestic market could provided one had the money to buy. No country was obliged to manufacture everything "from almonds to zippers" on its own soil unless governed by people suffering from war psychosis.[10]

Krenek's comments on Austria's alleged "*Lebensunfähigkeit*," penned down in the 1940s, sound like a distant echo of an address delivered as early as March 1919 by economist Joseph A. Schumpeter, who at the time acted as Austrian state secretary (minister) of finance. Schumpeter spoke at the Viennese Chamber of Commerce, a body whose members were in their majority positive about the perspectives of an independent Austrian state. Provided that government ceased to intervene into the mechanism of the free market, and the victorious Allies granted it favorable terms of peace, Schumpeter said, Austria was bound to prosper in the long run. Absence of domestic resources, as in the case of coal, was no hindrance. After all, the Bohemian and Silesian coal mines had not vanished from the surface of the planet, and Austrian industry could buy from them just as it would have bought from mines on home territory, if there had been any.[11]

Why did Schumpeter's cautious optimism, and that of a small group of likeminded intellectuals and businesspeople, fail to impact upon Austrian public opinion? In the early postwar days, strong political forces intervened to silence anyone who opposed the doom mongering that Austria's government had chosen as a strategy to impress the Paris peacemakers. Tellingly, the head of the Austrian delegation at Saint-Germain, the Socialist Karl Renner, urged officials at home to put pressure on Schumpeter, whose publicized remarks he considered to border on high treason.[12] When it became clear in the summer of 1919 that Austrian black painting of the country's economic future could not prevent the Allies from imposing harsh peace terms, the nonviability issue continued to draw newspaper headlines and scholarly comments, but now the reasons were different. As economic historian Karl

Bachinger has shown, Austria's powerful Social Democratic Party had a keen interest in keeping the debate alive to promote its chief political agenda—that of the Anschluss (i.e., unification of Austria with the Weimar Republic). Following the failure to achieve a quick, negotiated Austro-German union in early 1919, Otto Bauer, the party's strategic mastermind, kidnapped whatever economic argument could be found against Austrian independence for the purpose of Anschluss politics—without wasting too much time to tell people the real reason why he and his friends at the helm of the workers' movement favored the German alliance. Those who wanted to know were well advised to read Bauer's literary account of the "Austrian Revolution" of 1918/19 (O. Bauer, *Die österreichische Revolution*, 1923). In this text, Bauer expressed his conviction that transforming Austria into a proletarian democracy would be impossible as long as bourgeois forces held the upper hand in all other successor states of the Habsburg Empire and as long as the Austrian bourgeoisie could rely on the economic and political support of its counterparts in the Entente and the neutral powers. Only if Austria joined Germany, a country where Democratic Socialism was strong, could there be any hope for a bright, "red" future of the Alpine and Danube lands.[13]

Of course, the Social Democrats were not alone in their craving for the Anschluss. Throughout the 1920s, Pan-Germans of the *Grossdeutsche Volkspartei* and Austrian National Socialists, as led by lawyer Walter Riehl, were equally committed to it. A short-lived political formation under the name of "*Bürgerlich-Demokratische Partei*," with a liberal-social profile, also embraced the Pan-Germanic idea and received substantial financial support from Berlin. Its founder was Gustav Stolper, originally a Social Democrat and an expert advisor of the Austrian peace delegation at Saint-Germain who belonged to the most influential economic journalists of his country. Stolper's paper, *Der Österreichische Volkswirt*, supplied Austrian Anschluss fans of varying shades with facts and figures suggesting that nothing but union with Germany could save their nation from disaster. A series of *Volkswirt* articles, written by Stolper himself and published in late 1919 and early 1920, later appeared in book form and was widely circulated.[14] Against the success of *Deutsch-Österreich als Sozial- und Wirtschaftsproblem*, a handful of publications defending Austria's economic viability without German support had no serious chance to assert themselves. Among those who courageously held up the banner of Austria's "*Lebensfähigkeit*" were the Viennese economist Friedrich Hertz and League of Nations experts Walter Thomas (Baron) Layton of London University College and Charles Rist, one of the fathers of French monetary stabilization at a fraction of the franc's prewar gold equivalent in 1928.

Austrian financial reconstruction in the first half of the 1920s, aided by international loans and monitored by the Geneva League of Nations, laid the foundation for limited economic recovery, even if that recovery proceeded but slowly, and its measurable impact remained way below what could probably have been achieved under different circumstances. Compared with the speed and durability characterizing Austria's economic resurgence after World War II, the growth trajectory of the First Republic for sure was a disappointment even before it was so dramatically interrupted by the global economic downswing of the 1930s. Economic historians writing in the 1970s and 1980s, with very few exceptions, were quick in identifying the laissez-faire mentality of those in charge of interwar Austria's economic policies and the alleged financial imperialism of its foreign lenders and League advisors as the decisive factors, which ultimately drove the impoverished country into Hitler's arms. Before dealing with the historical justification of such an apportionment of blame, a brief glance at the structure and performance of the Austrian economy prior to 1938 is in place. Austria emerged from World War I as a predominantly agrarian state equipped, however, with an industrial potential second in the region only to that of the new Czechoslovakia. As to its energy base, the development of rich hydropower resources held some promises for the future but seemed unrealistic in the short term since Viennese banks were interested in the continuing exploitation of Bohemian and Moravian coal mines in which they held a stake. Austria's balance of trade, with the exception of the hyperinflation period of 1921/22, ran a deficit throughout the 1920s and did not recover until the Great Depression reduced the volume of traded commodities to one-third of the pre-Depression level. Austrian exporters suffered from the postwar surge in protectionism throughout the East-Central and Southeast Europe regions, which had previously been chief buyers of their goods and services. Very few branches of industry managed to successfully sell abroad, with chemicals and paper as frontrunners. Those sectors, which in 1918 employed most of the Austrian workforce (that of the metal and machine-building industries), were hardest hit by the implosion of what once had been a smoothly functioning "division of labor" between Habsburg's agrarian and industrialized possessions. Influential business circles in the First Republic, bankers in the first place, dreamed of a return of the old days and hence did not sufficiently press for a new, global (as against the traditional Central European) orientation of the Austrian economy. Without the perspective of fundamental economic change, investments in the industrial and service sectors remained at a low level throughout the 1920s and 1930s. The average gross investment rate did not exceed seven percent per annum, which merely allowed for a replacement of worn-down equipment, while unemployment hovered between eight percent (average 1923–30) and more than twenty percent (1931–37).[15]

But the overall picture of the Austrian economy between World War I and the Anschluss showed some bright spots as well. Agricultural output in 1929 was considerably higher than that of the last prewar year, and due to the energetic support farming enjoyed[16] under the authoritarian regime of Chancellors Dollfuss and Schuschnigg (1933–37), it grew to one hundred sixteen percent of its 1913 level. The energy sector also benefited from government action, notably the electrification of parts of the western railroad financed out of the proceeds of the League of Nations loan. Tourism made considerable progress despite being the temporary target of Hitler's anti-Austrian campaign following the abortive Austrian Nazi putsch of July 1934. Taking all these positive aspects into account, one is tempted to arrive at a conclusion similar to that voiced by the Austrian bank historian and chronicler of the Credit-Anstalt crash of 1931, Fritz Weber: Austria's economic problems had nothing to do with an a priori incapacity to survive. They resulted from the absence of a clearly defined and consistent economic policy strategy. But should we underwrite Weber's proposition that Austria's conservative governments and their foreign lenders and financial advisors, because of their commitment to an outdated monetary and fiscal orthodoxy, effectively blocked the road to sustained economic reconstruction?

Regarding the activity of the League of Nations in Austria between 1922 and 1926—when Commissioner-General Alfred R. Zimmerman (until early 1925) and his much less powerful successor, Meinoud M. Rost van Tonningen, supervised Austrian spending practices and, in a step-by-step process, liberated the proceeds of the international reconstruction loan of 1923 for a limited range of purposes—recent research[17] has rendered accusations against them of a doctrinarian free-market bias and lack of sympathy for the hard-struggling Austrians untenable. Zimmerman displayed authoritarian manners, it is true, but more than once proved his readiness to grant the Austrians some financial leeway for outlays not necessarily in line with the principal aim of reducing the national debt. When Rost van Tonningen found out that surplus tax returns were channeled around the League's control mechanism to discretely fill gaps in the budget, this breach of confidence failed to have serious consequences.[18] Also, the Austrian side persistently and with impunity ignored Geneva's admonitions to eliminate the unnecessary cost of *Doppelverwaltung* (i.e., the practice of involving both state and provincial bureaucracies in the administration of matters that could have easily been assigned to either the state or the *Länder*). The narrative of Austria being exposed, in the 1920s, to ruthless foreign financial dictatorship is a forceful myth of astounding longevity.

The economic policies of "Austrofascism" in the 1930s were also chastised for their erratic and inefficient nature, but here, criticism seemed to rest on more stable ground. The late historian Siegfried Mattl, after discussing the disastrous effect of the 1929 crisis on Austrian industrial production, investments, and employment, described how the government in Vienna and Austria's central bank reacted with a policy mix of tight money (to defend the hard schilling currency), reduced public expenditure for productive investment purposes, and a commitment to balanced budgets.[19] In official circles, it was believed that stimulating Austrian economic growth should be left up to domestic or foreign lenders, and indeed Austria floated two loans to this end (in 1933 and 1935), but large portions of their proceeds were spent for the liquidation of ailing banks or the repayment of state debts. Ironically, believers in Austria's economic potential in 1919 and the early 1920s (like Schumpeter or the slightly dubious inflation tycoon Camillo Castiglioni)[20] pinned their hopes on the large Vienna banks whose Central and East European business network promised to benefit the new republic. But when crisis struck in 1931, and the government decided to bail out the last remaining Austrian mega bank, *Credit-Anstalt für Handel und Gewerbe*, the dream of continuing Austrian financial hegemony in the erstwhile Habsburg territories was over. In sum, the loss of tax money spent for more than a decade on various bank salvation schemes was enormous. Because of the bank lobby's capacity to tap state funds for its ends, while all other businesses were denied affordable credit terms, "financial dictatorship" may indeed be an appropriate description of the prevailing economic dogma in the 1930s. The League of Nations' new representative in Vienna, Rost van Tonningen, first supported restrictive (or in Mattl's wording: deflationary)[21] monetary policies applied by Austria's chief central banker, Viktor Kienböck. Somewhat like Zimmerman in the 1920s, Rost was charged with supervising Austrian spending practices out of a reconstruction loan Vienna had been allowed to float abroad in 1933. Later, the Dutchman Rost converted to National Socialism and lobbied, to the embarrassment both of his Austrian hosts and his employers at Geneva, for applying Hitler's unsound, employment-increasing financial practices to Austria. When Rost resigned from his post in mid-1936, Austrian economic recovery was well under way, but it proved too feeble and came too late to prevent the annexation of Austria by Nazi Germany. There was the Anschluss that nonviability propaganda had always suggested to Austrians as a solution to their economic problems. Soon it would turn out that

German rule would increase, not mitigate, the difficulties of Vienna and the Alpine lands.

Post-World War II: The Second Republic

There was not another year in Austrian history when it was so difficult to face the future confidently, concludes a special *History Magazine* on 1945 in the Vienna daily *Die Presse*, and it also makes a comment on people's hardships in daily life: "Death, rape, hunger, trauma, displacement, banditry, prisoners of war, loss of home and *Heimat* all defined the wounds of the previous war that Austrians experienced."[22]

Indeed, it was a hard transition from war to peace in 1945. "The Second Republic was born out of the devastation of World War II," Dieter Stiefel has noted. He added that the postwar modernization of Austria was based both on lopsided German investments in the Linz area and Western Austria, as well as the wartime destruction of the *Ostmark*.[23] This gave Austria a chance to start anew after the wartime devastation.[24] Two American historians came to the conclusion that "[t]he National Socialist autocracy and German capital pulled the country out of her industrial backwardness and created the modern industrial base on which the country's future economic position would depend."[25]

In most accounts of Austrian economic reconstruction after World War II, American aid programs (including the "European Recovery Program," aka the Marshall Plan) are given most of the credit for Austria's postwar economic recovery. Franz Mathis credits the Marshall Plan for helping to overcome more rapidly "the bottlenecks in goods, raw materials and investment products."[26] Roman Sandgruber concedes that foreign aid programs helped the survival of the population. Between 1945 and 1955, Austria received $1,585,000 in foreign aid (almost a billion through the Marshall Plan). This was six times more in aid than Austria received in 1922 through the League of Nations loan. The "Geneva Loan" had to be paid back; Marshall aid was an American gift.[27] Franz Mathis stresses, like most economic historians do, the "much more positive basic mood" ("*positivere Grundstimmung*") that prevailed in Austria after World War II compared to the post-World War I period. He adds that this fueled both the will to rebuild inside the country and international cooperation.[28] Hans Seidel, too, sees the "collective consciousness of togetherness" ("*kollektives Bewusstsein der Zusammengehörigkeit*") as an important factor fueling economic recovery, next to the social partnership and the anti-revolutionary mood of the population. Seidel leaves no doubt about the crucial role American economic aid programs played in Austria's rehabilitation.[29] Ferdinand Lacina concludes that "Austria was, relatively speaking, one of the principal recipients of American transfers of goods and capital, the best means for economic reconstruction and political stabilization." It was the Marshall Plan that put Austria on track both for a Western-style market economy and democracy.[30]

Authors like former ÖVP leader Josef Taus give much of the credit to the hard-working Austrian people in what he calls the "heroic age" for the post-World War II recovery and adds that "the postwar political leadership was convinced of the viability of the oppressed country, and most Austrians probably as well."[31] In a similar vein, former SPÖ Finance Minister Hannes Androsch credits the "success story" of postwar Austria to the great faith Austrians had in their country at the end of the war and gives little credit to foreign aid programs.[32] Authors like the British historian Robert Knight cryptically see in "the heroic tale of the first decade of economic reconstruction" a "blind spot" in Austrian historical writing.[33] While economic historians provide careful assessments of the balance sheet between wartime Nazi German investments with wartime destruction and postwar bottlenecks overcome by foreign aid, former politicians are more given to mythmaking. All stress the economic viability of post-World War II Austria and agree that Austrians embraced their small state after World War II unlike their skepticism about Austria's viability after World War I. Such confident attitudes also aided the building of a positive national identity.

Nazi Germany heavily invested in Upper Austria during World War II and built outsized new industries (i.e., Hermann Göring Steel Works, Linz Chemical Works, Ranshofen Aluminum Plant, Synthetic Fibers Works Lenzing) next to building massive armaments factories in Upper Austria and Wiener Neustadt. The US Strategic Bombing Survey conducted after the war in Germany found that the bombing war had less of an impact in destroying German industry (the *Ostmark*, of course, was part of the Third Reich) during the war. The bomber generals had promised too much since the Third Reich managed to move much of its industrial production underground in the latter part of the war. Austria may have had twenty-five percent more machine tools available after the war. Due to postwar Soviet removals of factories and machine tools, however, only eighty-two percent of the prewar level (1937) was left. [34] US and international pre-Marshall Plan aid programs helped Austria overcome its economic bottlenecks. US foreign aid funded Austria's notorious trade deficits, and the European

Recovery Program paid for badly needed foodstuffs and raw materials. The counterpart funds generated through ERP aid donations to Austria provided the necessary investment capital to revamp Austria's industrial base.[35]

Postwar Austria ended up with an oversized sector of state-owned industries. More than half of Austrian industry was in the hands of the state. This had to do with the fact that the Western powers handed the "German assets" in their zones to the Austrian government in trusteeship and later allowed the state to take ownership of these industries. Even though no investment capital was available before the Marshall Plan, large-scale planning for the state sector started as early as 1947. Meanwhile, the Soviets seized all "German assets" in their occupation zone. A total of 280 companies (including the large oil industry and the Danube Shipping Company), employing some 50,000 people, were put into the Soviet holding company "USIA." During the first postwar years, the Soviets squeezed up to $50,000,000 of "reparations out of current production" from these USIA properties. Almost fifty-two percent of ERP counterpart investments went to the oversized sector of state industries, thereby financing forty-five percent of the investment needs of the state sector's basic industries. It is a great irony that the capitalist US financed the oversized sector of state industries in Austria. The Socialists, in charge of this state industrial sector, pressured the American Marshall Planners in Vienna and Washington to invest in the state-owned industries (i.e., the iron, steel, and electricity industries), while the conservatives would have liked to fund the private consumer goods industries.[36] In the final years of the Marshall Plan, the Austrian tourism industry started to receive a larger share of counterpart investments. The two to four percent of counterpart investments into tourism amounted to thirty percent of the investments of this industry. Earnings from tourism set the country on a path toward a positive balance of payments by the mid-1950s.[37]

Austria managed to scoop up the third-highest per capita amount of Marshall Plan aid (almost one billion dollars in direct and indirect aid). The Austrian government successfully argued with the American Marshall Planners and its European ERP partners that it was a "special case." With the Soviets occupying Eastern Austria and exploiting the USIA industries, the argument of Austria facing a dire threat of Communist takeover was persuasive during the first half of the Marshall Plan (1948–50) but less so in the final months of the program (1951–52) when the US forced a stiff, anti-inflationary stabilization program on the Austrians while reducing Marshall aid and holding back counterpart releases. Austria's difficult geopolitical location on the edge of the Iron Curtain made the country "particularly vulnerable" to Communist depredations, argued Foreign Minister Karl Gruber regularly with the Marshall Planners. Austria was one of the poorest countries in Europe with a government that faced the stern tutelage of the occupation powers, and still the country opted for the West. The Soviet zone of Austria was the only area in Europe that received ERP aid, but it was only a meagre eighteen percent of total ERP aid to Austria.[38] The "special case" scenario was bitter reality in the late 1940s. In the early 1950s, it became less credible. The myth of the threat of Communist takeover subsided as the occupation continued, and the country recovered economically.

Austria's political elite were well aware of the impact of American aid on Austrian economic viability. In a TV interview in New York, Chancellor Julius Raab stressed how Austria could hardly survive ten years of occupation without American economic aid, a message he regularly repeated in his public speeches. He also said that as a result of the American aid, the Austrian standard of living was higher than before the war.[39] After a 1958 trip to the United States, Chancellor Raab addressed the Austrian people on the radio: "It is very pleasing that the slogan of the unviable Austria ("*lebensunfähiges Österreich*"), which has long been advanced, is now dead and forgotten." He added: "Austria's economic situation, compared to other countries, is considered very favorable by the United States."[40] In a speech before a meeting of the International Press Institute, Chancellor Raab again insisted on Austria's postwar economic viability: "Austria's recovery, in spite of the heavy losses suffered in these years from the ongoing Soviet despoliation ("*Ausplünderung*") of its economy, proves that the country is viable." This economic viability, the chancellor insisted, was part and parcel of the wealth of its rich economic resources, as well as the hardened Austrian self-reliance during challenging times.[41]

Without blaming the Soviets directly, Raab noted that Austria received as much foreign aid through UNRRA and the Marshall Plan as the country lost as a result of the dispossession of the "German assets," the removal of industries, and occupation costs. He concluded with the myth that Austria managed to achieve its reconstruction through her own efforts.[42] Historians have indeed done the math and have concluded that Austria received between 1.5 and 1.8 billion in foreign aid while paying reparations to the Soviets in roughly the same amount.[43] Compare Raab's soaring rhetoric about Austria's post-World War II economic success story with newly elected Chancellor Figl's *Regierungserklärung* (a sort of "state of the union" address to parliament) of December 21, 1945: "We will celebrate Christmas in a few days… It will not be the Christmas this year as we like it. The Christmas trees will be full of sorrows." Figl then asked the Austrian people to all contribute to Austria's democratic renewal.[44] Biographers have constructed the myth that Figl said this on the radio on December 24: "I cannot offer you anything for Christmas. If you have a Christmas tree at all, I cannot give you any candles. No bread, no coal for your stoves, no glass for your windows…We have nothing to give. I can only exhort you to have faith in Austria."[45] The myth of the "legendary radio address Christmas 1945" is stronger than the facts and is repeated by biographers to this day.[46]

The depth of Austria's postwar economic misery can best be gleaned from the weekly discussions of the Austrian cabinet ("*Ministerrat*"). The lack of food and fuel were a constant part of these discussions. Maybe the most daunting challenge for the Austrian government was the constant worry about how to feed the Austrian population. At the beginning of 1948, the goal of the food ministry was to feed the average Austrian 1,800 daily calories—increased to 1,900 daily calories with the onset of Marshall Plan deliveries. The Austrian farmers only managed to contribute 820 calories to this modest goal. The severe rationing of food supplies led the government to pressure Austria's farmers to deliver the required amounts of grains, milk, meats, potatoes, etc. to make up this domestic Austrian portion toward achieving the daily caloric level needed for the population to survive. But many of the farmers did not listen to governmental mandates and preferred to sell on the black market, where they could fetch better prices. One of the most bizarre discussions—plainly showing the high level of desperation in the Figl government—happened over acquiring 40,000 tons of Swiss potatoes. The Swiss would then be compensated for 10,000 tons of potatoes with Austrian iron and wire. The minister of food, Otto Sagmeister, asked Hans Rizzi, the president of the Austrian National Bank, to guarantee 7.5 million in Swiss francs to pay for the rest of the Swiss potatoes. Rizzi refused to issue such a guarantee as the National Bank was out of foreign currency and close to bankruptcy.[47]

Conclusion

Austrian economic reconstruction was achieved by 1954. The occupation ended a year later with the signing of the Austrian State Treaty. The country was now on an economic growth path. By the end of the 1950s, people would speak of the Austrian "economic miracle," for doubts about Austria's "economic viability" were now a thing of the past. Yet instead of the myth of "economic nonviability," new myths were proffered. Chancellor Raab also mentioned that Austrians achieved economic reconstruction all by themselves with their hard work. What Josef Taus later called Austria's "heroic age" referred to the postwar "economic miracle" without mentioning foreign aid as the principal means to allow for Austria's rapid post-World War II economic reconstruction.

Comparing Austria's two postwar eras then, the general mood of the population and their leaders was very different. Austrians faced enormous economic obstacles in both postwar eras. After World War I, Austrians had little confidence in their future, but after World War II, people were more hopeful about the future of their small state in spite of the difficult beginnings. In Sigmund Freud's words, they had gotten used to living with the "torso" of the former Habsburg Empire. Austrians hardly could know that the period of National Socialism left considerable economic assets behind that were not destroyed by Allied bombing. However, Austrians knew in 1945, unlike after World War I, that they did NOT want to be a part of Germany. The World War II experience as part of the Third Reich made Austrians realize that "*Der Anschluss ist tot*" ("The Anschluss was dead"), as the later Vice Chancellor and President Adolf Schärf noted as early as 1943, adding: "*Die Liebe zum Deutschen Reich ist den Österreichern ausgetrieben worden*" ("Austrians have been thoroughly purged of their love of the German Reich").[48] Above all, American economic aid programs were generous gifts and fueled a rapid economic recovery by the mid-1950s. As it turned out, Austria was economically viable and today is one of the most prosperous nations in the world.

President Heinz Fischer summarized it well in a government publication published on the occasion of the "memory year" 2005:

> The Second Republic is a negation of the First Republic, in as much as the mistakes made, enabling the National Socialist takeover, were avoided. In this context, three basic points need to be made: first, there was faith in the "economic viability" of "small" and independent Austria; secondly, the firm will of the political parties, not to be enemies but to be competitors for the general welfare of the nation; thirdly, faith in democracy and the parliamentary system.[49]

Endnotes

1 Maureen Healey, "Am Ende und doch kein Ende," in *Im Epizentrum des Zusammenbruchs: Wien im Ersten Weltkrieg*, ed. Alfred Pfoser and Andreas Weigl (Vienna: Metroverlag 2013), 574.

2 George Prochnik, *The Impossible Exile: Stefan Zweig at the End of the World* (New York: Other Press, 2014), 174.

3 Gerhard Strejcek, "Als amerikanische Hilfe in Österreich eine ganze Generation rettet," *Neue Züricher Zeitung*, Dec. 30, 2019, 5; see also Franz Adlgasser, "The Roots of Communist Containment: American Food Aid in Austria and Hungary after World War I," in: *Austria in the Nineteen Fifties*, Contemporary Austrian Studies 3, ed. Günter Bischof, Anton Pelinka and Rolf Steininger (New Brunewick, NJ: Transaction, 1995), 171-188.

4 Margaret Macmillan, *Paris 1919: Six Months that Changed the World* (New York: Random House, 2001), 244.

5 Miroslav Krleža, *Die Fahnen* (Klagenfurt/Celovec: Wieser Verlag, 2016), 41.

6 Macmillan, *Paris 1919*, 243.

7 Christopher Clark, *Die Schlafwandler: Wie Europa in den Ersten Weltkrieg zog* (Munich: DVA, 2013), 713.

8 Norbert Schausberger, *Der Griff nach Österreich: Der Anschluß* (Vienna: Jugend und Volk, 1978), 83-85.

9 Karl Bachinger, "Umbruch und Desintegration nach dem Ersten Weltkrieg: Österreichs wirtschaftliche und soziale Ausgangssituation in ihren Folgewirkungen auf die Erste Republik" Habilitation thesis, University of Vienna, 1981, 337.

10 Ernst Krenek, *Im Atem der Zeit: Erinnerungen an die Moderne* (Hamburg: Hoffmann und Campe, 1998), 200.

11 Der Economist, "Staatssekretär Dr. Schumpeter über die industrielle Zukunft Deutschösterreichs," *Neue Freie Presse*, May 31, 1919, 10-11, accessed December 26, 2019, http://anno.onb.ac.at/cgi-content/anno?aid=nfp&datum=19190531&seite=10.

12 Bachinger, "Umbruch und Desintegration," 344.

13 Otto Bauer, *Die österreichische Revolution*, in Werkausgabe, vol 2 (Vienna: Europaverlag, 1976), 638 f.

14 Bachinger, "Umbruch und Desintegration," 349.

15 Fritz Weber, *Vor dem großen Krach: Österreichs Banken in der Zwischenkriegszeit am Beispiel der Credit-Anstalt für Handel und Gewerbe* (Vienna: Böhlau, 2016), 8-13.

16 In all fairness it should be added that not every sector of the agriculture benefited from government help. Small farmers on less privileged terrain often saddled heavy debts and ultimately went broke.

17 Nathan Marcus, *Austrian Reconstruction and the Collapse of Global Finance 1921-1931* (Cambridge, MA: Harvard UP, 2018). A more detailed discussion of Zimmerman's and the League's role in Austria during the 1920s will be found in Peter Berger's contribution to this volume.

18 Peter Berger, *Im Schatten der Diktatur* (Vienna: Böhlau 2000), 119.

19 Siegfried Mattl, "Die Finanzdiktatur," in *Austrofaschismus: Politik, Ökonomie, Kultur, 1933-1938*, ed. Emmerich Tálos and Wolfgang Neugebauer (Münster: LIT Verlag, 2014), 202-221.

20 Dieter Stiefel, *Camillo Castiglioni oder Die Metaphysik der Haifische* (Vienna: Böhlau, 2012), 105-106.

21 Mattl, "Die Finanzdiktatur," 208.

22 Günther Haller, "1945 und der Glaube an Österreich," *Die Presse*, Jan. 25, 2020, 26.

23 Günter Bischof values the wartime German investments to be higher than the wartime Allied bombing destruction, see his "Foreign Aid and Austria's Economic Recovery After World War II," in *New Directions in Economic and Security Policy: U.S. – West European Relations in a Period of Crisis and Indecision*, ed. Werner Feld (Boulder: Westview Press, 1984), 79-91.

24 Dieter Stiefel sees continuities from World War II to the postwar period. See his "Fünf Thesen zu den sozioökonomischen Folgen der Ostmark," in *Politik in Östereich*, Studien zu Politik und Verwaltung 10, ed. Wolfgang Mantl (Vienna: Böhlau, 1992), 49-61 (here 49, 61).

25 Hermann Freudenberger and Radomir Luža, "National Socialist Germany and the Austrian Industry, 1938-1945," in *Austria since 1945*, ed. William E. Wright (Minneapolis: Center for Austrian Studies, University of Minnesota, 1982), 96.

26 Franz Mathis, "Die österreichische Wirtschaft: Grundlagen und Entwicklungen," in *Österreich im 20. Jahrhundert*, vol. 2, *Vom Zweiten Weltkrieg zur Gegenwart*, ed. Rolf Steininger and Michael Gehler (Vienna: Böhlau, 1997), 415-453 (here 435).

27 Roman Sandgruber, *Ökonomie und Politik: Österreichische Wirtschaftsgeschichte vom Mittelalter bis zur Gegenwart*, Österreichische Geschichte (Vienna: Ueberreuter, 1995), 451f.

28 Franz Mathis, "Die österreichische Wirtschaft – Grundlagen und Entwicklungen," in *Österreich im 20. Jahrhundert*, vol. 2, *Vom Zweiten Weltkrieg bis zur Gegenwart*, ed. Rolf Steininger and Michael Gehler (Vienna: Böhlau, 1997), 415-453 (here 434f).

29 Hans Seidel, *Österreichs Wirtschaft und Wirtschaftspolitik nach dem Zweiten Weltkrieg* (Vienna: Manz, 2005), 74, 281-342.

30 Ferdinand Lacina, "Wirtschaftspolitischer Spielraum – von der Mangelwirtschaft zur globalen Vernetzung," in *Österreichische Nationalgeschichte nach 1945: Die Spiegel der Erinnerung. Die Sicht von innen*, ed. Robert Kriechbaumer, vol. 1 (Vienna: Böhlau 1998), 507-517 (here 508); for more detail on postwar reconstruction, see also Günter Bischof and Hand Petschar, *The Marshall Plan – Since 1947: Saving Europe, Rebuilding Austria* (Vienna: Brandstätter, 2017).

31 Josef Taus, "Österreich über alles, wann es nur will," in: *Österreichische Nationalgeschichte nach 1945*, ed. Kriechbaumer, I, 519-558 (here 520-523).

32 Hannes Androsch, *Wirtschaft und Gesellschaft: Österreich 1945-2005* (Österreich – Zweite Republik: Befund, Krititik, Perspective, vol. 2) (Innsbruck: StudienVerlag, 2005), 34-37.

33 "Die freiheitliche Historikerkommission ist ein Witz," Interview with Robert Knight, *Der Standard*, May 4/5, 2019, 15.

34 Bischof, "Foreign Aid and Austria's Economic Recovery," 81f; Dieter Stiefel, *Verstaatlichung und Privatisierung in Österreich: Illusion und Wirklichkeit* (Vienna: Böhlau, 2011), 81.

35 Bischof/Petschar, *The Marshall Plan – Since 1947*.

36 Stiefel, *Verstaatlichung und Privatisierung in Österreich*, 81-92 (here 84, 86); also see the essays by Kurt Tweraser on the steel industry and Georg Riegele on the electricity industry, in *The Marshall Plan in Austria*, Contemporary Austrian Studies 8 (New Brunswick: Transaction, 2000), 290-356.

37 Günter Bischof, "'Conquering the Foreigner': The Marshall Plan and the Revival of Postwar Austrian Tourism," in *The Marshall Plan in Austria*, ed. Bischof, Pelinka and Stiefel, 357-401.

38 Günter Bischof, "Der Marshall Plan in Österreich: War Österreich ein 'Special Case' im Europäischen Wiederaufbau Programm?" in *Festschrift in memoriam Karl W. Hardach*, ed. Stefan Karner (Graz: Leykam, 2016), 165-176; Seidel, *Österreichs Wirtschaft und*

Wirtschaftspolitik, 492-495; Michael Gehler, *Österreichs Aussenpolitik der Zweiten Republik: Von der alliierten Besatzung bis zum Europa des 21. Jahrhunderts*, vol. 1 (Innsbruck: Studien Verlag, 2005), 55f.

39 Interview transcript with Chancellor Raab, [1952], Folder R1/e/12, Julius Raab-Gedenkverein, Archiv des Karl v. Vogelsang Instituts, Vienna. I thank Johannes Schönherr, the archivist of the Vogelsang Institute for directing me through the Raab Papers there.

40 Radio Address [after trip to the USA], June 8, 1958, Folder Z2/9/12, Box 2, Raab Reden, Vogelsang Archives.

41 Presse clipping "Österreichs Lebenswille," *Wiener Kurier*, May 13, 1954, Folder Z/g/48, Raab Papers, Vogelsang Archives.

42 Raab "Wir fühlen uns durchaus wohl in unserem Kleinstaat," *Österreichische Zeitung*, May 12, 1954, Folder Z/g/49, Raab Papers, Vogelsang Archives.

43 Günter Bischof first tried such an accounting by arguing that Austria paid ca. 1,3 billion in reparations to the Soviet Union (1945-1964), while receiving ca 1,4 billion in American financial aid, see *Austria in the First Cold War, 1945-55: The Leverage of the Weak* (Houndmills-New York: Macmillan-St. Martin's Press, 1999), 87, 102; Hans Seidel argues that Austria paid ca. 1,8 billion in reparations and received ca. 1,9 billion in foreign aid, see Österreichs Wirtschaft und Wirtschaftspolitik, 467.

44 The myth was later constructed that Figl's government declaration of December 21 had been his Christmas radio address on December 24, 1945, of which no recording exists and no notice can be found in in the newspapers, see Robert Sedlaczek, "Leopold Figl's Echte Weihnachtsbotschaft," *Wiener Zeitung*, Dec. 21, 2005, https://www.wienerzeitung.at/meinung/glossen/290534_Leopold-Figls-echte-Weihnachtsbotschaft.html, accessed Jan. 3, 2020.

45 Cited in Susanne Seltreich, *Leopold Figl: Austrian Patriot and Statesman*, ed. Richie McEwen (Vienna: Erwin Metten, n.d. [ca 1955]), 92.

46 Peter Pelinka, *Österreichs Kanzler: Von Leopold Figl bis Wolfgang Schüssel* (Vienna: Ueberreuter, 2000), 27f.

47 See my review essay of 4 volumes of *Ministerratsprotokolle: Die Protokolle des Ministerrates der Zweiten Republik der Republik Österreich: Kabinett Leopold Figl I.*, ed. Gertrude Enderle-Burcel, Rudolf Jeřábek, Wolfgang Mueller, Vol. 7-10 (Vienna: Verlag der Österreichischen Akademie der Wissenschaften, 2016 –2017), in *Environmental History of Austria*, Contemporary Austrian Studies 27, ed. Marc Landry and Patrick Kupper (New Orleans/Innsbruck: UNO Press/innsbruck university press, 2018), 302-313

48 Adolf Schärf, *Österreichs Erneuerung 1945-1955: Das erste Jahrzehnt der Zweiten Republik* (5th ed., Vienna: Verlag der Wiener Volksbuchhandlung, 1955), 20.

49 Heinz Fischer, "Dank und Verantwortung – 50 Jahre Staatsvertrag," in *Österreich 2005: Das Lesebuch zum Jubiläumsjahr*, ed. Bundeskanzleramt Österreich (St. Pölten: Residenz Verlag, 2004), 12

Austria, *Insel der Seligen*: Fortunate Isle?

Konrad Paul Liessmann

1. Myths of Memory

The collective memory of any society contains firmly anchored turns and phrases that reappear time and again for all sorts of occasions. One such topos in the history of the Austrian Second Republic has been the *Insel der Seligen*, or the Isle of the Blessed. It is rarely stated that this topos is closely connected to the great burden of Austrofascism, the Third Reich, and World War II, having never ceased to call into question Austria's role: Hitler's first victim? Or co-perpetrator in the horrors of Nazism? Narratives such as the dichotomy of victims and perpetrators keep reappearing. Firmly ensconced as they are in the political and cultural memory, they can be revived and instrumentalized time and again, and by a range of discourses. There are good reasons to resort to legends and myths in this context in order to structure and highlight aspects of public (and sometimes also academic) discourses.

A phrase that serves remembrance can be considered mythological if it goes beyond the historical-academic and the mundane communicative discourses, as well as being to some degree collectively binding while its authors gradually sink into anonymity. Places of memory can therefore also be described as places where political myths solidify in the course of their construction. What does political mythologization mean exactly, however? It is obvious that the primary characteristic of myths applies to political mythology as well; they have a narrative. Hans Blumenberg, in his *Work on Myth,* postulated that myths root in an elementary condition of human existence, the need to tell stories: "Stories are told in order to kill something. In the most harmless, but hardly most irrelevant, cases, that is time. Otherwise and more seriously: fear."[1] The telling of myths provides information about the structure of the world in a pre-rational, as well as a proto-rational, sense. It fights what Blumenberg called the "absolutism of reality," for it is reassuring and it explains why things are as they are. The perspective of memory is structurally inherent to myth. Myths begin with "In the beginning" or, like fairy tales, "Once upon a time." Myths are therefore stories with "an extremely stable narrative core and equally distinctive marginal variability."[2] Without unduly stretching the notion of myth in the context of memory culture and its rhetorics, we may easily assume that their function is indeed to kill time, fear, and sometimes also the ghosts of the past and that the narrative element in these kinds of tales is exceedingly tenacious. Although their forms may vary, the same stories are being told again and again, each time reproducing their set phrases in the process.

Claudio Magris, the Triestine scholar of German language and literature, first published his famous paper, *The Hapsburg Myth in Modern Austrian Literature*, in 1963. In it, he defined myth as the "way in which a culture endeavors to reduce the plurality of realities to a unity, the chaos of the world into an order, the fragmentary coincidences of existence to its essence, the historical and political juxtapositions to a harmony that can reconcile if not abrogate."[3] Without any ill will, we can nowadays note that this definition itself was already infected by the spirit of the Habsburg myth. Magris did recognize, after all, that the affirmative, as well as the critical references to the Habsburg Empire, were the defining characteristics of Austrian literature in the first half of the twentieth century. This, however, meant that this body of literature and the collective consciousness it underpinned were therefore guided by a negative myth: the downfall of the Danubian Monarchy, the catastrophe, and the great loss that was the root of this myth and that gave the literary works their distinctive melancholia. When it came to the rebirth of Austria after World War II, this myth had long become unsuitable as a collective frame of reference. The writer Robert Menasse has postulated that it was replaced by the "myth of social partnership."[4] Without addressing the applicability of this claim in detail, it is certainly true that there are indications that "social partnership," at least when understood as a way of life and a political culture, was probably more significant for the Austrian sense of self during the time of the Second Republic than any other apparent form of collective awareness, and its contribution to the notion of Austria as an "Isle of the Blessed" was considerable.

The notion of myth is by now largely considered concordant with a search for or commemoration of origin and identity stories in the context of political reflection. Myths tell a story to give meaning to an event, a place, or a situation. They thereby furnish political concepts with narrative plausibility: "The origins as told by political myths are more than mere beginnings of time, within them lies the promise of a meaning that connects the past with the present in such a way that the past points beyond the present and into the future."[5] Although such myths already occurred in prescientific cultures (take the founding legend of the city of Rome, for example), they took on a particular, paramount significance in the context of the modern formation of nations since the nineteenth century. However, it is wrong to assume that myth-making is an irrational political strategy employed by the political Right and that the enlightened Left is immune to such practices: "Political myths [cannot] generally be considered to belong either to the Left or to the Right."[6]

Modern nations needed to invent themselves as communities of birth and destiny in the first place and have therefore, to this day, been particularly dependent on the myths they tell of themselves. For Second Republic Austria, this process first and foremost hinged on a sense of loss. "After 1945, the Austrians were looking for a universally accepted Austria myth."[7] Where such "myths" are supposed to take on a more precise form, however, Austria displays a strange breadth that permits landscapes, "sacred sites," cities, buildings, memorials, coats of arms, anthems, holidays, as well as ski stars, to be entered into its "store of symbols" under the heading of "myths, images, stereotypes."[8] What the Second Republic appears to be quite significantly lacking, by contrast, is the specific aspect of a political myth, the founding legend of a state or nation: "The Austrians cannot resort to a successful revolution or military victories in the recent past, nor to any successful independence or liberation movement."[9] The Habsburg myth of Old Austria serves the tourism industry, at best, and elements of this myth are still found in the constructs of a modern Austrian cultural identity, at least.

It seems tempting to speak of the Second Republic's "replacement myths" with regard to the stories and places that act as solidifiers of collective memory and thereby of a collective sense of identity. The myth of the *Geist der Lagerstrasse*, the "Spirit of the Camps," is instrumentalized for this role and a controversial point of discussion to this day. It is by now openly admitted that this claim—namely that the consensus democracy established after 1945 had been born in the Nazi concentration camps, where the former Austrian Civil War opponents had been imprisoned together—is a mere legend.[10] Closely connected to this rendering of shared imprisonment as the point of germination for a new Austria is the even more controversial myth of victimhood, which anchors the founding ideology of the Second Republic on (at least morally) shaky ground. This myth takes the form of either the claim that Austria had suffered under Nazi rule or the contention that this very claim is the ultimate sham of Austrian existence (the *Lebenslüge*).

Myth is used here, on the one hand, in its original meaning: a collective, narratively structured turn that enables communication among human groups about central aspects of the foundation of their community. We would like to add to this, on the other hand, the thesis that such political myths, meaning narratives that may well have a historical core, work best when they can be attached to their particular wider culture's applicable store of great myths. In this case, this refers to the need to consider the political topoi at play and how far the attendant construction of narratives can be linked into ancient, old European, and Christian mythology.

2. The "Victim Myth" and the Lebenslüge

The "victim thesis," which developed into the unofficial state doctrine after 1945, was based on a somewhat one-sided interpretation offered in the 1943 Moscow Declaration to claim that Austria had been the first victim of Nazi Germany's violent expansion policy. This notion lay at the very heart of the young republic's idea of itself, yet the very first critical reflection revealed it as mythical. After all, it tells a story that never happened as such: that Austria and its inhabitants had been innocent victims of foreign tyrants. From a viewpoint of greater moral accuracy, this myth was subsequently interpreted as the quintessential Austrian *Lebenslüge*. The victimhood thesis was decoded and laid bare as a strategy of cynical self-deception that permitted not only a denial of reality but also, as it is claimed, the evasion of responsibility.[11] This transformation therefore also indicates an enduring paradigm shift in the political discourse. Its primary goal is no longer the reconstruction of events, nor their narrative implementation into the general consciousness, but, rather, their moral evaluation. The discourse thereby comes to follow a very particular mythological narrative that essentially amounts to a new historical interpretation in itself: guilt and atonement.

What this discourse uncovers is a rarely analyzed side effect of the mythologization of places of memory: the "battle of memories."[12] Historical documents do not speak for themselves. They need "occupation," almost literally, by narratives. For a long time, the choice of narrative about March 1938 defined which Austria one considered proper to be acknowledged: Had a state been violently occupied, or did a people joyously throw itself into the arms of a *Führer*?[13] The *Lebenslüge* thereby grew into the negative myth of the Second Republic, for it sketched out an aspect of this country's history that betrayed it to be "*Infelix Austria*," politically and morally.[14] It has been suggested that guilt-ridden Austrians would have had to oppose the victimhood thesis as a short-term political strategy of the Allies.[15] Conversely, the politically enlightened Austria for a long time defined itself by the struggle against this *Lebenslüge*, the demand to face up to the country's past, which was to be uncovered in exhibitions, educational projects, and public debates. Last but not least, the enlightened "Other Austria," which saw itself in a long line of anti-fascist continuity, hinged on its role in critically unmasking the victimhood myth.[16]

We must ask, however, how far the construct of this ultimate sham fits into another, older "black legend" within the mythological narrative. This older tale had always framed Austria as a "breeding site of intolerance and indolence, submission and stupidity."[17] Is the *Lebenslüge* therefore a continuation of an already historical mythologizing interpretative narrative? This black legend has a lighter, albeit no less complicated, counter-piece in the Second Republic. This other tale has for a long time enjoyed rather great success and popularity as a central trope of remembrance and self-definition: the Isle of the Blessed. This topos has become proverbial and no longer refers to an actual space of memory located in Austria but simply mythologizes the entire country itself.[18] This myth includes the notion that the dark chapters of the past are to be closed, and Austria, in its own special way, has found not only its identity but also its place in the world as a small but successful state. The topos of the Fortunate Isle casts light where the shadows of 1934-45 had engulfed Austria while at the same time taking such an exaggerated form that it has always invited its own more or less malicious denial. It therefore certainly warrants taking a closer look at this rather unusual metaphor for a country.

3. Isle of the Blessed

Pope Paul VI used the phrase of the Isle of the Blessed—or, to be exact, the *isola felice*, the Fortunate Isle[19]—for Austria during Austrian President Franz Jonas's visit to Rome in November 1971. At first glance, it is astonishing that this utterance could become such a typifying topos for the country. The obvious thing would have been to consider this expression a matter of diplomatic manners and leave it at that. It coincided, however, with reforms and a resultant upturn in the country under Federal Chancellor Bruno Kreisky, together with an active policy of neutrality. The Isle of the Blessed therefore became synonymous with a sociopolitical success story. Ever since Hellmut Andics chose *Die Insel der Seligen* for the title of the last volume of his popular history of Austria,[20] the phrase has been a familiar trope of Austrian self-description. It is not necessarily applied affirmatively, though. The social and political changes that have affected Austria in the post-Kreisky era (ranging from the Waldheim affair via the fall of the Iron Curtain to EU accession and the effects of globalization) frequently go hand in hand with maliciously triumphal assertions that Austria is no longer a Fortunate Isle, or indeed had never been one. Whosoever feels the need to point out that Austria is as exposed to the storms of international competition, to terrorism, and to global political developments as all other countries are will struggle not to add that Austria is no longer an Isle of the Blessed.

Austrian Chancellor Wolfgang Schüssel, for example, stressed this point in his speech for the inauguration of the official *Gedankenjahr 2005* commemorations on January 14, 2005: "Austria was not and has never been a Fortunate Isle. All political upheavals on this continent have reached us, too, we have even almost been at their epicenter."[21] That Austria is not an Isle of the Blessed is a phrase befitting almost all spheres of policy and administration. In 2011, a parliamentary inquiry into forced prostitution was titled "Austria is not a Fortunate Isle."[22] Some years later, the Austrian association of journalists noted that Austria was no longer a Fortunate Isle with regard to press freedom.[23] In 2017, the incumbent Minister of the Interior responded to the arrest of a terrorism suspect by declaring that "Austria is no longer an Isle of the Blessed."[24]

The denial of the Fortunate Isle makes this trope's trans-contextual significance in Austrian public discourse apparent. The somewhat careless deployment of this phrase also demonstrates what happens when topoi that used to hold great narrative power gradually settle into public consciousness: they are reduced almost entirely to the role of set pieces in a rhetoric of criticism and political interests. The achievements of the social and welfare state are more easily undermined when they are accused of being tied to a naïve "politics of entitlement" purportedly premised on an "Island of the Blessed" mentality. Politicians can tap into looming threats and grievances by warning the population not to foolishly believe that we are living on an Isle of the Blessed. Finally, the denial of the trope—Austria is no longer a Fortunate *Isle*—indicates that membership in the European Union and a globalized society are preventing Austria's withdrawal to insularity. The implicit claim here is that the Isle of the Blessed had always also been somewhat isolated and provincial.

We still encounter the phrase in its original form too. In December 2018, Federal Chancellor Sebastian Kurz was content to note on the first anniversary of the ÖVP-FPÖ coalition (which was to implode only a few months later) that the actions of this government had made Austria an Isle of the Blessed while at the same time issuing a warning that this status could not be taken for granted.[25] Such proclamations, which are quickly undermined by reality, are rare, however. Remarkably, the Fortunate Isle topos survives largely in its denial. A Catholic church grandee's diplomatic manners have become a self-description that is denied by its very employment. This, one might say, makes out the logical structure of this Austrian myth: it exists only as an ambivalent figure, its affirmation must be followed by its denial, and often the mere denial suffices to implicate the claim regardless of whether it has been made or not. To stress that Austria is no longer an Isle of the Blessed implies that there are people who are still mistakenly harboring that belief. The Isle of the Blessed, and in particular its denial, are doggedly holding on to their place in public discourse; the metaphor must have hit a resonant note in Austrian sensitivities. Any phrase that warrants recurrent denials over the course of decades must have an original hold that feeds the rhetorical plausibility of its very denial.

Indeed, it appears that this small country's success story after World War II, and especially after 1955, is perfectly expressed by this phrase. Austria's thriving development was, after all, largely based on the country's position between the large military blocs of the postwar era as expressed in international law by Austria's obligation to perpetual neutrality. Its position between East and West granted Austria a peripheral existence from where it only had to take marginal note of the upheavals of the Cold War or indeed of the social changes taking hold of the postwar societies. Of course, Austria was never actually positioned outside of history. The 1956 Hungarian uprising, as well as the Prague Spring of 1968, were clear reminders of what being bordered by the Iron Curtain also meant. It is nevertheless often noted that everything (from economic crises to student movements, from left-wing terrorism to Islamic parallel societies) reached Austria later and in a diluted form. This has reinforced the impression that the country had been isolated and had greatly profited from such isolation. The post-1945 Austrian self-image included the notion that in Austria the bad was not as bad but also that success meant less than elsewhere. This insular perspective helps explain why so many debates in Austria centered on the question as to whether the country had finally managed to catch up with modernity, the West, civil society, and globalization. Incidentally, this attitude can also be interpreted as a representation of the final, weakened, and by now harmless form of an "annexation or exclusion trauma"[26] that had trailed Austrian sensitivities during the era of the First Republic. To those who consider themselves progressive, it is an essential part of their image of Austria that somewhere in the world there is something to latch onto in order to avoid the limited nature of Austrianness.

4. Fortunate Isles: History of a Phrase

It is unlikely that the topos of the Fortunate Isle would have enjoyed such a long-lasting effect in its various versions and degrees of intensity if this figure of speech had not already long been mythologically charged. Even ancient utopian thought used the trope of a Fortunate Island to represent a state of happiness that is characterized by peace and solitude.[27] In Homer's *Odyssey*, the Fortunate Isles are inhabited by the Phaeacians, central characters to the Austrian sense of self since the days of Enea Silvio Piccolomini, the later Pope Pius II.[28] In contrast to his successor, this pope also associated the Fortunate Isles with a morally rather doubtful lust for life; it was hardly a commendation when he endowed Austria with this status. It was eventually probably Friedrich Nicolai who "irrevocably" established this "Phaeacian stereotype" into the "German spiritual landscape": "all that which luxury and the luxurious can bring forth in order to weaken human might is equally present in Vienna, and there even more so than in Paris and London."[29] Even Anton Wildgans referred to this stereotype in his legendary RAVAG speech for the New Year of 1930 (his *Rede über Österreich),* distancing himself from it but still intent on finding its positive side. While he rejected the notion that Austrians were like the Phaeacians in being amicable but enamored with luxury and a playful lifestyle, Wildgans did affirm the analogy "in *this* sense, that our country, blessed with all God's miracles of beauty and inhabited by a friendly people, an island of song that emanates the noble cheer and brave emotion of human hearts, let us Austrians be Phaeacians in *this* sense, and let us stay that way."[30] With these words, Wildgans conjured up a First Republic ideology of Austria that already aimed at salvaging the notion of Austria as a cultural nation from the ruins of the Habsburg Empire. This idea was already toying with the notion of the "isle," which was to rise from the storms and breakwaters of nationalism by dint of its specific artistic sophistication.

The seeds of this image of the Isle of the Blessed with its mythical undertones were therefore planted during the First Republic, and the metaphor grew beyond mere popularity during the era of the Second Republic. It can be considered the true answer to the annexation/exclusion trauma. Apparently, there was only one alternative to melding into the greater German nation: retreat into an insular existence for a Phaeacian life rather than exile. The Phaeacians, driven as they were to fulfill their primary desires without conflict, were still fit to embody the paradigmatic image of Austrian *savoir vivre* in the Great Millennial Exhibition of 1996 and, in a somewhat more diluted form, at the World Expo in 2000. This constellation also lies at the root of the country's self-ascription as a "small country"—its size having always served as proof of its essential harmlessness.

The Isles of the Blessed are moreover a recurrent theme in German literature. As a set phrase, they usually denote a condition of naive and heathen *savoir vivre* rather than the Christian state of mercy that its later application by the pope might have implied. Thus, Goethe noted after he had visited the public gardens of Palermo, the "most wonderful place in the world": "But these wonderful gardens have made a deep and lasting impression on my mind. The black waves on the northern horizon, as they broke on the irregular points of the bay,— and even the smell of the sea,— all seemed to recall to my imagination, as well as to my memory, the happy island of the Phaeacians. I hastened to purchase a 'Homer,' and began to read this book with the highest delight."[31] Even quite without the aid of Homer, the notion of the Fortunate Isle as a well-tended gem of nature contributed to the consistent application of the phrase in Austria. This country's mythological notions of itself certainly include the idea of its intact state of nature being surrounded by territories that destroy the environment like a raging sea. That Austria is in fact by now lagging behind others in its ecological strategies and climate policies quickly puts paid to this interpretation. If nothing else, the tourism industry certainly needs to invest quite heavily in retaining the beautified image of the natural gem.

The Isles of the Blessed have yet an even greater scope of meaning. The Happy Isles, to Friedrich Nietzsche's titular character in *Thus Spoke Zarathustra*, for example, are those imaginary spaces where man can liberate himself from an external dictate or, theologically speaking, from the dictate and presence of God. The chapter "In the Happy Isles" in *Thus Spoke Zarathustra* contains a statement that is central not exclusively to Nietzsche's thinking: "If there were gods, how could I endure it to be no God! *Therefore* there are no Gods."[32] The philosopher Günther Anders, who lived in Austria after the Second World War, considered this Nietzschean statement an expression of the basic sensitivities of modern humanity: humankind, however proud and desperate, is willing to face its own contingency and hold up its own designs of the world and humans themselves against the religions' notions of gods.[33] Nietzsche's Happy Isles are therefore places of human self-assertion and self-creation. They are the expression of an effort that cannot, however, be conceived and tackled as a project fit for general consent; it requires the insular situation of exposure and solitude. The metaphor of the Isle of the Blessed may contain a grain of this notion: so little that it is hardly there yet still tempting enough. We can be quite certain, however, that the pope who imbued Austria with the status of Fortunate Isle was not thinking of Nietzsche at the time.

5. Blessed Neutrality, Blessed Social Partnership

The image of the Fortunate Isles had previously been placed in a different paradigmatic context by Friedrich Hölderlin: "What's the shipwreck of the world to me, I know of nothing but my blissful isle."[34] Here, the isle signifies apartness. This sense of disinterest in the happenings of the world fits well with the constellation neutral Austria liked to see itself in after 1955. Hans Blumenberg interpreted the image of the "shipwreck with spectator" as a metaphor for existence, which implies not least an aesthetic relationship to the world and its tragedies.[35] In response to the traumas of having been the perpetrators during the First and Second World Wars, Austria doubtlessly styled this aesthetic position of the onlooker into an attitude that fed its very identity. This is still apparent in soapbox sermons that appeal to the "cultural nation" as much as those on "neutrality." The political tale of the Fortunate Isles chimes not so much with Hyperion's inebriated and politically utopian Greek cravings as with an attitude that contentedly believes itself entitled to bypass the "shipwrecks of the world." Austria's situation in postwar-divided Europe had indeed been that of an onlooker who was able to watch, from a more or less sedate distance, the shipwrecks of the world, or at least some dangerous collisions. In spite of the array of rhetorical turns of speech on active neutrality, there is a kernel of truth to the cynical definition that neutrality means looking on.[36] Neutrality continues to be invoked even decades after Austria has joined the EU, most notably so on October 26 of each year, the national holiday in commemoration of the parliamentary act committing the country to perpetual neutrality in 1955. This in itself highlights not only the way this trope serves to provide a deep sense of safety among the public, but it's also a final bid for life by an otherwise questioned Fortunate Isle.

The Isle of the Blessed largely persists by way of its critical and denunciating negation. This tenacity may subconsciously be related to the continuity of this very particular Austrian myth. Somewhat blasphemously, it may be said that the papal phrase of Austria as the Isle of the Blessed has evolved into an essentially secularized modern continuation of the feudal *Felix Austria*. While others may have armed themselves to the teeth with a nuclear arsenal during the Cold War, you, happy Austria, have kept your role as isle and bridge between warring worlds. Neutrality was able to become so very important to many Austrians, not least due to the experience that abstinence and noninvolvement can be a recipe for security and stability. Romantic hindsight implies that Austria acquired something of a position of diplomatic status in the world during the Kreisky era due to this stance, fueling that particular dimension of the Fortunate Isles topos. In retrospect, there is a somewhat idyllic aspect to the time when the gentlemen of the world, nuclear weapons galore at their backs, enjoyed their occasional meetings in Vienna or Salzburg. Obviously, a nuclear conflict on European ground would hardly have spared Austria. Yet there is apparently a bliss, even in retrospect, to not formally having belonged to either side—to the likelihood of being trapped between the all-engulfing flames. As Austrian foreign policy has become ever more insignificant since the Iron Curtain fell and Austria joined the EU, the country's prior role as something of a turntable of international diplomacy and major power espionage may indeed appear like a time when Austria's imagined size was far greater than reality would have it. This part of Second Republic history is also an aspect of normality that has recently often been addressed. Austria is a wealthy and economically strong state with little geopolitical significance; it needs to find itself again within the borders of the European Union.

Social and economic policy are also writ large in the notion of the Fortunate Isle topos, especially so for Austria. The Isles of the Blessed were also the place that knew no class wars, no strikes, no blockades, and no social unrest, that almost wholly passed by the social conflicts that were commonplace in Italy, France, Great Britain, as well as western Germany during the 1960s and 1970s. The Fortunate Isles are therefore frequently associated with social partnership,[37] an expression of the social balance of interests that was to protect the country from tensions. The phrase continues to spin the yarn of blessed arrangements made behind closed doors with practiced hands-on pragmatism, which some representatives of industrialists and trade unions still nostalgically hark back to. Former class enemies became social partners. There are downsides, too, to this model of a balance of interests, which cast a shadow on the political state of the Fortunate Isle. While acting as a secondary government, the social partnership model contributed its success considerably to the rather stunted development of parliamentarianism in Austria. Even left-wing intellectuals have veritably criticized the social partnership model for this effect.[38] Opposing views were not debated but settled without serious public involvement. This went well with the ideology of a country that had made consent its central motto. "Consensual democracy" is a normative term ensconced in the Austrian political vocabulary. It is a questionable notion in itself and highlights the degree to which the topos of the Isle of the Blessed has still not lost its significance in political discourse. The notion that conflicts ought to be resolved at speed if not prevented outright is probably one of the most effective turns of memory of the Second Republic. The *Lagerstrasse* myth is still effective in the ritual incantations of common ground even where the reality of opposing interests has long been begging to differ.

In European legend, the Fortunate Isles were originally utopian locations that presented other models of life. From Plato's myth of Atlantis to Thomas More's *Utopia*, interestingly, all of these countermodels had to be isles. One aspect of this approach has possibly not attracted sufficient attention: that the striving to be untouched by the doom of the world and that some form of isolation and separation is a necessary condition for a happier state. Accordingly, Wilhelm Heinse, a late writer of the German *Sturm und Drang* movement, penned a novel in 1787 in which the title-giving hero, Ardinghello, eventually reaches a utopia that is a Blessed Isle. His text is filled to the brim with learnedness and was soon critiqued for its erotic phantasms. Indeed, the author associated insular happiness with hedonistic-sexual liberation of a kind that in Catholic, baroque Austria was only attainable with moral duplicity, if that. Remarkably, the Fortunate Isles continue to leave their tracks in contemporary Austrian literature. The phrase serves as the critical backdrop to the tale of a European family's turbulent history in Austrian author Vea Kaiser's novel *Makarionissi oder Die Insel der Seligen*.[39]

The era of globalization has put paid to notions of utopias that arise out of any kind of isolation. Attempts to invoke such ideas go against the zeitgeist and often follow debatable reasons; their critics will never tire of pointing out that there are no Fortunate Isles to live on anymore these days.[40] The Austrian myth of the Fortunate Isle was normally devoid of utopian aspects. It was not a promise for the future but a status that had always been considered under threat or redundant. Whether in affirmation or criticism, the phrase has always addressed the present or looked at the past with either rose-tinted glasses or malicious intent. The only future-oriented aspect of the topos is the notion of the Fortunate Isles' perennial destruction. This may well be typical for Austrian intellectuality as a self-designed juxtaposition to provincial Phaeatian existence. EU integration has allegedly long put an end to the small country's insular glory, and Austria has a new, defiant, and at times infantile and proud guiding motto: Austria is no Isle of the Blessed. This, especially the relishing denial, is in itself a continuation of the topos that gives away the Isle of the Blessed as a lost location of virulent longing and therefore an ambivalent, tragicomic Austrian myth.

Endnotes

1 Hans Blumenberg, *Arbeit am Mythos* (Frankfurt/Main: Suhrkamp, 1979), 40.

2 Ibid.

3 Claudio Magris, *Der habsburgische Mythos in der modernen österreichischen Literatur*, new ed. (Vienna: Zsolnay, 2000), 10.

4 Robert Menasse, *Die sozialpartnerschaftliche Ästhetik: Essay zum österreichischen Geist*, new ed. (Vienna: Sonderzahl, 1996).

5 Herfried Münkler, "Politische Mythen und nationale Identität," in *Mythen der Deutschen*, ed. Wolfgang Frindte and Harald Pätzold (Opladen: Leske+Budrich, 1994), 21.

6 Ibid., 26.

7 Ernst Bruckmüller, "Das Konzept der Ausstellung," in *Menschen, Mythen, Meilensteine: ostarrîchi/österreich 996 – 1996*, ed. Ernst Bruckmüller and Peter Urbanitsch (Horn: Berger, 1996), 2.

8 Ernst Bruckmüller, *Nation Österreich: Kulturelles Bewußtsein und gesellschaftlich-politische Prozesse* (Vienna: Böhlau, 1996), 87ff.

9 Ibid., 111.

10 Werner Mück, *Österreich: Das war unser Jahrhundert* (Vienna: Kremayr&Scheriau, 1999), 62.

11 "Opfermythos," in *Inszenierungen: Stichwörter zu Österreich*, ed. Susanne Breuss, Karin Liebhart, and Andreas Pribersky (Vienna: Sonderzahl, 1995), 238ff.

12 Ernst Hanisch, "Wien, Heldenplatz," in *Deutsche Erinnerungsorte I*, ed. Etienne François and Hagen Schulze (Munich: Beck, 2001), 118.

13 Cf. the dispute between Felix Butschek and Gerhard Botz in *Europäische Rundschau: Vierteljahreszeitschrift für Politik, Wirtschaft und Zeitgeschichte*, 1/1996: 17, 29.

14 Gerhard Botz, "'Infelix Austria': Lebenslüge und nationale Identität in Österreich heute," in *Das Jüdische Echo: Zeitschrift für Kultur und Politik*, 1/1990: 116-120.

15 Thomas Albrich: "'Es gibt keine jüdische Frage': Zur Aufrechterhaltung des österreichischen Opfermythos," in *"Heiß umfehdet, wild umstritten...": Geschichtsmythen in Rot-Weiß-Rot*, ed. Werner Koroschitz and Lisa Rettl (Klagenfurt: Drava, 2005), 51.

16 "Anderes Österreich," in *Inszenierungen*, ed. Breuss, Liebhart, Pribersky, 55ff.

17 Bruckmüller, *Nation Österreich*, 132f.

18 *Insel der Seligen* earned an entry in the critical *Stichwörter zu Österreich*, but no commentary. However, the authors make a number of references that indicate their view of the shaky interpretative range of this metaphor (*Inszenierungen*, ed. Breuss, Liebhart, Pribersky, 153).

19 Bruckmüller, *Nation Österreich*, 125.

20 Hellmut Andics, *Die Insel der Seligen. Österreich von 1943 bis 1975* (Vienna-Zurich: Molden, 1976).

21 http://www.oesterreich2005.at, accessed Aug. 13, 2005.

22 https://www.parlament.gv.at/PAKT/VHG/XXIV/AB/AB_09803/index.shtml, accessed Nov. 20, 2015.

23 "Pressefreiheit: Österreich keine 'Insel der Seligen'," *Der Standard* (May 2, 2016), accessed Nov. 20, 2019, https://www.derstandard.at/story/2000036168118/pressefreiheit-oesterreich-keine-insel-der-seligen.

24 https://www.krone.at/549926, accessed Nov. 20, 2019.

25 https://www.kleinezeitung.at/politik/innenpolitik/5540903/1-Jahr-TuerkisBlau_Kanzler-Kurz_Oesterreich-ist-eine-Insel-der, accessed Nov. 20, 2019.

26 Rudolf Burger, "Austromanie oder der antifaschistische Karneval," *Merkur* 613/2000: 388.

27 Reinhold Bichler, *Von der Insel der Seligen zu Platons Staat* (Vienna: Böhlau, 1995).

28 Peter Melichar, "Phäakisch – Intellektuell: Zum Verhältnis von sinnlichem Genuß und Kopfarbeit," in *Menschen, Mythen, Meilensteine*, ed. Bruckmüller and Urbanitsch, 545ff.

29 Bruckmüller, *Nation Österreich*, 119.

30 Anton Wildgans, "Rede über Österreich," in *Anton Wildgans: Ein Lesebuch*, ed. Franz Hadriga and Eva Maria Schwalb (Vienna: Hölder-Pichler-Tempsky, 1994) 108f.

31 Johann Wolfgang von Goethe, *Italienische Reise*. Hamburger Ausgabe, vol. 11 (Munich: Beck 1978), 240f. (English translation by Alexander James William Morrison).

32 Friedrich Nietzsche, "Also sprach Zarathustra," in *Sämtliche Werke: Kritische Studienausgabe (KSA)* (Munich: dtv, 1980), 4:110 (English translation by Thomas Common).

33 Günther Anders, *Die Weltfremdheit des Menschen: Schriften zur philosophischen Anthropologie* (Munich: Beck, 2019), 64.

34 Friedrich Hölderlin, *Hyperion*, in *Sämtliche Werke und Briefe* (Vienna and Munich: Hanser, 1992), 1:691 (English translation by Howard Gaskill).

35 Hans Blumenberg, *Schiffbruch mit Zuschauer: Paradigma einer Daseinsmetapher* (Frankfurt/Main: Suhrkamp, 1979).

36 Rudolf Burger, "Kriegsgeiler Kiebitz," in *Überfälle: Interventionen und Traktate* (Vienna: Sonderzahl, 1993), 41.

37 Thomas Chorherr, *Eine kurze Geschichte der 2. Republik* (Vienna: Ueberreuter, 2005), 50f.

38 E.g., Robert Menasse: *Das war Österreich* (Frankfurt/Main: Suhrkamp, 2005), esp. 123ff.

39 Vea Kaiser, *Makarionissi oder die Insel der Seligen* (Cologne: Kiepenheuer & Witsch, 2015).

40 On this, cf. Horst Afheldt, *Wirtschaft, die arm macht: Vom Sozialstaat zur gespaltenen Gesellschaft* (Munich: Verlag Antje Kunstmann, 2003) and the review by Warnfried Dettling, "Auf einer Insel der Seligen," in *Die Zeit* 47/2003, Literaturbeilage.

"Land of Mountains…":
Austria's Exceptional Environment and Its Myths

Georg Rigele

Fig.1: Assembly works on the steel structure of the Europa Bridge (1962)"
Image: voestalpine archives, Linz

"Land of mountains, land by the river" is the first line of the national anthem of Austria. The text Paula Preradović submitted to the Austrian Federal Government's competition for a new anthem was adopted by the National Council of the Austrian Parliament in 1947.[1] Postwar Austria largely defined itself by its landscape due to geographical, cultural, and political reasons. As Austria had not been able to win any war since the victories under Field Marshal Radetzky, a rather martial text for the new hymn was out of the question. (The audience at the Vienna New Year's Concert is all the more eager to clap along when it's time for the Radetzky March.) Nevertheless, the country's beautiful landscape helped the republic get over many situations of confusion and internal contradiction.

In 2019, the historian Ernst Hanisch published a comprehensive and multilayered book on the issue of landscape and identity in Austria.[2] Several sections in the following paper may refer to Hanisch's findings yet cannot do justice to his impressive work.[3] I would also like to present a few ideas and considerations based on my own research of the past thirty years.

Austria can certainly be proud of its geography and topography, with unique mountain massifs such as the Dachstein. While the Dachstein's winter ascent was portrayed in Adalbert Stifter's *Der Nachsommer* (*Indian Summer*) of 1857,[4] the mountain itself became a key motif in Ernst Krenek's song cycle *Reisebuch aus den österreichischen Alpen* (*Travel Book from the Austrian Alps*) of 1929. As it says in Song No. 12, "Politics," may the "bloody ogre" of quarrel and discord that used to ravage Austria be locked into the deepest cavern behind a rock "as large as the Dachstein."[5] Similar to the composer and well-known painter Arnold Schoenberg, Krenek had a second career as a travel writer, which made him quite successful and enabled him to eventually emigrate to the United States in 1938.[6]

The Glockner Group with its Pasterze Glacier is the highest elevation in all of Austria (3,797 meters) and a worthy replacement for Mount Ortler, the highest mountain of the former monarchy (3,905 meters). Another important mountain of the Austrian Empire, Mount Triglav, is the national symbol and motif in the coat of arms of today's Slovenia. Just as the other mountains mentioned above, the High Tatras, an iconic mountain range in the northern Habsburg Kingdom of Hungary (today's Slovakia) at the border to Poland (formerly Galicia), was part of Austria's geography until 1918.

When the borders were moved, the national attributions of landscapes and mountains changed as well. The remains of the former Danube Monarchy, the Republic of Austria (the Alpine Republic), were still rich in beautiful landscapes and sceneries despite its much smaller size. The land of mountains, thus Alpine Austria—from the Vienna Alps with both Rax and Schneeberg in the east to the Silvretta Alps with Piz Buin[7] in the west—turns into the land by the river, thus Danube Austria. After all, the Danube changes its character from a mountain river to something much wider only when it reaches Vienna.[8] On the one hand, South Tyrol and the Dolomite Alps, which had been developed for tourism with roads,[9] mountain railways, and cable cars rather early, became part of Italy in 1918. On the other hand, a part of western Hungary (today's Burgenland) was incorporated into Austria as its ninth federal province in 1921, thus further contributing to Austria's diverse range of landscapes.[10] The lake Neusiedlersee, a Pannonian steppe lake with a wide horizon, is considerably different from the small-scale lake scenery in Carinthia and the Salzkammergut region. Nevertheless, the lakes Wörthersee (Carinthia), Attersee (Upper Austria), and Altausseer See (Styria) continued to serve as hideaways of Vienna's upper class, accommodating summer villas along their shores since the nineteenth century. If there is a need to charge landscape with political significance and use it as an element of both national pride and collective identity—thus wrapping it up in myths, so to speak—the conditions for doing so are excellent in the Republic of Austria.

Shaping the Austrian Landscape in the Republic of Austria, 1918–38

The foundations for Austria's landscape, which supported the interests of the state in the Second Republic, had already been laid in the years between 1918 and 1938. The country was once again able to resort to its cultural, economic, and technical expertise of earlier times. In the period of mountain warfare in the Dolomites between 1915 and 1918, for example, cable cars were the only way of supplying exposed mountain fortifications with whatever they needed. This technical experience helped Austria promote the construction of new ropeways for touristic purposes in the 1920s; twelve aerial cable cars were put into operation between 1926 and 1937.[11] These developments undoubtedly contributed to the great success and popularity of skiing and winter tourism in Austria. The new cable cars turned such mountains as the Rax near Vienna, the Hahnenkamm in Kitzbühel, or Innsbruck's Nordkette into ski regions without all the troubles of climbing up first. The Bürgeralpe Ropeway in Mariazell, a Marian pilgrimage site in Styria, added a worldly purpose to an otherwise religiously charged landscape. In the early twentieth century, the recent electrification of the railway was combined with further developments in the field of hydropower, such as with the Mariazell Railway, electrified in 1911, and the Lower Austrian provincial electricity company *Landes-Elektrizitätswerk*.[12] After World War I and the dissolution of the monarchy, Austria was confronted with an energy supply crisis due to the lack of available coal. The country's railway system had collapsed, and without the necessary currency exchange and organizational framework, it had become impossible to import coal from the now-independent Czechoslovakia or other sources immediately after the war. The resulting political ambitions for self-sufficiency in the energy sector marked the beginning of a veritable boom in hydropower, which gradually faded in the late 1920s when the coal supply had normalized.

Austria's landscape was soon shaped by numerous power plants, such as at the rivers Mur in Styria or the upper Ill in Vorarlberg. Furthermore, the major railway lines west of Salzburg were electrified.[13] The federal province of Salzburg assumed a pioneering role in its specific combination of landscape, culture, tourism, and technology. The Salzburg Festival was founded in 1920 and soon gained popularity all across the world. In the same period, the car became more and more important as a means of transportation. Good roads were recognized as a clear competitive advantage in the overall struggle for guests with money. Initiated by the hotelier Theodor Christomannos, the Great Dolomites Road attracted the small, elite group of car owners in the monarchy in the early twentieth century.[14] After World War I, it was considered an excellent architectural model for scenic road projects in the Republic of Austria. The cable cars, mountain railways, and tourist roads not only made it possible to appreciate the scenery but also became part of the landscape itself. The gondola passing the pylon is nice to look at and enables its passengers to marvel at the beautiful landscape.

Fig. 2: The Bürgeralpe Ropeway in Mariazell, 1928.
Image: EVN Archive, Maria Enzersdorf

Directly connected to Salzburg and its famous festival is the Gaisberg Road, which replaced the rack railway to the panoramic mountain at the edge of the city in 1928. The successful completion of the Gaisberg Road was, to a certain extent, a test run for the *Großglockner-Hochalpenstraße* (Grossglockner High Alpine Road), an ambitious scenic road project that was to turn the Grossglockner into a destination for day trips by car, both from the festival city of Salzburg and the lake region of Carinthia.[15] Construction work began in 1930 but would have failed due to cost overruns if it had not been for the chancellors Engelbert Dollfuss and Kurt Schuschnigg, who completed the road as a signature project of the authoritarian government between 1933 and 1935. In some respects, the Grossglockner High Alpine Road was a great success as a showcase project of conservative modernization. It was much more than a mere technical traffic structure of aesthetic value to the landscape. It was also a masterpiece of marketing and historical self-interpretation by those who built it.[16] Its success was defined by gains in political prestige, extensive media coverage, and, above all, the unexpectedly great number of visitors willing to pay road toll. At the world's fairs of Brussels in 1935 and Paris in 1937, the Grossglockner High Alpine Road served as the poster child for modern tourism.[17] The artist Robert Haas created a photo collage of 9 x 30 meters with the Grossglockner and various road sceneries for the Paris World's Fair that caused a sensation.[18] After the dissolution of the Social Democratic city government in Vienna in February 1934, the new government commissioned the construction of the Vienna Höhenstrasse, another popular project that could be related to themes from Austrian history.[19] Kahlenberg Mountain, to which the Vienna Höhenstrasse was leading, was the rallying point of the relief forces that defeated the Ottoman Army in 1683 and thus ended the so-called "Second Siege of Vienna" (the Ottomans had already failed to seize Vienna in 1529). Press releases and political speeches on the Grossglockner High Alpine Road frequently emphasized Austria's bridging role in Europe. The theme of the mediator between all sides has been a popular one for a long time, ranging from such classics in literature as Franz Grillparzer's Habsburg drama *König Ottokars Glück und Ende* of 1825[20] to recent statements of today's politicians on Austria's position in foreign affairs.[21] Speeches on the Vienna Höhenstrasse, however, always had a certain undertone of resistance against pagan powers (e.g., Marxists, National Socialists). The dictatorial Austrofascist government stressed its close ties to the Catholic Church and introduced the concept of the Christian *Ständestaat* (Corporate State). Such ideological attributions ultimately proved to be nothing more than labels that could easily be replaced from one day to the next—in 1938, for example, when the Grossglockner became the highest mountain in all of Germany and the Catholic framing of Vienna's urban landscape faded into the background. The national character of a landscape is only superficial. The technologically enhanced landscapes undoubtedly remained popular. Car owners continued to undertake joy rides on the new scenic roads—at least until Hitler started World War II in September 1939, and private car use was restricted. Pedestrians, bus passengers, motor cyclists, and bicycle riders continued to enjoy the scenery presented from the roads. On the other hand, landscapes that were basically neutral in an ideological sense were used as a retreat by changing political or religious groups. One example is the Bödele, a small resort of outstanding scenic beauty in the western Austrian province of Vorarlberg. Developed by industrialist Otto Hämmerle from the city of Dornbirn in the early twentieth century, the Bödele primarily had a recreational purpose. In the 1930s, the Bödele, with its alpine cabins and chalets, became a retreat for then-illegal Nazi activities. After the annexation of Austria, the Nazis took over the cabin of the Roman Catholic youth organization *Reichsbund* at the Bödele—as they did with the property of their opponents at many other places.[22]

Austrian Landscape Once Again

In the year 1945, the still-preserved points of mythical reference of earlier times before 1938 could once again come to light. The Re-Austrification of the landscape—with its mountains, rivers, lakes, railways, roads, power plants, churches, monasteries, and old cities—took place from one day to the next as well. Among Austria's early postwar movies is *Der Hofrat Geiger* of 1947, which is set in the city of Spitz in Austria's Wachau region, a picture-postcard section of the Danube Valley between Melk Abbey and the medieval city of Krems.[23] The idyllic landscape contrasted to the reality of most Austrians at the time in an escapist fashion. The major economic projects of National Socialism, first and foremost the Glockner-Kaprun Tauern power plant and the Reichswerke Hermann Göring steel factory in Linz, were immediately transformed into practical tests of Austria's reconstruction efforts.[24] At both sites, Soviet prisoners of war had been forced to work under inhumane conditions. It took more than fifty years for the Republic of Austria to finally compensate the forced laborers that were still alive. The Linz steelworks became the primary site of the state-owned *Vereinigte Österreichische Eisen- und Stahlwerke*, or VÖEST for short, which today is a privatized global corporation under the name *voestalpine*. The Western occupation forces approved the nationalization of banks, major industrial enterprises, and the electricity sector in 1946 and 1947. They also left the Austrian government in control of "German assets," which the Soviet Union had claimed in its occupation zone and consolidated in its administrative body, USIA. Kaprun and Linz were in the American zone of Allied occupation. Kaprun became a sort of quarantine facility for Nazis that had been released after the shutdown of the Marcus W. Orr Internment Camp (*Glasenbach*) and had found work at the construction sites for the Tauern power plant. This development was also reflected in the results of the plant's works council elections. Instead of the Social Democratic Workers' Party of Austria (SPÖ), the Federation of Independents (VdU), the organization representing the interests of former National Socialists, had the majority of votes in the elections of 1949 and 1951.[25] The work was hard, dangerous, and full of deprivation in the beginning. As of 1948, ERP counterpart loans secured the funds for building the power plant. Local working conditions improved in the course of time. The entire power plant system with three reservoir lakes was completed in 1955.[26] Tauernkraftwerke AG established a separate subsidiary to take care of tourists wishing to see the plant. The massive changes in the landscape due to the power plant were seen as mostly positive and even used as tourist attractions. Its dam walls and other technical facilities (e.g., cable cars, roads, pressure pipes, plant buildings, power lines) were not hidden but integrated into the landscape.

Another highlight of technical landscape architecture is the Europa Bridge, built in 1963 and located south of Innsbruck at the Brenner Motorway A13.[27] Its supporting structure is made of VÖEST steel and was assembled by VÖEST in cooperation with the bridge construction company Waagner-Biro. In the following year, the supporting structure of the Trisanna Bridge at the Tyrolean side of the Arlberg Railway was replaced by an elegant steel arch framework. In terms of VÖEST references, there was also the Austrian Pavilion at the Brussels World's Fair of 1958; the excessively overhanging steel construction rested on four enormous structural steel pillars. The pavilion was dismantled after the Brussels World's Fair and reassembled in Vienna's Schweizergarten park as the "Museum of the 20th Century" for modern art in 1962.[28]

The Salzburg Festival and the city's summer tourism flourished soon after the end of World War II, certainly benefitting from the higher economic growth in the US occupation zone and the return of German tourists. The number of visitors using the Grossglockner High Alpine Road increased year after year, reaching its peak in 1962 (with 1,314,533 visitors).

The Austrian Postal Service issued many special stamps celebrating alpine engineering marvels like the Europa Bridge, the Kaprun power plant, or the Grossglockner Road.[29]

A Confusing Perception of the "Golden Days"

Shot at original locations in Salzburg and Upper Austria, the film *The Sound of Music* was released in 1965 and based on the stage musical by Richard Rodgers and Oscar Hammerstein. Its director, Robert Wise, who had opened the film adaptation of *West Side Story* with a spectacular camera shot from a helicopter, presented another idealized aerial perspective—this time of Austria's alpine landscape in his opening sequence, filmed by cinematographer Ted McCord.[30] *The Sound of Music* is one of the most successful motion pictures of all times and has lured vast numbers of American and Asian tourists to Austria. In Austria, however, nobody could understand what the American audience especially was so excited about for a long time. An unbelievably arrogant, albeit quite handsome, Christopher Plummer as the Imperial and Royal Corvette Captain bossing around his children and the singing Julie Andrews as Maria were so very different from the characters in Austria's traditional, so-called *Heimatfilme*. Captain von Trapp was a World War I hero, a patriotic Austrian, and anti-Nazi, but he was also unpleasant and authoritarian. This was rather confusing and inconsistent from an Austrian point of view. Perhaps the dashing film officer rubbed more salt into Austria's wound of not having fought back in 1938 and of not having taken the single gunshot that might have changed history. After revivals in London and New York, it took the stage musical until 1993 to finally arrive at Vienna's Schauspielhaus theater and to celebrate its Austrian premiere, even if with a smaller cast. *The Sound of Music* ultimately hit the big stage of the Vienna Volksoper in 2005 and was last performed in October 2019. Sixty years after the end of World War II and fifty years after the Austrian State Treaty, ending the period of Allied occupation, the Viennese audience was finally ready to enjoy the songs by Rodgers and Hammerstein without fear or favor. Now they could even accept the rotten Austrian Nazis as part of the story that portrayed them as adversaries of the rough captain and the singing nuns.[31] In 2018, *The Sound of Music* was the theme of the Life Ball, a charity event to combat HIV/AIDS, that was broadcast on television from the Vienna Rathausplatz and watched by millions of people around the world.[32] In the 1960s when the film was released, the country worked hard to improve its identity by idealizing

Austria's landscape through grand feats of construction and engineering. Today this landscape feels more staged than real. At the same time, it has also become more abstract and has assumed additional roles. It is both environment and nature, cultural landscape, settlement area, or a landscape with historical and somewhat ritualistic practices of use. Just imagine driving the Grossglockner High Alpine Road or taking a cable car up Mount Pfänder from Bregenz, Vorarlberg. People still do it in large numbers, but today nobody has to prove his or her ability as a driver to master steep grades on an alpine road. And the cable car in the capital of Vorarlberg is no longer one of twelve as it was in the 1930s but one out of a very large number. People are still visiting once-famous sites like a custom with a forgotten meaning.

The picture-postcard Salzburg from the "last Golden Days of the Thirties" that can be seen in the first scene of *The Sound of Music* was undoubtedly a joke to the Austrian audience of 1965. The days were hardly golden, the general conditions rather precarious, and Austria on the brink of disaster.[33] All this can be seen as piece of fiction sooner or later when the ambivalence of one's own history is finally accepted.

Skiing and the Gradual Disappearance of Technical Landmarks

Skiing became a national pastime and sport for the masses after 1945. Austria's skiing idols won medal after medal in world championships and Olympic Games. There was hardly a child, even among the unathletic, that could escape the school ski trips as they were mandatory.[34] This development culminated in the 1970s with the World Cup stars Franz Klammer and Annemarie Moser-Pröll, as well as the Austropop hit "*Schifoan*" ("Skiing") by Wolfgang Ambros. Skiing enthusiasm was not a choice but a duty. In the meantime, this all-encompassing identification of Austrians with skiing has somewhat subsided. Not only society but also leisure time opportunities have become more diverse—and skiing holidays are simply too expensive for many. Although Austria's skiing tourism is flourishing like never before thanks to its foreign guests, it is not of such dominant significance as it was four decades ago. Today's ski regions are technically designed to perfection and prepared with artificial snow at considerable effort. In addition to the cable cars that were built after 1920 and could climb to great altitudes with one cabin going upwards and one downwards, the ski slopes were soon covered in countless surface lifts and chairlifts.[35] The Tyrolean Zugspitze Cable Car of 1926, mastering a difference in altitude of 1,600 meters, serves as a brilliant example. Just as in power plant construction and the steel industry, winter tourism could rely on affordable ERP counterpart loans.[36] From a technical point of view, lifts and cable cars gradually merged into circulating ropeways and gondola lifts to carry the masses of skiers into the mountains. The queues of earlier times, when skiers had to endlessly wait for a single chairlift to ascend the mountain, are long gone. While the individual ski regions were constantly growing, they were often also interconnected through lifts and ropeways. In 2019, the rumor that a mountain peak in Tyrol might be blown up to make room for a cable car station and thus connect two major ski regions caused quite a stir.[37] If this had been true, it would still have not been the first time in Austrian history. The mountain peak of Salzburg's Edelweissspitze was cut back, for example, in order to build a parking lot and lookout post for the Grossglockner High Alpine Road. While the traditional cable cars were prominent individual structures, the character of the next generation of ropeways was changed toward a more discrete yet perfectly working infrastructure. In contrast to this development, older aerial tramways were iconic structures that could not—and were not supposed to—be overlooked. Among them are the Kitzsteinhorn cable car, opened in 1966, with a pylon measuring 360 feet (110 meters) to reach the all-year glacier ski region, or the Dachstein Südwand cable car, opened in 1969. The Stubnerkogel cable car in the ski region of Bad Gastein was funded by ERP loans and opened in 1950. The futuristic cable car stations designed by Gerhard Garstenauer for Sportgastein in 1970 mark an epochal change. The surface and underground infrastructure of today's ski regions does not attract a lot of attention anymore (although there are, of course, some remarkable exceptions). The extroverted blend of technology and landscape, or the creation of landscapes through technology, was scaled back and is hardly expected anymore. Today's reservoir lakes for the snow cannons along the slopes, with their underground water and power supply, are neither celebrated nor promoted any longer. They are, at best, disguised like the *Holzknechtland* (logger´s land), a theme park at the Bürgeralpe in Mariazell.[38] As mentioned above, this little ski mountain originally had a cable car that was opened in 1928 and decommissioned in 2018. Although the cable car was classified as a historical monument, its protection was later reversed. The historic cable car, with two cars going up and down on separate ropes, was replaced by a circulating ropeway with a number of small gondolas in 2019. The Bürgeralpe serves as an excellent example of the new relationship between landscape and technology in which technology plays a fundamental role in the economic exploitation of landscapes and is, at the same time, kept hidden from consumers.

Traditional roads and railways gradually disappear from the landscape—a process that began in the 1980s. The new roads and railways are built in long tunnels or between noise barriers. Even in lowland areas, longer sections are built over ("encased") or covered over by "green bridges" for environmental reasons, such as Motorway A4 near Parndorf (opened in 1991) or the new Western Railway section between Vienna and St. Pölten in the Tulln Basin (opened in 2012). Today's railway wagons have dark tinted windows that cannot be opened anymore. Their seats are arranged without consideration for the position of windows. It may happen that you have reserved a window seat and get a wall seat instead. In his novel *Winterbergs letzte Reise* (*Winterberg's Last Journey*), the Czech writer Jaroslav Rudiš has his protagonist moaning about the loss of landscape aesthetics, particularly in Austria. Traveling by train between Linz and Vienna, Winterberg complains that he can hardly see anything.[39] The landscape-creating constructions of the nineteenth and twentieth centuries were an integral part of the landscape. Moreover, they also made the landscape visible and enabled people to experience it. The Semmering Railway, a UNESCO World Heritage site since 1998, or the Grossglockner High Alpine Road, under monument protection since 2015, had a purpose and worked well both from the perspective of outside observers and in terms of vehicle dynamics that railway passengers and drivers in their cars could enjoy. As these examples are listed structures, their historical usage and the way people enjoyed them in earlier days can, to a certain extent, be experienced. The same does not apply to today's roads and railways that are disappearing behind noise barriers or in tunnels and enclosures.

Opposition Against Roads and Hydropower Plants—and the Unexpected Success of an Artificial Island

Opposition against individual traffic structures arose as early as the 1950s. Opened in 1959, the Wachau Road had to be directed through a tunnel under the city of Dürnstein after influential landscape conservationists had spoken out against a route along the Danube. In contrast, the completion of the Ybbs-Persenbeug Danube power plant in 1959 was celebrated by the general public, similar to the Tauern power plant in Kaprun. In the same period, it became quite clear that a potential Danube power plant in the Wachau region would run into opposition. Although the new Wachau Road was planned in the aesthetic landscape practice of the 1930s, it was still met with resistance. Among the opponents of the riverbank route of the Wachau Road in Dürnstein was the architect Clemens Holzmeister, one of the most influential personalities in the field of cultural and educational policies in Austria. Aside from his activities as the architect of the Salzburg Festival, Holzmeister had planned substations for electrifying the Arlberg Railway, large-scale hotels, cable car stations, and a monument for the Grossglockner High Alpine Road at Fuscher Törl. Although he designed his structures to be seen all across Austria's countryside, he did not want any new and striking designs in the Wachau region. In this section of the Danube Valley, a rather aggressive use of technology was the wrong way to go as a well-balanced cultural landscape had developed here since the Middle Ages. Today's single-track railway was incorporated with great sensitivity and discretion in the early twentieth century. The designs of its railway station buildings were based on the idea of cultural heritage protection; the railway line takes into account not only the towns but also the tradition of growing fruit and wine. Holzmeister's first design project was an elementary school in Marbach, a few miles west of Melk at the northern riverbank of the Danube, in 1913. In the Wachau region, any structures of civil engineering that altered the landscape could harm the region.[40] Located west of the Wachau region, for example, the Melk Danube power plant was completed in 1982 and noticed by the general public with considerable discontent. The Hainburg Danube power plant project, located east of Vienna and close to the Slovakian border (at the time, the border to the ČSSR), was aborted after massive protests from environmental and nature protection groups.[41] When the Danube wetlands near Hainburg were about to be cleared in autumn 1984, environmental activists, including university students, occupied the wetlands. One of their most prominent supporters was the Nobel Prize laureate Konrad Lorenz. The extensive police presence managed to forcibly clear parts of the wetlands from protesters. A few acres of wetlands were cleared of vegetation, thus fueling the protests once more. At the same time, with the occupation of the Danube wetlands, mass demonstrations in Vienna threatened to escalate. The Austrian Trade Union Federation took to the streets in favor of the power plant for reasons of employment. Represented by Josef Hesoun, chairman of the Trade Union for Construction and Woodworkers, they threatened to remove the activists from the wetlands, perhaps in reminiscence of the clearance of Communist road blockades by the same union in the context of the Austrian general strikes in October 1950. It was then that Federal Chancellor Fred Sinowatz declared a so-called "Christmas truce" in 1984 and a pause for reflection, ultimately resulting in the stop of construction of the Hainburg hydroelectric power plant and the preservation of the Danube wetlands. In 1996, the Donau-Auen National Park was established, covering the entire area between Vienna and the March River at the border to Slovakia.[42]

In comparison to these developments, the "second Vienna Danube regulation" appears to be an outright exception in terms of landscape history. It included the so-called "New Danube," a river channel of thirteen miles as a means of providing flood relief by containing excess water, and the resulting *Donauinsel* (Danube Island)[43] This large-scale project was realized between 1972 and 1988. The first Danube regulation of 1870–75 created a straightened river channel for the Danube and its former wide network of distributaries across the Danube wetlands. The Danube regulation was executed for the purpose of flood control, as well as for improvements for the shipping industry. On the left bank, a strip of land of about 550 yards was left clear as a flood-prone area. The adjacent Hubertus Dam protected the entire area north of the Danube from flooding. The new wharves for the shipping industry were directed toward the city.[44] The left riverbank was inundated during severe floods, especially during the historic Danube floods of 1954. For this reason, the urban development concept for Vienna of 1961 included plans for a discharge channel that would be able to cope with even the greatest floods.[45] At normal water levels, the discharge channel is separated from the Danube by means of weirs and serves as a stretch of standing water for swimming and water sports. The creation of Danube Island was a side product of flood control measures, using the spoil from the riverbed of the New Danube to build up the remaining strip of the former inundation area. Vienna's population discovered Danube Island as a recreation area even before it was finished. The new leisure paradise became one of the greatest successes of urban development in the twentieth century. Bicycling, running, swimming, nude bathing, walking, barbecuing, fishing, partying, and relaxing—the city is spoilt for choice at Danube Island. Nevertheless, it was originally created without any ambitions of improving Vienna's urban landscape. From a landscape point of view, Danube Island is rather neutral and unideological. Without claiming to serve any greater purpose, however, Danube Island and both the main branch of the Danube and the New Danube are among the most popular and most visited places in Vienna.

Although large-scale changes in the landscape by means of technology are much more frequent than ever before in history, their public perception has changed considerably as well. Today, Austria's population drives to the country's national parks between noise barriers and enjoys the landscape as a recreation area, as if they were mentally flipping a switch upon leaving the car. The Austrian landscape—the myth-like pride of the nation—is under either nature or monument protection, or even both. It is not an element of general progress in the sense of humanity's creative force anymore but has become something to be preserved and protected. Conservationists, on the other hand, had to learn that a national park also is the product of a specific social understanding of nature.[46] The antithesis of this development would be Danube Island, where flood control measures were turned into a recreation area that was quickly appropriated by Vienna's population. After all, it offers great benefits without having to represent or embody any particular image neither in the sense of nature nor in the sense of landscape.

Fig. 3: View from Vienna's DC Tower in the northwest direction. From left to right: Danube, Danube Island, New Danube, Highway A22 along the New Danube, 2012. Image: © Bwag/Wikimedia

Translation: Clifford Stevens

Endnotes

1 "Bundeshymne," *bundeskanzleramt.gv.at*, accessed Jan. 1, 2020, https://www.bundeskanzleramt.gv.at/bundeskanzleramt/geschichte/bundeshymne.html.

2 Ernst Hanisch, *Landschaft und Identität: Versuch einer österreichischen Erfahrungsgeschichte*. Schriftenreihe des Forschungsinstitutes für politisch-historische Studien der Dr.-Wilfried-Haslauer-Bibliothek 67 (Vienna: Böhlau Verlag, 2019).

3 See the review by Werner Telesko: Werner Telesko, review of *Landschaft und Identität: Versuch einer österreichischen Erfahrungsgeschichte*, by Ernst Hanisch, H-Soz-Kult, July 22, 2019, accessed Jan. 1, 2020, https://www.hsozkult.de/publicationreview/id/reb-28507?title=e-hanisch-landschaft-und-identitaet&recno=1&q=hanisch&sort=newestPublished&fq=&total=42)

4 Adalbert Stifter, *Der Nachsommer*, 3rd ed. (Munich: dtv, 1980), 573-585.

5 Ernst Krenek, *Prosa, Dramen, Verse* (Munich: Albert Langen Georg Müller Verlag, 1965), 385-398 (here 393).

6 Georg Rigele, "Ein Kontrapunkt zum Fremdenverkehr: Ernst Krenek und die österreichische Kulturpolitik 1928-1938," in *Kunst und Diktatur: Architektur, Bildhauerei und Malerei in Österreich, Deutschland, Italien und der Sowjetunion 1922-1956*, ed. Jan Tabor (Vienna: Verlag Grasl, 1994), Vol. 1, 242-251.

7 Michael Kasper, ed., *Mythos Piz Buin: Kulturgeschichte eines Berges* (Innsbruck: Haymon, 2015).

8 Ortrun Veichtlbauer, "Port of Vienna: Infrastructures and War on the River Danube in Vienna, 1850-1950," in *Austrian Environmental History*, Contemporary Austrian Studies 27, ed. Marc Landry and Patrick Kupper (New Orleans: UNO Press, 2018), 73-102 (here 75).

Susanne Breuss, Karin Liebhart, and Andreas Pribersky, *Inszenierungen: Stichwörter zu Österreich* (Vienna: Sonderzahl, 1995), 176-180.

9 Elisabeth Baumgartner, *Eisenbahnlandschaft Alt-Tirol: Verkehrsgeschichte zwischen Kufstein und Ala im Spannungsfeld von Tourismus, Politik und Kultur* (Innsbruck: Haymon, 1990).

10 Hanisch, *Landschaft und Identität*, 297-317.

11 Georg Rigele, "Sommeralpen – Winteralpen: Veränderungen im Alpinen durch Bergstraßen, Seilbahnen und Schilifte in Österreich," in *Umweltgeschichte: Zum historischen Verhältnis von Gesellschaft und Natur*, ed. Ernst Bruckmüller and Verena Winiwarter, Schriften des Instituts für Österreichkunde 63 (Vienna: öbv&htp, 2000), 121-150 (here 134).

12 Gerhard Artl, Roman-Hans Gröger, and Gerhard H. Gürtlich, ed., *Mariazell, Mariazellerland und die Mariazellerbahn*, 2nd ed. (Vienna: Holzhausen, 2018).

13 Peter Staudacher, "Euphorie, Stagnation, Pragmatismus: Streiflichter auf die Elektrifizierung der österreichischen Eisenbahnen vom Ende des Ersten Weltkriegs bis zum Staatsvertrag," in *Technik Politik Identität: Funktionalisierung von Technik für die Ausbildung regionaler, sozialer und nationaler Selbstbilder in Österreich*, ed. Klaus Plitzner (Stuttgart: Verlag für Geschichte der Naturwissenschaften und Technik, 1995), 149-169.

14 Th.[eodor] Christomannos, *Die neue Dolomitenstrasse Bozen–Cortina–Toblach und ihre Nebenlinien* (Vienna: Christoph Reisser's Söhne, 1913).

15 Georg Rigele, *Die Großglockner-Hochalpenstraße: Zur Geschichte eines österreichischen Monuments* (Vienna: WUV-Universitätsverlag, 1998).

16 Georg Rigele, "Die Großglockner-Hochalpenstraße: Der Bau ihrer Geschichte," in *Die Großglockner- Hochalpenstraße: Erbe und Auftrag*, ed. Johannes Hörl and Dietmar Schöndorfer (Vienna: Böhlau, 2015), 75-99.

17 Thomas Mitterecker, *Großglockner Hochalpenstraße: Prestigebau des Ständestaates* (Vienna: Klein Publishing GmbH, 2018), 121-149.

18 Anton Holzer and Frauke Kreutler, ed., *Robert Haas: Framing Two Worlds, Exhibition Catalogue Wien Museum* (Berlin: Hatje Cantz, 2016), 14-21.

19 Georg Rigele, *Die Wiener Höhenstraße: Autos, Landschaft und Politik in den dreißiger Jahren* (Vienna: Turia & Kant, 1993).

20 Franz Grillparzer, *König Ottokars Glück und Ende, 3. Aufzug, Rede des Ottokar von Hornek* (Ditzingen: Reclams Universal-Bibliothek, 1971), 65-66.

21 "EU-Ratsvorsitz Österreichs: Bundeskanzler Kurz will 'Brücken bauen,'" *europarl.europa.eu*, July 3, 2018, accessed March 30, 2020, http://www.europarl.europa.eu/austria/de/aktuell-presse/meldungen/meldungen-2018/juli-2018/pr-2018-juli-4.html

22 Nikola Langreiter, "Kleine Geschichte der Bödele-Hotellerie," in *Wem gehört das Bödele? Eine Kulturlandschaft verstehen,* ed. Nikola Langreiter and Petra Zudrell (Salzburg: Residenz Verlag, 2020), 142-167 (here 155).

23 Hanisch, *Landschaft und Identität*, 221-227.

24 Wolfgang Kos, *Eigenheim Österreich: Zu Politik, Kultur und Alltag nach 1945* (Vienna: Sonderzahl, 1994), 131-138

25 Georg Rigele, "Das Tauernkraftwerk Glockner-Kaprun – neue Forschungsergebnisse und offene Fragen," in *Blätter für Technikgeschichte 59* (1997), 55-94 (here 74).

26 Georg Rigele, "The Marshall Plan and Austria's Hydroelectric Industry: Kaprun," in *The Marshall Plan in Austria*, Contemporary Austrian Studies 8, ed. Gunter Bischof, Anton Pelinka, and Dieter Stiefel (New Brunswick, NJ: Transaction, 2000), 323-356.

27 *Die Brenner-Autobahn: Die erste alpenüberquerende Vollautobahn*, ed. Brenner-Autobahn Aktiengesellschaft (Innsbruck: Verlag "Tiroler Nachrichten," 1972), 104-11, 140-141, 148-151, 187-197; Leo Feist, *Vom Saumpfad zur Tiroler Autobahn* (Innsbruck: Amt der Tiroler Landesregierung, 1980), 401-405; Magdalena Pernold, *Traumstraße oder Transithölle? Eine Diskursgeschichte der Brennerautobahn in Tirol und Südtirol (1950-1980)* (Bielefeld: transcript Verlag, 2016), 137-145, 266-276.

28 Ulrike Felber, Elke Krasny and Christian Rapp, *Smart Exports: Österreich auf den Weltausstellungen 1851-2000* (Vienna: Christian Brandstätter, 2000) 143-157.

29 Christian Rohr, "The Austrian Environment en Miniature: 'Official' Perceptions of the Austrian Landscape Reflected through Postal Stamps since 1945," in *Austrian Environmental History*, Contemporary Austrian Studies 27, ed. Marc Landry and Patrick Kupper (New Orleans: UNO Press, 2018), 155-181.

30 Elisabeth Monarth, "'The Sound of Music'– Eine vergleichende Film- und Musicalanalyse," in *The Sound of Music zwischen Mythos und Marketing*, ed. Ulrike Kammerhofer-Aggermann and Alexander G. Keul (Salzburg: Salzburger Institut für Volkskunde, 2000), 195-215.

31 Technisches Museum Wien, ed., *Österreich baut auf: Wieder-Aufbau & Marshall-Plan/ Rebuilding Austria: Reconstruction and the Marshall Plan* (Vienna: Technisches Museum Wien, 2005), 158-159.

32 Peter Temel, "Warum 'Sound of Music' in Österreich fast niemand kennt," *Kurier*, June 6, 2018, accessed Jan. 1, 2020, https://kurier.at/kultur/warum-the-sound-of-music-in-oesterreich-fast-niemand-kennt/400044644.

33 Jacqueline Vansant, *Austria Made in Hollywood* (Rochester, NY: Camden House, 2019), 1, 123-130.

34 Hanisch, *Landschaft und Identität*, 81-85.

35 Robert Groß, *Eine Umweltgeschichte des Wintertourismus in Vorarlberg/Österreich (1920-2010)* (Vienna: Böhlau, 2019).

36 Günter Bischof, "Conquering the Foreigner: The Marshall Plan and the Revival of Postwar Austrian Tourism," in *The Marshall Plan in Austria*, Contemporary Austrian Studies

8, ed. Gunter Bischof, Anton Pelinka, and Dieter Stiefel (New Brunswick, NJ: Transaction, 2000), 357-401; Groß, *Die Beschleunigung der Berge*, 117-189.

37 Steffen Arora, "Die Gletscherehe – Tourismus in seiner zerstörerischen Form," *Der Standard*, Nov. 9, 2019, accessed Jan. 1, 2020, https://www.derstandard.at/story/2000110843796/die-gletscherehe-tourismus-in-seiner-zerstoererischen-form; "Gletschergipfel soll für Skigebiet gesprengt werden: 45.000 Unterschriften," *Die Presse*, Nov. 11, 2019, accessed Jan. 1, 2020, https://www.diepresse.com/5716445/gletschergipfel-soll-fur-skigebiet-gesprengt-werden-45000-unterschriften; *Neue Zürcher Zeitung, internationale Ausgabe* March 7, 2020, 6.

38 http://www.buergeralpe.at/sommer/erlebnispark/ (accessed Jan. 1, 2020).

39 Jaroslav Rudiš, *Winterbergs letzte Reise: Roman* (Munich: Luchterhand, 2019), 211, 234, 243, 248-249 (here 243).

40 Wilfried Posch, "An der Wende vieler Zeiten. Clemens Holzmeister zwischen Kunst und Politik" in *Clemens Holzmeister*, Buch zur Ausstellung "Clemens Holzmeister," RLB Kunstbrücke, Innsbruck, ed. Georg Rigele, Georg Loewit (Innsbruck: Haymon-Verlag, 2000), 48-66 (here 64).

41 Andreas Kuchler, "Hainburg (1980-1985). Menschen und Medien kippten ein Megaprojekt," in *Wasserkraft. Elektrizität. Gesellschaft. Kraftwerksprojekte ab 1880 im Spannungsfeld*, ed. Oliver Rathkolb, Richard Hufschmied, and Andreas Kuchler (Vienna: Kremayr & Scheriau), 245-256.

42 Ortrun Veichtlbauer, "Donau-Strom. Über die Herrschaft der Ingenieure," in *Graue Donau, Schwarzes Meer: Wien, Sulina, Odessa, Jalta, Istanbul*, ed. Christian Reder and Erich Klein (Vienna: Springer, 2008), 170-195 (here 190-194).

43 Zentrum für Umweltgeschichte (ed.), *Wasser Stadt Wien: Eine Umweltgeschichte* (Vienna: Universität für Bodenkultur Wien, Technische Universität Wien, 2019), 125-128; Kurt Freisitzer and Jakob Maurer, *Das Wiener Modell: Erfahrungen mit innovativer Stadtplanung: Empirische Befunde aus einem Großprojekt* (Vienna: Compress, 1985).

44 Veichtlbauer, "Port of Vienna," 78.

45 Roland Rainer, *Planungskonzept Wien*, ed. Wiener Stadtbauamt, Institut für Städtebau an der Akademie der bildenden Künste Wien (Vienna: Jugend und Volk, 1962), 174-177.

46 Martin Schmid and Ortrun Veichtlbauer, *Vom Naturschutz zur Ökologiebewegung: Umweltgeschichte Österreichs in der Zweiten Republik* (Innsbruck 2006), 41.

Mitteleuropa–Nostalgia in New Disguises?

Christian Hütterer

In his 1984 essay "The Tragedy of Central Europe," Czech author Milan Kundera wrote: "Does Central Europe constitute a true cultural configuration with its own history? And if such a configuration exists, can it be defined geographically? What are its borders?" Kundera himself answered these questions: "Central Europe is not a state: it is a culture or a fate. Its borders are imaginary and must be drawn and redrawn with each new historical situation."[1]

A few years after the publication of this essay, a "new historical situation," as mentioned by Kundera, developed. Mass protests toppled the Communist regimes in Central and Eastern Europe and led to the fall of the Iron Curtain. Borders that had previously almost been impossible to cross were opened, and a spirit of optimism fostered the belief that after decades of separation, the shared historical and cultural roots of Central Europe[2] would help the region to grow together again. The assumed closeness of these nations was supposed to create the fundament for political, economic, and cultural cooperation. Consequently, the notion of Central Europe soon became "a myth of the harmony of states and peoples capable of concealing different national interests," as Barbara Serloth wrote.[3] However, was this myth transformed in reality, in concrete political projects? This paper will present two initiatives with Austrian participation that may be considered political manifestations of the theoretical concept of Central Europe: the Central European Initiative (CEI) and the Regional Partnership. These two attempts to create a coherent Austrian policy for the Central European region will be presented from the initial ideas to their rather unsuccessful ends.

Only fifteen years after the fall of the Iron Curtain, the geopolitical constellation in Central Europe changed again fundamentally. By joining the North Atlantic Treaty Organization (NATO) and the European Union (EU), the countries of Central Europe integrated into Western European structures. For the second time within a few years, Austrian foreign policy had to adapt to new realities. The enlargement of the European Union toward the countries of Central and Eastern Europe led to a third initiative that may be regarded as a political manifestation of the Central European idea. Together with Romania, Austria initiated the European Union Strategy for the Danube Region (EUSDR), which resulted in the creation of a so-called macro-region in the Danube River Basin. Can this macro-region be considered a manifestation of the concept of Central Europe, or was it to be seen as a novel approach aiming to enhance regional cooperation?

Before presenting these three initiatives, it is necessary to come back to Kundera's essay and the question about the geographic limits of Central Europe. At a time when Europe was still divided in an Eastern and a Western half, geographer Karl Sinnhuber tried to define the location and delimitation of Central Europe. He analyzed various definitions and concluded that this term "lack(s) precise meaning and consequently give(s) rise to misunderstandings."[4] So how can Central Europe be defined and demarcated from other regions? At the end of the 1970s, intellectuals in Poland, Czechoslovakia, and Hungary used the notion of Central Europe to challenge the Communist regimes. For them, the discussion about Central Europe meant, above all, a rejection of Soviet supremacy and a political and cultural reorientation of their countries. Given the historic and cultural similarities between these three countries, these intellectuals used the concept of Central Europe in a specific version that comprised their three countries only. At the same time, other definitions of Central Europe were much broader; the amplest of them comprised the entire area between the river Rhine to the Russian border.[5] Further delimitations of the region were not based on geographic terms but on historic, ethnic, cultural, or economic parameters. Charles S. Maier identified three definitions of *Mitteleuropa*: One emanated from East Central Europe and has to be seen as a "claim for autonomy of the lands between the Germans and the Soviets."[6] Another delimitation of *Mitteleuropa* was shaped in Berlin, and it is "active and present-minded, endowed with a deep purse and for now a benevolent capitalist vision."[7] Finally, Maier described an Austrian definition of *Mitteleuropa* based on cultural affiliation and a "neo-Habsburg revery."[8]

As French essayist Jacques Le Rider pointed out, "The term Central Europe has never denoted a geographically precisely determinable area."[9] Therefore, none of the delimitations of *Mitteleuropa* remained uncontested and was generally accepted. As its working base, the Austrian Ministry of Foreign Affairs adopted a definition that comprised, besides Austria, her neighboring countries—Czech Republic, Slovakia, Hungary, and Slovenia—as well as the "cultural neighbours" Poland and Croatia. At the same time, this definition remained vague as the ministry pointed out: "The term Central Europe refers less to a geographic location than to a deeply rooted historical and cultural bond between the inhabitants of this region, which cannot be clearly defined."[10] Though the preceding definition was relativized by this addition, it still shows which geographical area is usually considered Central Europe in Austria. The present essay follows this, albeit vague, definition.

Central European Initiative

The year 1989 was crucial for Austrian foreign policy. On July 17 of this year, Austria formally applied for membership in the European Community (EC), which would later become the European Union. At the same time, the profound changes in Central and Eastern Europe cast their shadow ahead. Austria's diplomacy had to face two major challenges at the same time: integration into the European Community and the revolutionary changes in her immediate neighborhood.

Already, in early 1989 and months ahead of the upheaval in Central and Eastern Europe, Italy, Hungary, and Yugoslavia had initiated a new format of regional cooperation. Austria was invited to participate but reacted rather reluctantly to this proposal as membership in the European Community was clearly the main priority of the Austrian diplomacy. However, Austria could not risk being left aside of developments in her neighborhood and therefore decided to take part in this project. In summer 1990, it became evident that the new format of regional cooperation was to be kept loose. This decision met Austrian expectations and made clear that participation in this grouping would not hinder Austria's integration into the European Community.[11]

On November 11, 1989, only two days after the fall of the Berlin Wall, the new organization was officially founded in Budapest and named Quadragonale. It was a groundbreaking step as four states with different political backgrounds cooperated in this forum: neutral Austria, EC and NATO member Italy, non-aligned Yugoslavia, and Hungary, at that time still a member of the Warsaw Pact and with Soviet Forces deployed in the country. In order to have a central point of contact for the organization, a small secretariat was set up in Trieste. Apart from this institution, the four founding states agreed to keep the organization project oriented and consequently refrained from creating an elaborate statute for the Quadragonale. This flexible organization had drawbacks. It soon became obvious that the loose framework was detrimental to the organization's efficiency. Furthermore, the financial contributions of the member states were limited, and since its creation, the organization had to face persistent financial shortages. Finally, the participating countries welcomed the alliance as a novel form of cooperation in Europe, but none considered it a priority of its foreign policy. Austria, as one of the founding members, shared this ambiguous attitude toward the organization. One of its leading diplomats summed up the position of the Austrian government: "Austria therefore approaches the Pentagonale[12] with engagement, but without too exaggerated zeal… We therefore constantly try to avoid every—unjustified—appearance that with the Pentagonale a new and in a sort of intermediate Europe placed organism might be in the making…that could be regarded as a substitute for the endeavours undertaken by the participating countries towards a rapprochement to or membership in the EC."[13]

These shortcomings resulted in a politically limited relevance of the organization. However, the Quadragonale soon turned out to be an attractive forum for all countries between the Baltic Sea, the Black Sea, and the Adriatic Sea. In spring 1990, Czechoslovakia was the fifth state to join the organization that was consequently renamed to Pentagonale. Other countries soon followed, and the organization adopted the name Central European Initiative. By the year 2000, the number of members in this organization had grown to eighteen.[14] However, none of the participating states considered cooperation within the CEI a priority of its foreign policy, and consequently the political relevance of the CEI remained limited.

From a political point of view, Brussels soon turned out to be far more attractive than Trieste. At the time the Central European Initiative was founded, only one member—Italy—had also been a member of the European Community. The enlargements of the European Union between 1995 and 2013 profoundly changed the composition of the CEI. By 2013, ten CEI member states had joined the European Union, meaning that EU member states now constituted the majority in the CEI. The remaining eight states shifted the priorities of their foreign policies from regional cooperation toward rapprochement to the European Union. As a result of this foreign political reorientation of its member states, the CEI lost attraction and importance. Given the changed political environment, the organization had to adapt its activities to the new reality and redefined itself as an instrument to support preparation for membership into the European Union. In its latest basic document, the CEI described its principal activities as "capacity building and best-practice transfer from institutions in CEI-EU countries to benefit recipients in non-EU CEI Member States" and as an "implementation of EU projects focusing on transnational and regional cooperation."[15] With this new focus on the integration of non-EU states into the EU, the organization reduced itself to the status of an antechamber for membership in the EU. However, experiences before the enlargements of the European Union in 2004, 2007, and 2013 have shown that membership negotiations between a candidate country and the EU were most effectively conducted in direct talks with Brussels and not via an intermediary. With the decision to become a preparatory body for membership in the EU, the CEI maneuvered itself into a dead end.

More than three decades after the founding of the CEI, even strong supporters of regional cooperation in Central Europe, like Erhard Busek, had to acknowledge that the organization "had not produced big results."[16] Given the organization's continuous loss of significance, Austria was the first—and until today only—member state that decided to leave the CEI. In 2018, a review of the Austrian membership in various international organizations led to the conclusion that "participation in the CEI is less suitable to address current European challenges than it used to be in its early years of existence. Therefore, Austria, in May 2018, decided to withdraw from the Central European Initiative." According to the Federal Ministry for Europe, Integration, and Foreign Affairs, the termination of membership in the CEI had to be seen as a measure to "optimize Austria's international engagement" and to "concentrate on fewer actors in order to increase its impact."[17]

Regional Partnership

On October 3, 1999, a general election was held in Austria. While the Social Democratic SPÖ won most seats in the National Council, conservative ÖVP and populist FPÖ entered coalition negotiations. These talks were concluded successfully, and Federal President Thomas Klestil swore the new government led by Wolfgang Schüssel into office in February 2000. For the first time in Western Europe, a populist party was represented in a national government. This unprecedented step lead to heavy criticism on a European and international level. The remaining fourteen EU members states reacted strongly and decided to adopt bilateral measures (which became known as "sanctions"), such as reducing contacts to the Austrian government and downgrading official relations from a political to a bureaucratic level. The new Austrian government was isolated and needed to find international support to counterbalance these unexpected reactions.

Against this background, Austrian Foreign Minister Benita Ferrero-Waldner invited her counterparts from the four direct neighbors—Czech Republic, Slovakia, Hungary, and Slovenia—and from the "cultural neighbour" Poland to a conference in Vienna in June 2001. This meeting was meant to be the starting point for a new form of cooperation in Central

Europe. According to Ferrero-Waldner, the partnership was not supposed to "establish Austria as the political centre of the region"[18] but to identify cross-border challenges in view of a common future. She highlighted that Austria intended to play a "constructive political, economic and cultural role as a mediator and bridge-builder in the region" in order to find "common solutions to regional challenges."[19]

The potential cooperation partners reacted hesitantly to the Austrian proposal. The Hungarian government was the only invited country to explicitly welcome the Austrian initiative but pointed out that any negative effects of cooperation in the Regional Partnership onto the Visegrád Group[20] had to be avoided.[21] The Czech government adopted an even more reserved attitude toward the Austrian proposal. At the time Ferrero-Waldner proposed the Regional Partnership, bilateral relations between Austria and the Czech Republic were particularly complex. On numerous occasions, Austria criticized the use of nuclear energy in the Czech Republic and especially the Temelín power plant. In addition, the Beneš decrees[22] were exploited by the governing FPÖ for domestic purposes and overshadowed the bilateral relations. Comparable conflicts—as well as the question of the Slovene minority in Carinthia—cast shadows over the relations with Austria's southern neighbor Slovenia. The "cultural neighbour" Poland had been invited to the founding conference in Vienna but was not represented at ministerial level. This fact was interpreted as a sign that Poland—a country considerably bigger than the other participants in the conference—regarded the Austrian initiative as a concurrence to its own foreign political priorities.[23]

The reactions from the invited countries were lukewarm at best, and after the unfortunate start, the Regional Partnership never managed to gather momentum. This became clear at the second meeting of foreign ministers that took place in Bratislava in November 2001, where only two of the six countries were represented at ministerial level. Half a year later, Slovenia was supposed to organize the ministerial meeting, but this reunion had to be rescheduled—another sign of limited interest in the initiative.[24]

The reluctant reactions to the Austrian initiative were due to several differences between Austria and the other partner countries of the Regional Partnership. At the time the Regional Partnership was launched, all of Austria's supposed partner countries were already members of NATO (Poland, the Czech Republic, and Hungary since 1999) or wanted to become members of the alliance as soon as possible (Slovenia and Slovakia). When it came to security policy, cooperation with neutral Austria was certainly no priority for these countries. Concerning the negotiations for membership in the EU, it soon became evident that neither Austria's role as facilitator nor cooperation in the Regional Partnership was necessary for the integration efforts of the candidate countries as their talks were conducted directly with the institutions in Brussels and not by a detour via Vienna.[25] In addition, the candidate countries rightly doubted that Austria could accelerate their accession process into the EU. In the question of the enlargement of the EU, there was a large discrepancy in Austria between the statements of the predominantly enlargement-friendly decision-makers and the negative attitude of the public. Populist politicians (but also the trade unions) fueled fears that after the EU enlargement, the Austrian labor market would be flooded by workers from the neighboring countries. Even the government was divided on the issue of enlargement. At various occasions, the junior coalition partner FPÖ explicitly announced objections to the EU's enlargement and even threatened to veto it.[26]

Given all these obstacles, the Regional Partnership never got off the ground. In the Visegrád Group, Poland, the Czech Republic, Slovakia, and Hungary already had a vehicle for regional cooperation in which they worked together on an equal footing and without a *primus inter pares*, as Austria wanted to be seen in the Regional Partnership. The four countries saw no need for a duplication of their already existing regional cooperation.[27] In a later analysis, Benita Ferrero-Waldner stated that her initiative "failed due to resistance from the Czech Republic and Poland and reservations within Austria."[28] This analysis falls short, for the Regional Partnership failed for various reasons. The Austrian government initiated this forum but was internally split in EU and foreign policy matters: While the ÖVP had a positive attitude toward the EU and enlargement, her coalition partner FPÖ was opposed to it. In addition, large parts of the Austrian public were reluctant to embark on closer cooperation with the neighboring countries. Finally, the invited neighbors saw no need for this format of cooperation as it did not advance their integration into the EU and even hindered the one in NATO.

EU Strategy for the Danube Region

In 2009, the European Union established the first European macro-region around the Baltic Sea and thus added a novel regional policy approach to its toolbox. The so-called EU Strategy for the Baltic Sea Region comprises all countries on the shores of the Baltic Sea and aims at the promotion and strengthening of regional and cross-border cooperation. When the strategy was adopted by the European Council, the ministers agreed on limitations for this new form of cooperation, which became known as the "three no's": "no new EU funds, no additional EU formal structures and no new EU legislation."[29] Cooperation in the macro-region had to be based on existing legal provisions and had to get by with existing financing programs. This formula (which applies for all macro-regions) turned out to be a major impediment to the effectiveness of the macro-region.

Still, the novel concept was closely watched in other parts of the EU. At the time the Baltic macro-region was created, cooperation along the Danube was already very intensive but split in a plethora of forms and fora. In order to better coordinate these efforts, Austria and Romania pushed ahead with the proposal of creating a macro-region along the Danube. In 2010, this idea was endorsed at the European level: The European Commission proposed an EU strategy for the Danube region (the aforementioned EUSDR), which was adopted by the General Affairs Council on June 24, 2011.

In contrast to the difficult debate on the geographic limits of Central Europe, the European Commission adopted a pragmatic approach and defined the geographic area in which the Danube strategy should be applied according to natural criteria. For the European Commission, the strategy was meant to cover an "area defined by its river basin."[30] Covering the entire basin from the origin of the Danube to its estuary, the geographic scope of the strategy went far beyond the customary definition of Central Europe that was used in Austrian politics.

Today, this strategy comprises fourteen states, nine of which are currently EU member states.[31] The Commission identified the questions of mobility, energy, environment, risks such as flooding and droughts, socioeconomic disparities, and security as main challenges for the region and proposed to increase cooperation in these fields. When the Commission drafted the EUSDR, the macro-region in the Baltic Sea area served as an example. It soon turned out that there was one major difference between the two macro-regions: the socioeconomic discrepancies along the Danube were considerably bigger than the ones in the Baltic Sea area. While the German *Länder* of Baden-Württemberg and Bavaria and the Austrian *Länder* are among the most prosperous regions of the European Union, the ones on the lower course of the river figure among the least developed ones in the Union.

Even though the work in the new macro-region began with great enthusiasm, the first critical voices could soon be heard, and the effectiveness of the EUSDR was put into question. Two years after the adoption of the strategy, a Commission report on the EUSDR noted some progress but also criticized shortcomings. The report proposed to "establish sustainable leadership and strategic planning for the Strategy" and called upon the member states to "strengthen their internal implementation structures."[32]

Despite these early warnings and recommendations, the years to come only brought limited progress, and the high expectations were not fulfilled. A study about the effectiveness of the EUSDR came to sobering results: "The findings of the evaluation indicate that there have been some achievements of the EUSDR at strategic level, but the overall impact of the strategy is not very high." It pointed out that "coordinated funding of projects, better cooperation and better governance are needed most in the Danube region."[33] In addition, it was criticized that the EUSDR made the mistake of not sufficiently communicating the successes it had achieved to the public.[34] The lack of media presence lead to limited interest on the part of political decision-makers and little public attention.

In 2019, a Commission report on the macro-regions made a note about the EUSDR: "The main challenge for the EUSDR is the decrease of political momentum."[35] In this document, the Commission pointed out that the macro-regional strategies had reached a "moment of truth." The strategies had "generated very high political hopes. However, without joint political impetus at national and regional level, the commitment of players on the ground…will not be enough to ensure the macro-regional strategies survive."[36] The future effectiveness of the EUSDR will depend on the funds at their disposal, but the signs are not very promising. The negotiations about the EU's Multiannual Financial Framework 2021–2027 were not only overshadowed by the loss of one of the main net contributors (United Kingdom) but also by the division of member states when it came to their contributions to the budget of the European Union. In addition to plans to cut the EU's overall budget, considerable funds were to be redirected from regional development (which largely covers expenditure in the EUSDR) to new European policies, such as climate change and the protection of the Union's external borders. The reduction of financial resources at their disposal will make it even more difficult for the EUSDR (and all other macro-regional strategies) to deliver results.

Regional Cooperation in Central Europe Thirty Years after the Fall of the Iron Curtain

In the three decades since the fall of the Iron Curtain, numerous regional organizations were founded in Central Europe. Looking at a political map of the region, an observer will find a patchwork of national, regional, or local organizations that promote cooperation in the region. Many of them are overlapping, and while some are rather general, others are linked to specific policy areas and fulfill specified tasks.

The regional organization in Central Europe that has attracted most public attention in recent years is certainly the Visegrád Group. Poland, the Czech Republic, Slovakia, and Hungary founded this group in 1991 with the aim of promoting the accession of the four states into the European Union. When its members joined the EU in 2004, the *raison d'etre* of the group was lost, and a new one was not found until 2015. In the refugee crisis of that year, the four Visegrád states refused a compulsory division of migrants arriving in the EU. Other issues—such as the question of the posting of workers, the discussion about the rule of law, the claimed inferior quality of food in the eastern member states of the European Union, and a general feeling of being disrespected by the old member states—contributed to a division between old and new member states and gave additional impetus to cooperation in this forum.

Austria has close ties to all Visegrád member states, and Austrian politicians occasionally participate in meetings of the Visegrád Group.[37] However, full membership in this forum was never a real option for Austria's foreign policy. Austria and the countries of the Visegrád Group share common interests, but there are also numerous differences. Unlike Austria, all Visegrád states are members of NATO, the members of the Visegrád Group don't share Austria's rejection of the use of nuclear energy, and finally, Austria is currently a net contributor to the European Union's budget, while the Visegrád states are net receivers. Despite these differences, the question of the Austrian membership in the Visegrád Group was brought up by the FPÖ during the 2017 election campaign. The reason for this proposal was the fact that the Visegrád states were notorious for their intransigent stance on migration, which corresponded to the FPÖ's position in this question.[38]

The Visegrád Group may be the best-known forum for regional cooperation, but there are many other political bodies in Central Europe in which Austria is a member. Examples at the national level are the cooperation in the Austerlitz/Slavkov format (Austria, Czech Republic, and Slovakia), the Central European Defence Cooperation (Ministries of Defence of Austria, Czech Republic, Slovakia, Hungary, Slovenia, and Croatia), or the Salzburg Forum (cooperation of the Ministries of the Interior of Austria, Czech Republic, Slovakia, Hungary, Slovenia, Croatia, Romania, and Bulgaria). Beside the national level, a multitude of institutions was created at regional or local levels to foster cooperation in Central Europe. While some organizations are based on the territorial principle (e.g., the Alps-Adriatic Alliance comprising Styria, Carinthia, and Burgenland in Austria, as well as regions in Hungary, Slovenia, and Croatia),[39] others were founded to promote cooperation in specific policy areas. Two of these fora shall be mentioned by way of example: DANUBEPARKS is a network of protected areas along the Danube River. The group consists of sixteen national parks from nine countries and aims at the restoration of river habitats, the protection of rare species, and the promotion of nature tourism.[40] The Danube Rectors' Conference is a network of almost seventy universities in the Danube region. The cooperation in this forum intends to improve higher education in both teaching and research in Central Europe.[41]

Following the brief description of multilateral cooperation in Central Europe, one should also look at bilateral cooperation between Austria and Central European countries. A think tank recently analyzed patterns of bilateral cooperation between EU member states and possible coalitions between them.[42] The survey depicted an overwhelming focus of Austrian politics on Germany, which was not reciprocated from Berlin. At the same time, it showed that Central European countries attach much importance to cooperation with Austria but only get limited responses. Two questions stand out in particular. The answers to the questions "Which EU member state would your government generally contact most on European policy matters?" and "Which EU member states have been most responsive and are easiest to work with for your country's government?" show surprisingly little overlap between Austria and her neighboring countries. The replies to these two questions indicate that the five countries most interested in cooperation with Austria are Croatia, Czech Republic, Hungary, Bulgaria, and Slovenia.[43] When the two questions were put to Austrian decision-takers, Germany ranked clearly as number one, while the first Central European country was only named fourth.[44] An interpretation of the study came to a rather harsh conclusion, which contradicts Austria's official positive attitude toward cooperation with Central European countries: "Austria's immediate neighbours to the east and south look to Vienna, but Vienna rarely looks back."[45] Similar results can be found in an analysis by a leading Austrian journalist who stated an "alienation" between Austria and her

Central European neighbors.[46] Also, Erhard Busek and Emil Brix, two of the leading advocates of the Central European cause in Austria, concluded: "Since 1989 one has succeeded only insufficiently in converting the potential of cultural nearness into real common politics."[47]

Is the Myth of Central Europe Still Alive?

After the fall of the Iron Curtain, Austrian policymakers undertook three major attempts to translate the theoretical approaches and discussions about Central Europe into concrete policy plans. For different reason, none of the three were successful—if one ignores the fact that any form of regional cooperation, however marginal, is a success in itself as it contributes to mutual trust and cooperation. The three attempts to create regional cooperation ended with limited success, and this leads to the question as to whether the myth of Central Europe is still alive today.

Some Austrian intellectuals and diplomats continue to advocate the concept of a Central Europe based on common history and cultural heritage. But today, even those who still cherish this idea must admit that the high expectations raised in the 1980s and 1990s were not fulfilled. The different historical experiences between Austria and the other countries of the region until 1989 seem to have been too divergent to allow for the creation of a Central European bloc within the European Union. Added to this were political differences of interest in the 1990s and early 2000s, such as Austria's vehement opposition to the use of nuclear power, long transition periods for workers from Central European countries in Austria, and different views on security policy between neutral Austria and NATO members in the region. While the Benelux countries or the Nordic countries are forming regional groupings within the EU, the dividing lines that emerged in 1945 are still visible in Central Europe, and the countries of the region "have not found any recognisable Central European common ground."[48]

When looking at the three manifestations of cooperation in Central Europe presented in this paper, it is rather difficult to come to a positive conclusion. The CEI was a groundbreaking attempt to overcome rifts shortly before and immediately after the fall of the Iron Curtain. It ended with an organization that covered Central Europe in the broadest geographical sense but had to pay the price of political insignificance. The second attempt was the Regional Partnership, born out of the need to find allies against the sanctions imposed on the ÖVP-FPÖ government. The domestic political discussions in Austria and tensions within the Austrian government, however, did not make this effort very credible vis-à-vis the potential partner countries. Furthermore, it soon turned out that Austria's role as facilitator for the Central European countries in their negotiations with the European Union was not necessary as these countries held direct talks with Brussels. The third attempt to formulate a coherent Central European policy, the EUSDR, has already taken place under new geopolitical conditions, namely in an enlarged European Union. On the positive side, the strategy succeeded to place many projects in a larger framework, but it was unable to realize its potential, and the initial momentum was soon lost.

Heidi Hein-Kircher defines a political myth as a "spiritual frame of reference" ("*geistiger Bezugsrahmen*") that serves primarily as a "generator of meaning" ("*Sinngenerator*") and is intended to provide orientation, especially in times of profound political changes.[49] Hein-Kircher also notes that political myths create a frame of reference and thus "define emotionally charged narrations that interpret historical truths not according to the facts, but in a selective and stereotyped manner."[50] Yves Bizeul also emphasizes the emotional significance of political myths: "By mobilizing strong emotions, they bring to light potentialities that were previously invisible."[51] The fall of the Iron Curtain was a political development that aroused deep emotions that seemed to suffice to lay the foundation for regional cooperation. Seen from a distance of thirty years, these feelings seemed to be exuberant, and they were soon to wane. If emotions play an important role in the creation of myths, it must also be noted in the case of Central Europe that the emotions in Austria and in the other countries of the region were often not the same. What was seen in Austria in a very positive light and as a recourse to the common history and culture awakened in some of the neighboring countries memories of Austrian dominance in the region.

Was Central Europe a dream of "chain-smoking professional intellectuals"[52] that is now over? Or—as Erhard Busek believes—is Central Europe only in the process of emerging and needs more time to grow together like Benelux or the Franco-German tandem?[53] Three decades after the fall of the Iron Curtain, a dense network of organizations and forums has emerged in the center of Europe to ensure cross-border cooperation in this region. It seems that the mythical and culture-oriented idea of *Mitteleuropa* has been abandoned and replaced by this pragmatic cooperation.

But is it time to say farewell to *Mitteleuropa*, as Charles S. Maier suggested already in 1993? According to Maier, *Mitteleuropa* would be dominated by an economically strong Germany, while Austria's approach on *Mitteleuropa* was "long on culture and sentiment, short on funds."[54]

Germany, as the main economic power in Europe, plays a pivotal role for Central Europe, but Maier's assumption was too pessimistic as Austria has considerable economic influence in the region. Vienna continues to be an attractive destination for migrants from Central Europe, and Austrian companies (especially in the financial, insurance, and construction sectors) play an important role in the economy of the Central European region. But Maier was right when he foresaw that *Mitteleuropa* alone "is not a viable enough concept"[55] and therefore called for the integration of the entire region in bigger European structures.

Today, the countries of Central Europe are united in the European Union. For centuries, the nations in Central Europe were connected with each other, but in the course of history, they also made different historical experiences. It seems that the idea of *Mitteleuropa*, based on a common culture and history as it was advocated under the specific circumstances of the 1980s and early 1990s, is no longer relevant today. In the three decades since the fall of the Iron Curtain, the "glorious but vague dreams of Central Europe"[56] based on intellect and culture have been replaced by a pragmatic cooperation aiming at concrete results rather than sustaining a vague feeling of belonging together.

Endnotes

1 Milan Kundera, "The Tragedy of Central Europe," *New York Review of Books*, April 26, 1984.

2 For the history and development of the term Mitteleuropa/Central Europe see, for example, Jacques le Rider, *Mitteleuropa: Auf den Spuren eines Begriffes* (Vienna: Deuticke, 1994) or Erhard Busek and Emil Brix, *Mitteleuropa Revisited* (Vienna: Kremayr & Scheriau, 2018).

3 "... Mythos vom Gleichklang der Staaten und Völker, der imstande ist, die unterschiedlichen Nationalinteressen zu verdecken." Barbara Serloth, "Mitteleuropa zwischen Mythos und Wirklichkeit," in *Bewältigen oder bewahren: Dilemmas des mitteleuropäischen Wandels*, ed. Peter Gerlich and Krzysztof Glass (Vienna: Torun, 1994), 31.

4 Karl Sinnhuber, "Central Europe – Mitteleuropa – Europe Centrale: An Analysis of a Geographical Term," *Transactions and Papers* (Institute of British Geographers), no. 20 (1954), 15.

5 Ibid., 19.

6 Charles S. Maier, "Whose Mitteleuropa? Central Europe between Memory and Obsolescence," in *Austria in the New Europe*, Contemporary Austrian Studies 1, 10.

7 Ibid., 15.

8 Ibid., 13.

9 Jacques le Rider, *Mitteleuropa: Auf den Spuren eines Begriffes* (Vienna: Deuticke, 1994), 7.

10 "Inhaltlich bezeichnet der Begriff Mitteleuropa weniger eine geographische Lage als vielmehr eine tief verwurzelte historische und kulturelle Verbundenheit der Bewohner dieser Region, die sich nicht klar abgrenzen lässt," quoted in: Andreas Führer, "Was bedeutet Mitteleuropa? Die Verwendung und Abgrenzung von Mitteleuropabegriffen in geographisch relevanten, aktuellen Publikationen" (Diploma thesis, University of Vienna, 2014), 43.

11 Emil Brix, "Mitteleuropa als Herausforderung für die österreichische Außenpolitik," in *Die Dimension Mitteleuropa in der Europäischen Union*, ed. Michael Gehler, Paul Luif and Elisabeth Vyslonzil (Hildesheim: Georg Olms Verlag, 2015), 379.

12 Pentagonale was the temporary name of the organisation after it had grown to five members.

13 "Österreich geht somit an die Pentagonale mit eigenem Engagement, aber ohne allzu übertriebenen Eifer heran.... Wir sind daher stets bemüht, jeglichen – unbegründeten – Anschein zu vermeiden, dass durch die Pentagonale ein in einem Zwischeneuropa angesiedelter neuer Organismus im Entstehen ist ... der als Ersatz für die von allen teilnehmenden Ländern, ..., verfolgten Bestrebungen für eine Annäherung bzw. EG-Mitgliedschaft angesehen werden könnte," quoted in Emil Brix, "Mitteleuropa als Herausforderung für die österreichische Außenpolitik," in *Die Dimension Mitteleuropa in der Europäischen Union*, ed. Michael Gehler, Paul Luif and Elisabeth Vyslonzil (Hildesheim: Georg Olms Verlag, 2015), 379.

14 Until 2018, the member States of the CEI were: Albania, Austria, Belarus, Bosnia and Herzegovina, Bulgaria, Croatia, Czech Republic, Hungary, Italy, Moldova, Montenegro, North Macedonia, Poland, Romania, Serbia, Slovakia, Slovenia, Ukraine.

15 Trieste Declaration, adopted by the Foreign Ministers of the Member States of the Central European Initiative, adopted in Trieste on June 12, 2019, https://www.cei.int/sites/default/files/2019-06/102.005-19%20Trieste%20Declaration%20-%20FINAL.pdf, accessed 7 November 2019.

16 "... so ist de facto hier eigentlich nicht sehr viel entstanden...," in Busek and Brix, *Mitteleuropa Revisited*, 53.

17 "Central European Initiative," Federal Ministry of the Republic of Austria, accessed 29 October 2019, https://www.bmeia.gv.at/en/european-foreign-policy/european-policy/central-european-initiative-cei/.

18 Benita Ferrero-Waldner, "Die Regionale Partnerschaft: Österreichs Nachbarschaftspolitik als Baustein der Europäischen Integration," in *Österreichisches Jahrbuch für Politik 2004*, ed. Andreas Khol, Günther Ofner, Günther Burkert-Dottolo, Stefan Karner, and Dietmar Halper (Vienna: Böhlau, 2005), 481.

19 Ibid., 478.

20 A regional alliance of Poland, the Czech Republic, Slovakia and Hungary.

21 László J. Kiss, Lucie Königova, and Paul Luif, "Die Regionale Partnerschaft: Subregionale Zusammenarbeit in der Mitte Europas," *Österreichische Zeitschrift für Politikwissenschaft* 32, no. 1 (2003): 57-75 (here 65).

22 A series of decrees issued by Edvard Beneš (then President of Czechoslovakia) leading to the expulsion and resettlement of Sudeten Germans from Czechoslovakia after the end of the Second World War.

23 Michal Kořan, "The Visegrád Cooperation, Poland, Slovakia and Austria in the Czech Foreign Policy," in *Czech Foreign Policy 2007-2009*, Michal Kořan et al., (Prague: Institute of International Relations: 2010), 115-147 (here 71).

24 László J. Kiss, Lucie Königova, and Paul Luif, "Die Regionale Partnerschaft," 70.

25 Michael Gehler, "Vom EU-Beitritt zur EU-Osterweiterung," in *Die umstrittene Wende: Österreich 2000-2006,* ed. Robert Kriechbaumer and Franz Schausberger (Vienna: Böhlau, 2013), 461-550 (here 515).

26 Ibid., 516.

27 Emil Brix, "Man kann diese Region nur über die Kultur erneuern," interview by Josef Kirchengast, *Der Standard*, March 11, 2013, accessed December 8, 2019, https://www.derstandard.at/story/1362108118475/man-kann-diese-region-nur-ueber-die-kultur-erneuern.

28 Benita Ferrero-Waldner, "Ferrero-Waldner drängt auf ÖVP-Außenminister," interview, *Niederösterreichische Nachrichten*, November 11, 2017, accessed December 8, 2019,

https://www.noen.at/niederoesterreich/politik/ex-aussenministerin-ferrero-waldner-draengt-auf-oevp-aussenminister-cee-eu-int-beziehungen-minderheiten-verfassung-wien-67040525#.

29 Paragraph 5, Council conclusions on the European Union Strategy for the Danube region, 3083rd General Affairs Council meeting, Brussels, April 13, 2011.

30 Communication from the Commission to the European Parliament, the Council, the European Economic and Social Committee and the Committee of the Regions: European Union Strategy for the Danube Region, COM(2010) 715 final, 3.

31 Germany (the Länder Baden-Württemberg and Bavaria), Austria, Czech Republic, Slovak Republic, Hungary, Slovenia, Croatia, Romania and Bulgaria as well as Serbia, Bosnia and Herzegovina, Montenegro, Moldova and Ukraine.

32 Report from the Commission to the European Parliament, the Council, the European Economic and Social Committee and the Committee of the Regions concerning the European Union Strategy for the Danube Region, COM(2013) 181 final, 9.

33 Evaluation of the effectiveness, communication and stakeholder involvement of the EUSDR, accessed November 28, 2019, https://danube-region.eu/the-final-report-on-the-eusdr-operational-evaluation-has-been-published/.

34 Jörg Mirtl, "Sechs Jahre EU-Strategie für den Donauraum – ein Plädoyer für nüchternen Realismus," *Südosteuropa Mitteilungen* 02/2017, 61. This issue is also addressed in the Report

from the Commission to the European Parliament, the Council, the European Economic and Social Committee and the Committee of the Regions on the implementation of EU macro-regional strategies COM(2019) 21 final, 4.

35 Report from the Commission to the European Parliament, the Council, the European Economic and Social Committee and the Committee of the Regions on the implementation of EU macro-regional strategies COM(2019) 21 final, 8.

36 Report from the Commission on the implementation of EU macro-regional strategies COM(2019) 21 final, 11.

37 E.g. participation of the President of the National Council in an informal meeting of the Speakers of the Visegrád parliaments in Balatonfüred in June 2018, accessed January 14, 2020, https://www.parlament.gv.at/PAKT/PR/JAHR_2018/PK0754/index.shtml.

38 For more information on the development of the Visegrád-group and its standing in the European Union see Christian Hütterer, "Visegrád – ein regionaler Machtfaktor in der Europäischen Union?" *Österreichische Militärische Zeitschrift* 04/2018, 473-480. The relationship between Austria and the Visegrád-group is described in Erhard Busek and Sebastian Schäffer, "Austria and the Visegrád Four after the National Council Election," *Foreign Policy Review* 10/2017, 19-30.

39 Alps-Adriatic-Alliance website, accessed January 14, 2020, https://alps-adriatic-alliance.org/

40 For further information see http://www.danubeparks.org/; Austrian members are Nationalpark Donau-Auen and the Wachau Protected Landscape.

41 For further information see https://www.drc-danube.org/; Austrian members are Danube University Krems, Graz University of Technology, Johannes Kepler University Linz, Montanuniversität Leoben, University of Graz, University of Natural Ressources and Life Sciences (BOKU) Vienna and the University of Vienna.

42 EU Coalition Explorer by the European Council on Foreign Relations, accessed November 29, 2019, https://www.ecfr.eu/eucoalitionexplorer.

43 Order of agreement varies, see EU coalition explorer pages 36 and 232, accessed January 14, 2020, https://www.ecfr.eu/page/ECFR269_EU_COALITION_EXPLORER_2018_V1.10.pdf.

44 EU coalition explorer pages 37 and 233, accessed January 14, 2020, https://www.ecfr.eu/page/ECFR269_EU_COALITION_EXPLORER_2018_V1.10.pdf.

45 Josef Janning, "The Overconfident New President: Austria's Coalition Building Challenges," accessed November 29, 2019, https://www.ecfr.eu/article/commentary_eu28survey_austria_presidency_coalition_building_challange#.

46 Christian Ultsch, "Österreichs Außenpolitik in einer Welt im Umbruch," *Europäische Rundschau* 2/2016, 25.

47 "Es ist aber seit 1989 nur unzureichend gelungen, das Potential kultureller Nähe in reale gemeinsame Politik umzuwandeln," in Erhard Busek and Emil Brix, *Mitteleuropa Revisited,* 181.

48 "....haben zu keiner erkennbaren mitteleuropäischen Gemeinsamkeit gefunden." Anton Pelinka, "Mitteleuropa - eine mögliche Renaissance innerhalb Europas?" in *Geschichtsbuch Mitteleuropa: Vom fin de siecle bis zur Gegenwart,* ed. Anton Pelinka, Karin Bischof, Walter Fend, Karin Stögner, and Thomas Köhler (Vienna: New Academic Press, 2016), 11-15 (here 12).

49 Heidi Hein-Kircher, "Politische Mythen," *Aus Politik und Zeitgeschehen* 11/2007, 30.

50 Ibid., 27.

51 Yves Bizeul, "Politische Mythen," in *Politische Mythen im 19. und 20. Jahrhundert in Mittel- und Osteuropa,* ed. Heidi Hein-Kircher and Hans Henning Jahn (Marburg: Herder Institut, 2006), 3-16 (here 9).

52 Stefan Brocza, "Das Märchen von der Donau," *Der Standard*, September 7, 2017, accessed December 14, 2019, https://www.derstandard.at/story/2000063761742/das-maerchen-von-der-donau.

53 Erhard Busek, "Wirkliche Wirklichkeit der EU-Donauraumstrategie," *Europäische Rundschau* 4/2013, 89.

54 Charles S. Maier, "Whose Mitteleuropa? Central Europe between Memory and Obsolescence," in *Austria in the New Europe*, Contemporary Austrian Studies 1, 14.

55 ibid., 16.

56 Emil Brix, "Austria and Central Europe," in *Global Austria: Austria's Place in Europe and in the World*, Contemporary Austrian Studies 20, 208.

Non-Topical Essay

The Drimmel Effect: The Anti-State Performance of Heinrich Drimmel

Michael Burri

I. The Making of the Drimmel Effect

Rising from the long shadow cast by the failure of the First Republic, the state-led effort to advance a specifically Austrian consciousness in the early years of the Second Republic Austria testifies to the possibility of a modern nation-building. This effort is an enduring post-1945 success story. And yet, in 1988, the late historian Fritz Fellner observed that the knowledge of this directed nation-building continued to trouble Austrian historians, journalists, teachers, and cultural figures. This group, to be sure, embraced the self-evident fact that the geopolitical entity of Austria, as established in 1945, had now become an Austrian nation. But they could not quite forget that what they embraced had been handed down to them. The Second Republic, wrote Fellner, was a "product of power politics and expedience, and not the fruit of aspirations for national or social independence by the majority of the population."[1]

A child of the First Republic, Fellner highlighted the non-Austrian role of "power politics" as a source of distress. And yet, power politics alone did not make postwar Austria. For if power politics did create the geopolitical "state" of Austria, these power politics did not create the modern Austrian "nation." Credit for creating this Austria belongs, rather, to a small group of Second Republic state elites who tasked themselves with bringing it about. In the years after 1945, these elites encountered steady headwinds. Not only did state finances and differing party agendas constrain the scope of new initiatives, but each of the occupation powers sought an influence upon cultural policy.[2]

It was the *annus mirabilis* of 1955, marked by the State Treaty, the declaration of permanent neutrality as a national symbol, and perhaps also the *Tag der Fahne*, that finally brought an indisputable occasion of "national self-realization."[3] Mindful of the domestic reeducation that would take place after 1955, Emil Brix later described what had heretofore been missing. For "what had been repressed between 1945 and 1955," he writes, was "a discussion of what constituted Austrian self-understanding."[4] Indeed, after 1955, state elites, especially from the ÖVP, forcefully promoted such discussion, with the instruction of history in schools becoming one of the practices most notably charged with creating an Austrian consciousness.[5]

Austria might come to stand for a "culture nation" ("*Kulturnation*"), but it would also stand for a top-down state culture directed toward education.

More than three decades later, Fritz Fellner would single out the role of power politics in the history of modern Austria. But if the source of Austrian discontent lies in the disregard for the national aspirations of an Austrian majority, then it is not only the external fiat of power politics that is to blame. Is what troubled Fellner's "historians, journalists, teachers, and cultural figures" not only the problematic determinative role of power politics in creating the Austrian state but also the determinative role of Austrian state elites in creating the modern Austrian nation?

In an essay he published in the April 1962 issue of the Viennese political and cultural journal *Forum*, Heinrich Drimmel anticipated such a possibility. Issuing a warning signal about the prepotent role of state elites, he wrote, "One often encounters the objection that the modern mass party no longer serves the political will of the people, but rather controls it... Instead of the will of the people, it is the will of anonymous party bureaucrats, who by means of agitation, propaganda, and organizational measures manage an artificially fabricated people's will."[6]

And yet, considering the source, such a protest against how public policy is set would seem to beggar belief. Since 1954, Heinrich Drimmel himself had served as the minister of education, a position he would occupy until 1964, serving five governments. In early Second Republic Austria, moreover, the minister of education held a vast portfolio, overseeing primary and secondary education, sports, arts, and culture (both domestic and international). And finally, Drimmel was an activist minister. He summoned into existence, and his ministry financially supported, one educational project after another, including the *Arbeitskreis für österreichische Geschichte* with its journal, *Österreich in Geschichte und Literatur*, a powerful institutional advocate for building "Austrian consciousness."[7] If Drimmel did not see himself as a prepotent state elite managing the people's will, who exactly did play that role?

In what follows, I wish to explore this double pose—a pose in which acting on behalf of the state is accompanied by a critique of state functioning—via the figure of Heinrich Drimmel. In describing this double posture as the "Drimmel effect," my purpose is not to rescue Heinrich Drimmel from recent critical assessments of his tenure as the minister of education, particularly in the areas of research and higher education, nor is it to rehabilitate his conservative vision for postwar Austria.[8] There is little doubt that Drimmel, who was born in 1912, was greatly shaped by his Catholic upbringing. Philosophically, his thinking expresses the long-standing claim of the church against the state to leadership in culture and education, while professionally, he served in the Catholic Student Union from 1934 to 1938 and represented the union nationally during the *Ständestaat*.[9] I do, however, wish to argue that a closer examination of the relationship between Drimmel and the postwar Austrian state reveals a far more complex figure than either a straightforward analysis of his policies or a traditional biographical reading would suggest. Drimmel's antagonism toward the state is suggestive. The hurried rise of the Austrian state achieved remarkable results, but it also generated a forceful and lasting ambivalence in many toward its power.

Much has been said about the nation-building narratives of the postwar Austrian state. First, and in an impressive fashion, scholars have underscored the ways early Second Republic leaders responded to short-term imperatives of national state-building by creating stories that sought to disassociate Austria from the crimes of National Socialism. Second, scholars have highlighted how state leaders mobilized long-term features of the Austrian past -- dates, events, individuals, attitudes – to create collective national stories and a specifically "Austrian consciousness." I believe that a review of Heinrich Drimmel would have much to contribute to each of these approaches. What I wish to consider here, however, is a different feature of nation-building—namely the expression of dissatisfaction with the state itself. I say that the "Drimmel effect" is a performance. In this performance, the main actor serves the state, promotes and multiplies its institutions and activities, while expressing an anti-state posture.

II. The Drimmel Effect: A Captive of the State

As the minister of education, Heinrich Drimmel greatly expanded the reach of the Austrian state. In the area of education, for example, he pushed forward the founding of the University of Salzburg (1962), the College of Social Sciences, Economics and Business, or JKU, in Linz (1962), and the Academy of Music and Performing Arts in Graz (1962), and he initiated the takeover of the Mozarteum in Salzburg by the federal government.[10] And yet, despite this steady march of professional success, Drimmel always foregrounded his own subjection to the apparatus of state. This is the first, and an essential, component in the performance of the Drimmel effect: attack the state by emphasizing your own captivity in it.

"Whoever wants to be taken seriously as a politician," Drimmel wrote in 1964, "must first and foremost be familiar with two rules of thumb, and master them, so that one is trusted to succeed in directing the social dynamic." The first is that "the politician must grant an unlimited priority to the production process."[11] By forcing submission to the "production process," Drimmel continued, the state also compelled the politician to pledge allegiance to a linked group of policy priorities—namely "intensifying the labor process," pursuing "full employment," and ensuring the creation of a mountain of consumer goods. Much as in the 1962 essay he published in *Forum*, Drimmel characterized the state as imposing its will on those who should, in fact, be guiding it. The crucial difference here is that Drimmel himself, not the people, were rendered powerless.

The new *raison d'état* compelled the state leader to cede authority to the "production process" in order that the perpetually moving "affluent society" ("*Wohlstandsgesellschaft*") keep running.[12] Indeed, Drimmel particularly rejected an alignment of the state with the goal of increasing the supply of consumer goods and the spurious reasoning that cheered on this alignment. Full employment and increased affluence, Drimmel argued, did not lead to an increase in good social behavior. According to Roland Grasberger, the criminologist and rector of the law faculty at the University of Vienna, rates of property crime in Austria during times of higher employment were double those following the period of mass unemployment in the Depression. "Not only desperation fosters crime," Drimmel writes, "but also prosperity, luxury."[13]

Inspired in part by the traditional Catholic call to defy the temptations of materialism, such arguments recall that questioning the unspoken logic of the postwar state could constitute a resistance to the "irresistible empire" of consumerism.[14] But such arguments also converge with the critique of modern culture and the loss of individual autonomy modeled after the Marxist notion of the "culture industry."[15] Thus, in his influential 1962 essay, "The Industrialization of the Mind," Hans Magnus Enzensberger argued that, taken together, radio, cinema, television, recording, advertising, and public relations constituted a new and pernicious form of "mind industry."[16] Growing faster than any business, "not excluding armament," this industry turned every fresh or critical idea it encountered into a hit or a slogan for the customer. As a result, the modern individual absorbed not the idea but the hit or the slogan. Enzensberger characterized this as a new form of "immaterial exploitation," and the purpose of the mind industry was to "sell the existing order."[17]

For Enzensberger, the mind industry performed a function not unlike the function ascribed by Drimmel to the state. It celebrated the ideal of sovereign individual choice but in fact subjected the individual to a non-negotiable set of priorities. And if for Enzensberger an awareness of such subjection required the leftist intellectual to try to subvert the mind industry, Drimmel could seek to thwart the subjection of the individual by urging a less interventionist state. Not that the politician Drimmel sought to disavow responsibility for cultural policy or to dispense with an association between culture and state. In the 1962 essay on Austrian cultural policy he published in *Österreich in Geschichte und Literatur*, Drimmel acknowledged the popular characterization of Austria as a "culture state," wryly noting that the phrase was frequently invoked at speeches on festive occasions.[18]

But he added, and this was the focus of his attention, "cultural policy" ("*Kulturpolitik*") had both a broad and a narrow meaning. In the broad sense, cultural policy included the efforts of diverse institutions around culture—among these, federal, provincial, and municipal governments, churches, associations, and political parties. Only in the narrow sense did cultural policy refer to the relationship between the state and culture. And Drimmel made clear where he stood. "I wish right now to emphatically point out the basic fact that we in Austria *affirm the culture state* but reject the *principle of state culture*."[19] For Drimmel, the best way to sustain cultural activities, as he understood those activities, was to resist the state organization of culture. Charged with a leading role in making policy, Drimmel called for a kind of noninterventionist activism. In the name of culture, the cultural administrator argued for the retreat of administration.

In seeking to align such a cultural politics with broader trends that discouraged innovation in Austria during the 1950s and early 1960s, scholars have often characterized Drimmel as a traditionalist who wished to mobilize the state on behalf of a hopelessly obsolete vision of culture. Indeed, few statements of Drimmel have been repeated more often than his observation that "the material life of the state demands prestige culturalism (*repräsentativen Kulturalismus*). The imprint of the *Festwochen*, the marble facades of the cultural palaces are more essential for the formation of political will in a mass democracy than the urgent need for modest brick structures to overcome the shortage of classroom space and the state of emergency in scientific research and artistic activity."[20] Oliver Rathkolb, for example, finds here a classic expression of the "backward-looking policy preferences" of that era.[21] But such a reading wrongly takes the assessment of Drimmel for his own position, and it ignores his powerful antagonism toward the state in order to deliver a broader historical argument about backward-looking policy preferences. After all, Drimmel's anti-state posture also rejected a cultural politics agenda fueled by "prestige culturalism." As he himself had written in the previous paragraph, "I consider the essence of my work to be in the frequently desperate *struggle* against the *prestige culturalism* that spreads everywhere and in the *struggle* against *state culture*" (italics in original).[22]

In his 1960 essay on "Culture and Administration," Theodor Adorno observed that "the aversion towards the words culture and administration… must not conceal that there is a certain truth in it." [23] Drimmel shared Adorno's discomfort regarding the convergence of culture and administration. For him, as for Adorno, administration subsumed culture rather than comprehended it. The modern state empowered administrators whose understanding of the problem they were given to solve was not equal to the powers they yielded. To be sure, Drimmel would not have endorsed Adorno's parenthetical remark that such an "aversion [is] by no means free of barbarism and overshadowed by the urge to release the safety catch on a revolver."[24] Drimmel was conservative. But his thinking proceeded from a critical attitude toward the state, and his cultural politics did not entail a reflexive embrace of prestige culturalism.

To this policymaker Drimmel belongs the performance of an education minister who rages helplessly against the proliferation of the state in everyday life. The second rule of thumb to be learned by whoever wishes to be taken seriously as a politician, he wrote, is that "[t]he politician must take note that…the individual no longer wishes to entrust his fate to the care of his family, to neighborhood assistance, to the trade association or even his class."[25] Instead, the individual seeks to replace these networks of shared dependence by pooling their security risks with other similar individuals and entrusting them to the care of the state. Secularization strengthens the state, and in an act of betrayal, the individual weakens the politician whom the people have empowered to act. In turn, the individual who was formerly a subject in a network based on related identities becomes a mass subject of the state. For Drimmel, those who live in the present now work both in and for what he elsewhere called the "state factory of the new human."[26] This factory held even the education minister captive.

III. The Drimmel Effect: The Vanguard Intellectual without the Party

Ernst Hanisch describes Drimmel as a "prototypical conservative intellectual par excellence," and Drimmel struck virtually everyone who encountered him in just this way.[27] Former Chancellor Wolfgang Schüssel, who has said that it was not reading the party program but Drimmel who inspired him to join the ÖVP, recalls that "I myself heard him as a speaker.

He spoke extemporaneously, as if reading from a written text. ...A brilliant intellectual, conservative, to be sure."[28] Here, Schüssel provides testimony for the successful self-presentation of Drimmel as an intellectual. But he also calls attention to the *prima facie* incongruity between Drimmel and the public figure of the intellectual. After all, the intellectual, as this figure has emerged since the Enlightenment, avoids commitments of any kind in order to preserve cognitive autonomy. The intellectual does not reproduce the relationship of the priest to the church. Outside the Leninist tradition, where the intellectual represents the vanguard of the party, intellectuals do not work for the state.

No one would confuse Drimmel with the KPÖ functionary and mandarin Ernst Fischer. But to describe Drimmel as an intellectual who sought to represent the vanguard—minus the party—aptly captures a second element in the performance of the Drimmel effect. For though the personal authority of Drimmel during these years has often been recalled, this authority did not stem from the party. [29] In fact, Drimmel largely shunned party involvement with the ÖVP. He belonged to no party, for example, when Prime Minister Julius Raab nominated him to become education minister in 1954, and Christoph Mertens has described the considerable resistance to the nomination of a political outsider by the ÖVP's parliamentary club.[30] Drimmel never held party office, and he avoided party organizational activities.

More importantly, Drimmel represented the vanguard intellectual because, as he himself had always argued, the modern state had rendered cognitive autonomy irrelevant. In contrast to the present, for example—the age of the Austrian baroque—state and culture had constituted a unity. The intellectual contributed to a body of knowledge whose meaning was self-evident because immanent. By contrast, the intellectual situated in the modern state is confronted with a multiplicity of culture. No body of knowledge is self-evident, and the freedom to choose where to apply critical thinking becomes a burden. The price of the loss of unity, in his words, is a "forced state culture (*Staatskultur*) or something similar."[31] Against this fabricated state culture, Drimmel offered his own leadership as a conservative intellectual. Cognitive autonomy was an illusion. Drimmel stood for steadfastness against changing ideas. "In the era of democracy...," he declared in his 1966 *Forum* essay, "*Lauter Intellektuelle*," "the individual must resist public opinion, mass media, powerful interests, yes, even one's own party."[32]

Drimmel handed down this last obligation, concerning the duty to resist one's own party, after his defeat in the election for party leader at the September 1963 ÖVP Party conference in Klagenfurt. From 1961, under

Chancellor Alfons Gorbach, Drimmel had occupied an intellectual position within the party that far exceeded his direct responsibilities as minster.[33] His loss to the reformer Josef Klaus, who followed Gorbach as chancellor in 1964, signaled an end to any higher national political ambitions Drimmel may have had. Still, it is difficult to imagine how the anti-state posture of Drimmel could have been reconciled with his leadership of the Austrian state. Of course, this posture had a certain self-ironic dimension to it. How could it not? But, as elsewhere, the party conference speech delivered by candidate Drimmel clearly echoed his ongoing critique of the state. As Drimmel told the assembled delegates, "we do not venerate the state as an empty conceptual shell in the Hegelian sense but rather as a place in which we see decreed the protection, shield, and strength of our community." "Nothing should be given to the state" he added, "that others are more capable of doing better, more inexpensively, and—we want to be quite honest—also from inner conviction, more manageably than the state." [34] In his autobiography, Drimmel recalled with some bitterness that conference organizers had scheduled this speech to take place after votes for the election had been cast.[35] Drimmel felt that the election had been tilted against him. Perhaps, though, more than a few in the ÖVP understood Drimmel just as he had presented himself: an intellectual without a party.

IV. The Drimmel Effect: Delegates of Innovation

Drimmel lamented the fact that the state had transformed individuals into a mass subject. But he also conceded that there was no turning back to a unified culture. Meanwhile, his view of the modern intellectual denied the possibility that this figure could provide consistent leadership. So, is the Drimmel effect best described as a cynical, last-ditch performance, the play of a losing hand that seeks to hold innovation in check and aims to preserve a worldview that it concedes no longer exists?

This view, or what might be called the "suppression thesis," represents the shorthand version regarding the legacy of Heinrich Drimmel as education minister. In presenting Drimmel's direction in cultural policy, for example, Stefan Maurer offers a version of this thesis, writing that "Drimmel only supported writers and artists, whose work had been published during the time of the First Republic of Austria and also those, who were active in the literary field during the Nazi era." [36] The heroic period of modern Austrian literature can only begin after Drimmel. Meanwhile, Berthold Molden has described the ÖVP Ministry of Education in the late fifties and early sixties as more of a "stumbling block than a supporter" of relations with the East Bloc. Only the arrival of Bruno Kreisky and the newly established Ministry of Foreign Affairs in 1959, Molden concludes, could force Drimmel to rethink this approach.[37]

Drimmel did not grant a meaningful purpose to the modern intellectual, a hardly shocking stance given his own claim to intellectual leadership. But given his simultaneous claim to political leadership, Drimmel also needed to legitimate the professional work of his ministry, and he can be found elsewhere describing the exercise of proper intellectual activity. The "political functionary," he wrote in "Die Intellektuellen und der Apparat," would have the "courage and the ability" to elevate the political above "politicization."[38] And the "political functionary" was exactly the type "required by today's state and society." This figure possesses "principles and character" but is also aware that politics consists of working to do what is most practical, or even the least harmful. Such a "political functionary," Drimmel added, was an "intellectual in the apparatus of state." Here, finally, was a job description for the type of functionary with whom the minister of education could cooperate. The "intellectual in the apparatus of state" would carry out the new work of Drimmel. This is the third element of the Drimmel effect: attack the state and delegate innovation.

In 1959, the Education Ministry ceased cooperation with the *Grillparzer Gesellschaft*, an organization that since 1956 had, on behalf of the ministry, distributed information on Austrian literature to cultural organizations and educational institutions abroad. This was unfortunate, wrote the ministry's Alfred Weikert to Rudolf Henz, because the *Grillparzer Gesellschaft* would have been the "much-desired, long arm of the Ministry of Education."[39] But by 1960, the ministry had recreated that arm in the *Gesellschaft für österreichische Literatur* with Wolfgang Kraus as its director. Operating with subsidies from the ministry that dwarfed those it made to other start-up cultural organizations, the *Gesellschaft* would, in the coming years, not only continue the distribution of information on Austrian literature abroad, but it would also invite exile Jewish Austrian authors and promote a new generation of Austrian writers via its program series at the Palais Palffy. And Kraus himself would organize three legendary conferences, held in Vienna from 1965 to 1967, that convened intellectuals from both sides of the Iron Curtain.

Among his own ministerial staff, Drimmel is said to have been able to count on both great loyalty and no dissent or independent action internally, and he assigned Weikert to supervise the *Gesellschaft*.[40] Years later, in the obituary he wrote for Weikert in 1990, Wolfgang Kraus credited Weikert with being a cofounder of the *Gesellschaft*, a detail not often noted in that organization's official institutional history.[41] But in 1966, with his first and most influential book, *Der fünfte Stand: Aufbruch der Intellektuellen in West und Ost*, Kraus repaid Drimmel perhaps a still more fundamental conceptual debt.[42] In that book, Kraus argued that in the East, as well as the West, the individual has suffered. For while the individual in the East endures the exercise of state power and feudal-like structures, the individual in the West is increasingly trapped by the pursuit of material goods. Nevertheless, a new force was emerging. That force, which Kraus sought to describe, was the "fifth class" of intellectuals, a force that would rise above East-West divisions and restore the individual. In this "fifth class," Kraus foresaw the end of the state that his sponsor Drimmel never dared imagine.[43]

Drimmel was a superior delegator of a forward-looking cultural policy. Meanwhile, the Drimmel effect suggests how Drimmel could also distance himself from this policy by calling it "the most practical." Such a dynamic might be seen with respect to the role of the Ministry of Education in reengaging East bloc countries, despite the description of the Drimmel ministry by Berthold Molden and others. For in addition to the activities of Kraus, the Ministry of Education funded the new *Arbeitskreis für österreichische Geschichte* with its journal, *Österreich in Geschichte und Literatur*. Drimmel himself charted a course for this journal in its second issue with his essay, "Austria's Historical Mission in the Danube Region."[44] And again, in 1956, the Ministry of Education launched the *Arbeitsgemeinschaft für Ost- und Südeuropaforschung*, with Drimmel himself as chair, another move that signaled a major shift in foreign policy and foreign cultural diplomacy toward Eastern and Southeastern Europe.[45] The *Arbeitsgemeinschaft* would be officially established in 1958 and renamed the *Ost- und Südosteuropa-Institut* in 1964. Recalling the early years of the institute, its long-serving director, Richard G. Plaschka, summarized its relationship with Drimmel in a familiar manner. "In its activities…," Plaschka wrote, "the Institute was required to follow the goal it had agreed upon with the Ministry of Education."[46]

V. The Remains of the Drimmel Effect

The writings and speeches of Heinrich Drimmel provide a notably public display of an early Second Republic state elite grappling with the strengthening Austrian state and the consolidation of the Austrian nation. Considered as an aspect of the ministerial performance of Drimmel, these texts are multidimensional. On one level, they suggest a disavowal of power by Minister Drimmel and a frontal attack on the state. On a second level, they suggest that such disavowals of control could be accompanied by a delegation of authority to others to accomplish modern and forward-looking policy. Wolfgang Kraus and the opening of Austrian domestic cultural policy and Austrian foreign cultural diplomacy is one such instance of delegation.

At the same time, however, Drimmel's attack on the "state itself" could swiftly be redirected to the specific policies he found objectionable. Thomas König has described such activity as a "strategy of containment" in which Drimmel worked to secure "conservatives' hegemony in the entire realm of cultural and educational affairs by dominating the higher education sector."[47] Higher education, König argues, was the battlefield upon which Drimmel believed the future of Austria would be decided, and he waged a "top down struggle against modernization." Not that this sector was highly contested. In Austria, as Christian Fleck has noted, "only a few in the Socialist Party SPÖ and the two opposition parties, the FPÖ (from 1949) and the KPÖ (until 1959) were interested in universities or familiar with them."[48] In the early 1960s, moreover, two-thirds of university students themselves voted for the ÖVP.[49] Drimmel's view that the decisive political battles would be fought over the control of education was shared, at least by like-minded thinkers on the German political left. In his 1962 essay, Hans Magnus Enzensberger warned of the risks of the "mind industry," that "up to now it has not managed to seize control of its most essential sphere, which is education."[50]

Hans Tuppy—the former rector of the University of Vienna and Austrian minister of science and research in the 1980s, whom Drimmel advanced to full professor (*Ordinarius*)—praised Drimmel for his evenhandedness even though the ÖVP-aligned Tuppy was anything but a supporter of the association politics (*Verbändewesen*) cultivated by Drimmel. "The impression I had of Drimmel at that time was that he would go down with the flag waving him," recalled Tuppy, "though his thing was not that new." [51] Such testimony suggests a largely fair-minded figure who was committed to his cause. But Drimmel was also a state minister capable of pursuing an agenda and disinclined to submit to others. Carl Schmitt famously said that the distinction of friend and enemy is the essence of political existence.[52] Indeed, by this standard, Drimmel may be said to have led a thoroughly political existence. Like others in his early Second Republic cohort who had come of age in the 1930s, Drimmel relished vanquishing his enemies, and he favored a binary approach to history and intellectual thought. He thwarted the promotion of notable Austrian historian Friedrich Heer to a full professorship (*Ordinarius*). In a private setting, Heer once asked him quite directly why. Drimmel replied, "I don't like enemies in my own ranks."[53] In later years, Drimmel wrote popular histories that expanded upon his view that the materialistic ambitions of Americans represented the antithesis of the spiritual tradition of Austria. He devoted his book *Die Antipoden* to the proposition that the two superpowers, the conservative Habsburg Monarchy and the liberal United States, represented two diametrically opposed political and ideological systems.[54]

Every politician knows, or must believe, that the state will outlast their own service to it. And despite some mildly messianic statements concerning prospects for the future, perhaps even Drimmel himself expected that his opposition to the state would be forgotten.[55] In any case, the enlargement of the Austrian state – expansion of services, the government apparatus, expenditures, taxes -- is a persistent feature of the Second Austrian Republic.[56] Indeed, today, the afterlife of the Drimmel effect may survive most fully in writers, performers, artists, and others whose livelihood places them in an uneasy relationship with the state. Upon learning that she had been named the recipient of the 2004 Nobel Prize for Literature, Elfriede Jelinek told Swedish Radio, in a turn of phrase that she would later reuse in an interview with the *Frankfurter Allgemeine Zeitung*, that Austria "cannot stick me in its lapel."[57] Heinrich Drimmel recalls a period in recent Austrian history when such ambivalences toward the state could still be keenly felt and creatively expressed—even by a minister of education.

Endnotes

1 Fritz Fellner, "The Problem of the Austrian Nation after 1945," *Journal of Modern European History* 60 (1988): 264-289 (here 264).

2 Oliver Rathkolb, "Die Entwicklung der US-Besatzungskulturpolitik zum Instrument des Kalten Krieges," in *Kontinuität und Bruch 1938-1945-1955*, ed. Friedrich Stadler (Vienna: Jugend und Volk, 1988) 35-50; Johnnes Feichtinger, "Die Kulturpolitik der Besatzungsmacht Großbritannien in Österreich," in *Österreich unter Alliierter Besatzung 1945-1955*, ed. Alfred Ableitinger, Siegfried Beer, and Eduard G. Staudinger (Vienna: Böhlau, 1998) 495-529.

3 Ernst Bruckmüller, "Die Entwicklung des Österreichbewusstseins," in *Österreichische Nationalgeschichte nach 1945*, ed. Robert Kriechbaumer (Vienna: Böhlau, 1998), 369-396 (here 384).

4 Emil Brix, "Widersprüche und Wandlungen im Österreichbewusstsein der Zweiten Republik," in *Österreichische Nationalgeschichte nach 1945*, ed. Robert Kriechbaumer (Vienna: Böhlau, 1998), 449-466 (here 452).

5 Fritz Fellner, *Geschichtsschreibung und nationale Identit*ät (Vienna: Böhlau, 2002).

6 Heinrich Drimmel, "Die Intellektuellen und der Apparat," *Forum* 100, 9 (April 1962): 136-138 (here 136).

7 Bruckmüller "Die Entwicklung," 385.

8 On the impacts of this conservative vision for research and higher education, see Christian Fleck, "Wie Neues nicht entsteht," *Österreichische Zeitschrift für Geschichtswissenschaft* 11, no. 1 (2001): 129-178; Thomas König, "A Strategy of Containment. Heinrich Drimmel's Political Activism in the Realm of Higher Education Policy in the Early Second Republic," *Österreichische Zeitschrift für Geschichtswissenschaft* 29, no. 1 (2018): 180-205.

9 Drimmel was active in the Vienna Heimwehr in 1929, at age 17, and as a university student was accepted in the German student fraternity, *Nordgau*, a member of the *Österreichische Cartellverbindung* (ÖCV). These experiences strengthened what Anton Staudinger has described as Drimmel's "antimarxist and antiliberal worldview," and formed the basis for his 1930s position with the Catholic Student Union (*Hochschülerschaft*). Staudinger suggests that Drimmel successfully mediated university conflicts between Catholics and Nazis, and argues that these "friendly relationship with the National Socialists" enabled him to secure a position in the German Finance administration after 1938. By contrast, Reinhold Knoll, who also summarizes the pre-Anschluß activities and politics of Drimmel, declares with respect to National Socialism that "it is out of the question that he… (Drimmel) had any close relationship to this regime." Friedrich Torberg, who edited *Forum* from 1954 to 1965, published several essays by Drimmel. Of Torberg, Sigurd Paul Scheichl writes that "he never invited collaborators whose records were tainted in brown." Anton Staudinger, "Heinrich Drimmel," in *Die Politiker: Karrieren und Wirken bedeutender Repräsentanten der Zweiten Republik*, ed. Herbert Dachs, Peter Gerlich, and Wolfang C. Müller (Vienna: Manz, 1995), 118-123, here 120; Reinhold Knoll, "Zur politischen Philosophie eines Politikers. -- Gedanken über Heinrich Drimmel," in *Verdrängter Humanismus – verzögerte Aufklärung*, ed. Michael Benedikt et al. (Vienna: Facultas, 2010), 871-877 (here 872-873); Sigurd Paul Scheichl, "Why and How Friedrich Torberg's *Forum* Did Not Confront the Past," *New German Critique* 93 (2004): 87-102 (here 92).

10 For an overview of the policy accomplishments of Drimmel, see Helmut Wohnout, "Heinrich Drimmel. Skizzen zur Biographie eines homo politicus," *Demokratie und Geschichte* 9-10, no. 1 (2007): 65-78.

11 Heinrich Drimmel, "Der Staatsbürger im Wohlfahrtsstaat und in der Konsumgesellschaft," in *Der Österreicher und sein Staat*, ed. Erika Weinzierl (Vienna: Herder, 1965), 125-44 (here 125).

12 Heinrich Drimmel, "Wider den herrschenden Geist der Konsumgesellschaft," in *10 Reden Wider den Geist* (Vienna: Herold, 1965), 9-18 (here 11).

13 Drimmel, "Wider den herrschenden Geist," 9.

14 Victoria de Grazia, *Irresistible Empire: America's Advance through 20th Century Europe* (Cambridge: Harvard UP, 2005).

15 Max Horkheimer and Theodor W. Adorno, *Dialectic of Enlightenment*, ed. Gunzelin Schmid Noerr, trans. Edmund Jephcott (1947; Stanford, Stanford UP, 2002), 94-136.

16 Hans Magnus Enzensberger, "The Industrialization of the Mind," in *The Consciousness Industry* (1962; New York: Seabury, 1974), 3-15.

17 Ibid., 10.

18 Heinrich Drimmel, "Österreichische Kulturpolitik seit dem Staatsvertrag," *Österreich in Geschichte und Literatur* 6, 8 (1962): 343-351 (here 344).

19 Drimmel, "Österreichische Kulturpolitik," 344.

20 Ibid., 349.

21 Oliver Rathkolb, *Die paradoxe Republik: Österreich 1945 bis 2015* (2005; Vienna: Zsolnay, 2015), 49. For a similar reading of this statement by Drimmel as determining for the period, again in a standard reference work, see Klaus Zeyringer and Helmut Gollner, *Eine Literaturgeschichte: Österreich seit 1650* (Innsbruck: Studien, 2012) 617.

22 Drimmel, "Österreichische Kulturpolitik," 349.

23 Theodor Adorno, "Culture and Administration," in *The Culture Industry*, trans. Wes Blomster (Routledge: New York, 1991), 107–131 (here 108).

24 Ibid.

25 Heinrich Drimmel, "Wider das sinnlose Leben des Einzelnen und der Gemeinschaft," in *10 Reden Wider den Geist* (Vienna: Herold, 1965), 120-130 (here 126).

26 Heinrich Drimmel, "Wider die staatliche Fabrik des neuen Menschen," *10 Reden Wider den Geist* (Vienna: Herold, 1965), 19-29.

27 Ernst Hanisch, *Der lange Schatten des Staates* (Vienna: Ueberreuter, 1994) 426.

28 "Interview with Wolfgang Schüssel," *Deutsche Welle*, April 8, 2013.

29 On the authority of Drimmel during the period, see Leo Leitner, "Die Ära Drimmel am Minoritenplatz," *Demokratie und Geschichte* 9-10, no. 1 (2007): 119-126: "Heinrich Drimmel und die österreichische Kultuspolitik," *Demokratie und Geschichte* 9-10, no. 1 (2007): 209-225.

30 Christian Mertens, "Heinrich Drimmel und die ÖVP in den 1960er Jahren," *Demokratie und Geschichte* 9-10, no. 1 (2007): 227-240 (here 227).

31 Heinrich Drimmel, "Wider die Dominanz der Reproduktion in der Kunst," in *10 Reden Wider den Geist* (Vienna: Herold, 1965), 38-43 (here 40).

32 Heinrich Drimmel, "Lauter Intellektuelle," *Forum* 146, Jg. 13 (1966): 85-88 (here 88).

33 Mertens, "Heinrich Drimmel und die ÖVP," 229.

34 *Bundesparteitag 1963 in Klagenfurt* (Österreichischer Verlag 1964) 50-59 (here 56).

35 Heinrich Drimmel, *Die Häuser meines Lebens: Erinnerungen eines Engagierten* (1975; Vienna: Amalthea,1979), 345.

36 Stefan Maurer, "Wolfgang Kraus: Impresario of Austrian Literature and Cold Warrior," in *Austrian Lives*, ed. Günter Bischof, Fritz Plasser, and Eva Maltschnig (New Orleans: UNO Press, 2012), 256-276 (here 262).

37 Berthold Molden, "Das Bundeskanzleramt, Auswärtige Angelegenheiten, und seine Rolle in der österreichischen Kulturpolitik gegenüber den osteuropäischen Staaten 1945-1959," PhD diss., University of Vienna, 1999, 17.

38 Drimmel, "Die Intellektuellen,"138.

39 Viktor Suchy, "Hundert Jahre Grillparzer-Gesellschaft," *Jahrbuch der Grillparzer-Gesellschaft*, 3rd ser., vol. 18, (Vienna: Hora, 1992), 1-207 (here 124).

40 Staudinger, "Heinrich Drimmel," 120.

41 Wolfgang Kraus, "Dank an Alfred Weikert," *Die Furche*, April 26, 1990.

42 Wolfgang Kraus, *Der fünfte Stand: Aufbruch der Intellektuellen in West und Ost* (1966; Munich: Deutscher Taschenbuch Verlag, 1969).

43 On the alternative to the state and its diplomacy envisioned by Wolfgang Kraus, see Michael Burri, "Searching for an Alternative Austrian Cultural Diplomacy: Wolfgang Kraus with Heinrich Drimmel," *German Studies Review* 44, no. 2 (forthcoming, 2021).

44 Heinrich Drimmel, "Österreichs historische Sendung im Donauraum," *Österreich in Geschichte und Literatur* 1, no. 2 (1957): 1-3.

45 Vladislav Marjanović, *Die Mitteleuropa-Idee und die Mitteleuropa-Politik Österreichs 1945-1995* (Frankfurt aM: Peter Lang, 1998), 51.

46 Richard G. Plaschka, "Zur Bilanz: Zwanzig Jahre Österreichisches Ost- und Südeuropäisches Institut," *Österreichische Osthefte* 20 (1978): 7-9 (here 7). See also, Emilia Hrabovec, "Richard Georg Plaschka (1925-2001)," in *Osteuropäische Geschichte in Wien*, ed. Arnold Suppan, Marija Wakounig, and Georg Kastner (Innsbruck: Studienverlag, 2007), 331-346 (here 333).

47 König, "A Strategy of Containment," 190. On the similar role Drimmel played with the Fulbright Commission, see Thomas König, *Die Frühgeschichte des Fulbright Program in Österreich* (Vienna: Studienverlag, 2012).

48 Christian Fleck, "Über die Rolle von bedeutender Intelligenz, hingebendem Fleiss und liebenswürdigen charakterlichen Anlagen als Qualifikationen für wissenschaftliche Karrieren in Österreichs Zweiter Republik," in *Wandlungen und Brüche: Wissenschaftsgeschichte als politische Geschichte*, ed. Johannes Feichtinger et al (Vienna: Vienna UP, 2018), 389-397 (here 393-394). With respect to the "strategy of containment," described by König, Fleck elsewhere provides a fascinating account of the disengaged role played by Drimmel in the efforts of the Ford Foundation and Paul Lazarfeld to establish an Institute of Advanced Study in Vienna in the mid-1950s. Fleck seconds the view of Lazarfeld that Drimmel was a key figure. But in response to Lazarfeld's assessment that "fortunately he (Drimmel) would undoubtedly also be a good person to work with," Fleck honestly admits his own limitations in understanding how others saw Drimmel, writing that this "seems to me however barely comprehensible." "Wie Neues nicht entsteht. Die Gründung des Instituts für Höhere Studien in Wien durch Ex-Österreicher und die Ford Foundation," *Österreichische Zeitschrift für Geschichtswissenschaft* 11, no. 1 (2001): 129-178 (here 136).

49 Adolf Kozlik, *Wie wird wer Akademiker? Zum österreichischen Schul- und Hochschulwesen*, (Vienna: Europa-Verlag, 1965) 164.

50 Enzensberger, "The Industrialization of the Mind" 6.

51 Hans Tuppy, "... zwischen Wissenschaft und Politik," *Demokratie und Geschichte* 4 (2000): 58-78 (here 66).

52 Carl Schmitt, *The Concept of the Political*, trans. George Schwab (Chicago: Chicago UP, 1996), 26.

53 Norbert Leser, "Friedrich Heer (1916-1983). Der intellektuelle Österreichs schlechthin," *Skurrile Begegnungen: Mosaike zur österreichischen Geistesgeschichte* (Vienna: Böhlau, 2011), 71-78 (here 72-73).

54 Heinrich Drimmel, *Die Antipoden: Die Neue Welt in den USA und das Österreich vor 1918* (Vienna: Amalthea, 1984).

55 On the signs for a turn toward a different future see, Heinrich Drimmel, "Niemand lebt vom Brot allein…" *Österreichische Academia* 12, 11-12 (1960-61): 6-8.

56 Manfried Welan, *Republik der Mandarine: Ein Beitrag zur Bürokratie- und Beamtendiskussion*, Diskussionspapier Nr. 57-R-96 (Vienna: Institut für Wirtschaft, Politik und Recht. Universität für Bodenkultur, 1996), 4.

57 Schweizerische Depeschenagentur, "Jelinek will nicht zur Nobelpreisverleihung kommen," *Neue Zürcher Zeitung*, October 7, 2004, http://www.nzz.ch/newzzE00UWOM0-12-1.317084/. Elfriede Jelinek, "Der Nobelpreis muß an mir vorüberziehen: Interview with Elfriede Jelinek, Part II," by Rose-Maria Gropp and Hubert Spiegel, *Frankfurter Allgemeine Zeitung*, November 8, 2004, http://www.faz.net/aktuell/feuilleton/elfriede-jelinek-der-nobelpreis-muss-an-mir-vorueberziehen-1195180.html/.

Forum: South Tyrol in the Twentieth Century

South Tyrol in the Twentieth Century: Introduction

Günter Bischof

In the twenty-eight volumes of *Contemporary Austrian Studies* published since 1993, we have only printed one essay on the South Tyrol issue, which is an issue so vital to Austrian and Italian contemporary history.[1] The papers in this panel were first presented at the annual meeting of the Austrian Studies Association in Bowling Green, Ohio, in April 2019. As the essays in this FORUM suggest, the historiography on the South Tyrol issue has commonly been written from both the patriotic/nationalist Austrian/Tyrolean and Tridentine/Italian sides. These two historiographies hardly took note of one another. In the essays published in this FORUM, the authors are going beyond such traditional patriotic/nationalist perspectives. Based on archival sources and the asking of new questions, they are incorporating the historiographies of the other side.

All three scholars contributing to this FORUM are deeply steeped in the historiography of South Tyrol and teach at American universities. All three scholars approach this subject matter from a distance *sine ira et studio*. Eden K. McLean is an American who wrote her published dissertation at Yale University on Mussolini's education policies and teaches at Auburn University.[2] Roberta Pergher was born in South Tyrol and teaches Italian/European history at the University of Indiana and has published her University of Michigan dissertation on Mussolini's borderlands.[3] Gerald Steinacher worked as an archivist and historian in South Tyrol for more than thirteen years and currently teaches at the University of Nebraska. His University of Innsbruck dissertation on Allied intelligence services and their role in South Tyrol during World War II was also published.[4] All three represent the next generation of historians working on the South Tyrol issue without any patriotic/nationalist axes to grind. They also suggest a growing interest in American academia on the South Tyrol minority conflict.

Eden K. McLean looks at Italy's assimilation policies of the South Tyrolean population in the time between the two World Wars. She recognizes a transition from the "gradual" assimilationist approach of the post-World War I Liberal Italian governments to a more radical assimilation policy of Mussolini's Fascists. In 1926, Mussolini's government issued a declaration that it would divide the region of Venezia Tridentina (hitherto the larger administrative unit of the region, incorporating the German speakers in a majority Italian population) into the two politically distinct provinces Trentino and Alto Adige. "Gradual assimilation" had not worked. The new Fascist "divide and rule" policy aimed to "[identify] the majority German speakers bureaucratically and to isolate them politically and economically from the majority speakers of the Trentino." A segregated German population could be targeted with more intense Italianization efforts. In spite of Mussolini's efforts to make the Alto Adige region "a model of *italianità* and a fundamental part of a unified Italian nation-state, the Fascist regime created a multi-national space that only highlighted its weaknesses."

Roberta Pergher analyzes the controversial 1939 *Option* agreement between Adolf Hitler and Benito Mussolini and goes beyond the traditional narrative of "victimhood and injustice."[5] When the *Führer* and the *Duce* agreed to give the German speakers a choice to either stay in South Tyrol and accept Italian citizenship or leave the region and resettle in Germany, they practiced a policy of "ethnic cleansing" that foreshadowed policies of "population resettlement pursued by the Nazis across Europe." In this broader context, Pergher argues, the *Option* is "very much a European borderland story." Only in the 1970s and 1980s did a new generation of historians "connect the *Option* to broader historiography on the Third Reich." In this new reading, the South Tyroleans were enthusiastic about joining the Third Reich, and the Italians asserted their sovereignty by "right peopling" the territory. Mussolini's assimilation policies in South Tyrol had failed, but Hitler refused to "deliver" irredentist South Tyroleans from Fascist-forced Italianization. Nazi Germany "renounced" South Tyrol in favor of its alliance with Italy. Italy had been "resettling" the Italian population in its colonies of Libya and Ethiopia, so resettling the German borderland population of South Tyrol in Germany was not much of a stretch. In a stark conclusion, Pergher shows how the *Option* tore families apart as they made individual choices for both sides.

Gerald Steinacher shows how the patriotic/nationalist historiography of South Tyrol has claimed a dual victimization by both Italian Fascism and German Nazism for a long time. This "*Volk in Not*" ideology prevailed into the post-World War II era. Only after 1968 did South Tyrolean journalists and historians begin to question this victim narrative, demonstrating how strongly South Tyroleans identified with the Nazi regime. These revisionist historians were castigated by the local elites. After the end of the Cold War in 1989/90 the new narrative questioning the victimization of the South Tyroleans took a hold in historiography. Now Professor Rolf Steininger and the faculty of the new Institute of Contemporary History at the University of Innsbruck became the center of revisionist South Tyrolean history—the same university that earlier had been the mainstay of patriotic/nationalist historiography. Steinacher concludes with the ironic twist that only in South Tyrol could supporters of Nazism also claim to be anti-fascists.

All three papers in this FORUM open new avenues of understanding South Tyrolean history and historiography. In the process, they present South Tyrolean history as more mainstream European than previous patriotic/nationalist historians have done, dwelling on South Tyrolean victimization by Fascist Italy and then Nazi Germany and then by post-World War II Democratic Italy again. McLean portrays the Italianization of South Tyrol as part of a process going on throughout the borderlands (and in other parts of Europe). Pergher shows how resettlement of the South Tyroleans was part and parcel both of Italian resettlement of excess population to the colonies and later German vast resettlement projects—the interwar beginning of "ethnic cleansing," if you will. Steinacher demonstrates how the South Tyroleans were infatuated with Nazism like the rest of German-speaking Europe. Call it the inevitable "normalization" of South Tyrolean history and historiography, less *sui generis*, more part of the European mainstream of minority conflicts. Normalization is being used in the sense that the "past exceptionality" of South Tyrolean history is fading away and being "overturned."[6]

Endnotes

[1] Rolf Steininger, "75 Years After: The South Tyrol Conflict Resolved. A Contribution to European Stability and a Model for Solving Minority Conflicts," in *Austria in the Nineteen Fifties* (Contemporary Austrian Studies 3), ed. Günter Bischof, Anton Pelinka and Rolf Steininger (New Brunswick, NJ: Transaction, 1995), 189-203. This essay is based on idem, *South Tyrol: A Minority Conflict of the Twentieth Century* (New Brunswick, NJ: Transaction, 1993).

2 Eden K. McLean, *Mussolini's Children: Race and Elementary Education in Fascist Italy* (Lincoln: University of Nebraska Press, 2018).

3 Roberta Pergher, *Mussolini's Nation-Empire: Sovereignty and Settlement in Italy's Borderlands, 1922-1943* (Cambridge: Cambridge University Press, 2018).

4 Gerald Steinacher, *Südtirol und die Geheimdienste 1943-1945* (Innsbruck: StudienVerlag, 2000).

5 See also *Die Option: Südtirol zwischen Faschismus und Nationalsozialismus*, ed. Klaus Eisterer and Rolf Steininger (Innsbruck: StudienVerlag, 1989).

6 In the sense used by Gavriel D. Rosenfeld, *Hi Hitler: How the Nazi Past is Being Normalized in Contemporary Culture* (Cambridge: Cambridge University Press, 2015), 7-9.

A Border within the Borderland: Assimilation through Separation in Fascist Italy's South Tyrol[1]

Eden K. McLean

For those readers somewhat familiar with the modern history of South Tyrol, one of the first things that comes to mind is probably the 1939 agreement between Nazi Germany and Fascist Italy to allow German-speaking residents (and *only* German-speaking residents) to choose whether to exchange their Italian citizenship for German citizenship and move to an as-of-yet undecided territory in Adolf Hitler's expanding empire. Yet this traumatic chapter in the region's history did not mark an entirely radical departure from previous Italian policy in South Tyrol; it was only the latest, most extreme solution to the government's difficulties with the region's German-speaking population that emerged in the days after annexation in the aftermath of World War I. Though Italian nationalists contended that the portion of Tyrol south of the Brenner Pass was historically, geographically, and spiritually "Italian," Rome's interwar governments faced significant difficulty in determining how best to integrate its new multilingual border region into the nation-state. A number of shifts in policy between 1919 and 1939 demonstrated an increasing impatience with what officials saw as an unwillingness on the part of many German speakers to embrace their rightful homeland and the regime's ultimate assessment that the former Habsburg territory did not simply contain "Germanized" Italians but, in fact, two distinct and largely antagonistic national populations.[2] Of particular note but little scholarship, Rome's December 1926 resolution to establish an internal border that administratively separated the region's German and Italian speakers into discrete provinces marked a significant turning point in the state's multifaceted "Italianization" campaign from a strategy of "gradual assimilation" to one of "divide and conquer" that would help pave the way for the infamous 1939 *Option*.

The modern idea that national borders demarcate boundaries between national populations as much as between political entities spurred Rome's ambition to secure an unquestionably "Italian" border between its newly enlarged kingdom and the much reduced—but still potentially dangerous—Austrian nation-state. The problem, of course, is that borders never separate populations neatly or accurately into obvious, self-determined nations; borders are far more frequently multilingual spaces where "political sovereignty [is] 'indeterminate'" rather than definitive.[3] Not only did Italy's new borderland illustrate this messiness, but it had the added complexity of containing a population and land that had belonged to a multilingual empire until 1918. While paying allegiance to what some historians of the Habsburg Empire have called a "non-national state," the people of southern Tyrol had functioned within a political and cultural reality that largely had not required adherence to a single "national" identity.[4] Though the nineteenth-century development of more centralized education systems, censuses, and other bureaucratic innovations began to force different Habsburg populations into "ethnic boxes"—eliding and erasing numerous alternative categories of identification along the way—there was a general sense within many Habsburg communities of local autonomy in such decisions.[5] Now under the control of the Italian nation-state, however, these former Habsburg subjects could not be indifferent to nationality. Instead, they had to convincingly embody Italian-ness—*italianità*—and, by extension, rid themselves of all outward forms of non-Italian-ness.[6]

Language was broadly considered a fundamental component of the "Italian" identity that was to serve as a bulwark against foreign encroachment at the Brenner Pass, and while a majority of residents in the south of Italy's new territory, Trentino, primarily spoke variations of Italian, a majority of residents in South Tyrol (Alto Adige to authorities in Rome) predominantly spoke variations of German. This linguistic reality posed a significant obstacle to the Italian state's objective, particularly when read alongside the prevailing nationalist assumptions that, first, speakers of Italian *were* Italian just as speakers of German *were* German and, second, that there was little room for self- or collective identification with more than one—or no—nationality.[7] Given this interpretation of the relationships between language, national identification, and modern political hegemony, Rome recognized a need to undertake a deliberate campaign to "Italianize" the entire population in order to establish a definitively Italian border.

After the kingdom successfully took military and then political control of South Tyrol and Trentino in the months following the November 1918 armistice, Italian statesmen faced a robust debate over how best to ensure the *italianità* of their new Alpine border while simultaneously illustrating their government's clear superiority over that of the former Habsburg Empire. After years of accusing the government in Vienna of "de-nationalizing" the spiritually "Italian" population under its control, Italy's Liberal regime was hard-pressed to demonstrate its commitment to respect its new "German" residents.[8] Additionally, Italian authorities faced significant pressure from the bishops of Brixen/Bressanone and Trent to respect the territory's preexisting ecclesiastical boundaries that largely fell along linguistic fault lines. Even Trent's Bishop Celestino Endrici, whom the Habsburg regime had imprisoned during World War I for supposedly supporting the Italian cause, urged Rome in a 1919 letter to recognize the "singular" nature of the region when finalizing the new administrative system. In Endrici's estimation, it was "much better to recognize the unique character of the Tyrolean, to gradually earn his trust without impinging on his deep-rooted beliefs, which he considers sacred."[9] And yet, what officials in Rome most desired was the irrefutable delineation between Italian and Austrian jurisdiction—to confirm Italian political and cultural power in the region—not the protection of the "unique character" of its new border community and particularly not if that character happened to seem remarkably similar to an "Austro-German" character.

Italy's Liberal regime attempted to thread this needle when, in 1921, it announced that the newly annexed region would maintain a single provincial administration. Authorities in Rome chose to adopt a philosophy of "gradual assimilation" that asserted they could best strengthen the *italianità* of the region and produce the least amount of popular opposition by treating it as one cohesive Italian province containing mere pockets of German speakers in its north.[10] The attendant decision to name the territory Venezia Tridentina aimed to highlight the depth of its Italian-ness by deliberately linking the whole region to its southern city of Trent, the heart of the Italian-speaking population.[11] Such a resolution highlighted Rome's awareness of the power inherent in borders and, in turn, its disinterest in mapping the region's civil boundaries onto its ecclesiastical cantons.[12] To do so would, first, suggest a concession to the Catholic Church (which would not have been ideal for the Liberal regime) and, second, entail creating a separate northern province with an overwhelmingly German-speaking population along what was meant to be a border of unquestionable *italianità*. To divide the new territory into two jurisdictions would suggest to Germans speakers and their allies that the Italian state acknowledged their existence as a minority population, resulting in an increase of "pan-Germanist" efforts to renegotiate Italy's northern border.[13] As the ardent Italian nationalist and senator Ettore Tolomei wrote in 1919, "it is too easy to imagine the problems caused by creating a predominantly 'German' province" so close to the Austrian border. Instead, Tolomei continued, "only by joining the upper valleys with the Trentino will the region have a large and decisive Italian majority; and then the unified administrative entity will make the political and ethnic fusion easier and quicker."[14] As Tolomei's commentary suggested, the establishment of a single province under the leadership of Trent, at least theoretically, signaled Rome's trust in the local

Italian-speaking population to administrate the new region but also to infiltrate its non-Italian-speaking communities and to absorb them quickly and peacefully into the "Italian" way of life.[15] This more organic, gradual approach to assimilating German speakers to their (re)new(ed) national identity was, as Mussolini's personal secretary, Alessandro Chiavolini, would write in 1923, a policy of "prevention instead of repression." Chiavolini elaborated, explaining that "while the assimilation efforts must always proceed with energetic firmness, it should use generous and persuasive methods as far as possible" to avoid producing resentment or opposition.[16] And, until late 1926, both Roman and local authorities championed this idea, working under the principle that the local Italian-speaking population, with its knowledge of and entwined relationships with its "non-Italian" neighbors, was best positioned to lead the Italianization campaign.[17]

Italianization policies in the early 1920s generally adhered to this approach of gradual assimilation. For example, by 1923, all public schoolteachers were required to be proficient in Italian, but German- and Ladin-speaking students were only incrementally introduced to lessons in Italian.[18] Only first-graders were obligated to take classes in Italian during the 1923-24 school year, and that requirement was to expand by a grade each subsequent year.[19] Under this policy, it would take several years before the state would compel all students to take classes exclusively in Italian.[20] In theory, such guidelines allowed for students to maintain some sense of continuity while the state steadily increased exposure to the new linguistic and national identities students were to assume. It also indicated that the regime's earliest dictates about who was Italian and what was *italianità* were somewhat fluid and open to all who spoke Italian and educated their students to do so. That is, the central government appeared to support the notion that the Habsburg occupation of the territory had merely submerged the "great Latin blood" coursing through the veins of all the region's inhabitants and that greater exposure to *italianità* would lead these so-called "de-nationalized" Italians to rediscover their inherent national identity.[21]

The 1921 decision to advance a program of gradual assimilation in Venezia Tridentina did not end the discussion over how best to manage the border region, however. The appointment of Benito Mussolini as prime minister in 1922 only intensified pressure on local authorities to prove the security of Italy's political and cultural hegemony along its border with Austria. Moreover, the *Duce*'s efforts to affect a reconciliation with the Vatican most likely inspired him to give greater consideration to the request from regional Church authorities to harmonize civil and ecclesiastical jurisdictional boundaries. Rumors of a border within the borderland persisted within the region as well, and local Italian-speaking nationalists continued to express anxiety over the threat of a political division between Trentino and South Tyrol. The vocal Italian nationalist and former mayor of Trent Vittorio Zippel wrote in a 1923 letter to Mussolini that such a possibility evoked in him—and the entire Trentine population—"a sense of painful shock."[22] Despite Interior Minister Luigi Federzoni's declaration in early 1926 that a "single province of Trent was definitively established, clearly rejecting the idea of another province with Bolzano as its capital," it seems Rome's shift in position later that year did not take everyone by surprise.[23]

Rome's December 1926 declaration that the regime would divide the region of Venezia Tridentina into two politically distinct provinces—Trentino and Alto Adige—as part of a broader reform of the nation's provincial system marked an important change in the regime's approach to the assimilation project in the hopes that a more direct policy of "divide and conquer" would more quickly achieve complete Italianization.[24] South Tyrol would no longer be run indirectly through the prefecture of Trent but directly, with an uninterrupted line of communication between Rome and the new capital of Alto Adige, Bolzano (Bozen), the center of the region's German-speaking population.[25] Senator Tolomei explained that Mussolini's decision—and his own rush to support it—served as proof of Fascism's successful conquest of the central government and its improvement of the nation-state at large: "the unified region that was a necessity during...a time of weak and ignorant governments,...even during the first phase of the Fascist revolution as the most effective means of assimilating Alto Adige, today, ten years after annexation, with a strong and wise government, is a necessity no longer."[26] Certainly the postwar Liberal regime had considerable difficulty asserting its control over the region, though to say it was the only reason state authorities had to rely on local actors to help organize and run Venezia Tridentina ignores the ongoing debates taking place among Italian nationalists—within both academic and bureaucratic circles—over the substance of national categories, the extent of its malleability, and whether the region's German speakers were capable of becoming truly Italian.[27]

More than reflecting an increase in Fascist bureaucratic power, Rome's reorganization of Venezia Tridentina's provincial administration revealed Mussolini's disappointment in the limited success gradual assimilation had thus far accomplished. Instead of the seemingly more passive approach of organically "diluting" regional non-Italian-ness through daily interactions between German speakers and their Italian-speaking neighbors, the increasingly totalitarian regime envisioned the regional partition as a way to identify the majority of German speakers bureaucratically and to isolate them politically and economically from the majority of Italian speakers.[28] In his famous Ascension Day speech of May 26, 1927, the *Duce* assured his followers that such a measure was not meant as any kind of "concession to the German element," much of which (on both sides of the Pass) had long called for a similar acknowledgement of the linguistic and cultural fissures in the region.[29] Instead, the segregation of German speakers delimited where more targeted and intense Italianization efforts would take place among those residents who posed the greatest threat to Italian cultural hegemony in Venezia Tridentina.[30] Consequently, the second half of the 1920s witnessed a conscious acceleration of state efforts to create a clear and present *italianità* in South Tyrol and the essential abandonment of such efforts in Trentino.[31]

Fascist authorities from Rome dismissed the argument that they were aiming to separate "Germans" from "Italians" physically, politically, and culturally, claiming that "in Italy there are only Italians."[32] In other words, as all residents of the Kingdom of Italy were Italian, all were treated equally. To grant South Tyroleans access to German-language education, for example, would be to consider them an exceptional population within the nation-state. Echoing this rationale, Fascist officials increasingly worked to formally eliminate the term "German" to describe German speakers, instead opting for the terms *allogeni* (aliens) and *alloglotti* (foreign-language speakers).[33] Such rhetorical logic worked to avoid granting German speakers the right to practice or pass on family traditions deemed particularly Germanic and attempted to negate the very existence of the German-speaking community or individuals' identification as German or Austrian. And yet, their identification as "alien" still differentiated these residents from a supposedly pure Italian nation.

Despite these linguistic gymnastics, the bureaucratic transformation of Venezia Tridentina into Trentino and Alto Adige suggested an official acceptance of the idea that the region contained multiple distinct national populations—and homelands—rather than a single Italian community. The creation of a predominantly German-speaking province apart from Trentino shaped a space that was almost exclusively not-Italian and in turn generated, or at least rigidified, boundaries—and therefore identifications—within the population; German speakers were effectively defined as foreigners on Italian soil. Of course, German and Austrian nationalism had existed in the region well before the start of the Fascist assimilationist campaign, and World War I had proved especially divisive for South Tyroleans and Trentini, especially as many residents in the region's southeast experienced the ravages of war firsthand.[34] Still, a result of the Fascist state's increasingly draconian efforts to deny the complex and nuanced ways residents identified and categorized themselves appears actually to have been an increase in Austro-German nationalist efforts. In the face of accusations that that their language usage and names and habits were not Italian enough for the Italian state, it is not surprising that German speakers fought back, often turning to a nationalism that ostensibly supported their sense of connectedness. The fact that German-language clergy in the region overwhelmingly and adamantly supported the right to live, learn, and pray in one's mother tongue gave German speakers a political voice during the thaw in relations between Rome and the Vatican.[35] The Church also provided them with safe spaces in which to speak German and conduits through which to communicate with supporters on the other side of the border. That the late 1920s saw an increase in the now-famous underground system of German-language schools known as *Katakombenschulen* and stronger ties between South Tyroleans and Austro-German nationalist groups should therefore be no surprise.[36] This type of "transborder nationalism" undoubtedly emerged out of the Italian state's efforts to create a model national community and its clear message that, while technically Italian citizens, German-speaking South Tyroleans were not, in fact, Italians.[37]

The continued lack of success in the project to assimilate the residents of Venezia Tridentina after the provincial restructuring in 1926 only led to increasingly aggressive Italianization efforts, including even stricter linguistic regulations and more frequent population transfers—both to and from Italy's "old provinces" with the goal of populating the border with truly "Italian" residents. In turn, these measures led to heightened resistance throughout the region, as well as to threatened relationships between the Italian state and Germany, Austria, and the Catholic Church. In other words, the regime unintentionally transformed the region from a multilingual territory into a multinational space with clear divisions between those residents who were, in the eyes of the Fascists, Italian and those who were not. Instead of creating a region that was a model of *italianità* and a fundamental part of a unified Italian nation-state, the Fascist regime created a multinational space that only highlighted its weaknesses.

Endnotes

1 I would like to thank Günter Bischof for organizing this Roundtable, and Christian Karner and Roberta Pergher for their comments on the draft. I could not have done any of this research without financial support from Trinity College's Barbieri Foundation and the American Philosophical Society, as well as Auburn University's College of Liberal Arts and Department of History.

2 There was no consensus among Italian nationalists on what to make of the region's Ladin-speaking population; many argued, however, that it was essentially Italian. For example, Giuseppe Sergi, "I 'ladini' sono italiani," *Archivio per l'Alto Adige* VIII, no. 1 (1913), 42; Ettore Tolomei, *L'Alto Adige* (Turin: Tip. Palatina di G. Bonis e Rossi, 1915); Dante Marini, "La crisi di coscienza dei ladini," *Trentino: Rivista della Legione trentina* IV, no. 6 (1928).

3 Roberta Pergher, *Mussolini's Nation-Empire: Sovereignty and Settlement in Italy's Borderlands, 1922-1943* (Cambridge: Cambridge University Press, 2018), 15.

4 On the concept of the "non-national" Habsburg state, see, for example, Jeremy King, "The Nationalization of East Central Europe: Ethnicism, Ethnicity, and Beyond," in *Staging the Past: The Politics of Commemoration in Habsburg Central Europe, 1848 to the Present*, ed. Maria Bucur and Nancy M. Wingfield (West Lafayette, Indiana: Purdue University Press, 2001); Gary B. Cohen, "Nationalist Politics and the Dynamics of State and Civil Society in the Habsburg Monarchy, 1867-1914," *Central European History* 40 (2007); Rok Stergar and Tamara Scheer, "Ethnic Boxes: The Unintended Consequences of Habsburg Bureaucratic Classification," *Nationalities Papers* 46, no. 4 (2018).

5 Stergar and Scheer, "Ethnic Boxes: The Unintended Consequences of Habsburg Bureaucratic Classification"; Cohen, "Nationalist Politics and the Dynamics of State and Civil Society in the Habsburg Monarchy, 1867-1914"; This does not mean to ignore the presence of growing numbers of nationalist organizations throughout the empire. For more on the rise of nationalist activism in the empire's "language frontiers," see Pieter M. Judson, *Guardians of the Nation: Activists on the Language Frontiers of Imperial Austria* (Cambridge, MA: Harvard University Press, 2006); Nancy M. Wingfield, *Flag Wars and Stone Saints: How the Bohemian Lands Became Czech* (Cambridge, MA: Harvard University Press, 2007). Even my use of the term "Trentino" to describe the southern-most portion of the annexed region has its roots in this late nineteenth-century process of nationalizing populations in the Habsburg Empire. Laurence Cole, "Patriotic Celebrations in Late-Nineteenth- and Early-Twentieth-Century Tirol," in *Staging the Past: The Politics of Commemoration in Habsburg Central Europe, 1848 to the Present*, ed. Maria Bucur and Nancy M. Wingfield, (West Lafayette, Indiana: Purdue University Press, 2001), 113.

6 On the concept of national indifference, see Tara Zahra, *Kidnapped Souls: National Indifference and the Battle for Children in the Bohemian Lands, 1900-1948* (Ithaca and London: Cornell University Press, 2008), 4; Tara Zahra, "Imagined Noncommunities: National Indifference as a Category of Analysis," *Slavic Review* 69, no. 1 (2010); Pieter M. Judson and Tara Zahra, "Introduction," *Austrian History Yearbook* 43 (2012). (Judson and Zahra's piece introduces a special issue of the *Austrian History Yearbook* dedicated to the theme "Sites of National Indifference.")

7 Italian nationalists were certainly not alone in this position; in the modern quest for national unity among populations across Europe, language was often the first characteristic used to identify national membership. Rogers Brubaker, *Grounds for Difference* (Cambridge, MA and London, England: Harvard University Press, 2015), 5, 87. On the contemporaneous case study of Alsace-Loraine, see Stephen L. Harp, *Learning to Be Loyal: Primary Schooling as Nation Building in Alsace and Lorraine, 1850-1940* (DeKalb, IL: Northern Illinois University Press, 1998), x-xi, 4-5. Of course, J. G. von Herder was perhaps the most famous promoter of this principle in his *Letters for the Advancement of Humanity* (c. 1791-97). Even within the

multilingual Austro-Hungarian Empire, subjects were required to report a single language "of daily use" for the imperial census, ignoring the fact that many subjects were themselves multilingual or primarily identified themselves through different categories, such as territory, religion, or class. Stergar and Scheer, "Ethnic Boxes: The Unintended Consequences of Habsburg Bureaucratic Classification."; Dominique Kirchner Reill, *Nationalists Who Feared the Nation: Adriatic Multi-Nationalism in Habsburg Dalmatia, Trieste, and Venice* (Stanford: Stanford University Press, 2012); Jeremy King, *Budweisers into Czechs and Germans: A Local History of Bohemian Politics, 1848-1948* (Princeton, NJ: Princeton University Press, 2002). On the problems this discrepancy produced within the new Italian borderlands, see, for example, Marina Cattaruzza, "Slovenes and Italians in Trieste, 1850-1914," in *Ethnic Identity in Urban Europe*, ed. Max Engman, (New York, NY: New York University Press, 1992); Maura Hametz, "Naming Italians in the Borderland, 1926-1943," *Journal of Modern Italian Studies* 15, no. 3 (2010).

8 Giuseppe Guadagnini, "Memoriale sulle condizioni religiose nell'Alto Adige," 1925 (Fondo sacra congregazione degli affari ecclesiastici straordinari, Segretaria di stato del Vaticano (hereafter AA.EE.SS., Arch. Seg. Stato), IV Periodo, Italia, Pos. 644, F. 71), 6-7; Lodovico Mortara, Letter to Celestino Endrici, September 15, 1919 (Archivio Diocesano Tredentino (hereafter ADT), Acta Episcopalia Endrici Celestino, 816/1919).

9 Celestino Endrici, Letter to Luigi Facta, May 17, 1919 (AA.EE.SS, Seg. Stato, III Periodo, Austria Ungheria, Pos. 1408, F. 561).

10 Tullio Minghetti and Giuseppe Cristofolini, "Oggetto: Memoriale della Leg. Trentina 'Provincia unica Trento'," August 31, 1923 (Fondazione Museo Storico del Trentino (hereafter FMST), Archivio Legione trentina, B. 8, F. 23, "19. Fiume - Alto Adige").

11 Cesira Zambellini, "Assillante certamente per la vita italiana...", ed. ONAIR, 1923 (Archivio Provinciale di Trento (hereafter APTn), ONAIRC, B. 206, F. Relazioni anno 1923).

12 Many scholars have written on the role of borders as sites of power; a good introduction is Hastings Donnan and Thomas M. Wilson, *Borders: Frontiers of Identity, Nation and State* (Oxford and New York: Berg, 1999).

13 Alessandro Chiavolini, "La provincia di Bolzano. Appunto per S.E. il Presidente," August 30, 1923 (Archivio Centrale dello Stato, Presidenza del Consiglio dei Ministri (hereafter ACS, PCM), Gab., 1923, B. 695, F. 1/1-6). According to Ettore Tolomei, the local German nationalist group *Deutscher Verband* had wanted South Tyrol to be a separate province immediately after annexation, and Tolomei delighted in the fact that it did not get its wish. Ettore Tolomei and Giuseppe Preziosi, "Provvedimenti per l'Alto Adige: Intesi ad un'azione ordinata pronta efficace d'assimilazione italiana," ed. ONAIR, 1923 (APTn, ONAIRC, B. 207, F. Questione Alto Adige), 6.

14 Ettore Tolomei, "Trentino e Alto Adige, provincia unica," *La vita italiana* XIV, no. LXXIX (1919), 3. Even the Fascist Party, in its first days in the region, argued vociferously for a united province of Venezia Tridentina. Achille Starace, "Ai deputati Fascisti! A tutti i Fascisti d'Italia!," June 1, 1921 (ACS, Segretaria Particolare del Duce, Carteggio Ordinario (hereafter SPD (CO)) 556.428 Bolzano: Situazione politica).

15 Tolomei, "Trentino e Alto Adige, provincia unica," 7.

16 Chiavolini, "La provincia di Bolzano. Appunto per S.E. il Presidente," August 30, 1923.

17 Giuseppe Cristofolini, "I trentini e la provincia di Bolzano," *Trentino: Rivista della Legione trentina* III, no. 10 (1927), 209.

18 Guglielmo Pecori-Giraldi, "Oggetto: Toponomastica dell'Alto Adige," 1919 (ACS, Archivio Luigi Credaro, B. 35, F. 235). As of October 1, 1923, all German-language schools were technically "suppressed" and transformed into Italian-language schools, though German could still be taught as a "second" language. Pietro Fedele, Letter to Benito Mussolini,

January 25, 1926 (ACS, PCM, Gab., 1924, B. 740, F. 1/1-11.2525); Michael Gamper, Letter to Pietro Tacchi Venturi, Noveber 21, 1925 (Archivum Romanum Societatis Iesu (hereafter ARSI), Arch. Tacchi Venturi, B. 12, F. 294). For the most thorough study of Italy's interwar Italianization campaign in the region, see Andrea di Michele, *L'italianizzazione imperfetta: L'amministrazione pubblica dell'Alto Adige tra Italia liberale e fascismo* (Alessandria: Edizioni dell'Orso, 2003).

19 Giovanni Gentile, "R. D. 1 ottobre 1923, n. 2185 -- Ordinamento dei gradi scolastici e dei programmi didattici dell'istruzione elementare," *Bollettino ufficiale del Ministero dell'Istruzione Pubblica* II, no. 47 (1923), 4062.

20 Gabriella Klein, *La politica linguistica del fascismo* (Bologna: il Mulino, 1986), 72-73. The policy of gradual assimilation also allowed many German-speaking teachers to keep their jobs as long as they became proficient in Italian. "Cronaca quinquennale, 1924-1928. Lingua e cultura," *Archivio per l'Alto Adige* XXIII, (1928), 522. The Fascist state abandoned this program in 1927, however. Luigi Molina, "Periodo Trentino 1a parte," n.d., 283-284.

21 The phrase "great Latin blood" was taken from Alessandro Marcucci, "Il 'bello' come elemento di educazione," *Annali dell'istruzione elementare* X, no. 4-6 (1935), 317. On the de-nationalization (or Germanization) of Italians in the region, see Chiavolini, "La provincia di Bolzano. Appunto per S.E. il Presidente," August 30, 1923; Luigi Molina, Letter to Nardi, August 11, 1923 (ACS, PCM, Gab., Affari generali, 1924, B. 738, F. 1/1.11); G. P., "La difesa dell'italianità nel Trentino per opera della Lega nazionale," *Schola: Bollettino del R. Provveditorato agli studi della Venezia Tridentina* I, no. 10-11 (1924); Italiano Marchetti, "Scuole d'italianità," ibid., II, no. 8-10 (1925).

22 Vittorio Zippel, Letter to Benito Mussolini, September 6, 1923 (ACS, PCM, Gab., 1923, B. 695, F. 1/1-6).

23 Luigi Federzoni, Letter to Benito Mussolini, January 12, 1926 (ACS, PCM, Gab., 1926, B. 880, F. 1.1/13-16.26).

24 Carlo Viesi, "Le aspirazioni delle provincie finitime sul territorio trentino," *Trentino: Rivista della Legione trentina* III, no. 12 (1927), 257; Paolo Drigo, "Alto Adige," ibid. IV, no. 7 (1928), 228.

25 Ettore Tolomei, "I provvedimenti per l'Alto Aige dopo un quinquennio (1923-1928)," in *Archivio per l'Alto Adige, annata XXIII - 1928*, ed. Ettore Tolomei, (Roma: Tip. Coop. Sociale, 1928), 7.

26 Ettore Tolomei, "Le due provincie. Trento e Bolzano," in *Archivio per l'Alto Adige, annata XXII - 1927*, ed. Ettore Tolomei, (Roma: Tip. Coop. Sociale, 1927), 193.

27 On the debate over whether residents were simply Germanized Italians or actually "German," see Molina, "Periodo Trentino 1a parte," n.d., 43-46. On the broader academic and bureaucratic discussions about national/racial character during the Fascist period, see Eden McLean, *Mussolini's Children: Race and Elementary Education in Fascist Italy* (Lincoln, NE: University of Nebraska Press, 2018).

28 On the increasing lack of confidence the regime had in the Trentini to Italianize the region, see Roberta Pergher, "Staging the Nation in Fascist Italy's 'New Provinces'," *Austrian History Yearbook* 43 (2012).

29 Benito Mussolini, "Il discorso dell'ascensione" in *Opera Omnia di Benito Mussolini XXII: Dall'attentato Zaniboni al discorso dell'ascensione*, ed. Edoardo and Duilio Susmel, 44 vols., vol. XXII, (Florence: La Fenice, 1964), 369. It does bear noting, however, that 1926 was a year of particularly high tensions between Germany and Italy, with the Weimar foreign minister Gustav Stresemann accusing Mussolini of "raping the German culture in South Tyrol." Cited in Georg Grote, *The South Tyrol Question, 1866-2010: From National Rage to Regional State* (Bern: Peter Lang, 2012). Historian Leopold Steuer also describes a secret meeting in Munich on November 11, 1926 between German and Italian representatives that

suggested Mussolini was open to appeasing some of South Tyroleans' requests for greater linguistic freedom. Leopold Steurer, *Südtirol zwischen Rom und Berlin, 1919-1939* (Vienna: Europaverlag, 1980), 145-46. After the division, the Italian nationalist organization Legione Tridentina claimed that German nationalists celebrated the move as in their favor. Dante M. Tuninetti, *Trentinismo e antitrentinismo* (Trento: Arti grafiche tridentum, 1928), 55.

30 The corollary to such a position was that the Italian speakers who supposedly justified Italy's initial irredentist claims and spearheaded the early Italianization project (Trentini, by and large) were not capable of fully assimilating the German-speaking population. Apparently, Mussolini's instructions to Bozen/Bolzano's first prefect, Umberto Ricci, claimed as much. As cited in Steurer, *Südtirol zwischen Rom und Berlin*, 145.

31 Continuing to use our example of the education system, after 1927 German was officially (though not practically) banned in public schools. In fact, even private lessons in the mother languages of German or Ladin were forbidden. Luigi Molina, "Prot.19107 Tit. B Classe 34. Oggetto: Insegnamento della religione in Alto Adige," December 29, 1927 (AA.EE.SS., Seg. Stato, Italia, IV Periodo, Pos. 644 P.O., F. 73). The exception to this rule was the use of German or Ladin in catechism classes that took place on Church grounds. Gustavo Testa, "Esposto di Monsignor Endrici, Vescovo di Trento, consegnato a Mons. Testa il giorno 8 febbraio 1933," February 8, 1933 (AA.EE.SS., Seg. Stato, Italia, IV Periodo, Pos. 644 P.O., F. 75). Simultaneously, the Ministry of Education announced in October 1928 that all German-speaking secondary-school teachers had been expelled or transferred from Alto Adige, and very few German speakers remained in the ranks of primary-school teachers, officials, and school inspectors. Giuseppe Belluzzo, Letter to Benito Mussolini, October 5, 1928 (ACS, PCM, Gab., 1928-1930, B. 1090 F. 1/1-13.3001).

32 Giovanni Geisler, "Promemoria del Principe Vescovo di Bressanone sopra alcuni aspetti politico-religiosi della sua diocesi," December 17, 1934 (Archivio Segreto Vaticano (hereafter ASV), Arch. Nunz. Italia, B. 82, F. 2, Bressanone), 9-10; Eugenio Pacelli, "Protcollare, riferito il 10 Gen. 1934," January 13, 1935 (AA.EE.SS., Seg. Stato, Italia, IV Periodo, Pos. 644, F. 79).

33 Geisler, "Promemoria del Principe Vescovo di Bressanone sopra alcuni aspetti politico-religiosi della sua diocesi," December 17, 1934, 9-10. For more on this distinction, see Pergher, "Staging the Nation in Fascist Italy's 'New Provinces'," 113.

34 Grote, *The South Tyrol Question, 1866-2010*, 10-14.

35 Pietro Gasparri, Letter to Pietro Tacchi Venturi, March 27, 1927 (ARSI, Arch. Tacchi Venturi, Affari, B. 19, F. 486). Fascist officials were quite convinced the German-speaking clergy was at the forefront of the "anti-Italian" campaign in South Tyrol. Alfredo Rocco, Letter to Pietro Tacchi Venturi, December 9, 1926 (ARSI, Arch. Tacchi Venturi, Affari, B. 19, F. 486).

36 The Italian state spent the next decade in an intense campaign to root out these illicit schools, but, as regional superintendent of schools Luigi Molina explained in his memoir, "No one feared the fines imposed by the magistrates; there was always someone to pay them, and when a school was closed in one place, it would emerge immediately in another." Luigi Molina, "Periodo trentino 3a parte," n.d., 413.

37 On transborder nationalism, see Brubaker, *Grounds for Difference*, 8.

The South Tyrol Option and the Borderlines of National Historiographies

Roberta Pergher

For much of the twentieth century, the history of South Tyrol has been told from two opposing perspectives. The German-language historiography, as well as the dominant popular narrative in the region, long presented a story of victimhood and injustice.[1] After suffering through World War I, the South Tyroleans were egregiously mistreated by the Paris peacemakers, who apportioned the former Habsburg territory to Italy. They were then terrorized by the Fascists, who sought to Italianize them by restricting the use of the German language in public and undermining local customs and associations.[2] After enduring another world war, the South Tyroleans were neglected by the next lot of peacemakers, who refused them self-determination and a possible unification with Austria, and then ignored and abused by postwar Italian politicians, who would not grant them autonomy. The Italian historiography, by contrast, told the tale of a region won through sacrifice in war and defended against Hitler's murderous expansionism—a region recalcitrant and difficult, constantly defying patient efforts to facilitate its full absorption into Italy. While both tales revealed something about South Tyrol's history, both remained (and in some cases still remain) mired in the long history of grievances of the two sides in this contest over borders, identities, and allegiances.

This dichotomous narrative is nowhere more apparent than in relation to the 1939 Option agreement between Nazi Germany and Fascist Italy. The agreement called upon all native German and Ladin speakers residing in Italian territories acquired after World War I to register for either Italian or German citizenship. Most of these non-Italian speakers lived in the annexed South Tyrol. If they chose to retain their Italian citizenship, they could remain in their homeland, but they committed themselves to live like "a brother among brothers in the great Italian nation."[3] Choosing German citizenship meant they agreed to migrate "home to the Reich" and relinquish their native land. From the Italian state's perspective, the Option agreement was intended to forestall German irredentist claims to the German-speaking Alto Adige once and for all and ensure that the land south of the Brenner Pass remained under Italian sovereignty.[4] From the German perspective, this was an agreement that cemented the alliance with Italy while ensuring that all "Germans" would be reunited in a "Greater Reich," besides bringing valuable workers to the Reich.

The Option has been told for the most part as a localized, peculiar story of Axis scheming—as the brief survey of the Option's historiography, with which this piece opens, will show. In popular memory, particularly on the German-speaking side, it is perceived as a tragic and very particular turn of fate that befell a population squeezed between Fascist Italy and Nazi Germany. To those not familiar with the history of South Tyrol but with some knowledge of the Third Reich, however, many of the parameters of the Option agreement will sound familiar. They fit with what we know about Nazi Germany's gigantic population settlement schemes, its oversize nationalism, and its sense that territorial cohesion required ethnic homogeneity. My contribution recognizes this broader context but goes further in arguing that the Option is, in fact, best understood in the setting of interwar Europe, indeed of interwar patterns that extend beyond even the European framework.[5] Above all, the values and norms that emerged from the Paris Peace Treaties—national self-determination and the inviolability of national sovereignty—were crucial here, albeit taken to the extreme by Fascists and National Socialists. As we will see, the Option followed other similar policies of ethnic cleansing enacted in the colonies by European powers, including Italy, and foreshadowed policies of population resettlement pursued by the Nazis across Europe. The history of the Option, as indeed the history of South Tyrol in the twentieth century as a whole, is thus very much a European borderland story.

For a long time, the Italian and the regional German-language historiographies assessed the Option very differently.[6] In a transparent blame game, the Italians blamed the ruthless Germans for imposing it on the local population, while the local German-speaking scholarship and popular memory in the region framed the Option as a last resort initiated by Mussolini after all other Italianization efforts had failed. It was not until the 1970s and 1980s that the German-language historiography, initially outside the region in Vienna or German university cities, began to acknowledge the forceful hand of Nazi Germany in the formulation and implementation of the Option and thereby to connect the Option to broader historiography on the Third Reich.[7] This new work also acknowledged the enthusiasm with which many South Tyroleans responded to the possibility of joining the Third Reich. What it lost sight of, however, was that for the Italians, also, the Option was a natural extension of previous efforts to assert Italian sovereignty by "right-peopling" the territory.[8] Italy was not just a puppet, operating at the mercy of the Germans. Rather, for Fascist Italy, too, the Option corresponded to preexisting understandings of nationality, legitimacy, and the possibilities of demographic engineering.

For Fascist Italy, it is true that in some ways the Option was an admission of defeat. It constituted a recognition that Mussolini's Italianization plan had failed, that the great majority of German speakers still identified as German, and that the province was more susceptible than ever to German irredentist claims. Hitler's rise and early foreign policy successes led South Tyrolean irredentists, and increasingly the population at large, to hope for "deliverance" from Mussolini's program of forced assimilation. By the late 1930s, and particularly after the March 1938 annexation of Austria, Germany appeared strong enough to reclaim the territory inhabited predominantly by German speakers. A local illegal group, the Völkisch Combat Unit South Tyrol (*Völkischer Kampfring Südtirol*, VKS), which had emerged in the late 1920s, bound together a growing network of Nazi sympathizers under the *Führer* principle. Additionally, various German organizations seeking to support Germans abroad were also active in South Tyrol: the National Association for Germanness Abroad (*Volksbund für das Deutschtum im Ausland*, VDA) and, after 1937, the Main Welfare Office for Ethnic Germans (*Hauptamt Volksdeutsche Mittelstelle*, VoMI).

In theory, Hitler's iterations on the topic of South Tyrol should have dashed every South Tyrolean hope and assuaged every Italian fear of the territory passing over to Germany. From the early 1920s onward, Hitler had always maintained that acquiring South Tyrol entailed a war that was not in Germany's interest.[9] Rather than embroiling Germany and Italy in a regional conflict, he wanted the two countries to enter an alliance. He saw Italy as the only power that, like Germany, had too little land for its people. An alliance between the two have-nots would require Germany to renounce South Tyrol but would at the same time enable it to pursue a "truly large-scale policy of space."[10] Yet even though the two European fascist powers solidified their alliance in the second half of the 1930s, the South Tyrol continued to be their Achilles heel.

In a diary entry for April 3, 1938, with the recently completed "Anschluss" of Austria meaning that German troops were now standing at Italy's northern border, Italian Foreign Minister Galeazzo Ciano worried that the South Tyrol question could lead to the Axis being "blown sky high."[11] Reflecting on the possibility of a German exodus, he wrote: "Geographically South Tyrol is Italian territory and, as we can't change the position of mountains or the course of rivers, the men will have to move."[12] Nazi potentate Hermann Göring had reportedly stated already in January 1937, well before the Anschluss, that 200,000 South Tyroleans could not continue to strain relations between the two countries.[13] After the annexation, reasoning along the lines of a population swap, Göring offered in

April 1938 a couple of thousand Italians living in Germany in exchange for the South Tyroleans who wanted to move to the Reich.[14] Following the Anschluss, therefore, leading Italians and Germans were thinking independently of population resettlement as a possible solution to the South Tyrol "problem." Both sides operated with the idea of the nation as an ethnic-racial community, and both aspired to rule over homogeneous populations within their borders, be it through incorporation of territory, through assimilation of "others," or through expulsion of those who did not fit.

By that time, Italy was engaged in a major settlement program in Libya, where the regime hoped to settle 100,000 Italians in only five years in order to consolidate Italy's claim over the territory.[15] When the leading promoter of Italianization in South Tyrol, Ettore Tolomei, learned in 1938 about the first wave of 20,000 settlers in Libya, he hoped that something similar could be done in his adopted region.[16] Moreover, the regime was planning a massive settlement program in recently conquered Ethiopia, where 2,000,000 Italians were supposed to find a new home.[17] Tolomei fantasized that Ethiopia might serve as an outlet for the German speakers in South Tyrol and that their removal would complete the Italianization of the borderland.[18] For the regime, the colonial settlement projects, as well as the South Tyrolean program, were responses to contested sovereignty in marginal territories. True, the Fascists also pursued settlement projects away from the borderlands, and their signature program in the Pontine Marshes was marked by the same grand aspiration to social engineering and by the same rhetoric of social betterment that would accompany the settlers to Libya. But in the borderlands, be they uncertain national territories or rebellion-prone colonies, Italy's ultimate goal was to secure Italy's sovereignty by implanting trustworthy Italians.

In all these ways, the Option was no anomaly for the Italians. On the German side, Germany wanted to bring all the Germans together, had annexed Austria and the Sudetenland—with considerable Italian support—and in 1939 was planning to resettle German speakers from the recently annexed remaining territories of Czechoslovakia to Germany.[19] And specifically for Himmler and the SS, the Option signaled the beginning of their own increasingly radical resettlement policies.[20] Thus, the negotiations between Italy and Germany over the "natural" border between the two countries and the place of German speakers in the Italian nation emerged in a context where the Option, and the resettlement scheme it engendered, made logical sense.

Within that decisive broader context, however, it is important to recognize the ways in which the South Tyrol policy stands out. For all the overlap with other settlement programs, the Option was at the same time a peculiar policy, dictated above all by the fact that two ultranationalist powers were forced to reconcile their rival national interests in a contested space. It was the alliance with Germany, but also the concurrent fear of a German takeover, that shaped and rendered urgent the agreement for Italy. An "Option" would have been neither possible nor necessary for the Slovene and Croat speakers in the annexed Northeast, where Italy's relationship with the Yugoslav kingdom was premised on rather different agreements and foundations.

During his Rome visit in May 1938, Hitler publicly announced that he considered the current border to be "inviolable" ("*unantastbar*").[21] A year later, in June 1939, the two sides laid out the policy that would "safeguard" the border, which is what came to be known as the Option. The details of the agreement were published only in October 1939, and the last date to submit a preference was December 31, 1939. After the vote was cast, the German and Italian authorities reported different results. The Germans declared 90.7 percent had opted to leave—the same outcome as in the Saarland plebiscite. The Italian number was 69.4 percent. Scholarly consensus puts the number around 86 percent. The Italians were stunned, but the results were stunning only if one had trusted earlier propaganda about the South Tyroleans' attachment to the land. If we consider the lingering effects of the Depression, the poverty of many in the area, their sense of alienation, their insecurity about the future, and their illusion that a united vote would in effect amount to a plebiscite and consequently bring the annexation of the territory to Germany after all, the high percentage in favor of leaving becomes far more understandable. If indeed we focus on the broader context of efforts at "unweaving" and "unmixing" the populations of interwar Europe, we might well be more astonished that 14 percent chose to stay.[22]

Thus, though in some respects the product of a particular compromise between two hypernationalist regimes and in line with their current and future plans for population management, the Option's stated premise—namely that people had the right to choose their nationality but would, in fact, inevitably opt for their "innate" nationality—was not so unusual. It was already present in the Wilsonian doctrine of self-determination. Self-determination rested on the belief that people had the right to choose where they belonged. But while this policy posited the nation as a community of choice, the underlying understanding—the illiberal basis of the liberal solution, if you like—was that the choice had already been made for them by the presumed givenness of their nationality. People were thus, in theory, destined to opt in accordance with their linguistic, cultural, and ethnic affiliation—in effect, their "inner essence." In practice, the dirty secret of the early postwar plebiscites was that individuals made strategic choices of affiliation based on their sense of personal advantage.[23] This vindicated the idea of holding a vote, but it belied the essentialist understanding of national identity. The Option was no different in that respect. The crucial difference lay in the fact that earlier plebiscites had been collective votes to determine the affiliation of a given territory. Individuals who had not voted with the majority were forced to accept the nation chosen by the majority. In the Option, by contrast, the territorial outcome was already clear: the Italian claim to South Tyrol was accepted by both parties as a given. Thus, individual voters chose for themselves whether to identify as Italian and stay or declare themselves as German and leave. Everyone had to vote for themselves, with the exception of wives and underage children.

One implication of devolving choice to the individual was that families with adult children could be separated, as in the case of Giuseppe Gamper's family. A parachutist in the Italian air force, Gamper wrote to his mother in 1942 asking her to change her mind and opt for Germany after all (the initial deadline for voting was December 1939, but opportunities were subsequently provided for voters to change their election).[24] He himself had chosen Italy, but now he declared that the happiest day of his life would be when he emigrated to Germany. His father, who was a carpenter, his brother Alberto, who was a barber, and his sister Anna, a maid, had all opted for Germany. His mother, his brothers Giuseppe, also a barber, and Giovanni, a messenger, his sister Erna, who was a maid like Anna, and his brother Carlo, still a pupil, had decided to stay in Italy. We do not know what persuaded each individual in this lower-class family to make the choices they did. The disparate choices within one and the same family certainly undermined the very idea of clear-cut racial nationhood.

The example of the Gamper family shows us just how ambivalent and indeed at times paradoxical the Option was. Even though the Option was coercive—everyone was required to declare his or her preference, and either option came with impositions—it was also surprisingly conciliatory and voluntaristic. It combined the ruthless mass social engineering of twentieth-century population resettlement with an attentiveness to individual preference. The German speakers of the annexed territories were not forced to the polls by shotgun. They were, moreover, given the unusual luxury of being able to choose their citizenship and implicitly their "race." These paradoxical features were in large part a function of the peculiar compromises necessary for the two radical nationalist regimes to agree and so preserve their alliance. Making a resolution between the two Fascist powers possible was the reality that both sides were keen to maintain their alliance, even while they pursued competing national interests and espoused opposed ideologies of national supremacy. Isolated in Europe, both were determined to change the status quo. Indeed, what brought the two powers together were their separate and seemingly compatible expansionary goals, namely Italy's aggression toward Ethiopia and Germany's desire to have an alliance partner that would support its own ambitions in the East. With such "imperial" ambitions uniting them, the two dictators were careful not to stumble over a small nationality conflict.

The paradoxical consequence of this paradoxical plebiscite was a very particular kind of trauma—one that, in part, resulted from the fact that families might end up having "voluntarily" opted to go in different directions and thus finding themselves, at least in theory, divided forever. Because of the visceral memory of that ambivalent and painful experience engaging with the broader context of self-determination and plebiscites gets us only so far in understanding the local perspective. It also means that "educating" local memory with evidence of the parallels elsewhere in interwar Europe, and of the ways in which the Option was actually a relatively soft version of the population policies being applied elsewhere, cannot really speak to the agonies of individual choice. The result is an uneasy standoff, which has in part banned the Option from view and has in part left it visible only as a stroke of fate that had to be endured and where there was no right or wrong and everyone was a victim.

Endnotes

1 See Gerald Steinacher's contribution to this roundtable.

2 See Eden McLean's contribution to this roundtable.

3 Auswärtiges Amt, Berlin, Politisches Archiv, Rom-Quirinal Geheim 116: Proposal for a joint publication by the prefecture of Bolzano and German general consulate of Milan, 1939.

4 For the Italian perspective on the Option, see Renzo De Felice, *Il problema dell'Alto Adige nei rapport italo-tedeschi dall''Anschluss' alla fine della seconda guerra mondiale* (Bologna: Il Mulino, 1973) and Federico Scarano, *Tra Mussolini e Hitler: Le Opzioni dei sudtirolesi nella politica estera fascista* (Milan: FrancoAngeli, 2012).

5 See Roberta Pergher, *Mussolini's Nation-Empire: Sovereignty and Settlement in Italy's Borderlands, 1922-1943* (Cambridge: Cambridge University Press, 2018).

6 For an overview of the historiography and collective memory of the Option, see Eva Pfanzelter, "Die (un)verdaute Erinnerung an die Option 1939," in "Option und Erinnerung/ La memoria delle opzioni," ed. Eva Pfanzelter, *Geschichte und Region/Storia e Regione* 22, no. 2 (2013): 13-40.

7 Karl Stuhlpfarrer, *Umsiedlung Südtirol 1939–1940*, 2 vols. (Vienna: Löcker, 1985) and Leopold Steurer, *Südtirol zwischen Rom und Berlin 1919–1939* (Vienna: Europaverlag, 1980). The early exception is Conrad F. Latour, *Südtirol and die Achse Berlin-Rom 1938–1945* (Stuttgart: Deutsche Verlags-Anstalt, 1962).

8 On the concepts of "right-sizing" and "right-peopling" state territory, see Brendan O'Leary, Ian Lustick, and Thomas Callaghy, eds., *Rightsizing the State: The Politics of Moving Borders* (New York: Oxford University Press, 2001).

9 Hitler issued the brochure "Die Südtiroler Frage und das deutsche Bündnisproblem" in 1926, which was then included as chapter 13 in Hitler's sequel to *Mein Kampf.* On the significance of South Tyrol in the German-Italian relationship, see also chapter 15 in Hitler's *Second Book,* reproduced in Gerhard Weinberg, ed. *Hitler's Second Book: The Unpublished Sequel to Mein Kampf by Adolf Hitler* (New York: Enigma Books, 2003).

10 Weinberg, ed., *Hitler's Second Book*, 198.

11 Galeazzo Ciano, *Ciano's Diary 1937–1938*, trans. Andreas Mayor (London: Methuen, 1952), 96.

12 Ibid.

13 This was an internal document of the German Foreign Ministry and not part of a statement made to the Italians. Cited in De Felice, *Il problema dell'Alto Adige*, 23.

14 Magistrati report to Mussolini, cited in De Felice, *Il problema dell'Alto Adige*, 25–26.

15 See Federico Cresti, *Non desiderare la terra d'altri: La colonizzazione italiana in Libia* (Rome: Carocci, 2011).

16 Ettore Tolomei, "Notiziario – Vita e problemi," *Archivio per l'Alto Adige* 33, no. 2 (1938): 23.

17 In his landmark overview of the history Italian colonialism, Nicola Labanca notes that estimates of the Italian masses to be relocated in Ethiopia ranged between one and six million. Nicola Labanca, *Oltremare: Storia dell'espansione coloniale italiana* (Bologna: Il Mulino, 2002), 325.

18 Tolomei, *Archivio per l'Alto Adige* 31, no. 2 (1936), 640–641.

19 See Robert Koehl, *RKFDV, German Resettlement and Population Policy, 1939–1945: A History of the Reich Commission for the Strengthening of Germandom* (Cambridge, MA: Harvard University Press, 1957), 41.

20 Peter Longerich, *Heinrich Himmler* (Oxford: Oxford University Press, 2013), 417–418.

21 Umberto Corsini and Rudolf Lill, *Südtirol 1918–1946* (Bozen: Athesia, 1988), 296.

22 The point is made by Donald Bloxham, "The Great Unweaving: The Removal of Peoples in Europe, 1875–1949," in *Removing Peoples: Forced Removal in the Modern World*, ed. Richard Bessel and Claudia B. Haake (Oxford: Oxford University Press, 2009), 186.

23 Brendan Karch, *Nation and Loyalty in a German-Polish Borderland Upper Silesia, 1848–1960* (Cambridge: Cambridge University Press, 2018).

24 Archivio Centrale dello Stato, Rome, Ministero dell'Interno, Direzione generale di pubblica sicurezza, Documenti suddivisi per anni, 1942, b. 47, Cat. C2.1. Bolzano, sf. 29 Gamper Giuseppe di Giovanni ed altri: Letter written on 19 April 1942.

Borderline: South Tyrol and its Nazi Past Between Politics and Historiography[1]

Gerald J. Steinacher

Introduction

South Tyrol is the Land of Ötzi—the Iceman, the beautiful Dolomites, delicious speck (smoked prosciutto), and good wine! Yet there is more to this Italian-Austrian border region. South Tyrol's experience of both Italian Fascism and German National Socialism created a rather unique situation before and after 1945.

"The South Tyroleans suffered like the Jews," claimed the governor of Italy's northernmost province of Bolzano, also known as South Tyrol. He was speaking, in 2003, to an Italian journalist on the occasion of the commemoration of the Holocaust and the sixtieth anniversary of the invasion of Italy by Nazi Germany in September 1943.[2]

Let me be clear: this statement was outrageous. The South Tyroleans, a German-speaking minority in Italy, suffered discrimination and oppression by Fascist Italy, but it never amounted to anything close to a mass murder campaign or genocide. To make any such claim between these two historical events is not just false but deeply problematic. Historian Jan-Werner Müller makes the general argument that a rhetoric of alleged historical analogies is so problematic at least for two reasons: it short-circuits "critical reflection" and aims at the creation of "instant legitimacy" for dubious claims.[3] But this false *Gleichsetzung* (equalization) made by Governor (*Landeshauptmann*) Luis Durnwalder was not considered remotely scandalous. Most local journalists and the wider public simply ignored it or, worse, found nothing troubling about it.

Durnwalder's view on the history of South Tyrol is both common and revealing about the perception of many in his society. Many South Tyroleans downplay the Nazi past and that community's own responsibility in it, instead focusing on the victimization of the South Tyroleans during Italian Fascism. This short paper looks into South Tyrol's Nazi past between politics and historiography.

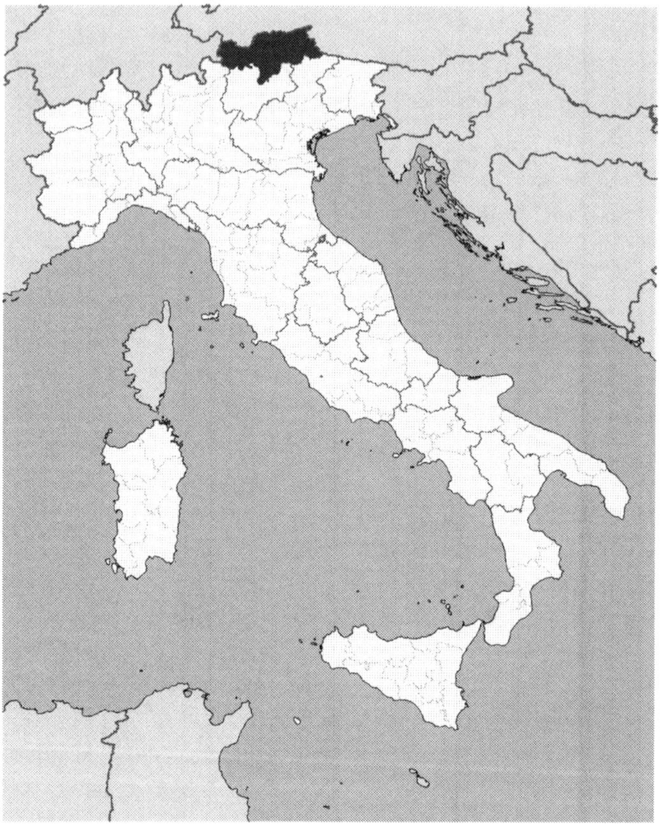

Fig. 1: Map of South Tyrol – Geography in Central Europe (Wikimedia Commons)

According to scholar Günther Pallaver, South Tyrol's history and politics are understood as a triad of dependence, delay, and "ethnic" division. The political system in South Tyrol relied primarily on developments from outside. This holds particularly true for democracy, which was introduced as a result of the defeat of Fascism and National Socialism. Democracy in South Tyrol was also significantly delayed. It was because of the Fascist regime between 1922 and 1945 that democratic development like the formation of political parties and culture was on hold. It was not until 1946 that the Italian monarchy ended, and the country enacted a fully democratic constitution in 1947.

Further, the ethnic divisions led to the formation of *lager* mentality. Ethnicity remains a critical cleavage in the borderland and dominates society, political institutions, political parties, as well as social action and interaction. The differences among the main ethnic/linguistic groups—German speakers, Italian speakers, and Ladin speakers—are still difficult to overcome.

For Pallaver, all three aspects of the South Tyrol triad represent shortcomings: Dependence reveals deficits in democratic political culture. Delay hints at problems accepting both democratic institutions and a materially participative culture between the three language groups. Finally, the ethnic division shows a lack of cooperation between the main ethnic/linguistic groups, which, in turn, exposes general difficulties in overcoming their differences.[4]

Each of these elements deeply impacted not just the political-historical process of South Tyrol but also its historiography.

The Völkisch Historiography

The end of the Habsburg Monarchy in 1918 meant the deep fall of the South Tyroleans. Almost overnight, they went from being a part of the dominant German-Austrian majority to a small ethnic/linguistic minority in Italy, which came as a huge shock. And soon, like Germany, Tyrol bore witness to the birth of a ready-made stab-in-the-back legend (*Dolchstosslegende*). According to this myth, the annexation of southern Tyrol was due to Italian treachery and Allied power politics. To this day many Tyroleans still blame US President Woodrow Wilson for not following through with his promise of self-determination. As a result, in 1919, the historic Tyrol region was cut in two—northern and southern parts divided by an international border between Austria and Italy.[5]

But the one-sided and oversimplified narrative of victimization did not stop there. As the story goes, the South Tyroleans next became victims of suppression by Italian Fascists and Nazi dictatorship. Further, the end of World War II did not end the suffering of the South Tyroleans. They then became victims of Italian nationalism and the Cold War strategy of the Allies. The promised autonomy was not fulfilled; the future looked bleak. South Tyroleans were condemned to lose their cultural identity and control over their land due to the influx of Italian settlers from the south. These views culminated with the notion that the South Tyroleans in the 1950s were on a death march (*Todesmarsch*—also a term from the Holocaust!). This *Volk-in-Not* (Nation in Peril) mentality found plenty of academic support in the work of historians. As Pallaver explains, both the myth of victimization and *Volk-in-Not* ideology crystallized in the collective memory of the World War II and first postwar generations of South Tyroleans.[6]

Historiography concerning South Tyrol in Austria and Germany after 1918—and even before—served German-nationalistic policies and revisionist goals. History was mostly identified as part of *völkisch* border region studies (*Völkische Grenzlandwissenschaft*) and served as an auxiliary discipline for political expediencies. The goal was to establish a clear consensus about which parties were on the right and wrong side of history in regard to territorial claims. In other words, who had the "historical" right to claim the territory? The ethnic-cultural divisions also meant that exchange and discussion between the Italian- and German-speaking locals remained limited. Each group was writing its own historiographies, and the differences could not have been more pronounced. Comparing the contradictory narratives, one gets the impression that the historians are not even writing about the same region, much less recording the same historical events. Publications from the "other side" were rarely referenced. Anyone perceived to be fraternizing with the "other side," historian or not, was seen as a traitor, much like Anna, a character in Joseph Zoderer's powerful 1982 novel, *Die Walsche*. Anna, a Tyrolean, was ultimately ostracized from her family and her village simply because she pursued her love for an Italian man.

These entrenched ethnic beliefs were academically enshrined until the 1970s by historians at the University of Innsbruck, which is just over the border and has been the alma mater for many generations of South Tyroleans. Having the claim of being the *Landesuniversität* for all Tyroleans, the University of Innsbruck felt obliged to defend and promote a united Tyrolean identity and history. They were supported by Austrian state officials and non-academic historians. The ethnic divisions and long-lasting legacy of nineteenth century border nationalism made dialogue and cooperation between the groups within South Tyrol difficult. Historians were certainly no exception.

As a kind of extended arm of politics, historians were used in political struggles. They willingly served the interests of their own ethnic groups in promoting the rights and claims against "the others." The delay in critical approaches of history writing led to black-and-white narratives, where South Tyroleans were 1) always the victims (of Italy) and 2) until rather recently portrayed in a very sympathetic light.[7] This would only slowly start to change in 1968.

South Tyrol and its Historikerstreit

The break with the *völkisch* border studies came with the first self-critical reflections about Tyrolean society. In the wake of the 1968 student movement, South Tyrolean students in Vienna, Bologna, Trento, and elsewhere started to challenge cultural norms first and then traditional politics.

Claus Gatterer's 1968 book, *Battling against Rome: Citizens, Minorities and Autonomies in Italy*, initiated a radical change in both paradigm and methodical approach.[8] This journalist and historian started to challenge the victim myth of the Tyroleans by pointing out that many South Tyroleans fell for the Nazis and their ideology. He explains that from the South Tyrolean perspective, "Mussolini's Fascism was more humane, more corrupt, and, precisely in its human weaknesses, more easily predictable—but it spoke Italian; it was 'alien.' Although Nazism was more brutal and inhuman, many South Tyroleans embraced it, [it was ours], 'because it spoke our language.'"[9] With the rise of National Socialism, many South Tyroleans oriented themselves more toward Munich and Berlin and less toward Innsbruck and Vienna. Their smashing motto was: only a powerful Germany can help South Tyrol. Gatterer situated South Tyrol within a wider context, comparing it to other European border regions and historic minority communities. While discussed in small circles, the new views of Gatterer were widely ignored. However, this new perspective would influence the publications of Karl Stuhlpfarrer and Leopold Steurer, both students of Gatterer.[10]

Steurer's 1980 book, *South Tyrol between Rome and Berlin 1919-1939*, served as an ice breaker for a new paradigm and triggered South Tyrol's very own *Historikerstreit*.[11] Steurer was aggressively attacked by representatives of the older historiography, as well as veterans of the SS and the *Wehrmacht*. What did Steurer say that caused this backlash? Based on careful archival research, Steurer identified Nazi Germany as the driving force behind the Option, the project of ethnic cleansing of South Tyrol that involved the removing and resettling of the local German-speaking population. The Option of 1939 is a very painful moment in the history of the region, deeply splitting the local population. The popular historical narrative of the "victim myth" blamed the Italians (under Mussolini) for the policy. Accordingly, it was Italian propaganda and pressure that forced around eighty-six percent of the South Tyroleans to vote for German citizenship, giving up their beloved *Heimat*. In stark contrast, Steurer revealed the extent to which South Tyrolean society willingly fell for Nazi ideology, a revelation that went completely against any narrative of victimization. Steurer had hit a nerve. The young historian and *Gymnasiallehrer* from Sterzing/Vipiteno was soon smeared as a *Nestbeschmutzer*, someone who runs down his own people, and even a communist sympathizer. Soon Steurer was declared to be persona non grata by the ruling establishment in South Tyrol. That same year also saw the release of the film *Sie sagten nein: Widerstand in Südtirol 1943-1945*, directed by Gerd Staffler. The film focused on oral histories of Nazi victims, which were difficult to record on camera as many still feared a negative backlash from their neighbors and the wider community. Resistance fighters and deserters were still (in the 1980s) considered traitors of the *Volk*. The film also reported in detail about the concentration camp of Bolzano and the murder of the South Tyrolean Jews, another taboo subject. To make matters worse, Steurer and Staffler were also questioning the image of the clean, or apolitical, *Wehrmacht*. As in Germany and Austria, the South Tyrolean *Wehrmacht* generation denied any involvement in the Holocaust (it was all Hitler and the SS, they claimed).

The Option of 1939 remained a central issue in South Tyrol's identity and history. In the course of a television interview (on Italian television Rai UNO) in November 1981, world-renowned mountaineer and author (and one of the discoverers of Ötzi) Reinhold Messner made the following claim: "I believe. That no other people ever have betrayed their own homeland so much like the South Tyroleans did." With this betrayal, Messner referenced the Option in which almost ninety percent of South Tyroleans decided to emigrate to the German Reich.[12] The topic of the Option was thematized and popularized for a wide audience in the 1989 TV series *Verkaufte Heimat*, written by prominent Tyrolean author Felix Mitterer. The title "Sold out homeland—betrayed homeland" would seem to reinforce the "victim narrative" of the betrayed and cheated South Tyroleans, their land having been stolen by a foreign nation, in this case Italy. But in reality, the film gave a very balanced depiction that sympathized with the small people, the little guys, on both sides of the linguistic divide. Tyroleans and Italians alike were depicted as pawns in a larger chess match between dictators—foremost Hitler and Mussolini—and other powerful leaders. But Mitterer also showed the fanaticism of some South Tyroleans for the Nazi regime.

The fall of the Berlin Wall in 1989 had huge repercussions on the politics and the historiography of this European border region. That year, the Tyrolean History Society (*Tiroler Geschichtsverein*) organized a major exhibition in Bolzano on the fiftieth anniversary of the Option of 1939. This balanced look at a troubled past turned out to be a major milestone for crossing the ethnic divide in the history and memory of the region. The project involved the cooperation of a younger generation of historians from each of the three major ethnic/linguistic groups and also from neighboring countries. The project reappraised the past seeking to overcome old concepts of "the other" as perpetrator and the "self" as victim. This was not an easy undertaking due to the deep legacy of Fascism and National Socialism and the even older shadows of ethnic nationalism. Such fresh views laid the foundation for a common future and for overcoming the dominating victim narrative.[13] A direct outcome of these efforts was the foundation of the Working Group of Regional Historians, which started to publish a high-quality bilingual (Italian-German) journal called *Geschichte und Region/Storia e regione*.[14]

Retreat to Normality?

The 1990s saw a clear shifting of paradigms. Similar to Austria, South Tyrol's victim myth was also decisively challenged during that decade due to research at the University of Innsbruck and its Institute of Contemporary History. Starting in the late 1980s, basically the entire faculty engaged in top-notch research on South Tyrol; it expanded the temporal focus, widening the time frame to the postwar years.

In addition to the Option of 1939, another central element in South Tyrol's recent history concerns the road to an extended autonomy after 1945. At the war's end, Austria demanded the return of South Tyrol, a demand supported by most German-speaking Tyroleans. Austria claimed victim status as well. After all, hadn't the Allies declared in 1943 that Austria was the first victim of Nazi aggression? But Italy was dealt an even better hand from the Allies. While the borderland of South Tyrol remained in Italy, the Allies demanded some compromises from the Italian government. The result was the Gruber-De Gasperi Agreement between Austria and Italy. Many Tyroleans claimed for decades that the agreement was an empty promise for South Tyrol's autonomy, a product of Italian tricksters (again!). In stark contrast, Rolf Steininger argued that the agreement was not a defeat at all, but it would ultimately prove to be the "Magna Carta for South Tyrol."[15] In other words, it laid the groundwork for its rich autonomy today.[16] And most importantly, South Tyroleans did not share the fate of other German-speaking minorities after 1945; they were not expelled. This revisionist view initially made Steininger, who came to Innsbruck from Germany, many enemies among the political and cultural elites in South Tyrol.

I started attending the University of Innsbruck in the late 1980s. I am also a product of that Innsbruck school, the second generation, at least in part, together with the schools at the Universities of Trento and

New Orleans. My research, too, challenged long-held beliefs and caused some stir in the Tyrol. This is particularly true for the 2008 German edition of *Nazis on the Run: How Hitler's Henchmen Fled Justice.*[17] It showed the prominent role of South Tyrol as a Nazi loophole for people like Adolf Eichmann, Josef Mengele, Franz Stangl, Ludolf von Alvensleben, Otto Wächter, and many others. Many South Tyroleans were involved in helping to smuggle them across the border, sometimes even providing South Tyrolean identities. In my book, South Tyroleans do appear as victims but more often as Nazis, as perpetrators and active bystanders. The book gained attention in the borderland also because some of the Nazis were still alive. Karl Nicolussi-Leck was a prominent citizen, co-founder of the Museum of Modern Art in Bolzano, and a businessman in Europe and Argentina. But earlier in his life, he was also a Nazi leader, a highly decorated SS officer, and, as documented in my book, an important postwar Nazi smuggler.[18] When he died in 2008, his obituary stressed that he was an anti-fascist, which seemed an absurd claim and only makes sense once you consider the background of the borderland's history. He was an anti-fascist in the sense that he was against Mussolini's repressive policies against the South Tyroleans, but he was a hardcore Nazi too. In other words, in South Tyrol, in some weird way, it was possible to be both a Nazi and an anti-fascist at the same time.[19] I would argue that this was, and remains today, a rather unique situation in Europe, and possibly in the world.[20]

Täterforschung is always more common in South Tyrol. Most recently Costantino Di Sante published a book about the perpetrators of the concentration camp in Bolzano. Sante provides the first history of the camp from the perspective of the perpetrators.[21] Other books document the history of South Tyroleans in the *Waffen-SS.*[22] And the image of the clean *Wehrmacht* crumpled quickly. In line with international Holocaust research, victims are also very much in the center of research interest in South Tyrol.

The memoirs by Franz Thaler, a Catholic concentration camp prisoner, had a huge impact on many South Tyroleans, arguably because of his unpretentious style and the human story it contains. Thaler passed away in 2015. His book, *Unforgotten: A Memoir of Dachau,* was first published in 1989 and has been reprinted in a number of editions.[23] It was even translated into English, which is rare for history books on South Tyrol.

Conclusion

After 1945, "unified fronts" in South Tyrol were formed along the ethnic divide, which often served to achieve political goals. This ethnic entrenchment played a similar role in South Tyrol as the Cold War did in other countries: the critical confrontation of the past was laid on ice. The role of Nazi perpetrators by many South Tyroleans was often left unaddressed due to ethnic division; the South Tyrolean society in many areas was split between the German- and Italian-speaking populations.[24] Italians focused on their victimization during the Nazi occupation between 1943 and 1945, while South Tyroleans cultivated identities as victims during Italian Fascism from 1922 to 1943. According to this simplistic version of the historiography interpreted along ethnic-linguistic lines, one's own group allegedly always, always made out to be the victims, the others the perpetrators.

Erinnerungskultur (memory culture) is always complex and diverse. To speak from an Italian and South Tyrolean memory culture as an absolute would be a denial of the complex realities of societies, as well as the world around us. It is also not the job of historians to somehow create a shared historical memory.[25] In any society, there will always be various competing narratives that coexist at the same time. Italy in particular had a postwar climate that cultivated "competing collective memories."[26]

In the last twenty years, South Tyrol has arguably seen a retreat into reality as a *New York Review of Books* article put it in 2004.[27] Cooperation between historians of different cultural and linguistic backgrounds is very common nowadays. There are now even shared textbooks for the schools in the Italian and German language. These are all indications of a less segregated society. But nationalism and neo-fascism is on the rise again, and old narratives die hard.

Also, the longtime handling of the history of Fascism and National Socialism through an ethnic lens has not disappeared completely.[28] In 2009, the Tyrolean deputy mayor of Bolzano stated that the South Tyroleans were "liberated" by the *Wehrmacht* in September 1943.[29] As a reminder, in September 1943, Hitler's army invaded and occupied its former ally Italy. A brutal and bloody period of occupation, war, and civil war followed. But for the mayor and others, it was a liberation because, in this thinking, the invading soldiers "spoke German, they belonged to us."

Endnotes

1 Thanks to Stas Nikolova, Günter Bischof, Christian Karner, Marc Landry and Christian Stenico for their feedback on my article.

2 Statement by the *Landeshauptmann* of South Tyrol Luis Durnwalder, "Il gruppo tedesco ha sofferto (…) come gli ebrei," *Alto Adige*, 29 March 2003. See also Thomas Albrich, *Jüdisches Leben in Nord- und Südtirol nach der Shoa* (Innsbruck: Haymon Verlag, 2014).

3 Jan-Werner Müller, ed., *Memory and Power in Post-War Europe: Studies in the Presence of the Past* (Cambridge: Cambridge University Press 2002), see introduction by Müller, 1-35, here page 27.

4 Gerald Steinacher, Günther Pallaver, "Leopold Steurer: Historiker zwischen Forschung und Einmischung," in *Demokratie und Erinnerung: Südtirol, Österreich, Italien. Festschrift für Leopold Steurer zum 60. Geburtstag*, ed. Christoph von Hartungen et al. (Innsbruck: Studienverlag, 2006), 51-91 (here 51). See also Günther Pallaver, "Abhängigkeit, Verspätung, ethnische Versäulung. Folgen einer verfehlten Epurazione und Entnazifizierung in Südtirol," in *Südtirol im Dritten Reich: NS-Herrschaft im Norden Italiens 1943-1945. L'Alto Adige nel Terzo Reich: L'occupazione nazista nell' Italia settentrionale*, ed. Gerald Steinacher (Innsbruck: Studienverlag, 2003), 361–374.

5 To the historiography on World War I in South Tyrol and recent changes in the paradigm see Hannes Obermair, "Geschichtsblindes Südtirol? (Fehlende) Erinnerungskulturen 1918-2018 als Ausfall kritischen Bewusstseins," in *Considerazioni sull'Alto Adige/Betrachtungen zu Südtirol*, ed. Patrick Rina, Ulrike Kindl and Tiziano Rosani (Bozen: Die Zeitfabrik, 2018), 48-55. For more on WWI and Tyrol see the research by Oswald Überegger.

6 Günther Pallaver, "Schlachtfest und Paradigmawechsel: Zur Situation der Geschichtsschreibung in Südtirol," *Zeitgeschichte*, Heft 1/2 (1998), 69-76.

7 Pallaver in Pallaver and Steinacher, "Historiker zwischen Forschung und Einmischung," 52.

8 Claus Gatterer, *Im Kampf gegen Rom: Bürger, Minderheiten und Autonomien in Italien* (Vienna: Europa Verlag, 1968).

9 *Claus Gatterer, "Südtirol 1930-45. Eine politische Landschaftsskizze," in: Keinen Eid auf diesen Führer: Josef Mayr-Nusser, ein Zeuge der Gewissensfreiheit in der NS-Zeit, Reinhold Iblacker* (Munich: Tyrolia-Verlag, 1979), 33-46 (here 39).

10 Karl Stuhlpfarrer, *Umsiedlung Südtirol 1939–1940* (Vienna: Löcker, 1985). Karl Stuhlpfarrer, *Die Operationszonen "Alpenvorland" und "Adriatisches Küstenland" 1943–1945.* Publikationen des Österreichischen Instituts für Zeitgeschichte und des Instituts für Zeitgeschichte der Universität Wien, Band 7 (Vienna: Hollinek, 1969).

11 Leopold Steurer, *Südtirol zwischen Rom und Berlin 1919-1939* (Vienna: Europa Verlag, 1980).

12 Pallaver, Steinacher, "Historiker zwischen Forschung und Einmischung," 62.

13 Gerald Steinacher, "Auschwitz liegt in Südtirol: über die Notwendigkeit einer Tätergeschichte Südtirols," *Forum Schule heute, Pädagogische Zeitschrift für die Schule in Südtirol*, Heft 1 (2011), 10-12.

14 Scholars in this group include Hans Heiss, Andrea Di Michele, Siglinde Clementi, Oswald Überegger, Martha Verdorfer, and Carlo Romeo just to name a few.

15 Rolf Steininger, *Los von Rom?: Die Südtirolfrage 1945/1946 und das Gruber-De Gasperi-Abkommen.* Innsbrucker Forschungen zur Zeitgeschichte (Innsbruck: Haymon-Verlag, 1987). Rolf Steininger, *South Tyrol: A Minority Conflict of the Twentieth Century* (Piscataway, NJ: Transaction Publishers, 2003).

16 See e.g. Giovanni Bernardini, Günther Pallaver, eds., *Dialogue against Violence. The Question of Trentino-South Tyrol in the International Context* (Bologna – Berlin: Duncker&Humblot 2017).

17 Gerald Steinacher, *Nazis auf der Flucht: Wie Kriegsverbrecher über Italien nach Übersee entkamen* (Frankfurt: Fischer, 2010). Gerald Steinacher, *Nazis on the Run: How Hitler's Henchmen Fled Justice* (Oxford: Oxford University Press, 2011).

18 Gerald Steinacher, "'A Man with a Wide Horizon:' The Postwar Professional Journey of SS Officer Karl Nicolussi-Leck," in *From Nazis to West-Germans: "Nazi Self-Help," Recast Identities and the Politics of the Past after 1945,* ed. David A. Messenger and Katrin Paehler (Lexington: University of Kentucky, 2015), 225-248.

19 And vice-versa: in other words, a Fascist and an anti-Nazi at the same time. Local Italian Fascists saw the local Nazis in South Tyrol as opponents if not worse.

20 A quick comparison with Austria might illustrate this point. Austrian Nazis in the 1930s might have considered themselves "antifascist," in the sense that they were against Engelbert Dollfuss, the Catholic fascist leader of Austria. The Chancellor defended the independence of Austria and was supported by Mussolini. In 1934 Dollfuss was assassinated by Austrian Nazis. After 1945 Austrian Nazis on trial hardly used the argument "to be antifascist" and it would not have given them much credit anyway. In South Tyrol on the other hand, this was a winning strategy. South Tyrolean Nazis were seen by many in Austria and Germany as patriots, who defended South Tyrol against Italian claims. And this narrative of Tyrolean Nazis ran over decades - from postwar defenses into their obituaries 50 years later. This said, Austrian right-wing politicians have repeatedly called anti-Nazi laws and antifascist politicians "fascists," therefore "turn[ing] meaningful political concepts upside-down." For more on this see Walter Manoschek, "FPÖ, ÖVP, and Austria's Nazi Past," in *The Haider Phenomenon in Austria,* ed. Ruth Wodak and Anton Pelinka (New Brunswick: Transaction Publishers, 2002), 3-15 (here 6).

21 Costantino di Sante, *Criminali del campo di concentramento di Bolzano* (Bozen: Raetia, 2019).

22 For recent studies see Thomas Casagrande, *Südtiroler in der Waffen-SS: Vorbildliche Haltung, fanatische Überzeugung* (Bozen: Raetia, 2015) and Thomas Mang, *Die Unperson: Karl Ebner, Judenreferent der Gestapo Wien* (Bozen: Raetia, 2013).

23 Franz Thaler, *Unforgotten: A Memoir of Dachau* (Munich: Kiener, 2013). For a most recent study on the fate of Jews in South Tyrol see Joachim Innerhofer and Sabine Mayr, *Mörderische Heimat: Verdrängte Lebensgeschichten jüdischer Familien in Bozen und Meran* (Bozen: Raetia, 2015) and Cinzia Villani, *Zwischen Rassengesetzen und Deportation: Juden in Südtirol, im Trentino und in der Provinz Belluno 1933–1945,* (Innsbruck: Universitätsverlag Wagner, 2003).

24 Steinacher, "Auschwitz liegt in Südtirol."

25 See Christoph Cornelißen and Paolo Pezzino, eds., *Historikerkommissionen und historische Konfliktbewältigung* (Berlin/Boston: De Gruyter, 2017).

26 For Italy see Ilaria Poggiolini, "Translating Memories of War and Co-Belligerency into Politics: The Italian Post-War Experience" in *Memory and Power in Post-War Europe,* ed. Jan-Werner Müller, 223-243; here also Müller, introduction, 5.

27 Tim Parks, "Tyrol: Retreat to Reality", *The New York Review of Books,* May 27, 2004, https://www.nybooks.com/articles/2004/05/27/tyrol-retreat-to-reality/.

28 For the controversies over the material legacy of Fascism in South Tyrol see Gerald Steinacher, "Fascist Legacies: The Controversy over Mussolini's Monuments in South Tyrol", *European Yearbook of Minority Issues,* Vol. 10 (2011), 647-666.

29 Vizebürgermeister Oswald Ellecosta, April 2009. "Wenn wir schon von Befreiung reden, dann sollten wir den 9. September 1943 nennen. Damals sind die Deutschen einmarschiert, sie sind von den Südtirolern mit Blumen empfangen worden," wird Ellecosta vom "Alto Adige" zitiert. Auf Nachfrage des Redakteurs, dass es sich um die Nazis gehandelt habe, antwortete Ellecosta: "Die Nazis waren Großkriminelle. Die Faschisten haben uns verboten Deutsch zu sprechen und unsere Namen italianisiert. Ab dem 9. September 1943 ist jedoch die deutsche Kultur zurückgekehrt," so Ellecosta." in "Tag der Befreiung? Der 9. September 1943!," antifameran.blogsport.com (April 27, 2009), accessed Nov. 26, 2019, http://antifameran.blogspot.com/2009/04/.

Review Essay

Janek Wasserman, *The Marginal Revolutionaries: How Austrian Economists Fought the War of Ideas* (New Haven: Yale University Press, 2019)

Hansjörg Klausinger[1]

When John Maynard Keynes wrote his path-breaking *The General Theory of Employment, Interest, and Money*,[2] one of his highly successful strategies of persuasion was to concoct a body of so-called "classical economics" as a well-designed target for his attacks. Critics have since then pointed out that such a "classical strawman" had never existed or only, as a critic put it, as "a composite Aunt Sally of uncertain age."[3]

The term "neoliberalism" appears to suffer from a similar fate. It has been sparingly used by the propagators of the liberal creed, predominantly in the 1930s and 1940s to distinguish it from "old liberalism," but all the more by its critics as a shortcut for all that they disdain of this view. Historians of economic thought have dealt with the revival of liberalism after its near-death in the 1940s and thereby emphasized the important role to be attributed to the Austrian School of Economics or, to be precise, to its liberal wing. However, it appears to be such a highly sensitive subject that it has proven almost impossible to write such histories *sine ira et studio*. Thus, the existing spectrum ranges from hagiographic exercises over a middle ground—where authors just mildly emphasize the benevolence or malevolence, respectively, of the liberal venture—to outright attempts at destroying the reputation of the project and/or its propagators. To give but a few examples, at the one extreme there is Hartwell's history of the Mont Pèlerin Society (MPS) or Hülsmann's Mises biography. The Hayek biographies of Ebenstein and Caldwell's intellectual portrait, as well as the history of the MPS by Plickert, may be counted among the (mildly) benevolent ones and the study by Burgin as the rare case of a balanced account. At the other end, the studies inspired by Mirowski stress the role of big-business-financed think tanks in the evolution of the networks of the neoliberal thought collective. The gist of these approaches is neatly brought out by the title of Walpen's monograph on the MPS, *Die offenen Feinde und ihre Gesellschaft*. Most recently, Slobodian investigated Geneva as a hub of global liberalism.[4] Notably—although often prejudiced in one or the other direction—most, if not all, of these monographs contain valuable historical insights and can only be neglected at the reader's own peril. In my view, the only exception to this rule are the editor's contributions to a stream of (an apparently open-ended number of) volumes, currently at fifteen, of a collaborative biography of F.A. Hayek, edited by Robert Leeson, which defy any scientific categorization.[5]

It is against this background that the book by Janek Wasserman on the history of the Austrian School's *Marginal Revolutionaries* is to be evaluated. Its title elaborates the pun that the Austrian School is commonly credited for its role in propagating the "marginal revolution" of economic theory in the 1870s and that later on its members felt themselves "marginalized" within the discipline for their steadfast defense of liberalism. Two features of the book stand out from the beginning. First, the explanation of the evolution of Austrian thought and its impact is primarily externalist—that is, it focuses on networks, connections, and alliances with think tanks and funding institutions rather than on scientific accomplishments. And second, it soon becomes obvious that the author shares hardly any of the views of the scholars that he portrays.

Before discussing the pros and cons of Wasserman's history, a summary of the story told is in order. The book consists of seven chapters, supplemented by an introduction and a conclusion, and it deals in chronological order with the evolution of the Austrian School of Economics—from its very beginning to its present-day ramifications.

The first chapter concerns the school's founding fathers. It covers all the core topics: Carl Menger's *Principles of Economics* as the founding document of subjectivist marginal utility theory, the battle of methods with the Younger Historical School led by Gustav von Schmoller, and Eugen von Böhm-Bawerk and Friedrich von Wieser as the intellectual entrepreneurs who in effect (more than Menger) created the school. Böhm contributed a theory of capital and interest, while Wieser's *Social Economics* attempted a synthesis of Austrian and neoclassical economics. The Austrians' collaboration in the creation of the *Gesellschaft* österreichischer *Volkswirte* and its associated *Zeitschrift* may be seen as their first steps toward institution-building. However, without an equivalent to the Prussian "System Althoff," academic economics in Austria remained much more diverse than in the German Reich. Already in this opening chapter, two of Wasserman's perennial topics come to the fore. These are, first, the role of "status" and "connections" as crucial for the school's success—where it seems to me that the status of lower nobility to which some of the best-known members belonged (e.g., Menger, Wieser, Böhm-Bawerk, Mises, Hayek, or Haberler) is overrated. And second, starting with Böhm's attempted refutation of Marxian exploitation theory, the theoretical arguments are downplayed in comparison to the school's political stance as an example of "antisocialism, antileftism, and liberal apologetics" (39).[6]

Next, the author turns to the school's Golden Age in the prewar era. For the theoretical discussions, the famous Böhm seminar is singled out as of paramount importance, with participants ranging across the whole political spectrum—from Ludwig von Mises to Otto Bauer, Rudolf Hilferding, and Otto Neurath. For evidence on the increasing impact on policy-making, Wasserman picks out Menger's chairing the Austrian currency commission and some Austrians' stints as ministers in various cabinets (e.g., Böhm as finance minister on three occasions and Wieser as minister of trade on the monarchy's eve). Yet I would attach less weight than the author to the liberal element in these political activities, for they occurred not during the short era of the Liberal Party's reign but in the conservative governments that followed, which famously adhered to a policy of "muddling through." With regard to methodological controversy, Wasserman stresses the significance of the 1909 Vienna meeting of the *Verein für Socialpolitik*, well known for its heated dispute on the problem of value judgments. He argues that the choice of the topic for the Vienna meeting was not accidental insofar as the Austrian School shared Max Weber's position on the demarcation between value judgments and science. This appears doubtful since of the Austrian contributors to the discussion (Philippovich, Zwiedineck, Spann, and Otto Neurath), none spoke in favor of Weber's verdict.[7] In the final section, we are introduced to the next generation of scholars, led by Joseph Schumpeter and Ludwig von Mises, both of which initiated the turn toward the role of "public intellectuals."

"Austria's end" and what it meant for the reinvention of the Austrian School is the topic of the third chapter. There were then fewer opportunities for the Austrians to shape policy directly in government, with the exception of Schumpeter's short and unlucky term as finance minister in the Renner cabinet, so that the "battle of ideas" fought in public discourse gained in importance. The most noteworthy was the socialist calculation debate instigated by Mises and at first directed at Neurath as its prime target. With regard to institution-building, the Austrians cultivated their own circles of debate outside academia. Here, the focus is on the liberal, Mises-led strand of the school and a new generation of younger scholars comprising Friedrich A. Hayek, Gottfried Haberler, Fritz Machlup, and Oskar Morgenstern. Wasserman duly mentions the *Geist-Kreis*, founded by the friends Hayek and Herbert Fürth, and the Mises Circle. His judgment on the preeminence of the former is, however, debatable, even if one need not go so far as characterizing the *Geist-Kreis* as merely "a private meeting of friends who tried to escape from their everyday work into esoteric discussions."[8] It indeed played a vital role in introducing its participants to the whole range of issues pertinent for their view of Western civilization, yet economics, per se, was *not* a major subject in the discussions. It was also *not* the case that the "complete *Geist-Kreis*" joined the Mises Circle on Hayek's and Morgenstern's behalves (121).[9] At last, it is apparently Haberler's innocuous remark that, insofar as economics attempts to *understand* individual actions, it must be regarded a "*Geisteswissenschaft*,"[10] which prompts Wasserman's claim that "inspired by the *Geist-Kreis*, Haberler argued that spirit, or *Geist*, rather than statistical regularities, were at the core of economic activity and social science" (137)—a rather baffling interpretation. Apart from these circles, according to the author, the Austrians' reactions to the changed circumstances were to seek "support from allies in business and finance" (95). The foundation of the Austrian Institute for Business Cycle Research in 1927 is referred to as a case in point (on which more below).

The next period to which the book turns is that of crisis and emigration. In the 1930s, Austroliberalism came under siege in various fields: its theses on the causes of and the remedies required for the Great Depression, derived from Austrian business cycle theory in opposition to the novel Keynesian approach, were found wanting by academic, as well as public, opinion; the focus on the time dimension of its capital theory was criticized by Chicago economist Frank Knight; and in a new round of the calculation debate, socialist economists who pointed to the equivalence of the outcome of general market equilibrium and an efficient central plan, simply to be derived as a solution to a multi-equations system, appeared to have the better end of the debate for themselves. Moreover, in the 1930s, more and more Austrian School economists left Austria for the US and Great Britain (e.g., Hayek, Haberler, Mises, Machlup, and others). Although contacts among them persisted, the consequence was a de-homogenization of the school, with Morgenstern's reorientation toward economics as an exact science being an outstanding example. Finally, the "Anschluss" in 1938 gave rise to a final rush of emigration, for political and "racial" reasons. Wasserman gives due weight to the efforts of the Austrian emigrants on behalf of those still left behind and also how they were able to garner support from organizations like the Society for the Preservation of Scientific Learning or the RF. Perhaps it would have been worthwhile noting that their support did extend well beyond ideological barriers; Hayek, for example, intervened on behalf of the Socialist coworkers Josef Steindl and Adolf Kozlik at Morgenstern's institute or of Moritz Schlick's former assistant Friedrich Waismann.

The fifth chapter turns to the fate of the Austrian School economists in postwar emigration. Significantly, although all of them had acquired their reputation by contributions to (pure) economic theory, they appeared to have arrived at a dead end, as proven by the failures of Hayek's *The Pure Theory of Capital*, Schumpeter's *Business Cycles*, and the neglect of the ill-fated Swiss publication of Mises's *Nationalökonomie*. This may have been the motive behind two highly successful transgressions beyond the field of technical economics into social philosophy and methodology: Hayek's *The Road to Serfdom* and Schumpeter's *Capitalism, Socialism and Democracy*. Although similar concerns had been ever present, the Austrian School's subject now became visible for a wider audience as that of the "study of civilization."[11] Morgenstern's path at Princeton was different as he was out to revolutionize economics by a novel approach: game theory, jointly developed with the eminent mathematician John von Neumann. For Morgenstern, knowledge and acceptance of game theory henceforth became the single criterion for distinguishing between good and bad economics, a kind of *acqua fortis*, and thus, although he remained in friendly personal contact with his former Austrian colleagues, he no longer took their economics seriously.

But the realm of the Austrian School was not limited to scholarly discussion. It extended, as Wasserman reiterates, well into the spheres of institution-building and influencing the drift of political decisions. Foremost in this regard was, of course, Hayek's foundation of the MPS in 1947, the core model of a neoliberal think tank. Other ventures of the Austroliberals included Hayek's role within the Chicago school of economics or Mises's presence in New York that led to the formation of a small, but articulate, group of true believers. Haberler succeeded as an economic adviser to the GATT in turning the tides toward an advocacy of global free-trade policies (instead of local development strategies). Machlup led the Bellagio group, which, after the breakdown of Bretton Woods, was pivotal in transforming the world monetary system into one of flexible exchange rates and the free movement of capital. This was noteworthy for the fact that the preference for flexible rates had only been a minority view before and continued to be considered a heresy by the adherents to a gold-based currency, educated in the pure teachings of their mentor, Mises. Here, and on other occasions, Wasserman does not fail to point out that these successes came about with a little help from liberalism's friends: "pro-business and anti-New Deal" institutions like the Volker Fund, the Earhart Foundation, the Foundation for Economic Education, or the Koch Foundation. These provided the funds for sponsoring chairs and creating various centers of Austrian thought (e.g., the Mercatus Center at GMU, the Cato Institute, or the Ludwig von Mises Institute).

The final chapter is devoted to the competing legacies of the Austrian School at a stage when its last Austrian-born generation was slowly passing away. In fact, its present-day representatives are almost exclusively "non-Austrian Austrians" who moreover split along various cleavages. One conflict that has been crucial from the times of the *Colloque Walter Lippmann* in 1938 and the foundation of the MPS up to the present day is that between "new" and "old" liberalism—that is, whether the active role of the state in implementing a legal framework conducive to a liberal economic order is indispensable or if such an order would evolve "automatically." (In my view, Wasserman, 146–49, does not fully appreciate the importance of this distinguishing feature of "neoliberalism.") Hayek adhered to the former view—in *The Road to Serfdom*, he advocated this kind of "planning for competition."[12] Although he later became less outspoken in this respect, there was always a clear dividing line between "neoliberalism" in this sense and the laissez-faire position advocated by Mises, as well as by latter-day anarcho-liberals. Second, opinions also differed on the place of Austrian economics within the discipline as a whole. While "moderates" aimed at an integration of the Austrian view with the economic mainstream—Hayek once remarked that "a school has its greatest success when it ceases as such to exist because its leading ideals have become a part of the general dominant teaching"[13] —others were more concerned of keeping the masters' teaching pure and immaculate. This overlapped to a great degree with the conflicting views, if Austrian economists faithful to their creed could content themselves with "doing good economics" or if analysis and ideology had (or indeed should) become inseparable. Finally, on the restoration of a liberal order—however defined—the school and its institutions split between those favoring a more piecemeal approach and others who could only envisage a most radical break from the present system. Of course, most of these divisions ran between the more traditional (Austrian) Austrians on one side and the neo-Austrian School created by Mises and his ever more radical non-Austrian disciples on the other side, centered at George Mason University and the Ludwig von Mises Institute at Auburn University, respectively. In this sense, Wasserman is certainly right in his verdict that the Mises group, although "one of the least impactful of Austrian postwar ventures, …was to have the greatest influence on the 'rebirth' of Austrian economics" (216) and thus, in a way, usurped the tradition. These conflicts also led to splits and redirections of the funding provided by those institutions that had created the financial leeway for the survival of the school in the postwar period (e.g., when Murray Rothbard broke with the Koch-financed Cato Institute [257]).

As regards the impact of Austrian economics in the sphere of politics, its association—justified or not—with the neoliberal U-turn brought about by the Reagan and Thatcher governments also reveals that these successes had a price, namely the acceptance of alliances with conservative movements, with some of the school's strands not shying away from making common cause with the right-wing lunatic fringe (see 278–83). In contrast, "The quest for a progressive Austrianism remains unfulfilled" (289). This might point to the fact that, camouflaged by the apparent success story of Austrian School liberalism, its creed still does not appeal to more than a small minority of the public, and therefore, in order to succeed in the political arena, uneasy coalitions have to be forged with more or less trepidation.

In conclusion, this is how Wasserman summarizes the evolution of the Austrian School: "It originated in opposition to German economic thought and Habsburg conservatism. It flourished in the interwar years through its connections to US philanthropic organizations. It successfully migrated to the Anglophone world during the war years thanks to these connections. Its members developed transnational networks of intellectuals and free-market activists using their Rolodexes of like-minded scholars and wealthy elites" (267).

Even this extensive summary of the book cannot do justice to the wealth of ideas critically discussed and the multitude of facts revealed—one of the book's virtues that, however, come at the cost of some lack of coherence. Unfortunately, this is not the only shortcoming of Wasserman's venture into the history of Austrian economics.

First of all, the book is "thick" on the (hidden) connections of the Austrians, the impact of their status (nobles as many of them were), or the funding that really or allegedly furthered their career moves. Yet it is "thin" on the substance of the peculiar Austrian contributions—that is, if one dare use this formulation, their scientific accomplishments. This is certainly due to the choice of the book's focus in writing a largely externalist history of Austrian economics, but it may also owe to the author's uneasy grip on economic theory, which leads to him often ending up in error when trying to depict the Austrians' theories.

To give but a few examples, the summary of Böhm-Bawerk's interest theory confuses the notions of time *preference* and time *productivity*—that is, the first and the third of Böhm's famous "three reasons" for the existence of interest (47). Similarly, the 1930s debate between Hayek and Keynes becomes impenetrable for the uninitiated reader. When Wasserman states that Keynes objected to the "conventional policy response of governments to economic downturns—raising interest rates to drive down prices and spending" (140), he possibly confuses the responses to a balance-of-payments crisis within a gold standard system with those to a cyclical downturn.

Still more enigmatic is the description of the Austrians as advocates of "price stability and self-adjusting monetary policy" (141). Conceding that what is meant is "price *level* stability," the Austrians stood out as skeptics of such "stabilization policies," and indeed a core innovation of Hayek's *Monetary Theory and the Trade Cycle*[14] was to show that, in a growing economy, a stable price level might just be the source of those monetary disturbances that generate business cycles. Furthermore, no Austrian economist ever used the expression "self-adjusting monetary policy," and it is difficult to imagine what it is supposed to mean. For lack of space, I cannot elaborate on the misrepresentations of Hayek's concept of dispersed knowledge and of Machlup's book on the stock market (see 151–52 and 136–37).

The author also devotes a few pages to a sketch of von Neumann and Morgenstern's (vNM) *Theory of Games and Economic Behavior*,[15] which, alas, will not be helpful to those not already acquainted with it. The crucial misunderstanding is to regard game theory as a progressive contribution to subjective utility theory (188). Yet game theory was not out to "provide insight into how to measure utility" (191) because these refer to the sphere of the *individual* decision, while its novel approach centered on the *interaction* among individuals. Nor did the novelty of game theory consist in the introduction of the "new assumptions" of "rationality, perfect knowledge [and] free competition" (ibid.)—in particular the analysis of two-person games by vNM was, of course, a major deviation from the notion of free competition.

Turning to economic history, Mises's advice to Chancellor Ignaz Seipel on the Austrian currency stabilization of 1922, resulting in the League of Nations granting a loan and supervising Austrian financial policies, is given pride of place (see 108, 131). Drawing on the famous Marienthal study about the sad fate of the unemployed, Mises is blamed for his support of "draconian liberal policies" (133) that apparently hampered the Austrian economy for the sake of a stable currency. This does not conform to what I hold to be the state of the art of historians' judgment on that episode.[16] In any case, the author forgets to tell the uninitiated reader that the stabilization program's aim was to end the Austrian hyperinflation that had rampaged the economy. At the end, prices had risen at an annual rate of about 1,700 percent. Indeed, the hyperinflation's distortion of price relations, the booms generated in some sectors of the economy due to devaluation and depressed real wages, and the profiteering of speculators like Camillo Castiglione or Siegmund Bosel provided the model for Austrian business cycle theory—that is, of an inflationary-induced sham prosperity doomed to break down sooner or later. Unfortunately, then as now, economists do not know a recipe for ending hyperinflations, and end they must, without remedies giving rise to a stabilization crisis, presumably the deeper the later the inflation is stopped. Thus, the criticism of Mises would be justified only if, alternatively, there had existed a magic formula of how to stop the hyperinflation without causing such collateral damage. In some sense, this is an example where the blame is put on those who provide the cure instead of those who cause the disease.

Let's turn then to the other highly unfortunate feature of the book, namely that it is littered with inaccuracies and superficial observations. All too often the story told contains facts that turn out to be inaccurate, if not wrong. Sometimes these errors appear just to reflect the author's intent to tell a better story than the facts alone would permit. Sometimes they also have the tendency to promote the author's favored conclusions. Here, I dare not bore the reader by attempting to provide a complete list of these shortcomings but only pick some examples.

The depiction of the Hayek family may serve as a first example. The family into which Friedrich Hayek was born was *not* "prosperous" (113) but at most upper middle class, after his father had sacrificed a more lucrative job for his scholarly ambitions as a botanist. It is also *not* true that both of Hayek's grandfathers were "economists" (22). Neither was. Franz von Juraschek was a statistician, and Gustav von Hayek taught biology at a Vienna Gymnasium. Hayek's mother, Felicitas (née Juraschek), was related to the Wittgenstein family, one of the richest in Vienna. Yet it is an exaggeration that the Juraschek and Wittgenstein families "summered together in the Vienna woods" (113). Rather, both spent the summer at neighboring residences in Neuwaldegg on the outskirts of Vienna—the Wittgensteins in a summer palace, the Jurascheks in a small Swiss cottage. So apparently the whereabouts of the Hayek family were a little bit less glamorous than the author would like to make us believe.

For a second sampling, take a single paragraph on page 38 and what it tells about Böhm-Bawerk's early career: "Böhm's first book attracted little notice. …Menger himself paid the work scant attention. …In spite of this desultory debut, Böhm's prominent social status and his bureaucratic connections helped him secure a professorship at the University of Innsbruck." The book in question was Böhm's habilitation thesis[17] that he presented to the law faculty of the University of Vienna, mentored by Menger, who duly wrote a favorable report and recommended awarding Böhm with the respective lectureship. And possibly an economics lectureship from Vienna was a better qualification for the University of Innsbruck than mere "status" and "connections." In this respect, Wasserman apparently overestimates the connections of a junior civil servant at a Lower Austrian financial office (not, as Wasserman believes, at the "Lower Austrian Finance Ministry," 37, for an institution with that name never existed).

In particular, with regard to the Austrian Institute for Business Cycle Research, Wasserman refers to the support received from "members of the increasingly conservative Austrian *Großbürgertum* and international philanthropic associations," which "demonstrates the convergence of liberal ideas and capital" and in the end led to a steering role in the institute for "private industry" (123, see also 123–25). However, Wasserman should have concentrated less on counting the members of the institute's board and their allegiances than on the institute's income statement, which shows that only a small share of contributions came from private industry.[18] Rather, the Chamber of Labour had also been involved in the foundation (and made an annual payment), giving rise to the institute's characterization as an example of social partnership, *avant la lettre.*[19] Furthermore, the policy recommendations of the institute often were not well aligned with the interests of big business—Morgenstern in the 1930s destroyed his chances for a career within the Association of Austrian Industrialists by his advocacy of free trade and deregulation.[20] The other source of "wealthy benefactors" was The Rockefeller Foundation (RF), which not only lent financial support to the institute but also sponsored fellowships for members of the Austrian School. Yet there is no evidence that the RF, in its support for Austrian institutions and scholars, revealed a bias toward liberal thought. For example, the foundation supported a great number of business cycle institutes across Europe, with a focus on furthering empirical research for the aim of economic stabilization—two issues not high on the Austrian agenda and of rather diverse orientations. For example, in Germany it supported the institutes in Berlin (Ernst Wagemann), Kiel (Bernhard Harms and the Astwik group), and Heidelberg (Adolf Weber and Emil Lederer), neither of whom could be said to exhibit a liberal bias. These, at least, were not "RF institutions" that served as "proxy agents of the US government" (125).

The characterization of the "family feuds" within the interwar school—between the disciples of Mayer and Menger and later on the Morgenstern group—is marred by numerous gaffes too. For example, Haberler did *not* belong to the Mayer group. Mayer did *not* favor mathematical methods. The dispute between Mises and Karl Menger (154) was *not* on "questions of ethics" but on the a priori validity of the laws of returns. And it *cannot* be true that "after their major spat [about Morgenstern's 1934 book] they [Morgenstern and Hayek] still attended the Mises seminar fortnightly and ate lunch together several days a week" (156) because in 1934, Mises had already left Vienna for Geneva and closed his seminar, and Hayek's LSE chair had kept him away from Vienna since 1931.

Turning to a minor issue, the author's emphasis on the role of "coffeehouses" and "salons" for the discourses led by the Austrian economists appears misleading too. The portrait of the Austrians as a "coffee-house school" (164) is certainly an overstatement, and who would believe that the controversy between Böhm and Hilferding on the justification of interest became the subject of Vienna *Kaffeeklatsch* (66)?[21] With regard to the "salons," where Wasserman would have expected to regularly meet members of the Austrian School, he does not hint at which particular salon he would have had in mind—one of those hosted by eminent Viennese women like Alma Mahler-Werfel, Berta Zuckerkandl, or Eugenie Schwarzwald? The Austrians have left no traces there. The author's mild obsession also spills over into the description of the mini-seminars held by Herbert Furth in the 1970s: "Herbert Furth convened a *Geist-Kreis*-style session at his home in the Washington, DC, suburbs for his Viennese friends. Haberler, Machlup, and Martha Steffy Browne joined him. The wide-ranging conversations reaffirmed the most significant features of their movement: its combative discursive style honed in coffeehouses and salons, its intellectual eclecticism and interdisciplinarity, and its skepticism about its own core principles" (267). Sounds great, yet the only fact that can be confirmed from the source quoted, a letter from Furth to Hayek, March 14, 1977, is the mere existence of the seminar. Anything else is pure speculation added by the author. Furth is silent in his letter on the style of the conversation in these seminars, although he gives the names of the participants: Ilse Mintz, Otto Donner, Erich Schiff, Herbert Zassenhaus, and Hans Richter-Altschäffer; only Haberler, Machlup, and Browne were not there.

This is, unfortunately, only a small selection of those instances when the author is strolling away from the simple facts, presumably drawing on "artistic freedom" in search of some kind of higher truth. Let's have a last example. Wasserman is entirely justified when he draws attention to Hayek's Chilean episode as revealing a serious blind spot in Hayek's weighing of the benefits of economic liberalism against the violation of human rights. Why, then, does he add the apocryphal story of Hayek having been invited by Augusto Pinochet himself (262)? Not only has this detail of Hayek's trip been disproved by Caldwell and Montes,[22] but Caldwell is referred to in the introduction as one of those who read the typescript, and it is unbelievable that he would not have pointed out this error to the author.

Finally, one may ask, how could so many inaccuracies have crept into a thoroughly documented text? The answer lies in the somewhat awkward system of documentation used. As a rule, notes with corresponding references to the sources are only appended to whole paragraphs and not to single passages. This has the drawback that when paragraphs contain arguments from various sources, as well as the author's own elaborations, it is impossible to find out which parts are backed by the sources and which are not. This may result in confusions. For example, I was surprised to find a paragraph contending that Hans Mayer was a member of the Nazi Party with a reference to one of my articles on the subject (131 n.5) because the contention is wrong, as well as not backed by the source. There is ample reason to believe that this is not a singular case.

In sum, despite all my criticisms, this is certainly a book that no one interested in the interrelationships between Austrian economics and the renaissance of liberal thought can afford to disregard. In my view, its value is thoroughly diminished by numerous factual inaccuracies and errors. Accordingly, it would have been a big improvement if a clearer demarcation between facts and evidence-based arguments on the one hand and speculation on the other hand—or, that is, between "science" and "fiction"—had been observed. In consequence, for the proper consumption of this book, a mere "grain of salt" will not suffice.

Endnotes

1 For useful hints I am grateful to Harald Hagemann and to Bruce Caldwell, with whom I am co-authoring a biography of Friedrich A. Hayek.

2 John Maynard Keynes, *The General Theory of Employment, Interest and Money*, reprinted as *The Collected Writings of John Maynard Keynes*, vol. 7 (Cambridge: Cambridge University Press, and London: Macmillan, 1973 [1936]).

3 Dennis H. Robertson, "Alternative Theories of the Rate of Interest," *Economic Journal* 47 (1937): 428–36 (here: 436).

4 See Ronald M. Hartwell, *A History of the Mont Pèlerin Society* (Indianapolis: Liberty Fund, 1995); Jörg Guido Hülsmann, *Mises: The Last Knight of Liberalism* (Auburn: Ludwig von Mises Institute, 2007); Alan Ebenstein, *Friedrich Hayek: A Biography* (New York: Palgrave, 2001), and *Hayek's Journey: The Mind of Friedrich Hayek* (New York: Palgrave Macmillan, 2003); Bruce Caldwell, *Hayek's Challenge: An Intellectual Biography of F. A. Hayek* (Chicago: University of Chicago Press, 2004); Philip Plickert, *Wandlungen des Neoliberalismus: eine Studie zu Entwicklung und Ausstrahlung der "Mont Pèlerin Society"* (Stuttgart: Lucius & Lucius, 2008); Angus Burgin, *The Great Persuasion: Reinventing Free Markets since the Depression* (Cambridge, MA: Harvard University Press, 2012); Philip Mirowski, ed., *The Road from Mont Pèlerin: The Making of the Neoliberal Thought Collective* (Cambridge, MA: Harvard University Press, 2009); Bernhard Walpen, *Die offenen Feinde und ihre Gesellschaft: eine hegemonietheoretische Studie zur Mont Pèlerin Society* (Hamburg: VSA-Verlag, 2004); and Quinn Slobodian, *Globalists: The End of Empire and the Birth of Neoliberalism* (Cambridge, MA: Harvard University Press, 2018).

5 Robert Leeson, ed., *Hayek: A Collaborative Biography*, vols. 1–15 (New York: Palgrave Macmillan, 2013–2019); cf. Roland Fritz and Hansjörg Klausinger, "Das phantastische Archiv: Zu Robert Leesons '*Hayek: A Collaborative Biography*,'" *ORDO* 67 (2016): 519–27.

6 Page references are to the book reviewed.

7 See Franz Boese, *Geschichte des Vereins für Sozialpolitik, 1872–1932* (Berlin: Duncker & Humblot, 1939), 133–35.

8 Christian Fleck, "Zum intellektuellen Umfeld der Wiener Jahre von Alfred Schütz," in *Krise und Exodus: Österreichische Sozialwissenschaften in Mitteleuropa*, ed. Kurt R. Leube and Andreas Pribersky (Vienna: WUV-Universitätsverlag, 1995), 98–116 (here: 108).

9 Cf. e.g. the membership lists provided by Claire Wright, "The 1920s Viennese Intellectual Community as a Center for Ideas Exchange: A Network Analysis," *History of Political Economy* 48 (2016): 593–634.

10 Gottfried Haberler, *Der Sinn der Indexzahlen: Eine Untersuchung über den Begriff des Preisniveaus und die Methoden seiner Messung* (Tübingen: Mohr Siebeck, 1927), 70 (Wasserman gives no page reference).

11 See Erwin Dekker, *The Viennese Students of Civilization: The Meaning and Context of Austrian Economics Reconsidered* (Cambridge: Cambridge University Press, 2016).

12 See Friedrich A. Hayek, *The Road to Serfdom: Text and Documents: The Definitive Edition* (vol. 2 of *The Collected Works of F. A. Hayek*), ed. Bruce Caldwell (Chicago: University of Chicago Press, and London: Routledge, 2007 [1944]), 90; cf. also ibid., 88: "In no system that could be rationally defended would the state just do nothing."

13 Friedrich A. Hayek, "The Austrian School of Economics," as reprinted in *The Fortunes of Liberalism: Essays on Austrian Economics and the Ideal of Freedom* (vol. 4 of *The Collected Works of F. A. Hayek*), ed. Peter G. Klein (Chicago: University of Chicago Press, and London: Routledge, 1992 [1968]), 42–60 (here: 52).

14 Friedrich A. Hayek, *Monetary Theory and the Trade Cycle* (London: Jonathan Cape, 1933 [1929]).

15 John von Neumann and Oskar Morgenstern, *The Theory of Games and Economic Behavior* (Princeton: Princeton University Press, 1944).

16 See e.g. recently Nathan Marcus, *Austrian Reconstruction and the Collapse of Global Finance, 1921–1931* (Cambridge: Harvard University Press, 2018).

17 Eugen von Böhm-Bawerk, *Rechte und Verhältnisse vom Standpunkte der volkswirtschaftlichen Güterlehre* (Innsbruck: Wagner, 1881).

18 The income statement for 1929 is preserved in Rockefeller Archive Center, Collection RF 1.1/705, box 4, folder 36: Austrian Institute for Trade Cycle Research, 1930–1934; see also Hansjörg Klausinger, "Das Österreichische Institut für Konjunkturforschung 1927 bis 1938: Wirtschaftsforschung und Wirtschaftspolitik in der Ersten Republik," *Wifo-Monatsberichte* 90, no. 12 (2017): 935–40 (here: 936).

19 Felix Butschek, "Eine Wurzel der Sozialpartnerschaft. Die Konjunkturforschung zwischen den Kriegen," *Wifo-Monatsberichte* 85, no. 6 (2012): 451–59.

20 See Hansjoerg Klausinger, "Policy Advice by Austrian Economists: The Case of Austria in the 1930s," *Advances in Austrian Economics* 11 (2008): 25–53 (here: 36–40).

21 The author is obviously not aware that "*Kaffeeklatsch*" usually does not take place in coffeehouses, and he is also wrong, owing to a mistranslation of the phrase "lauter Dinge" (p. 21), in believing that the poet Arthur Schnitzler liked coffeehouses because they were loud.

22 Bruce Caldwell and Leonidas Montes, "Friedrich Hayek and His Visits to Chile," *Review of Austrian Economics* 28 (2015): 261–309.

Book Reviews

Moritz Csáky, *Das Gedächtnis Zentraleuropas: Kulturelle und literarische Projektionen auf eine Region* (Vienna: Böhlau, 2019)

William M. Johnston

For the past twenty years, historians of the Habsburg Empire have been inquiring what, if any, cultural traits pervaded that entire realm. This quest for distinguishing features of the empire builds on earlier research on "Austria," construed either as the region of today's republic or as the larger conglomerate once known as Cisleithania, the very region (excluding Greater Hungary) that Musil mischievously called *Kakanien.* To provide a name for the whole empire to replace the contested slogan "*Mitteleuropa*," Tony Judt in his final book, *Thinking the Twentieth Century* (2012), offered the coinage "Habsburgia" (12), and this review will use that label for what Csáky prefers to call by Pieter Judson's term, "Habsburg Central Europe" (*Zentraleuropa*) (38-40, 139). Endless debates about how to name the various entities have given way to exploring what patterns and structures, no matter how elusive, the widely scattered regions may have shared. Judson's political and social history, *The Habsburg Empire* (2016), integrates much of this research for the period 1780-1925.

Recently no one has contributed more cogently to Habsburgia studies than Moritz Csáky, who has just published his sixth or seventh book that rethinks the subject's fundamentals (*Grundbegriffe*). His preceding volume bore a kindred title: *Das Gedächtnis der Städte: Kulturelle Verflechtungen – Wien und die urbanen Milieus in Zentraleuropa* (Wien: Böhlau, 2010). The earlier "essay" (13) opens with three chapters that re-assess at least two dozen categories (13-127). Following up on Béla Bartók's analysis (1942) of how ethnic musicians exchanged one another's melodies (14-17), Chapter 4 examines "polyphonic" exchanges of culture among ethnicities in Vienna's neighborhoods, large and small (129-271), while Chapter 5 does likewise for Budapest, Pressburg, Czernowitz, Triest, Breslau, Leutschau, and Prague (273-344). Few historians writing in any field command such a wide range of analytical categories derived from the social sciences worldwide, particularly sociology, anthropology, and social psychology, albeit not religious studies or art history. One could profitably assemble a glossary of up to a hundred technical terms that Csáky has dissected with clinical acuity since 1980. Throughout, he displays a gift for redefining terminology, for comparing novel perspectives, and for proposing syntheses across broad horizons, as well as for unmasking delusional self-images. What is even more unusual, his innumerable case studies focus equally on micro- and macro-data. Without doubt he is the most globally minded of recent Austrianists, and together with Steven Beller and Norman Stone he shines as the most methodologically astute critic of the regime's self-delusions.

This extraordinarily nuanced new book risks unsettling the reader in the same way that study of the Habsburg Monarchy can. Indeed, simply to peruse the kaleidoscope of topics may induce some of the cognitive disruptions that the author diagnoses within Habsburgia, such as disorientation (*Orientierungslosigkeit*, 136), the undermining of certainties (*Verunsicherung*, 136), and drowning in multiple meanings (*Mehrdeutigkeiten*, 33). To spare the reader any such symptoms, this review will outline the book's scope before listing salient omissions. After expounding certain indisputable strengths, the review will pose the ticklish question: To what scholarly genre does this formidable assemblage belong? Having defined the genre "anatomy" as an idiosyncratic taxonomy of a large subject's fundamental categories, the review will label this volume *An Anatomy of Habsburgia's Grundbegriffe: Part Two.* Part One would be the previous work, *Das Gedächtnis der Städte* (2010), which boasts an identical structure founded upon Aleida Assmann's analysis of culture as a "hybrid space of communication" (104-09). Even more than the earlier volume, the new one unmasks how frequently the peoples of Habsburgia veiled "false consciousness" (95-96) not with slogans but with silence.

The new book contains 350 pages of text, enhanced with more than a thousand footnotes, as well as a mind-boggling bibliography of more than 700 items in German, Hungarian, and English, with one or two in French and Italian. Here and on page 307 (footnote 94), the author lists fourteen of his own titles on kindred matters, such as Miroslav Krleža, "transnational remembering," and methods for studying food and drink (*Kulinarik*). The first chapter of 107 pages and 305 footnotes explicates more than thirty basic concepts (*Grundbegriffe*), such as "hybrid identities," "heterogeneous spaces" (above all in the "third space" of border regions), and music or cuisine as "metalanguages" whose commonalities link spaces of communication across a vast region. "Myths of sacrifice" (*Opfermythen*, 86-97) are shown to distort national memory, most tragically in the Balkans. Underpinning all this is Jurij Lotman's (1922-1993) notion of a "semiosphere," defined as a cultural borderland like Joseph Roth's Galicia, where clashing heterogeneities require mutual efforts at translation, whose success varies from instances of comprehensibility to those of untranslatability (56). More often than any other work, Csáky cites Lotman's little known *Die*

Innenwelt des Denkens: Eine semiotische Theorie der Kultur (Russian edition, 1991; Frankfurt: Suhrkamp, 2010).

In Chapters 2 to 5, Csáky centers his analytical concepts around four well-known authors. A highly original Chapter 2 weaves Franz Kafka's likening of Franz Joseph to an unspeakably remote Chinese emperor in the fragment *Beim Bau der Chinesischen Mauer* (ca. 1916) (123-44) into a subtle analysis of a dozen other critiques of the hollowness of the *Kaisermythos.* Chapter 3 expounds Hermann Bahr's unconventional rebranding of Habsburgia as a "Slavic *Vielvölkerstaat*," whose Germanocentric bureaucracy he was berating already by 1910 (163-66). A revisionist Chapter 4 exposes Joseph Roth's disillusionment at the failure of "interior colonization" in eastern Galicia, where in light of Lotman (183-84), Csáky re-interprets as "Mimikry" (185-88), the feigned compliance known as (Jewish) "assimilation." An exhilarating Chapter 5 scours the novels of the embittered Croatian Miroslav Krleža in search of hybrid identities, traumatic memories, and "multiple codings" (*Mehrfachcodierungen*) that agitated the arbitrarily defined "threshold space" (*Schwellenland*), which the contrarian Croat calls *Illyricum sacrum.* Csáky sees it as a laboratory for the kind of interethnic conflicts that now routinely erupt worldwide (212). Regrettably here as elsewhere, Csáky does not gauge the explanatory power of his categories or tell us which writers he admires most. And nowhere does he apologize for puncturing so many of Habsburgia's life-sustaining illusions.

Readers new to Csáky might want to start with the superbly coherent Chapter 6 on the familiar topic of "language conflict and language critique" in Bohemia. The case studies range from Fritz Mauthner's *locus classicus* in *Prager Jugendjahre* (1918) and Robert Musil on *Mehrsprachigkeit* to Kafka's *oeuvre* (245-52) and then on to Rilke's mounting misgivings about Habsburgia's intersecting languages (*Mischsprachen,* 259-63) before climaxing with František Palacký and a less famous plea by the Czech physiologist Jan Purkynje, who in his "political Märchen," *Austria polyglotta* (1867) (272-73), fantasized a "*Metaraum*" of trans-ideological communication thriving among rival ethnicities. Conceived around a redefinition of "Orientalism" as hate-love for a foreigner as *neighbor* (277-79), Chapter 7 introduces three recently rediscovered works of fiction. In *Die Heimatlosen* (1923), the polyglot Wilma von Vukelich (1880-1956) situates five Jews in a village of northeast Croatia similar to her own hometown of Osijek (278-93), Franz Werfel testifies to a Jewish officer's crises of identity during World War I in *Pogrom* (1926), and before World War I Robert Michel portrayed army officers as ambivalent colonizers in Bosnia in *Die Verhüllte* (1907) (303-08). In these and other texts, it is always "assimilated" Jews who emerge as the most tormented of outsiders (*Fremde*) (291, 294-301). Besides discerning Orientalist fantasies in the anti-Ottoman propaganda embedded in Hofmannsthal's notion of Austria's "cultural mission" (308-18)—in 1922, the dramatist went so far as to equate the Orient with Freud's unconscious (316)—this chapter strengthens the canon of Habsburgia's historical fiction. Finally, Chapter 8 refines theses that Csáky has long advocated—to scant response—regarding the potential of Habsburgia's "hybrid configurations" (345) for inspiring reform of today's European Union.

What topics are missing? Above all, the visual arts. Whereas music is shown everywhere to have enlivened "spaces of memory" (*Gedächtnisräume*) both large and small (61-69), this volume does not even mention works of visual art. Thus the discussion of Kafka's symbol of the emperor's unknowable role in a never-to-be-completed "Chinese wall" ignores a slightly earlier novel by the artist Alfred Kubin, *Die andere Seite* (1909), whose Orientalizing allegory imagines a stylized Habsburgia ("*Traumreich*") stagnating under an unfathomable dictator in the city of "Perle" in remotest Asia. This unbearably ironic novel cries out to be aligned with Kafka's enigmatic fragment. Nor does Csáky discuss periodization in cultural history or the related problem of delineating intellectual generations. Cultural historians will miss the names of two scintillating colleagues, both skilled in redefining *Grundbegriffe*. One was the last exponent of the Vienna School of Art History, Werner Hofmann (1928-2013), who from 1960 wrote meticulous essays on Austrian art's hidden intertwinings (*Verflechtungen*), and the other is the Salzkammergut-born Germanist Gerald Stieg (1941-), whose masterpiece of wit, *Sein oder Schein* (2016), brings Parisian *savoir faire* to elucidating three centuries of "mythographies" about "Austrian identity."

To what scholarly genre can we assign Csáky's recent books? This review proposes to classify them as specimens of an "anatomy." In *Anatomy of Criticism: Four Essays* (1957), the literary critic Northrop Frye argued that the genre purports to classify a vast subject across a large span of time and space onto which a single author imposes a personal, sometimes idiosyncratic taxonomy, often in the format of a collage, which juxtaposes but cannot systematize innumerable oddities. The modern type originated in Baroque Europe as a device for writers to emulate a princely *Wunderkammer*, as in Robert Burton's *The Anatomy of Melancholy* (1621) or Thomas Browne's *Religio Medici* (1642). Since 1945, the anatomy has become the genre of choice for reconceptualizing the basics of a vast subject on which opinions differ drastically. Almost invariably, such books carry an air of being *sui generis*. Werner Hofmann's labyrinthine catalog of European Mannerisms, *Zauber der Medusa* (1987), is a classic of the genre.

A virtuoso of unclassifiable rethinking is the Milanese essayist Roberto Calasso, whose wry gravitas has for the past forty years generated *ten* (10) anatomies concerning ancient myths of cosmic order and their breakdown since the French Revolution, a process said in *The Ruin of Kasch* (1983, tr. 1994) to have been understood earliest by Talleyrand. A thrilling example of a *Wunderkammer* is Peter Weibel's catalog of "artist-scientists" in exile in post-1918 Vienna in *Jenseits von Kunst* (1997), while a distressing example is Friedrich Heer's *Der Kampf um die österreichische Identität* (1983), a *Wunderkammer* of anguished reflections.

Csáky makes no effort to disguise the idiosyncrasy of the selection in his two- volume cornucopia of *Grundbegriffe*. In response, each student of Habsburgia must choose which notions to retain and which to discard. Probably not many English-language scholars will fancy the jargonistic spelling *Zentraleuropa* or the trenchant but unwieldy word "semiosphere." But many will endorse the validation of music and cuisine—to which one might add military uniforms, formulas of politeness, coffeehouses, and *kaisergelb* architecture—as "metalanguages" that bridged ethnicities throughout Habsburgia's "spaces of communication." Equally appealing will be awareness of the risks of mutual "(un)translatability" among the "multiple codings" that emerge in "threshold lands" like the Balkans, and no one can any longer shun the term "hybridity" in its many Csákyian permutations. Likewise, many scholars will accept, even if they do not welcome, the shrewd refocusing of familiar notions like Orientalism, internal colonization, and cultural heterogeneity, not to mention "traumatic memory" or "myths of sacrifice." Still other readers will balk at the relentless "deconstruction" (95-96) of Habsburgia's self-flattering tropes, like the *Kaisermythos*, faith in bureaucratic fair-mindedness, or retreat into aestheticism.

The taxonomies in this book lay out a vast spectrum of possible futures for Habsburgia-studies. But as often happens to revisionists, many of these proposals will grate on upholders of fixed positions, and no doubt certain suggestions will simply be ignored. Readers are advised slowly to digest each chapter and to pursue the seminal footnotes. For years or even decades to come, the task of deciding which of Csáky's rethinkings to embrace and which to avoid will test every reader.

Günter Bischof and Hannes Richter, *Towards the American Century: Austrians in the United States* (New Orleans: University of New Orleans Press, 2019)

Emil Brix

Writing a book about Austrians in the United States, from its beginnings to the present day, for a wider audience is quite a challenge. All the more so when at the same time it has to be the catalogue-book for an exhibition about Austrians in the United States, as well as for a companion website project (www.austriainusa.org). After all, we don't even have the exact numbers as to how many Austrians emigrated and how many of their descendants regarded or regard themselves to be "Austrians in the United States." And yet the book successfully tells and illustrates by its excellently chosen photographs the story of how the United States became home to so many Austrians and for what reasons.

It has to be a story of migration and integration, which describes and analyzes identities, as well as disruptions. From expelling Protestants from the Austrian Lungau in 1732, to the mass economic emigration of Habsburg citizens from the eastern crownlands and Hungary before World War I and from Burgenland after 1918, to the enforced emigration of large parts of the Jewish population during the Nazi regime, and to the migration of brides of American soldiers after 1945, US-Austrian relations mirrored some of the most important developments in Austrian history. Portraying the story of almost three hundred years in short, emblematic essays, the book convincingly shows that migration from Austria could depend on push and/or pull factors. Religious intolerance, poverty, and racial hatred were those push factors that, until the end of World War II, prompted large scale migration. What pulled Austrians to the United States were expectations of individual and collective freedom and prosperity. Concise portraits of Austrian emigrants who came to fame or wealth in the US are to be expected in such a survey because their biographies can prove the positive potential of bilateral relations. The role models range from movie stars and filmmakers to scientists, entrepreneurs, architects, ski pioneers, and chefs.

Unavoidably, in such a book, there is little room for questioning historical myths and stereotypes. It can only present mainstream images of both countries. A good example for the limits of such a presentation is the chapter on the breakup of the Habsburg Empire. It might be questioned whether it is fair to qualify the US position at the end of World War I as "based on racialist thinking" or that the Wilson administration "willy-nilly accepted the break-up of the autocratic Habsburg Monarchy."

The difference between an academic book and a volume that celebrates a bilateral relationship which "has blossomed into a friendship" (quote from the preface by Alexander Van der Bellen) is unbridgeable. The authors of this volume are well aware of this fact. Still, in the introduction, they make an interesting judgement about the Austrian role in the world of today, which deserves some more reflection. In their words, Austria doesn't even figure as an "important unimportant" place anymore.

Seen from a geopolitical point of view and stressing the returned relevance of "hard power" in global politics, such a verdict deserves attention. What is intriguing is the fact that the design of the book and the exhibition contradicts this introductory verdict. All chapters and illustrations exhibit the strength of "soft power" by highlighting the impressive Austrian presentations at the Chicago World's Fair of 1893 and in St. Louis in 1904, the remarkable role of former Austrian scientists and filmmakers for the modern American world, or the huge educational role of the Marshall Plan, the Fulbright Program, the Institute of Advanced Studies in Vienna, and the Salzburg Seminars at Schloss Leopoldskron in Salzburg for Austrian intellectual life after World War II. When today's leading expert on the famous Austrian painter Egon Schiele lives and works in New York and is the daughter of an Austrian emigrant, when the owner and founder of a leading museum of Austrian and German art in New York (Neue Galerie) is the descendant of an Austro-Hungarian Jewish family, and when the director of the most prominent art museum in the United States (The Metropolitan Museum of Art in New York) is an Austrian, one might come to the conclusion that not all is lost for Austrian soft power in the United States.

What makes this book worth reading are exactly these sorts of contradictions. There is a sting to the presented storyline of bilateral relations. However, maybe this sting has to do with our present-day, all-too-robust preoccupation with hard power and transactional diplomacy.

Ernst Hanisch, *Landschaft und Identität: Versuch einer österreichischen Erfahrungsgeschichte* (Vienna: Böhlau, 2019)

Marc Landry

In *Landschaft und Identität*, Ernst Hanisch has set out to explore the history of how Austrians have talked about and thought about the landscapes of the current Austrian state. In a career characterized by methodological variety—ranging from biography through political history, social history, and gender history—the retired professor for Austrian History at the University of Salzburg has added another station. *Landschaft und Identität* is not a book that offers cut-and-dried pronouncements on either the Austrian landscape or history. Reading it is more like accompanying one of the many observers whose reports on the Austrian landscape make up the focus of this book. Hanisch is an experienced, knowledgeable, and entertaining guide who provides impressionistic pictures of crucial connections between the landscape and developments within Austria. The great value of the book comes from seeing how a focus on nature can reveal new and fascinating perspectives on a history whose political and social outlines are by now familiar. Seeing a connection between topics as diverse as the Slovenian partisan campaign in Carinthia during World War II and the development of a regional identity in the Burgenland after 1921, for example, is rewarding. In both cases—in countless iterations of Austrian identity building—ideas about nature played a central role.

Hanisch's work has been stimulated by the growing interest in environmental history since the 1970s. Clearly, books like Simon Schama's *Landscape and Memory* (1995) were an important inspiration. *Landschaft und Identität,* however, is not an environmental history of Austria. Hanisch is much more interested in discourses about nature than about the ways that Austrians have actually changed the real landscape. The focus here is the "landscapes of the mind" (275). Thus, the key sources for this book are so-called "ego documents," first-person narratives from a variety of genres ranging from scientific reports to literature, film, songs, and even fairy tales. These are accessed by synthesis from other secondary literature or in many cases from the documents themselves. In analyzing these texts, Hanisch adopts a moderate constructivist viewpoint. He views language as important in constituting nature while recognizing that ideas about nature are inspired by some sort of objective environment beyond human consciousness. The remaining pillars of *Landschaft und Identität*'s approach are spelled out in the book's subtitle. First, Hanisch views this history as a "*Versuch*," an attempt, essay or experiment. Second, the emphasis is on experience, personal and collective. The point is to trace how Austrians experienced landscapes in the nineteenth and twentieth centuries, what dreams and fears they held, and how landscapes fed into identity.

This analysis is carried out over six parts. Though the work is not underpinned by any one specific theoretical concept, an introductory section lays out some orienting structure. Here, Hanisch establishes that Austrian views of the landscape have in many cases paralleled the major political turning points in the country's history. Nature was continually utilized to bolster support for a given regime. Considering the current situation of Austria and Austrians' relationships to the environment, Hanisch paints a picture of a "light-green society." This term, coined by environmental historian Michael Bess in reference to contemporary France, describes a society where environmentalist ideas are mainstream but do not fundamentally challenge the underlying economic order. This explains the widespread popularity of things like recycling and organic food but no serious rejection of consumerist values.

Thereafter, Hanisch unfolds his landscape analysis in five parts devoted to what he refers to as archetypal Austrian landscapes: mountains, the "large river" (Danube), the forest, industrial landscape, and the flatland. Obviously, the section on mountains deals exclusively with the Alps. The segment dealing with industrial landscapes uses the example of the Erzberg in Styria. And the final part on the plains deals with the most recent addition to the Austrian landscape, the former Hungarian territory of the Burgenland. Topics covered within the chapters are more or less randomly chosen, though all of the major environmental events of contemporary Austrian history (Kaprun, Zwentendorf, Hainburg) are here. Within the sections that do contain chronological analysis, a familiar pattern emerges. Enlightenment-era views of instrumentalized nature give way to Romanticized nature depictions after the rise of urbanization and industrialization. As the nineteenth century progresses, landscapes become ever more important for constructing national identity. Only after the crowning catastrophe of nationalism (World War II) do we see a growing number of voices questioning the human relationship to nature.

Though Hanisch admits that his coverage of Austrian landscapes is uneven, the analysis does at least touch on each *Bundesland* at some point. The Alps receive the most attention by far, with almost double as much space as the next largest topic, the Danube. Fascinatingly, the region whose actual physical landscape is perhaps most underrepresented is the capital of Vienna. Granted, Vienna is the smallest *Bundesland* by territory. But the absence of a section dealing specifically with an urban landscape is perhaps the greatest selection criticism to be made. For several decades now, a consensus within environmental history has it that cities, too, are part of the environment. Excluding them runs the risk of conceiving of the homes of an increasing portion of humanity as unnatural. While the urban environment is not really considered, a large number of the observations of landscapes in these pages come from people with connections to the imperial city.

This is a personal book, and to my mind the intimacy serves the larger goal of the project. At moments in the text we learn that the author is actually gazing upon the landscape being analyzed through the window of his workroom. Hanisch often uses the first person and at times refers to specific personal experiences. Not surprisingly for someone who comes from the Waldviertel, thinking about the forest in this region seems to have triggered the most substantial reminiscences—from the young boy killed in his family's yard by a leftover World War II ordnance to another young man who hung himself in the forest out of lovesickness. These reflections fit, however, in a volume devoted to experience.

It is the essayistic format of *Landschaft und Identität* that is likely to prompt the most criticism. Hanisch does not spend much time clearly delineating the parameters of the study. It is never made exactly clear what is meant by Austria, for example, though it seems likely that the territory of the current Austrian republic is meant. The author explains that the book's focus is on the nineteenth and twentieth centuries, though at times it reaches even farther back. There are surely defensible reasons for this, but they go unmentioned. Probably the biggest issue concerns the concept of "Austrianness" itself. The question of who is Austrian is never explored too deeply—presumably ethnic Germans who lived primarily in the territory of the current Austrian state as most of the perspectives surveyed in this book stem from such people. But again, it goes unstated. Austria is and always has been a land of immigrants, but immigrant experiences do not take center stage here.

Despite these issues, *Landschaft und Identität* succeeds admirably in its attempt to present a history of Austrians experiencing their landscapes. Fascinating observations are to be found on every page of this learned book, but the greatest impact comes from considering the work as a whole. At the end, one wonders what, if anything, might be specifically "Austrian" about the relationship between landscape and identity. Hanisch is hesitant to draw too-hard-and-fast conclusions, so "diverse" the aspects of his foray (318). The impression he leaves, however, is twofold: nature has always been central to Austrian identity, and the relationship between the two will continue to evolve.

Jacqueline Vansant, *Austria Made in Hollywood* (Rochester, NY: Camden House, 2019)

Felix Tweraser

This outstanding contribution to film history and criticism and exile studies works on many levels: it provides a useful overview of all the Hollywood productions in which Austria provided a/the setting, compiling this particular corpus for the first time; it develops a coherent argument—with compelling evidence—that, more often than not, the image of Austria that emerges in any given Hollywood film has more to do with the political, social, and cultural concerns of the time in the United States; and finally, it provides sophisticated, original, and critically informed close readings of representative films, including Erich von Stroheim's *Merry-Go-Round* (1923) and *The Wedding March* (1928), Edwin L. Marin's *Florian* (1940), Billy Wilder's *The Emperor Waltz* (1948), Michael Curtiz's *A Breath of Scandal* (1960), Otto Preminger's *The Cardinal* (1963), and Robert Wise's *The Sound of Music* (1965). By looking carefully at all aspects of the productions and exploring multiple historical contexts (i.e., the conditions of artistic creativity in Hollywood, global political developments, the development of mass audiences) while judiciously tracing the biographical resonances of the filmmakers themselves, many of whom were part of the significant cultural transfer of Austrian émigrés who were fleeing Nazism to Hollywood, Vansant anchors her close readings within a complex network of experience and reference that informs each work:

> At the intersection of several disciplines, this study draws on, complements, and ultimately builds upon previous research. It seeks to expand our knowledge of the film industry, and the influence of domestic controversies on images of a foreign country. Finally, it strives to explain the disappearance of Austria from the Hollywood screen… each chapter delves into the impact of changing historical circumstances on the screen projections and the interplay of the elements that resulted in the 'funhouse mirror' distortions of Austria. (p. 20)

Vansant frames her argument cogently through the metaphor of the funhouse mirror, namely that the images of Austria in Hollywood productions are inevitably distorted by distance in space and time from what is depicted and by the overriding concerns of the moment in the United States. The vast majority of the films that form the corpus of Hollywood productions with Austria as a setting date from the 1920s and 1930s and, as one might expect, Vienna at the turn of the century assumed the status of *locus classicus* for a certain sophistication, musicality, and modernity that was sweeping other Western capitals and prompted the widespread recruiting of talent by Hollywood studios in Vienna—recruitment that only accelerated with the rise of Nazism and the changes it brought to the conditions of film production.

With the coming of World War II, depictions of the Austrian Anschluss with Nazi Germany took on a paradigmatic function in Hollywood films, and Vansant judiciously demonstrates how, in these productions, Austria was stylized as Hitler's first victim, one which came to stand in for others as the war continued. In films such as *So Ends Our Night* (James Cromwell, 1941), *They Dare Not Love* (James Whale, 1941), and *Once Upon a Honeymoon* (Leo McCarey, 1942) the Anschluss forms the historical backdrop for genre films that were crafted to appeal to American audiences and, though largely forgotten today, can be seen as part of the concerted effort in the Hollywood of the early 1940s to influence public opinion away from the dominant isolationism of the 1930s and to support military intervention in Europe. Such excavation of forgotten films and the work of historical contextualization are real strengths of this volume, and scholars will be grateful for such spadework as they look more closely at such hidden gems.

The case studies and close readings themselves are carefully chosen to tease out important continuities, ruptures, and blind spots in Hollywood film production. Such continuities encompassed personnel, genre vocabulary and conventions, audience appeal, and political (sub)texts. At the same time, they effectively underscore the constraints (i.e., profit motive, star system, censorship) that the developing studio system in Hollywood imposed on its talent, exile or not. By embedding the case studies within these institutional imperatives, Vansant underscores specific aspects of dialogue, camera work, set design, and acting style that illustrate the unique sensibilities of director and personnel who were informed, in many instances, by the experience of exile.

One of the most compelling chapters offers close readings of two quite different films from the 1960s that used the Anschluss as historical framing: Otto Preminger's *The Cardinal* (1963) and Robert Wise's *The Sound of Music* (1965). While Preminger sought a reckoning with his erstwhile hometown that attempts to depict the widespread enthusiasm for Nazism that existed at the time and the dominant Catholic Church's accommodation with and cultivation of such sentiment—during a period when such forthright confrontation with this past was hardly the norm—Wise used the Anschluss as one among many threats from outsiders (i.e., urbanites and Germans) to the von Trapp's family idyll. Vansant summarizes cogently: "By drawing attention to the actions of Cardinal Innitzer, Preminger could argue for the importance of remembering this past as well as inviting audience members to see present day parallels. By contrast, Wise offered viewers a respite from the turmoil of the day with the highly fictionalized story of the von Trapp family" (129-30). It is interesting that these two commercially successful films had little resonance in Austria upon their release but perhaps for quite different reasons: Preminger's film held up a mirror to Austrians' attitudes and behavior in March 1938 at a time when the ethos of the *Sozialpartnerschaft* and a shared desire to move on from this past were potent political and social mobilizing forces; and Wise's film depicts a highly sentimentalized version of events that quite simply did not resonate with audiences who perhaps resented the simplistic portrayal of individuals and events and an Americanized version of Austrian folk idioms. Here it might have been interesting for the author to treat the "afterlives" of these two films in a bit more depth. Preminger's film, for instance, was completely elided from the City Museum of Vienna's exhibition—one that presented itself as exhaustive—on Vienna as a film setting, while Wise's film exists in the popular imagination as a curiosity that has drawn generations of mainly American tourists to Salzburg. One senses that there still exist—for different reasons—reservoirs of discomfort in the reception of these films in Austria, and the specific nature and historical resonance of such discomfort may be of interest to subsequent scholars. Vansant's survey of Hollywood films set in Austria skims briefly over more recent works such as Richard Linklater's *Before Sunrise* (1995) and the BBC's production of *Woman in Gold* (2015). Here one sees an opportunity for further work that would connect the cosmopolitan Vienna of the turn of the century with its contemporary return, in many ways, to embracing that heritage.

In sum, Vansant's study is essential reading for students and scholars of film history and criticism, Austrian studies, and intellectual history. It is thoroughly researched with a comprehensive and deeply thoughtful bibliographic apparatus, a judicious selection of illustrations (mostly film stills), and an excellent index. It will be an important enhancement to library collections and a key entry on syllabi in film studies, Austrian studies, and cultural history.

Ina Markova, *Die NS-Zeit im Bildgedächtnis der Zweiten Republik,* Der Nationalsozialismus und seine Folgen 6 (Innsbruck: Studienverlag, 2018)

Hans Petschar

Visual sources play a crucial role in the public perception of history. Like almost no other medium, photography and film can provide seemingly direct insights into the past, arouse emotions, and shape individual or collective memories.

This applies in particular to the memory of traumatic and fateful experiences of the recent past. In the Austria of the Second Republic, the culture of remembrance after 1945 is inconceivable without reference to the time of National Socialism.

In an impressive study, Austrian historian Ina Markova has presented a well-founded analysis of the Nazi era in the visual memory of the Second Republic.

Markova's study is grounded on a solid empirical basis comprising approximately 5,900 photographs, which the author has selected from newspapers, textbooks, exhibitions, and photo books from 1945 to 2013 and has integrated into her research database.

To identify the photographs, Markova went through every single copy of ten Austrian newspapers from 1945 to 1955 (*Arbeiter-Zeitung*, *Das kleine Volksblatt*, *Wiener Kurier*, *Neues Österreich*, *Oberösterreichische Nachrichten*, *Österreichische Zeitung*, *Die Presse*, *Salzburger Nachrichten*, *Tiroler Tageszeitung*, and *Österreichische Volksstimme*). For the period after 1955, Markova used a paper clippings collection of the *Dokumentationsarchiv des Österreichischen Widerstandes* (DÖW) and looked at a sample of critical discourse moments in four newspapers (*Kurier*, *Kronen Zeitung*, *Die Presse*, and *Der Standard*) and the weekly journal *Profil* (1970–2013).

The author incorporated at least one photo book per decade and examined ten temporary exhibitions circa 1945–2005, as well as the permanent exhibitions in Mauthausen (1970, 2013), the Austrian Pavilion in Auschwitz (1978), and the permanent exhibition in the DÖW (1978, 2005) along with their revisions.

While in the early years of the Second Republic relatively few photographs appear in the public, since the 1970s, an increasing usage of photographs has to be recognized. Markova identified and analyzed 162 photographs for the years 1945–49, 352 for the 1950s, 447 for the 1960s,

873 for the 1970s, 1,761 for the 1980s, 1,038 for the 1990s, and 1,251 for the years 2000–13.

In her longitudinal analysis, the author observes decade per decade processes of "iconisation" and the shift of meaning in the collective creation of Austria's memory of the Nazi past.

In the Austrian culture of remembrance of the National Socialist era, a number of caesuras, well documented by contemporary historical research, can be recognized. The end of the war in 1945 marked a decisive turning point in Austrian history. In April 1945, the Red Army liberated Vienna after seven years of National Socialist rule. In May 1945, US, British, and French armies entered the western provinces of Austria and overpowered the remaining troops of the *Wehrmacht* and SS forces. After a brief, anti-fascist consensus in 1945/46, a contradictory picture emerged in the 1950s, characterized by the portrayal of Austria as the "first victim of the Nazis," a shift of National Socialism completely to Germany, and a tabooing of Austrian perpetrators and guilt.

It was not until the mid-1960s that this view of history changed in part through reference to the long-secret resistance against National Socialism. However, the victim thesis as a basic building block of Austrian postwar history was not questioned decisively. It was only after the "Waldheim affair" in 1986 that Austrian perpetration was publicly discussed. A final turning point was Chancellor Franz Vranitzky's speech to the Austrian National Parliament on June 8, 1991, in which, for the first time, an Austrian head of government questioned the victim myth and openly expressed the perpetration of Austrians in World War II.

On a discourse level, these stages and shifts in the collective memory of National Socialism have been researched in detail. Markova's research impressively demonstrates that visual sources, in this case photographs that were disseminated through the media, played a decisive role in shaping the memory of National Socialism and in changing the perception of the past since 1945.

Markova argues that through a combination of visual and verbal framing, Austrian memories of the Nazi past have been created.

The visual record of destruction and devastation of Austrian cities and infrastructure (i.e., railways, bridges, industries) became widely known as "*Trümmerbilder*" ("rubble" pictures). In 1945 and 1946—in newspapers, journals, and exhibits—pictures of destroyed bridges were used to represent the immediate past.

In August 1945, the *Wiener Kurier* published a photograph of the destroyed Floridsdorfer Bridge in Vienna as a visual signifier of the end of the war. The photograph shows a crowd of civilians traversing a foot bridge over the damaged Floridsdorfer Bridge on the Danube, which had been destroyed by the retreating German troops. Interestingly enough, the caption text in the *Wiener Kurier*, a newspaper largely supported by US forces in Austria, emphasizes that it had been Soviet pioneers who had built this makeshift bridge in order to help the Austrian population. The original caption text in the archives of the United States Information Services branch, which provided Austrian and international newspapers with photographs, is dated "Salzburg, 17 August 1945" and proves that this photograph was part of a series documenting the first encounters of the USIS photographers with the Soviets located in Vienna.

Markova refers to the highly symbolic value of bridges and the Danube in Austrian imagery and interprets the verbal reference to the Red Army as a testimony that the Cold War had not yet ended the "policy of brotherly love" between the Soviets and the US.

Only the Communist papers, however, visualized in a very short time span between 1945 and 1946 combat actions and the military liberation of Vienna. Indeed, April 13, 1945, the day when the Red Army had liberated Vienna, became the primary *lieu de memoire* in the Austrian Communist papers *Österreichische Zeitung* and *Volksstimme*. Rebranding the year 1945 as a year of liberation and not defeat was by no means an easy task. Instead of negatively connoted photographs showing advancing tanks, attacking soldiers, death, and devastation, the *Volksstimme* tried to invent new pictorial traditions showing jubilant Austrians dancing around the national flag while the caption texts stated: "Liberated."

The time span of confronting the Austrian population with Nazi crimes and initiating a process of reeducation via photographs and exhibitions is limited to a short period from 1945 to 1946. Markova analyzes an information campaign of the US Information Services from June 1945 and the big exhibition "*Niemals vergessen*" ("Never forget") in the Wiener Künstlerhaus from autumn 1946, which attracted more than 260,000 visitors in only fourteen weeks.

Shortly thereafter, from 1946/47 onwards, the visualization of the Nazi past fell victim to the Cold War and thus began a phase characterized by the formation of poignant "counter-images" celebrating reconstruction works and, above all, the Austrian State Treaty and the "true liberation" of Austria in May 1955. The new "key images" of Austria superimposed the images of Austria's Nazi past, which disappeared from the pictorial discourse in Austrian textbooks in the 1950s.

According to Markova, Austria's picture canon has been broadened from the 1960s onwards. Photographs of the Anschluss, which had been avoided in the first years of the Second Republic, became fashionable in 1963 when newspapers referred to the events of March 1938. Pictorial representations of the Anschluss depicted the "anti-Austrian" dimension of the event and, for the first time, included depictions of anti-Semitic riots in the streets of Vienna. In a sense, Markova concludes, the visualization of the Anschluss in the media represented the postwar "anti-fascist" interpretation of the "victim theory."

However, the 1960s also witnessed the visual representation of the Holocaust in traveling exhibitions and from the 1970s onwards in permanent exhibitions. As a consequence of the Waldheim affair, the crimes and atrocities committed by Austrian perpetrators were openly discussed. According to Markova, the erosion of the "victim theory" mainly took place on the level of textual contextualization of a canon of images that had been introduced into the public throughout the second half of the twentieth century.

The process of deconstruction and recontextualization continues at the beginning of the twenty-first century with "memory agents" revising the permanent exhibitions in Mauthausen and other memory institutions. The book ends with questioning what can or cannot be shown in a process of deliberating the "ethics of seeing."

Ina Markova's study on the visual memory of the Nazi past in the Second Republic of Austria is a thoughtful and highly original work, written by a talented young scholar of whom one would love to read more of in the future.

Martin Haidinger, *Wilhelm Höttl: Spion für Hitler und die USA* (Vienna: Carl Ueberreuter Verlag, 2019)

Norman J.W. Goda

It is unfortunate that the debate of the past twenty years concerning Nazi and other perpetrators of mass crimes has made no room for men such as Wilhelm Höttl, neither an "ordinary man" reluctantly enmeshed in German crimes nor an ideological killer but, rather, an unprincipled, self-motivated scoundrel that defies categorization. Research into such types is difficult. Höttl, an almost cultish figure in postwar Austria as he held forth in his picturesque town of Altaussee, was a wartime member of the *Sicherheitsdienst*'s (SD) foreign intelligence branch, whose members often operated under the radar during the war and were adept at obscuring the record afterwards. In this biography, Vienna journalist Martin Haidinger employs the available sources, from obscure diaries to declassified CIA records, to chip through the crust of Höttl's obfuscations.

Höttl's greatest skill might have been what scholars these days call seizing control of his own narrative—or what everyone else calls lying. His best-selling, widely translated, and still-read memoir, *Die geheime Front* (1950), presents an "insider" account of German wartime intelligence in which Höttl recounts secret spy tales of derring-do even as he elides all criminal responsibility. Other self-serving books and interviews continued into the next decades. In fact, Höttl had been a member of Nazi organizations in Vienna in 1931, when he was sixteen, and in 1934, the year of the putsch against Chancellor Engelbert Dollfuss when Höttl was working with the SD as a university student, collecting intelligence on political enemies at the University of Vienna, where he was completing a doctoral degree in history. After the Anschluss in 1938, he headed the SD office in Vienna charged with political enemies, even coming to know Adolf Eichmann when the latter arrived in Vienna to clear the country of Jews.

There was always something fishy about Höttl even to other Nazis. His superiors in Vienna thought, probably correctly, that he was stealing party funds. They also found suspect his ties to characters like Taras Borodajkewycz, a Catholic conservative and fellow student of the Austrian historian Heinrich von Srbik, who received generous financial support from Nazi Party coffers, and to Countess Dorothy Pálffy, an American source married to a key Hungarian aristocrat, Fidél Pálffy, for whom Höttl had tried to secure confiscated Jewish property. Höttl's superiors labeled him "a pronounced operator," and complaints reached all the way to Reinhard Heydrich, head of the Reich Security Main Office (RSHA), who transferred Höttl to combat duty in Yugoslavia with the *Waffen-SS Prinz Eugen* Division even as he was being investigated.

Had it not been for Heydrich's assassination in 1942, Höttl might have remained, but the Czech partisans who set the bomb in Prague provided him with the first of many lucky breaks. Ernst Kaltenbrunner, Heydrich's eventual replacement, was Austrian, an ally since 1937, and a man in need of supporters in the RSHA hierarchy. The investigations of Höttl ended, and he was promoted to *SS-Sturmbannführer* despite not having reached the requisite age of thirty. He played roles in the massive effort to counterfeit British pounds (Operation Bernhard), the rescue of Mussolini from his captors in 1943, and the occupation of Hungary in 1944, where he headed SD foreign intelligence in Budapest as mountains of Jewish property were seized and more than 400,000 Jews were deported to Auschwitz. In his postwar discourse, he emphasized the former operations while downplaying the latter.

And indeed, the latter has confounded historians. Contemporaries in Budapest described Höttl as very well informed; Haidinger adeptly uses the diary of military adviser Edmund von Glaise-Horstenau, a fellow Austrian, who noted that Höttl threw himself into his work. He reconnected with Eichmann, who headed deportation efforts, was a friend of László Baky, the Hungarian Interior Ministry official who rounded up Jews for Eichmann, and advised the Reich plenipotentiary Edmund Veesenmayer, who kept tabs on the Hungarian cabinet. But practically no written records discuss the details of Höttl's time in Budapest. Similarly, the Jewish loot that Höttl segregated for himself in separate crates on the infamous "Gold Train," which wound its way into Austria as the Soviets advanced, disappeared into legends of hidden treasure in the Austrian Alps.

It was here that Höttl's penchant for deflection, fabrication, and self-preservation manifested itself. Historian Kerstin von Lingen has shown how the May 1945 "Secret Surrender" of German forces in Italy, negotiated by *SS-Obergruppenführer* Karl Wolff and Allen Dulles of the Office of Strategic Services (OSS), saved Wolff's skin. Glaise-Horstenau's diary suggests that Höttl acknowledged the possibility of defeat as early as 1943; he argued that Kaltenbrunner should start peace feelers through the Vatican. But Haidinger also cites Höttl's secretary, Hildegard Beetz, who said that Höttl was trying, like many in the SD, to split the Western Allies from the Soviets. In 1945, when matters were far worse, Höttl made his own efforts to Dulles, ostensibly on behalf of Kaltenbrunner, concerning intelligence on the Alpine Redoubt fortifications, which were, in fact, never as formidable as the Americans feared and as Höttl suggested.

Haidinger suggests that Höttl parlayed these contacts into a measure of protection from former OSS officials. The records, in my view, do not support this, but Höttl nonetheless moved freely in Nuremberg during the Trial of the Major War Criminals as a witness in the case against Kaltenbrunner. He also provided a critical affidavit in December 1945, describing a discussion with Eichmann in Budapest thirteen months earlier wherein Eichmann provided details of his role in the Final Solution. Eichmann, Höttl said, even provided the number of six million as this had been the number he reported to *Reichsführer-SS* Heinrich Himmler. There were numerous problems with the comments Höttl attributed to Eichmann, but from this point, Höttl was the insider who could speak to others' guilt but who also could, as an honorable intelligence agent, work for Germany's former enemies. Later-debunked legend had it that he even worked for Nazi hunter Simon Wiesenthal and the Mossad.

Though a fine candidate for the *Volksgericht* in Vienna, Höttl found other employment, connecting with Thomas Lucid of the 430th detachment of the US Army Counter Intelligence Corps (CIC) in Austria, himself a swashbuckling type unbothered by his agents' baggage. In 1948, Höttl put together networks of his roguish wartime contacts to generate reports on Southeastern Europe and the Soviet zone of Austria. CIC dropped him in 1949 owing to his worthless reporting (much of it came from newspapers) and his meddling in right-wing Austrian politics. Despite red flags from the Central Intelligence Agency, Höttl then found a place in West Germany's intelligence apparatus, thus validating suspicions by the CIA that its German allies ran a very loose ship. Höttl was dropped in 1952, but afterwards he had broad contacts with Soviet agents until the Americans uncovered them in 1953. Typically, Höttl's low blood pressure rendered a polygraph test useless, but the Americans publicly outed his activities, thus reducing his intelligence career to a sputter.

Afterwards Höttl reveled in local celebrity status in Altaussee. He remained cagey. During the Eichmann trial in 1961, the Israeli government promised safe passage, but he knew better than to go to Jerusalem. He gave testimony in Austria, again sidestepping any personal role in Eichmann's criminality. He continued to crave relevance. He spoke with actor Klaus Maria Brandauer, also from Altaussee, concerning the movie project *Ein Sonntag im Oktober* (1979), which portrayed the Nazi coup against Admiral Miklós Horthy in Budapest and in which Brandauer played a roguish intelligence officer modeled on Höttl himself. He weighed in on the Hitler diaries hoax of 1983, arguing that the East Germans might have been behind one of the great forgeries in history. Toward the end of his life he published another set of opaque memoirs (*Einsatz für das Reich* [1997]) and continued to give interviews concerning tales of sunken treasure in the Toplitzsee.

Haidinger's book is the best account we have of Höttl's career, especially as the author is generally careful with his sources. The missing element, however, is a richer context, particularly for what Höttl's career can tell us about intelligence and its practitioners in Nazi and postwar Germany and Austria. Höttl's memoirs and interviews are part of a broad exculpatory literature that includes other former German intelligence officials from Klaus Barbie to Otto Skorzeny to Walter Schellenberg to Reinhard Gehlen, all of whom inflated the accomplishments of German intelligence as they sidestepped guilt for Nazi crimes while forging, or attempting to forge, postwar intelligence careers all over the world. Several scholarly studies have appeared in recent years by Katrin Paehler, Robert Hutchison, Rolf-Dieter Müller, and Agilolf Keßelring, all of which confirm the vacuous nature and ideological pollution of German intelligence while revealing its criminality and the degree to which Nazi intelligence officials created postwar intelligence careers with results ranging from the inconsequential to the disastrous. In this sense, Höttl might have been rather ordinary after all.

Peter Pirker, *Codename Brooklyn: Jüdische Agenten im Feindesland. Die Operation Greenup 1945*. Mit einem Fotoessay von Markus Jenewein (Innsbruck: Tyrolia, 2019)

Rob Citino

Of all the many genres of World War II historiography, perhaps the most problematic is that of espionage. Books dealing with spies, double agents, and breathless derring-do almost always include exaggerated claims that an intrepid hero or heroes played a key role in bringing down the Third Reich. While unscholarly, such books are extremely popular, and it is certain that we haven't seen the last World War II spy thriller.

For all these reasons, historians should welcome Peter Pirker's *Codename Brooklyn*. Pirker tells a tale that is even more improbable than the potboilers discussed above: two Jewish refugees to the United States living in Brooklyn (Frederick Mayer, twenty-three, and Hans Wijnberg, twenty-two) enlist in the Office of Strategic Services (OSS) and parachute into Austria in 1945 to report on German rail traffic over the Brenner Pass. Their little band also consisted of a third member, Franz Weber, a lieutenant in the *Wehrmacht* who has come to his senses about the murderous nature of the Nazis' war. Service on a half-dozen fronts, including the vicious partisan struggle in occupied Yugoslavia, has made Weber see the reality of Hitler's dystopian plan to transform the continent into "KZ-Europa." Weber deserts to the Allies, makes contact with the OSS, and agrees to work with Mayer and Wijnberg. Think of them as the real "inglourious basterds," and indeed, Mayer himself is alleged to have said that the three of them "wanted to kill Nazis."

While they didn't embark on a killing spree, they did succeed in their mission. Operation Greenup, as it was called, yielded the Allies real material benefits, transmitting over sixty radio messages with detailed accounts of Brenner traffic to the OSS listening station in Bari, located in the Italian heel. Data gleaned from these reports helped US intelligence officers explode the myth that the Germans were concentrating men and weapons in the south for a last-ditch defense of an "Alpine redoubt." Despite being captured and nearly tortured to death, Mayer was able to make contact with enough local officials, including Tyrolean Gauleiter Franz Hofer, to negotiate the peaceful surrender of Innsbruck to the US Seventh Army. Compared to dozens of other cities and towns, defended till the last ditch by the German forces and then pulverized by US air power and artillery, Innsbruck survived nearly unscathed. We can say with some assurance, therefore, that Greenup saved many thousands of lives, Austrian and American alike.

While the operation has not gone completely unnoticed (it is discussed in Joseph Persico's 1979 book, *Piercing the Reich*, for instance), Pirker notes in this meticulous and masterfully researched reconstruction that it has had very little resonance in Austria itself. Postwar Austria, after all, was home to thousands of individuals deeply implicated in the crimes of the Nazi state. Calling attention to Greenup would only serve to call attention to all those Nazi officials who had hunted down Mayer and his friends, tortured them, and staged a horrible late-war razzia of denunciations, arrests, and extrajudicial murders. Moreover, endorsement of Greenup meant, by definition, condemnation of one's own fathers, brothers, and sons who were fighting and dying to defend the Nazi regime that Greenup was trying to destroy.

When it came to memories of the Third Reich, postwar Austria preferred to see itself as Hitler's first victim, a virtuous little republic swallowed up in the Anschluss and then forced to take part in the war. Austrians enjoyed reading the published accounts of Fritz Molden, who described the heroic exploits of his homegrown resistance group, O5, or watching the 1980s television documentary *Österreich II* by Hugo Portisch, accounts which Pirker exposes as almost completely fictional.

As this fine book reminds us, Germany, Austria, and the Tyrol itself were liberated not by homegrown resistance but by Allied military power, an unlikely alliance that included not only the armed might of the US Army but also officially marginalized figures within the Nazi state: Jews like Mayer and Wijnberg, bent on injuring the regime that had persecuted them and, in Wijnberg's case, killed his parents; Weber, a military deserter currently on the run from a death sentence; Anna Niederkircher, keeper of the *Zur Krone* inn, who gave the team shelter, support, and protection from the authorities and who once said, "If Hitler wins the war, then I don't believe in God anymore"; and not least, a handful of trained OSS operatives in the United States and in Bari. Indeed, the real service of Pirker's book is the way it nests its heroic narrative within these various contexts of Jewish resistance, internal dissent, and transnational networks.

Pirker also emphasizes the "transitory milieu" that generated and sustained this act of resistance—a temporary mixture of Allied war aims, personal motives, and war weariness. Surprisingly, Tyrolean particularism didn't seem to play a particularly important role, although Pirker does identify regional Catholicism as an ingredient, generating "in many individuals a distinct reticence towards the totalitarian claims of the NS Regime and its *Führer* who had supposedly been chosen by Providence" (308-09). But like all transitory moments, this one passed only to be replaced in the post-war world by the imperatives of anti-communism and the Cold War, and Greenup disappeared from Austrian memory.

Code-Name Brooklyn is a tour de force that belongs in any collection of literature on wartime resistance. With lavish assistance from Markus Jenewein's accompanying photo essay, Pirker succeeds in restoring Greenup to its rightful place in World War II memory and proves once again that even Quentin Tarantino's wildest fantasy has nothing on real life.

Veronika Duma, *Rosa Jochmann: Politische Akteurin und Zeitzeugin* (Vienna: Verlag des Österreichischen Gewerkschaftsbundes, 2019)

Jason Dawsey

The renewal of interest—political and scholarly—in the history of the European Left in the last decade has not left the subject of Austrian Socialism untouched. Especially noteworthy are recent anthologies of the writings of the principal figures associated with "Austro-Marxism."[1] As impressive and welcome as this new literature is, it still re-circles theorists and politicians (e.g., Otto Bauer, Max Adler, Rudolf Hilferding, Karl Renner, Friedrich Adler) long familiar to students of the Left in Austria. That cannot be said of Veronika Duma's biography, *Rosa Jochmann: Politische Akteurin und Zeitzeugin*.

While Jochmann (1901-1994) was a remarkable Socialist and feminist who participated in and witnessed many of the definitive events of twentieth-century Austrian history (e.g., World War I, the Revolution of 1918 and the founding of the First Republic, Red Vienna, the February 1934 insurrection, Austrofascism, the Anschluss, the Nazi camp system, and the Second Republic), she is largely unknown in the anglophone world. Correcting this oversight, Duma offers an enormous depth of coverage to Jochmann's rich political life in a book roughly 440 pages in length. A strength and a weakness, the level of detail in the monograph leaves very little else to be said about its subject.

Duma acknowledges the extensive research on Jochmann done prior to her work. She distinguishes her contribution from these often celebratory pieces in two ways: her reliance on gender as a primary category of analysis and the investigation of Jochmann's place in several successive networks of women in the Austrian and larger Central European Socialist and Communist movements. Duma draws on the scholarly literature about gender, which has burgeoned since the 1980s, including current discussions of "intersectionality." The painstaking documentation in the book provides great insight about the salience of networks for Jochmann, existenitially and politically, and doubles as a meditation on solidarity among women on the Left.

It is so refreshing to read of the story of a working-class woman active in Socialist politics who resisted both the Austrofascist and Nazi dictatorships. Rosa Jochmann proudly described herself as a "proletarian" and remarked at her 1935 trial: "I was a socialist, I am a socialist, and I will remain one" (279, 155). The fourth of six children from a family of Czech descent living in Vienna, she started factory work at the age of fourteen. Subsequently, she became involved in union activity and later joined the SDAP (*Sozialdemokratische Arbeiterpartei Österreichs*). As a young Social Democrat, Jochmann admired Otto Bauer, the key figure in the party's left wing, and regarded him as her mentor. According to Duma, Jochmann supported the Bolshevik Revolution more than many of her comrades and inquired into its impact on the condition of Soviet women.

Unlike Bauer and the Austro-Marxists, Jochmann was largely an autodidact. Much of the tutelage she received came from the group of women in the SDAP. Adelheid Popp and, especially, Käthe Leichter set such powerful examples for Jochmann as the party's Red Vienna project took shape in the 1920s. As Duma demonstrates, Jochmann labored for decades on behalf of these two to ensure that their goal of winning a place of equality for women within Social Democracy was not in vain. With Leichter, whose friendship and comradeship carried over into the Nazi concentration camp at Ravensbrück, Jochmann felt a lifelong connection.

Duma notes that Jochmann was elected to the SDAP's executive in October 1933 as the party's suppression under Dollfuss loomed. "The prohibition of the party during the February struggles of 1934 marked for Rosa Jochmann—less than the National Socialist assumption of power in 1938—a caesura in the history of Social Democracy and thus in her life's history," Duma contends (158). Indeed, Jochmann was a figure who never tired of saying after 1945 that Austria experienced *twelve* years of Fascism, not seven. After the party was banned, she undertook clandestine work with the *Revolutionäre Sozialisten* (RS) under different pseudonyms. Trials and stints in prison did not deter her from drumming up opposition to the Christian Social government. Her experiences in the Revolutionary Socialists offer a fascinating contrast to Joseph Buttinger's *In the Twilight of Socialism*.[2]

Having warned the Austrian Left for years about Adolf Hitler and the Nazi Party, developments after the Anschluss surpassed Jochmann's worst fears. The chapter on Jochmann's five years in the Ravensbrück concentration camp (1940–45), 140 pages long, is the most powerful section of the biography. Here, Duma's endorsement of a "paradigm shift in resistance research" is very illuminating (242). She shows how Jochmann's authority as a "Block Elder" among the inmates sent there for political offenses meant occupying a precarious place between collaboration and resistance. Jochmann was tested to her limits in protecting Socialists, Communists, anarchists, and others from the SS. The network of women she organized and led retained its bonds of solidarity long after the Third Reich fell. Duma's investigations also uncover the nightmare of solitary confinement Jochmann underwent, her care for children in Ravensbrück, and the importance of Cäcilie Helten, a German Communist who lived with her after the war.

Of all the degradation and death she beheld in Ravensbrück, nothing affected Jochmann as did the murder of Käthe Leichter in the winter of 1942. Duma points out that Jochmann never forgot the savagery meted out to Leichter and other Jewish inmates and that Jews were targeted more systematically and relentlessly than other groups of victims. After liberation, Jochmann "represented a voice against forgetting, repression, and relativization" (21). In several instances, she gave statements in cases where perpetrators were tried. While she spoke vividly about the hunger and disease in the camp, her statements about beatings, sexualized violence, medical experiments, and killing carry the greatest weight. The story of these five years Duma provides contributes significantly to our understanding of the dynamics of brutality and survival in Ravensbrück.

During the almost fifty years Jochmann lived after the defeat of Nazism, she remained a dedicated member of her party. She served proudly until 1966 as a functionary, doing valuable work on the Party Executive and the Central Committee for Women. In general, as Duma demonstrates, she rarely opposed the now-renamed *Sozialistische Partei Österreichs* (SPÖ) publicly but preferred to channel her criticisms internally. Here Duma's stress on the agency of women, while extremely important, could have been supplemented with more thematization of the political party as the vehicle of agency for Jochmann and so many Socialists of her generation. Her fierce commitment to party is one reason why her life may seem very different to activists in the early twenty-first century far more cynical about left-wing parties.

In researching and writing about this incredible life, Duma worked through a vast array of sources. She dug deeply into materials from the Jochmann *Nachlass* at the Verein für Geschichte der ArbeiterInnenbewegung and the Dokumentationsarchiv des Österreichischen Widerstandes. Correspondence with family and comrades, published texts and speeches prepared by Jochmann, as well as Socialist publications, indicate the thoroughness of the research, even if they threaten at moments to overwhelm the reader with the amount of details extracted. As far as sources go, Duma also communicates an absolutely awful moment for Jochmann as she struggled to write her own autobiography: how she destroyed a text of 1,500 typed pages in a "bout of fury and despair" (51).

If the book is somewhat repetitious and takes almost 100 pages to get to the main narrative, it succeeds in conveying Jochmann's significance as a working-class Socialist feminist. There is still so much work to do on the history of the Austrian Left. An abridged, English version of Duma's *Rosa Jochmann* would be a very good addition to what we have available. With neofascist and neo-Nazi ideologies resurgent, there cannot be too much attention paid to someone like her who acted as a "witness to the time (*Zeitzeugin*)" and its "chronicler" as did this extraordinary Socialist (s202).

Endnotes

1 Mark Blum and William Smaldone, eds., *Austro-Marxism: The Ideology of Unity*, Volume 1: *Austro-Marxist Theory and Strategy* (Leiden: Brill, 2015); Mark Blum and William Smaldone, eds., *Austro-Marxism: The Ideology of Unity*, Volume 2: *Changing the World: The Politics of Austro-Marxism* (Leiden: Brill, 2017).

2 Joseph Buttinger, *In the Twilight of Socialism: A History of the Revolutionary Socialists of Austria*, trans. E.B. Ashton (New York: F.A. Praeger, 1953).

List of Authors

Peter Berger is Professor Emeritus of Social and Economic History at WU Vienna University of Economics and Business.

Günter Bischof is the Marshall Plan Chair of History and the Director of Center Austria: The Austrian Marshall Plan Center for European Studies, University of New Orleans.

Emil Brix is the Director of the Diplomatische Akademie Wien/Vienna School of International Studies. He is a former Austrian Ambassador to the United Kingdom and to the Russian Federation.

Michael Burri teaches on Central Europe in the Film and Media Arts Department at Temple University.

Rob Citino is the Samuel Zemurray Stone senior historian and Executive Director of the Institute for the Study of War and Democracy at the National World War II Museum in New Orleans.

Tim Corbett is a freelance historian and translator based in Vienna.

Jason Dawsey is Research Historian at the Institute for the Study of War and Democracy at The National World War II Museum in New Orleans.

Lucile Dreidemy is Associate Professor in the Department of German Studies at the University of Toulouse Jean-Jaurès, France, and currently a Research Fellow in the Department of Contemporary History of the University of Vienna.

Norman JW Goda is the Braman Professor of Holocaust Studies and the Director of the Center for Jewish Studies at the University of Florida.

Christian Hütterer works for the Parliamentary Administration. He currently serves as representative of the Austrian Parliament to the European Parliament.

William Johnston is Emeritus Professor of History at the University of Massachusetts, Amherst. He lives in Melbourne, Australia.

Christian Karner is Professor of Sociology in the School of Social and Political Sciences at the University of Lincoln, UK.

Hansjörg Klausinger is retired Associate Professor in the Department of Economics at WU Vienna University of Economics and Business.

Marc Landry is Assistant Professor of Central European History and the Associate Director of Center Austria: The Austrian Marshall Plan Center for European Studies, University of New Orleans.

Konrad Paul Liessmann is Professor of Philosophy at the University of Vienna and scientific director of the Philosophicum Lech.

Eden McLean is Associate Professor of History at Auburn University.

Laura Morowitz is Professor of Art History in the Department of Visual Arts at Wagner College in New York.

Roberta Pergher is Associate Professor of History at Indiana University, Bloomington.

Hans Petschar is the director of the Picture and Graphics Department of the Austrian National Library.

Peter Pirker is post-doc researcher at the Department of Contemporary History, University of Innsbruck and lecturer in the Department of History at the University of Klagenfurt.

Maria Pohn-Lauggas is Professor for Multimethod Social Research at the Center for Methods in Social Science at the University of Göttingen, Germany.

Georg Rigele is the corporate historian and archivist of EVN AG, an energy supply and environmental service company in Maria Enzersdorf, Lower Austria.

Peter Stachel is Historian at the Austrian Academy of Sciences and Humanities in Vienna.

Gerald J. Steinacher is the James A. Rawley Professor of History at the University of Nebraska-Lincoln.

Dr. Felix Tweraser is Professor of German at the University of West Georgia in Carrollton.

Contemporary Austrian Studies

Günter Bischof, Anton Pelinka/Fritz Plasser/Ferdinand Karlhofer, Editors

Volume 1 (1992)
Austria in the New Europe

Volume 2 (1993)
The Kreisky Era in Austria
Oliver Rathkolb, Guest Editor

Volume 3 (1994)
Austria in the Nineteen Fifties
Rolf Steininger, Guest Editor

Volume 4 (1995)
Austro-Corporatism: Past—Present—Future

Volume 5 (1996)
Austrian Historical Memory & National Identity

Volume 6 (1997)
Women in Austria
Erika Thurner, Guest Editor

Volume 7 (1998)
The Vranitzky Era in Austria
Ferdinand Karlhofer, Guest Editor

Volume 8 (1999)
The Marshall Plan in Austria
Dieter Stiefel, Guest Editor

Volume 9 (2000)
Neutrality in Austria
Ruth Wodak, Guest Editor

Volume 10 (2001)
Austria and the EU
Michael Gehler, Guest Editor

Volume 11 (2002)
The Dollfuss/Schuschnigg Era in Austria: A Reassessment
Alexander Lassner, Guest Editor

Volume 12 (2003)
The Americanization/Westernization of Austria

Volume 13 (2004)
Religion in Austria
Hermann Denz, Guest Editor

Volume 14 (2005)
Austrian Foreign Policy in Historical Perspective
Michael Gehler, Guest Editor

Volume 15 (2006)
Sexuality in Austria
Dagmar Herzog, Guest Editor

Volume 16 (2007)
The Changing Austrian Voter

Volume 17 (2008)
New Perspectives on Austrians and World War II
Barbara Stelzl-Marx, Guest Editor

Volume 18 (2009)
The Schüssel Era in Austria

Volume 19 (2010)
From Empire to Republic: Post-World War I Austria

Volume 20 (2011)
Global Austria: Austria's Place in Europe and the World
Alexander Smith, Guest Editor

Volume 21 (2012)
Austrian Lives
Eva Maltschnig, Guest Editor

Volume 22 (2013)
Austria's International Position after the End of the Cold War

Volume 23 (2014)
1914: Austria-Hungary, the Origins, and the First Year of World War 1
Samuel R. Williamson, Jr., Guest Editor

Volume 24 (2015)
Austrian Federalism in Comparative Perspective

Volume 25 (2016)
Austrian Studies Today

Volume 26 (2017)
Migration in Austria
Dirk Rupnow, Guest Editor

Volume 27 (2018)
Austrian Enviromental History
Marc Landry and Patrick Kupper, eds.
Verena Winiwarter, Guest Editor

Volume 28 (2019)
Democracy in Austria
David M. Wineroither, Guest Editor